Bantu, Boer, and Briton

THE MAKING OF
THE SOUTH AFRICAN
NATIVE PROBLEM

Oxford University Press, Amen House, London E.C.4

GLASGOW NEW YORK TORONTO MELBOURNE WELLINGTON
BOMBAY CALCUTTA MADRAS KARACHI LAHORE DACCA
CAPE TOWN SALISBURY NAIROBI IBADAN ACCRA
KUALA LUMPUR HONG KONG

Bantu, Boer, and Briton

THE MAKING OF
THE SOUTH AFRICAN
NATIVE PROBLEM

BY

W. M. MACMILLAN

REVISED AND
ENLARGED EDITION

OXFORD
AT THE CLARENDON PRESS
1963

FIRST PUBLISHED IN MCMXXIX
BY FABER & GWYER LIMITED
24 RUSSELL SQUARE LONDON W.C.I

This edition © Oxford University Press 1963

PRINTED IN GREAT BRITAIN

Ὦ πόποι, οἷον δή νυ θεοὺς βροτοὶ αἰτιόωνται.
ἐξ ἡμέων γάρ φασι κάκ' ἔμμεναι· οἱ δὲ καὶ αὐτοὶ
σφῆσιν ἀτασθαλίῃσιν ὑπὲρ μόρον ἄλγε' ἔχουσιν.

HOMER, *Od.* I. 32

The fault, dear Brutus, is not in our stars,
But in ourselves. . . .

PREFACE TO THE SECOND EDITION

THIS book embodies what were to have been only the first gleanings from the private papers of the early nineteenth-century figure, the Rev. Dr. John Philip, whose influence on the politics of South Africa is still a matter of controversy, and whose name is still used as a condemnatory label for missionaries and liberals. The whole collection of his papers was put at my disposal in 1920 by the Philip family. Two years after the publication of this book the University Library in Johannesburg was destroyed by fire and with it the original papers. Unknowing that there would be no further opportunity I had, even unconsciously, avoided biographical treatment, hoping to come to that later. It therefore seems necessary in this new edition to enlarge on the nature and significance, and the entire novelty, of the evidence these papers brought to light, and also on the man who wrote or received them—both his ideas and his doings having been very widely misrepresented; in the first edition his constructive work for a just frontier settlement was evidently left too much to inference. This time I have focused throughout on John Philip; a new introductory chapter provides background matter, and since fresh examination of the sources is no longer possible I have tried to make more effective the presentation of any extracts and quotations from the original material which might have been overlooked in footnotes. I have drawn here and there on latter-day studies in the general field of colonial matters, and on acquired personal experience of comparable colonial conditions.

The 1928 preface is reprinted for its possible historical interest.

My grateful thanks are due for a contribution to accuracy such as only my old colleague Professor E. A. Walker could have supplied, from his unrivalled erudition on South African subjects. With exemplary kindness he provided several sheets of emendations and suggestions. Not for the first time Julius

Lewin made helpful suggestions; and his wife Eleanor contributed invaluable advice based on long experience of using the book in her teaching of South African history.

W. M. M.

Long Wittenham
Abingdon, Berks.
27 February 1962

PREFACE TO THE FIRST EDITION

THIS book, like *The Cape Colour Question*, evolved from the study of the private papers of Dr. John Philip, now acquired by the Witwatersrand Council of Education for the University of the Witwatersrand. These papers throw new light especially on Dr. Philip's personal share in the politics of his day. But chiefly they point to the necessity for a radically new interpretation of known and generally undisputed facts, suggesting in particular that the predicament of the natives, involved perforce in a struggle with encroaching European colonists, has never been taken into account.

To say this is in no way to make light of the hardships stoutly endured by European pioneers, or to minimize their sufferings at the hand of the natives whom in the end they subjugated and conquered. Even now the condition of the victorious white farming community of South Africa is a matter for grave concern. For years past, in articles, papers, and pamphlets I have done what I could to call attention to the facts and causes of the sordid poverty, white no less than black, that rests like a blight on the common weal of Golden South Africa; and I hope shortly to re-embody the results of first-hand study of modern conditions in a single book by way of commentary on the pages of history here dealt with.

The social problems of mixing and of intermarriage, which are a modern nightmare, happily do not arise so far as the South African Natives are concerned. The Native Problem is economic and political, and, so long as economic stress is not allowed to undermine and destroy the moral fibre of the race, the Bantu are a pure stock, with a fair share of the white man's antipathy to race-mixture. In truth, the diseases of the body politic of the Union today are the sins of the fathers visited upon the children of the third and fourth generation, who are as far as ever from an understanding of the true significance of the happenings of seventy years ago. The Native Problem as it is now is what the disintegration of the Ama-Xhosa by the Kaffir wars, and the widespread dispossession of tribes by the Great Trek, made it in the eighteen-fifties, when Government and

Trekkers alike failed to take just account of the economic needs and human interests of the native population. And now, in the full bloom of 'young nationhood', the Union bids fair to repeat this fundamental mistake. It is a sign of ill omen that South African opinion is absorbed in the political aspect of a problem that is one of administration, and, above all, of economics. For good or ill the country is made up of black as well as white, and to satisfy the complex needs of her varied population is the essential Native Problem. Civilization, being of the East as well as of the West, knows no Colour Bar.

Nowhere is there such danger of political disaster as in a country, constitutionally democratic, which denies political rights to a section of its own people. In South Africa, though Parliament is more than usually sensitive to electoral opinion, that opinion is not only incompletely representative, but, through fear, definitely antagonistic to the interests of a large part of the community. Instead of seeking the best possible representation of Native opinion, South Africans deny the first principles of their own cherished Parliamentary system, leaning heavily to a 'solution' of the Native Problem by measures expressly calculated to make their Parliament more one-sided than ever—proposals for 'reform' being inspired, chiefly, by a desire to restrict the Native vote in the interests of 'White' Civilization. The plan, much favoured, of a fixed maximum of separate or *communal* Native representation must place the effective control of the country's future in the hands of a Parliament whose members (all but the communal 'five' or 'seven') will be expressly freed from the compelling electoral necessity of remembering that Natives exist. The Natives ready to qualify for the jealously guarded privilege of the franchise are a mere handful, and their number increases all too slowly. Wisdom demands that White South Africa bind this handful to itself, and secure their co-operation in devising a policy for leading up to civilization the great backward masses who must, for many years, remain incapable of independent political thought and action. To doubt its ability to do this is to despair of the soundness of the political system and the civilization of which it boasts. For the Union—in blindness born of fear—to baulk or retard their progress will be to sow dragons' teeth that must soon spring to dreadful life in the not infertile seed-plot of

South Africa. If knowing is understanding, it may be that new light upon the pages of history will serve to prepare the ground for a happier issue.

Obligations acknowledged in the preface to *The Cape Colour Question* hold for this which was originally designed to form part of that book. I must now add that the later chapters owe a very great deal to the researches of Miss L. S. Sutherland and Dr. C. W. de Kiewiet in the Public Records of London and Cape Town. Dr. de Kiewiet has put me under an additional obligation by compiling the Index. In very early days Miss G. E. Edwards, of Wynberg, read the draft of certain chapters which her invaluable suggestions helped to transform past her own powers of recognition.

The map, unearthed for me by Mr. D. Chamberlin of the London Missionary Society, is of interest as showing certain limitations and imperfections in the knowledge of South African geography in the eighteen-thirties.

W. M. M.

University of the Witwatersrand
Johannesburg
December 1928

CONTENTS

LIST OF MAPS

ABBREVIATIONS, ETC.

AGAR-HAMILTON—*Native Policy of the Voortrekkers.* J. Agar-Hamilton. Cape Town. 1928.

BIRD—*Bird's Annals of Natal.* 2 vols. Pietermaritzburg.

BROOKES—*History of Native Policy.* Professor E. H. Brookes. Cape Town. 1924.

CAPE COL. QN.—*The Cape Colour Question.* W. M. Macmillan. Faber & Gwyer. 1927.

C. C. RECORDS—*Records of the Cape Colony.* 35 vols. Ed. by G. M. Theal.

CORY—*The Rise of South Africa.* 4 vols. Sir G. E. Cory. Longmans.

DURBAN MSS.—Typewritten volumes copied by Dr. Theal, in South African Library, Cape Town.

EYBERS—*Select Documents Illustrative of South African Constitutional History.* G. W. Eybers. Routledge.

GIE—*Geskiedenis vir Zuid Afrika.* 2 vols. Dr. S. F. N. Gie.

GUBBINS—Private Library of the late J. G. Gubbins, Esq., of Ottoshoop, Western Transvaal.

LETTERS AND DOCUMENTS cited by name or date only were among the Philip MSS., University of Witwatersrand, Johannesburg.

L.M.S.—London Missionary Society.

THEAL—*History of South Africa since 1795.* 5 vols. G. McC. Theal. Sonnenschein. 1908.

WALKER—*A History of South Africa.* Professor E. A. Walker. Longmans.

NOTE ON NOMENCLATURE

TERMS innocently used as the designation of the peoples concerned in this story may too easily give offence. Changes in usage thus caused in the past have brought nomenclature into a state of confusion which in itself is apt to cause this offence. Of the indigenous peoples, those best able to express an opinion now prefer to be called *Africans* and are generally so called, except in South Africa where many of other than African origin also claim to be African. There is thus the difficulty not only that the term has to do duty for an even greater variety of peoples than its counterpart 'European', but also that Afrikaans usage has completely established the form *Afrikaner* for South Africans of Dutch origin—so much so that even the famous historical term *Boers* (freely and inevitably used of the frontiersmen in this book) will probably also arouse criticism.

In earlier times the tribes who long challenged the white colonists' advance on the eastern frontier were distinctively known as the *Kaffirs*. English writers always used the word politely, and charged it even with feelings of respect for a brave foe. But in origin, *Kaffir*, or giaour, was the Islamic term for unbeliever and is still so used by Islamic Africans of their non-Islamic fellows. Even more decisively an Afrikaans form, *kaffer*, has become a term of contemptuous abuse. Historically speaking it is impossible to avoid the established name for the 'Kaffir Wars', and in innumerable quotations. But clearly the term has become inadmissible in modern usage.

The alternative, native or natives, became the established parliamentary and statutory usage, but came also to be disliked as derogatory. In the 1920's the use of a capital N was beginning to be accepted as more polite—(the first edition of this book involved me in a considerable printer's bill for changing n's into N's!). At that time also the term Bantu was coming in and I was snared by the lure of alliteration into giving this book its ungrammatical title—it should have been consistently in the plural, *Bantu, Boers, and Britons*. The word Bantu, Zulu for 'the people', was a convenient appellation for the great group of kindred but diverse languages used by most of the peoples south of the Sahara. South African Parliaments have now done their best to fix it on their still antipathetic African subjects. Here it will be believed I have tried my best to walk warily.

My apologies are due to my colleagues in university departments of phonetics for my dismal failure to keep abreast of what they will admit are bewildering changes in the approved spellings of tribal and personal names, e.g. Tshuana, Chwana, Tswana, for Bechuana. I have, as far as I could, consistently adhered to traditional historical spellings.

I. INTRODUCTORY

THE ENDURING SIGNIFICANCE OF JOHN PHILIP

THE once familiar phrase, *Native Problem*, has passed out of currency even in South Africa where it originated; the confusion in that country now manifestly affects all peoples and classes. Yet the sub-title of this book originally published in 1929—*The Making of the South African Native Problem*—is still appropriate to the unimaginative dragooning of the Bantu which passed for policy. The country's rulers, Boer and British alike, long persisted in seeing the tribal African society in their midst only as a potential military danger, giving way to feelings of mere relief the moment they thought the Bantu military power at last decisively broken; their long feud with one another was reason in itself for leaving aside Bantu affairs as possible further cause for contention. Memories of wars with the tribal hosts continued to be lively; a major disaster to British troops at the hands of the Zulu in 1879 was still in mind when disorder threatened in Natal so late as 1906, and the passing of this or any lesser threat of unrest served only to confirm the universal assumption that all was well on the Bantu front so long as all was quiet. Hardly a thought was spared for the necessity laid on the conquered and broken tribes of adapting their whole way of life to gravely straitened conditions, and for the well considered and sympathetic help this demanded. Social reconstruction by public authority had no place in the economic theory of the day.

The social and economic consequences of such long-continued neglect of the African masses at last began to react, as they were bound to do, on the national economy; during and after the 1914–18 War the general malaise was such as compelled attention. The Dutch Reformed Church had already taken alarm at the condition of many 'poor *whites*' when the Bishop of Grahamstown, the late Archbishop Phelps, directed my attention to social distress, also among whites, in his essentially non-Afrikaner diocesan city. Thus prompted I began investigations, first in Grahamstown, then in white rural districts, only after that in the so-called 'Native areas'.[1] New stresses then manifesting themselves in these last obviously had deep roots and were, I concluded, not to be understood, much less ordered, without a more satisfying knowledge than was anywhere to be had of their historical origins.

Talk on this theme had an unlooked-for outcome when, in 1920, the late Rev. G. P. Ferguson not only directed me to one indispensable, hitherto untapped source of history, but moved his nephew, Mr. A. D. Philip, to entrust me with the massive collection of letters and documents written, and many more received, during thirty crucial years of South Africa's history by his great-grandfather, the Rev. Dr. John Philip, in his capacity as Resident Director in Cape Town and South African Superintendent of the London Missionary Society (L.M.S.). Ever since the death of Dr. Philip this mass of historical material had been kept strictly private while the unpopularity he had earned in his lifetime as the champion of the weaker peoples' rights if anything grew in volume, making his name anathema to the majority of white South Africans. At intervals his son, Durant, and afterwards a grandson, Fred, worked at a defensive *Life* which, they hoped, would counter so much blind prejudice; their unfinished draft existed and contained matter not to be found elsewhere. Philip's correspondence, however, which included letters received from a great variety of the prominent actors in African matters at home and abroad, made me give priority to an examination of the development of policy, first towards the Hottentots or Cape Coloured People, then as affecting Bantu relations with their Boer and British neighbours. Much in the hitherto accepted version of these long contests must otherwise have remained almost inexplicable. There was matter there for many more investigators to have worked on, but on the Christmas Eve of 1931 the Philip Papers, together with the draft *Life* of Philip, were totally destroyed by fire in the Library of the University of the Witwatersrand, Johannesburg. This book, and its out-of-print companion, *The Cape Colour Question*, 1927, are now their only witness.[2]

---

[1] Various pamphlets and articles on social conditions in the 1920's were brought together in *Complex South Africa*, Faber, 1931.

[2] The working notes and excerpts made in compiling these two books are now

The lost Philip Papers were the intimate record of one man's sustained effort to give direction to a policy for southern Africa as the whole which, in spite of the diversity of its peoples, nature and history combined to make it. John Philip's claim to distinction is that he saw the situation in perspective as few have ever done; his life work called indeed for the full biography which is now impossible. The two surviving studies were to have been only a 'first-time-over' of his papers and took the shape they did because the entirely new evidence they contained called imperatively for a review of the generally accepted account of the decisive years in the country's history. The reappraisal I originally made in the 1920's has been almost ignored in the seminal school books, for the reason that their compilers (and still more the pupil examinees) must walk warily indeed lest they appear to be casting doubt on the basic tenets of Afrikaner Nationalism. This National Movement, which was growing strongly in the twenties and is now politically dominant, has as the very foundation of its creed an exclusive, emotionally interpreted historical tradition which it is heresy to question—a definitive authorized version. The very possibility of revision is excluded above all in the crucial phase covered by the Philip Papers where it can claim to be confirmed by independent witnesses. On many vexed questions of that day some British officials and perhaps most British Settlers were for reasons of their own as strongly critical of Philip's opinions or doings as most of the frontier Boers. The persistence of such a parallel anti-Philip tradition compels me, regretfully, even after thirty years, to leave standing numerous citations of the factual and inferential errors of those chiefly responsible for perpetuating it, two outstanding pioneers of South African historiography. Scholars owe a major debt to the late Dr. G. M. Theal for the first comprehensive national History as well as for invaluable Records, and to the late Sir George Cory for devoted work in recording much even of the oral tradition of the Eastern frontier. No ingratitude must be inferred if, besides frequently acknowledging their help, I also cite their errors;

foliated and docketed in the Library of Rhodes House, Oxford. Another casualty in the Johannesburg University fire was the first collection of MSS. made by the late Mr. J. G. Gubbins. These too have, so far as I know, no memorial other than a few of those same 'working notes' at Rhodes House.

their lapses could not well be avoided so long as the Philip Papers were inaccessible; but neither can they now be passed over; the most serious of them have become part of the very fabric of what I have called the authorized version. The outlook for the new Republic of South Africa, of 1961, seemed to many people almost ominous largely because its entrenched rulers' view of their own past was this disordered obsession.

The anxious responsibility now resting on South Africa's leaders should induce in them a more humble sympathy for the pioneer who tried harder than any other to save their predecessors from the courses that went, as my old sub-title tried to suggest, to the *making* of the 'Native Problem' which they now find daunting. With the hope, and in the belief that nothing can so help them as a better understanding of the past, I take the opportunity a revised edition of this book affords to include in this introductory chapter not only (since the former book may be unobtainable) a bare outline of the conditions that gave rise to Philip's earlier, and successful, campaign for just dealing with the Cape people, but also a summary of what is known about his personal (and real) opinions and doings—these last by way of background to many which are detailed in later chapters.

South Africa's present-day troubles are at any rate not new; the existing ferment is not to be judged as accompaniment to or outcome of that which has arisen in the rest of Africa—its mere echo. The rise and the dramatic spread of national self-consciousness among the peoples of the greater Africa is a phenomenon of the last twenty or thirty years and became even possible only as a result of the revolutionary development of transport and communications. South African stresses, though old, are also in a high degree modern, having come to a head in consequence of by far the most highly developed industrial state in Africa having been superimposed upon and yet most imperfectly harmonized with an older, essentially African society. In the 1920's, when this book was first in preparation, the peoples of tropical Africa were in a calm nonage; the League of Nations could then unhesitatingly pronounce them a Sacred Trust of Civilization; colonial rule, the inevitable instrument of this Trust was generally accepted as essential to world order. Lord Lugard, himself an enlightened colonial administrator, broke new ground when his book *The Dual Mandate*, 1922, mooted a

cautious plan for the advancement of tropical Africa. Few of the
then tiny class of educated Africans showed marked enthusiasm,
as was not surprising since his tribally based system of local
government, or Indirect Rule, left them dominated by an
hereditary ruling class; it was assuredly not because emergent
Africans were fired by ambition to make rapid advance to self-
rule of Western democratic or any other pattern. Yet in those
same, now almost distant 1920's, when tropical Africa was profoundly quiet, South Africa was already profoundly disturbed.
In the general awakening the rest of Africa may seem to have
moved faster than the south; but in South Africa a long-stand-
ing debate on the rights and status of Africans and, hence, on
the adjustment of relations between them and their strongly
established white neighbours, had reached only a new pitch of
intensity back in the 1920's; it was then that most of the themes
and catchwords that have since won notoriety abroad—all
except the word *apartheid*—came into daily use. South Africa,
in short, being more than an appendage of the greater Africa,
has long known stresses that are distinctively its own.

Many South Africans, acutely aware, in spite of their domin-
ating strength, of being outnumbered by three or four to one,
themselves over-play a claim that their situation is, as they like
to put it, 'unique'. This is in part the natural reaction to the
habitual over-simplification of the issues by critics who make all
a straightforward choice between black and white, right and
wrong. Not for nothing has South Africa had three centuries of
what students of the inter-war generation anxiously studied
under the name of 'racial contact': this has in truth made
necessary readjustments peculiarly hard to achieve—established usage always too readily allows deep-seated prejudice to
pose as ripe experience. But one factor acknowledgedly making
for difference is the chance that South Africa is the one political
unit south of the Sahara with a temperate and indeed notably
healthy climate. This has done much to determine the way of
life of the white population; the South African pioneers, for
example of mining development, have never had to contend
with tropical diseases. For more than a century after the Dutch
occupation of the Cape in 1652 colonists were free to settle at
will and dig themselves in. This, it is commonly claimed, was
because in south and south-west there was no Bantu opposition;

and for more than a century, it is true, the colonists met only once with these tribesmen, and then in a chance affray. But climatic conditions very definitely set limits to the colony's expansion northwards; the *voortrekkers* who ventured in the 1840's into the attractive but tropical *low veld* of the Transvaal quickly found themselves beaten by the novel experience of malarial fever. In present-day debate a few South Africans continue to harp on the Bantu theme, even drawing the dubious deduction that the Bantu, as themselves interlopers from the Tropics, have no inherent right to be where they are in the south; but many more than the exponents of this double-edged argument yet miss the true moral. That peaceful early history was decisive above all in confirming the white actors in the national ways and outlook that still persist. By the end of the eighteenth century, before relations with the Bantu had reached any major crisis, they were already a distinct people, the Afrikaner *Boers*.

Till well after 1770 the mass of the Bantu were only a distant threat, directly affecting only a handful of pioneers. Within the Colony proper the poorly equipped Hottentots presented no serious challenge; their scanty wealth in cattle actually so much immobilized them that the very primitive Bushmen, mere hunters and food-gatherers, were felt to be more of an embarrassment. The farmers who settled in the well-watered country within reach of the Cape Town market became sufficiently well off to buy the slaves which the Dutch East India Company imported from its possessions in the East, and from East Africa. With the help of these so-called 'Malay' artisans the Western Province acquired the appearance of a civilized country. Only the Western farmers could afford slaves and these, as valuable property, were carefully housed and kept. The Hottentots were not judged worthy of so much care and maintenance; but the farmers of the interior had to make do with their services since they lacked the financial resources to do otherwise. The Boers, inevitably generalizing from their indifferent experience of the Hottentots measured thus against the quicker and more skilled slaves from the East, emerged with very definite ideas about the inferiority of African races, and the treatment due to them in consequence. As for the Cape Hottentots, they drifted into a state of servile dependence without any recognized status, becoming—in literal truth—lesser breeds without the law.

The anomaly of their existence, within the Cape society but not of it, was such as only a weak and preoccupied government, that of the mercantile East India Company, could so long have tolerated, and its equally Dutch successor, the short-lived Batavian Republic, 1802–6, at once initiated measures to end it. The execution of reforms, however, devolved on still newer British rulers whose arrival was at once followed by the Act abolishing the slave-trade and, before long, by steady pressure for the abolition of slavery itself. The Government's desirable and necessary task of tightening up the general administration of this most laxly administered country became no easier when it was required to enforce slave regulations many of which were not drafted to suit conditions at the Cape. There would seem to have been little attempt at consultation between the new British rulers and the long-established inhabitants; the farmers of the West were well enough established to take Abolition on the whole calmly; but the humanitarian drive turned attention also on the Hottentots, to the very considerable disturbance of their masters in inland districts. These worthy inland people soon began to show that they had become a distinct and self-conscious community with views of their own on such topics. They quite simply demanded that Hottentots be their *servants*, willing servants they hoped but, at all costs and as Holy Writ required, they must be obedient. Ill usage of servants was and always has been unusual; but any change in Hottentot status must, they feared, imperil the high degree of security they had come to take for granted; and after all, they could not unjustly claim to be in effect the sole representatives of government authority on their far-scattered farms, and in case of need the only defence force. Proposed changes, therefore, even obvious administrative reforms, provoked more than one unfortunate incident.

Changes at any rate were upon these Boers and, it must be said, their free life was an ill preparation for the political debate this involved; even had the colonial system provided any forum, and it did not, the lonely seclusion of their farms cut them off from discussion and fostered a dangerous habit of brooding. It has been an enduring weakness of this normally amiable people to brood on wrongs, or fancied wrongs, and in particular the British-made Hottentot law of those early years

became the first of a sadly long line of Boer national grievances.
Thanks expressly to the example of the South African judicial
bench, which has won for itself unimpeachably high distinction
as champion of strict legality, few if any present-day South
Africans question either the principle of the rule of law or the
right of the meanest subject to a secure legal status. But two
of the earliest assertions of authority, the Black Circuit of 1812,
and the execution of white men for a rebellion at Slagter's Nek
in 1815, are long remembered grievances. An Afrikaner historian, Dr. J. S. Marais, has, however, written of the 'educative influence' and indeed the 'educative necessity' of these
incidents.[1]

The affair of the Black Circuit was in fact a direct outcome of
the right and proper ambition which the new British rulers
shared with their Dutch predecessors, to strengthen the administrative system. The obvious need was to let the law be seen
throughout the Colony and not only in the distant capital Cape
Town. The judges of the High Court were accordingly instructed to go on regular circuits in the eastern districts.
Shortly before this the Governor, acting on the report of detailed investigations set on foot by his predecessors, had in 1809
enacted a *Hottentot Code* which was by no means revolutionary
but at last gave these people a definite legal status as subjects.[2]
The Hottentots' principal mentors, the missionaries of the
London Missionary Society, decided to test the efficacy of the
protective provisions of this code, and on behalf of their protégés
laid charges against a few employers—of assault, one or two
even of murder, and many more of lesser offences. The court
itself was a novelty and the idea of calling masters to face
charges laid by Hottentot servants was revolutionary; with so
many family parties gathered together from far and wide for
this novel occasion the excited talk can be imagined. The
Hottentots' missionary advisers, for their part, either failed to
marshal a sufficient volume of evidence, or allowed too little for
the difficulty of eliciting reliable facts from their witnesses.

---

[1] *The Cape Coloured People*, J. S. Marais (Longmans), p. 121.

[2] The notorious pass laws of the Transvaal are sometimes fathered on British
precedent, justly to the extent that the carrying of 'passes' by Hottentots absent
from their fixed place of abode was imposed by the law of 1809. Passes were lifted
from the Cape in 1828, but so much approved by the frontier Boers as to be re-
introduced and much developed by them in their own Republic.

Many of the cases were dismissed, some of them as frivolous; and this has obscured the fact that grievances were proved to exist for which only courts of law could give redress. There were eight convictions on charges of assault, some of them serious, several more for minor offences. Sentences were not severe, but leniency did little to mitigate the indignation the affair aroused. This indignation, frontier-fashion, has never been allowed to die.

For the first time in this hitherto placid colony the Black Circuit revealed the existence of sharply divided interests and opinions. The first to feel the effect was actually the leader for the Hottentots, the L.M.S. The effort to protect and if possible better the conditions of the people its missionaries served set these at loggerheads with one another. The sudden death of their senior member, a Hollander, Dr. J. T. van der Kemp, had left his less well qualified assistant, Mr. James Read, to carry the main burden of responsibility for the cases taken to court. The ensuing commotion caused some colleagues to judge him to have acted with more zeal than discretion and to have set public opinion needlessly by the ears. When Read as the senior minister came also to act as the Society's secretary, at least five of the critics resigned membership. The threatened collapse of the Society's extensive work (see note on p. 10) created such scandal that in 1817 the Governor himself took action and pressed on the Directors at Home the imperative need to institute inquiry and reform. Their answer was to appoint and send off to the Cape, as Resident Director and Superintendent of Missions, Dr. John Philip.

The consequences for the Cape and for South Africa were momentous. This Superintendent of Missions, never himself a *missionary*, however often so described, was never isolated on any one station, yet by virtue of his office in touch with scores of stations all over the country. If his supervisory duties gave him nothing like the authority of a bishop, they left him free of the ecclesiastical chores that harass a bishop; at the same time the charge of a congregation in Cape Town kept him in close association with people of his own race, yet did not interfere with his long tours of inspection. Once he had arrived at the essential yet highly original conclusion that the obstacle to the greater success of the missions was the unsatisfactory status of the people they served he was in duty bound to act. Yet action by its nature took him beyond the ecclesiastical sphere, concerned public affairs and was, in short, political. In this way the subject people came to have an advocate well placed near the headquarters of the still very small colonial community at a time when none had yet felt any need to set up whole-time departments, much less to appoint Ministers of Coloured or Native Affairs.

For the efforts Philip made in his unpopular cause he emerged in the end one of the most hated figures in any national history. Americans may yet be found who believe the unwisdom of British Ministers to have been personally inspired by George III; likewise generations of South African children have learnt from teachers and textbooks of a Philip they must deem to have been *wicked*; even in the 1960's hardly a month or a week passed without some example of a Nationalist politician or scribe resorting to the use of the name 'Dr. Philip' as the most comprehensive term of abuse possible. The grievous wrong done to his memory makes the destruction of the Philip evidence the more deplorable. One minor excuse for misunderstanding may lie in the decline and disappearance from the scene of the L.M.S. itself. By tradition 'Independent', the Society's set policy had been to free its missionaries, who were scarce, for work in untouched fields by leaving congregations, once formed, to independent self-government—too often much too soon. The result was that not long after Philip's death (1851) the L.M.S. had very few stations left—whereas in his prime its work was by far the most extensive in the whole of southern Africa.[1] That this fact has certainly been forgotten might ac-

---

[1] A list of stations under Philip's direction compiled from letters in the Philip Papers included virtually all places of any significance in the Colony of the day and many beyond the frontiers: Cape Town, Stellenbosch (early left to Rhenish mission), Paarl, Tulbagh, Caledon, Zuurbraak (Swellendam), Pacaltsdorp (George), Dysselsdorp (near Oudtshoorn), Hankey, Uitenhage, Bethelsdorp, Port Elizabeth, Grahamstown, Theopolis, Kat River, Keiskama, King William's Town, Blinkwater (Fort Beaufort), Somerset East, Graaff-Reinet, Colesberg, Philippolis, Bethulie (later French), Griquatown, Taungs, Kuruman (the last three with sub-stations).

Besides these there were several L.M.S. stations in Namaqualand, and Philip had some general supervision over, and received direct reports from, both French and American stations in Basutoland and Natal respectively.

A few of these stations dropped out or were transferred to other supervisors in Philip's lifetime. Very few survived a large-scale withdrawal in the sixties and seventies.

count for the very great width of his experience coming to be
underrated and his actions deemed merely presumptuous. That
Philip's range was in fact so wide admits of another quite
different deduction. His most consistent aim was beyond all
doubt to have merely local interests subordinated to those of the
general good; confronted as the champions of many highly
local interests often were with representations based on Philip's
unrivalled first-hand knowledge of southern Africa in all its
length and breadth, they were left speechless with rage—and
that rage it is that has never died. This deduction is strongly
borne out by a significant fact (one not without manifest effect
in confirming the prejudice against him in Boer circles); his
most vocal critics in his own lifetime were the intensely local
interests of English Grahamstown. Later chapters will show the
varied sources Philip drew on for his facts, the judgements he
made, also something of the methods he used in his efforts to
influence policy. The material for biography is necessarily now
scanty, the numerous documents surviving in public archives
being for the most part formal writings; but sufficient remains
to show the real Philip a very different person from the 'Dr.
Philip' of South African mythology.

John Philip was born of sound weaver stock at Kirkcaldy in
the county of Fife in 1775; he was thus a man of mature experience when called on at the age of 44 to adapt himself to and
assess conditions in a strange and distant land. But he came not
ill prepared. Formal schooling had ended and he was at the
family trade about the age of 11; but his father was a reader;
the family 'prized works by Bacon, Newton, Swift, and Dr.
Johnson', and it is probable that in such a home he mastered
(as is strongly suggested by evidence from his own memoranda
and letters) more than the rudiments of his famous fellow-
townsman, Adam Smith. The young man was early caught in a
wave of the then active evangelical revival. Clearly making
some mark as a speaker and worker, he was taken up by the
Haldanes, well known as the founders of the Evangelical Union
(Scottish Congregationalism). At 21, he himself wrote, he was
'for six months managing a power mill in Dundee', but left it
to undergo regular training for the Ministry at a reputedly
'liberal' institution, the Independent College at Hoxton. In
1802 he was called to a charge at Newbury in Berkshire of

which one significant episode is recorded. Public speaking, after all, not writing, was Dr. Philip's profession and when a friendly Newbury curate told him that the 'intelligible' parts of a lecture he had given had been 'interesting' he took the hint and started trimming the rough edges of his native speech. Later he clearly preached, as his hearers would have put it, 'with acceptance'. Years afterwards the characteristic letter of an Aberdeen artisan parishioner expressly acquitted him of being one of 'Oh! *that* reading Preachers!'

Philip's fuller experience was in the city of Aberdeen, from 1804 to 1818, in strong fresh air, physical and mental, that never suffers fools gladly. There in 1809 he married Jane Ross, an unmistakably proficient 'minister's wife': the only live memories I ever got of either of them were from a very old woman at the Hankey mission where both their graves are; she was vague about the Doctor but spoke repeatedly, and with emphasis, of '*Juffrouw!*' (Madam). Philip's Independency, and his years at Hoxton, made a ready link with the L.M.S.: at least as early as 1810 he was campaigning for Missions as far away as Wick and Thurso. When, later, the Society's Cape affairs were called attention to, his copy of the Secretary's circular letter had enclosed in it a note saying curtly 'Can you go?' That was in October 1817. His immediate reaction must have been furiously to think. His congregation did not want to get rid of him and months later were even proposing to give him two years' leave of absence—long enough only for a tour of in-spection such as his companion, the traveller John Campbell, actually made. The Resident Directorship was accepted only on 8 September 1818. By this time influential friends were moving to arm him for his new post with a 'diploma'. The Principals of both the constituent Colleges of Aberdeen Univer-sity, King's and Marischal, were among his correspondents, but the Divinity degrees of the Home Universities were in those days a preserve of the Established Churches, and finally his doctorate was received from the U.S.A., both Columbia and Princeton enrolling him. His own letters in these months were, not surprisingly, few; for it appears from one note that inside three months, on December 5th, his ship had already 'put back into Liverpool'. He moved fast for, reaching Cape Town only on 26 February 1819, before the end of April he was off on the

first of his many long and physically arduous ox-wagon tours of
his vast new field.

This prompt start is wholly in character. Whatever else
Philip did he habitually deferred action until after he had taken
steps to inform himself as fully as he could about the matter in
hand. Records existed of full notes of not fewer than twelve
long treks made between 1819 and 1845, most of them of up
to six months' duration; in 1841–2 his tour of nearly twelve
months included a call on the chief Moshesh, in Basutoland,
as well as what was at least his second visit to Bechuanaland.
The *Journals* of all these tours, often in regions far beyond the
range of any post office, I had hopefully set aside for fuller use—
'papers a yard high' in a phrase used of a very different and
still extant bundle from Governor D'Urban. The facts or even
the impressions recorded were his own—there were then few
published books—but, unhappily, Philip's stoep-sitting critics,
most of them men of provincial outlook who have never so
much as seen a 'native area', can never now be introduced to
Philip, the Traveller, who first and last was at pains to make
factual evidence the basis of his opinions. Returned home, he
had the help of Mrs. Philip and other amanuenses in collating
his notes with evidence from a variety of other sources, his own
familiarity with both the places they came from, and the writers
and actors themselves, making the contents of letters from out-
stations more readily assessable. The Philip home in Cape Town
was always a rest-house for missionaries coming and going on
their travels; Robert Moffat, a younger man who had already
served in Namaqualand, set out to found his famous Bechuana
station in 1820 from the same house where in 1841 David
Livingstone made his first African landfall. Philip's visitors included many more than those of his own widely dispersed community; early and late he was consultant in chief to French,
German (Barmen), and American Mission Boards; he personally directed the Paris Society to the important Basuto field where
they made such a mark, and was in constant close touch with
its men there. Stalwart Independents like Robert Moffat chafed
especially if their quasi-episcopal Superintendent was thought
to be infringing the sacred principle of local self-rule; but Moffat
in particular also believed fervently that desirable ends were to
be attained only by religious exercises, in the last resort by

direct Divine intervention; from his remote inland station he looked askance at Philip's 'political' activities, certainly never appreciating how necessary they were.[1]

In Cape Town society Philip clearly had an established position. An adaptable and already travelled Scot, he had stout help from Mrs. Philip in maintaining the most 'respectable' standards. 'The smiles of the great' is a phrase of his own, and he found them agreeable, always working for choice with Governors, like Sir Rufane Donkin in early days, rather than against them. When on occasion he felt obliged to resist, his prowess as an Evangelical preacher brought him advice and some active help from visiting hearers, especially serving officers of the fighting and East India Services. Even the newly arrived British Settlers, who fell out with him later, found Philip helpful during their earliest struggles and provided one active colleague, Thomas Pringle, a writer and journalist who carried a letter of introduction to Governor Somerset from Sir Walter Scott. Nearer home the capable and active editor of the Cape Town daily newspaper, the *Commercial Advertiser*, John Fairbairn, was his son-in-law and a lifelong ally.

Philip's failure to establish any useful links with his Afrikaans-speaking fellow-colonists stands out as a fatal weakness—but surely only by virtue of hind-sight? The direct colonial rule of his day did nothing to break down the aloofness of the people on the lonely farms. Language may not have been the chief barrier; Philip took services regularly on his Cape mission-stations where Afrikaans was the only medium—the aged witness I have cited had not a word of English—and on his tours he took services for Boer farmers who were no less unilingual. The Rev. Abram Faure was one of his early friends and still in touch in 1844. In later years when the (ill) fame of his name had spread he often allayed hostility and began conversation by handing round his open snuff-mull. The disastrous drifting apart of Boer and Briton in that century is not to be fathered any longer on that figment of brooding Boer imaginations, 'Dr. Philip'.

Philip began his work at the Cape with no preconceived ideas—he was ready even to believe the station Bethelsdorp 'a disgrace' by the fault of the missionaries he was commissioned

[1] See Dr. I. D. Schapera's editions of Moffat's *Journals*, e.g. *Apprenticeship at Kuruman*.

to order. Like any younger man he enjoyed his new experiences and was for a time thinking of a 'philisophical review of missions', 'possibly for publication'. Fully two years passed before he came to his momentous conclusion that the unsatisfactory conditions of the people served were the basic cause of missionary dissensions. One apparent lapse from his invariable rule not to rush into action till he was sure of his ground was in truth an attempt to inform himself by asking the friendly acting Governor Donkin to take the opportunity of a frontier journey to 'look into' certain matters of alleged forced labour that were troubling him. Donkin returned sharply annoyed on having found that officers inculpated had convincing answers. Philip thereupon set off hurriedly to do his own investigating and, finding incontrovertible evidence not only of the *corvée* he had suspected but of personal restrictions, gave over philosophizing. The law governing the status of the Hottentots he now realized was bad law; hard cases, such as he had thrust upon Donkin, must fail to convince law courts so long as the law itself countenanced hard treatment of the subject peoples. Hence the law itself must be reformed. For the new phase thus begun[1] Philip laid it down as a working rule that the case for the Hottentots must henceforward rest 'on generals rather than particulars'.

Even this shrewd working rule was arrived at only after long deliberation. Philip returned to Cape Town in the last days of 1821 satisfied that what had once again been James Read's allegations were this time proved. His letter to the L.M.S. pronouncing for the liberation of the Hottentots, and calling off any project of publication of his writings, was in mid-1822. The rule to stand out for 'general' reform was formulated only in mid-1823, at the suggestion of a naval friend, Captain Owen, when he advised against pursuing one 'particular' case. Before this, however, Philip had seen that an essentially political reform was to be extracted from the autocratic Cape government only by discreet pressure on its masters in London. The evangelical connexion now brought him help from an Admiralty official Sir Jahleel Brenton, who had also worked to make peace with Donkin. In the course of 1822 Brenton, who had access to Wilberforce, was armed by Philip with evidence which moved the anti-slavery leader to have the Commission of Inquiry,

[1] See *The Cape Colour Question*, p. 163.

already projected, instructed to investigate conditions not only of slaves but also of 'free persons of colour' at the Cape. Philip for his part then set about marshalling factual information to give to the Commissioners when they arrived. Next, in 1825, he undertook a major inland tour in the course of which he consulted, more successfully than he perhaps realized, with by no means unsympathetic frontier officials, including Andries Stockenström. Resolved to leave no stone unturned, he was off again to London a matter of days after his tour, early in 1826.

In London the Colonial Office certainly took notice, but three changes of Colonial Secretary protracted the delay which consultations with the Cape made inevitable. While he waited Philip prepared a two-volume appeal to the British public, his *Researches in South Africa*; he also cemented what became a fruitful alliance with Wilberforce's anti-Slavery successor Fowell Buxton. After two years, in June 1828, when Buxton was just about to make a move in the House of Commons, the Colonial Secretary suddenly presented the campaigners with the Cape Government's long delayed answer; this was the draft of a measure, famous in history as the 50th Ordinance, for 'Improving the condition of the Hottentots and other Free Persons of Colour' and for consolidating and amending laws affecting them. This measure was actually enacted at the Cape at the time of the London discussions. Having consulted Buxton's legal adviser, Dr. Lushington, Philip accepted this law as a settlement, stipulating only that it be formally endorsed by Order-in-Council, as a safeguard against subversive local amending legislation. Back at the Cape in September 1829, Philip found himself the object of obloquy which in important circles he still is. Public outcry was at a height because as a result of the law abolishing 'passes' many Hottentots were said to be celebrating their freedom by turning 'vagrant'. This was judged to be Philip's doing; but in later days, when vagrancy was forgotten and Hottentot freedom a matter of course, the critics insisted that it had never been his achievement but the work of Cape officials—as in detail it was. For a while the hurt public found solace from Philip's paying the penalty for breaking his own rule of 'generals not particulars'. 'Particulars' detailed in his book, the *Researches*, proved to be within the letter of the law and he had to pay heavy damages and costs.

But the outcry continued and at last in 1834 a newly created Advisory Council (part nominated) won the support of the acting Governor for a renewed Vagrancy Law. The substantive Governor arrived at this stage and, sharing the doubts expressed by his officials and mindful of the Order-in-Council safeguarding the 50th Ordinance, reserved the draft law for His Majesty's, William IV's, consideration; whereupon the Colonial Secretary, agreeing with Mr. Buxton that the draft was 'an insidious document', disallowed it.

The sequel is by any measure quite extraordinary. Before the disallowance of the Vagrancy Law reached the Cape a major crisis on the Bantu frontier completely and finally diverted public attention from the hitherto burning topic of the Hottentots. For a moment, it is true, the Advisory Committee's approval of the stringent draft Vagrancy Law sent many Hottentots flocking for shelter to missionary 'Institutions' (their only substitute for 'reserves'), and not without reason; at least four field-cornets were subsequently suspended for applying the new provisions without waiting for their confirmation. The authorities had other reasons for anxiety; 1 December 1834 was Emancipation Day for the slaves of the more settled districts; this passed quietly, but a few weeks later war on the frontier caused unusual comings and goings of Bantu refugees, as well as of Hottentots, going increasingly in search of work. Laws specifically designed for Hottentots would no longer serve; but law-makers had also to avoid offending again against the anti-slavery or the more positively humanitarian sentiments of the British Colonial Office. At last, in 1837, the needs of the case suggested an entirely reasonable stiffening of the law, no longer aimed at vagrancy, sweepingly so-called, but confined to cases where criminal intent appeared. This time there was no outcry; on the contrary, a note of Dr. Philip's recorded, on the eve of his long tour in 1841, his novel experience of having had no single occasion in the two and a half years of a new Governor's tenure of office to approach him on behalf of any Hottentot. Slavery being no more (and the ominous modern word, Colour, having not yet come to bedevil the issues), Cape society in the 1840's was coming to classify its peoples calmly in terms of their occupations, mainly as employers and employed. After long consideration, undisturbed by agitation from any quarter,

C

existing ordinances were amended and consolidated into a single *Masters and Servants Law* in 1842. Neither the fact that the famous 50th Ordinance of 1828 was repealed nor, certainly, the significance of the change, finds any place in what I have described as the 'authorized version' of this history, perhaps because this time Philip was in no way involved. Modern as he often was Philip had from the first disliked what would now be described as the discriminatory legislation of 1828; but in 1842 he was on trek far away in the interior. He of course had reason to rejoice that the new law, instead of singling out the Hottentots for special protection, treated them at last as citizens among others; regardless of their race or colour Hottentot employees, ex-slaves, Bantu tribesmen, and even a few Europeans, were recognized as having, like their employers, both statutory rights and obligations, on which the courts could adjudicate in case of need. This first venture in 'colour-blind' legislation cleared the way for another even more notable step. In 1851 Philip, the trail-blazer, died. In 1853, in spite of a very local Hottentot Rebellion[1] in the disturbances of 1851, his son-in-law Fairbairn played a leading part in winning general popular support for a similarly colour-blind electoral roll for the newly constituted Parliament of the Cape of Good Hope.

This concession of equal rights marked the triumph of the famous 'Cape policy', which survived for just 100 years. The racial equality conceded may have been potential only; the distinctively Cape People, superfluously dubbed 'Coloured', (*Kaapsche mensche*, they call themselves), never rose from their wretchedly proletarian start to have any considerable influence; but they were free at any rate to take such opportunities as came their way, and many did. They were free, too, as were, presently, a steady number of their African or Bantu fellows, to qualify as parliamentary voters. That Afrikaans was the Cape People's home language helped to make them readily adaptable. The happy result of the Cape policy was that till only the other day, when first African, then Cape voters were deprived of their highly prized political privileges, these were even a stabilizing factor in the complex South African whole. The Cape 'solution' was home-made, never a plan worked out on lines suggested by British tradition and imposed by the Colonial

---

[1] *Cape Col. Qn.*, pp. 280–2.

Office from London. The smooth development of the Cape
Colony was no doubt eased by the withdrawal after 1836 of so
many of the more dogmatic frontiersmen on the Great Trek.
The Trek, nevertheless, left the original Cape Colony a still
predominantly Afrikaans-speaking community which, from
first to last, gave this enlightened policy almost unqualified
popular support.

The ups and downs of the struggle which finally reached this
settlement concerned matters wholly internal to the original
Cape Colony and these were detailed in the former book, *The
Cape Colour Question*. On the Cape frontier first, and ultimately
far beyond it, an even longer struggle for the ordering of relations with the more numerous but not so radically different
indigenous peoples had a less fortunate outcome. In *Bantu,
Boer, and Briton* the familiar story is not merely told, but retold
as it needed to be in the light of unimpeachable evidence extracted, before they were destroyed, from the Philip Papers.
The decisive part in trans-frontier affairs was of course played
by emigrant colonists; in a less roomy country their exodus
might well have been open revolt or rebellion, but these wan-
derers quickly put themselves out of reach of effective government interference. Americans in particular will appreciate that
scholarship spent in analysing the 'causes' of such a movement is
an otiose exercise—critical though many of them are of other
people's 'colonialism' they will at once see the Trek as an un-
mistakable expression (in highly 'colonialist' form) of the
'frontier spirit'. The Cape farmers, twenty or thirty thousand at
most, had in their first century scattered themselves thinly over
country up to 500 miles from their Cape Town base and could
never be stayed indefinitely even by Bantu rivals from a venture
into the continent lying ahead of them; it was always a question
only how long their advance would be delayed. When at last
hundreds of families uprooted themselves to join the so-called
'Great' Trek, it was in the confident hope of better living in
lands that by this time they knew (see below, p. 197) to be
better suited to their way of life than those they were leaving.
To their credit, and that of the Bantu, the lands they occupied
never became an American 'Wild West'. The opening tragedy
was unique. In spite of emotional names like Weenen, place
of *weeping* for Dingaan's victims, and *Blood* River, scene of the

avenging battle, the pattern ever since has been one of isolated farmers, much outnumbered by Bantu but living peacefully, each with his '*volk*' (labourers) in a near-by *stad* (village) of family huts. The pity is that, coming when it did, the invasion of the *hinterland* was exclusively by pastoralists, truly a peculiar people who thus cut themselves off more completely than ever from trade and other influences which might have mellowed their almost seventeenth-century political code. Their frontier life had its risks and, frontier-fashion, they were taking none; the peace depended on the humble submission of the dependent peoples to masters whose claims to possess the land and all that was on it were final and absolute.

The aims and objectives of the emigrants emerge very clearly from the little they put in writing. The well-known *Manifesto* of the leader, Piet Retief, is the *locus classicus*; having denounced the evil effects of vagrancy and of plunder by 'Caffres' and others he adds:

We complain of the unjustifiable odium ... cast upon us by interested and dishonest persons under the cloak of religion, whose testimony is believed in England, to the exclusion of all evidence in our favour; and we can see, as the result of this prejudice, nothing but the total ruin of the country.

It was the 'Black Circuit' which obviously still rankled, and the more for what followed it. Thus:

We are resolved, wherever we go, that we will uphold the just principles of liberty; but, whilst we will take care that no one shall be held in a state of slavery, it is our determination to maintain such regulations as may suppress crime, and preserve proper relations between master and servant.

The *im*proper relations complained of could only be those Retief saw as the inevitable result of the 50th Ordinance without the stiffening supplied by the newly disallowed, and 'proper', Vagrant Law. In other words, the 'resolve' of which Retief was the spokesman was nothing less than to repudiate the 'Cape policy' of which these two official actions, one positive the other negative, were the corner-stone; they were resolved, further, to do all in their power to thwart the extension of this policy beyond the frontier of the Cape as then constituted.

Seldom has any historical movement been so successful—and more than successful since in the end the Frontier Resurgent has swept back and overrun the bastions of the Cape itself. But it is not the way of the frontier to deal in such plain statement of *ideas* as Retief bravely attempted when a personal vendetta will serve. And there was 'Dr. Philip', the personal embodiment of everything they so bitterly resented—when the L.M.S.'s disgraceful part in the Black Circuit had all but wrecked the Society, this man came in to revive its fortunes, by base intrigue to foist upon the country the mischievous 50th Ordinance and then, even after being convicted of libel uttered in the earlier campaign, to baulk them all of a proper Vagrant Law. On a simple *post ergo propter hoc* principle, the woes of the frontier that followed hard on this man's coming must be his *fault*. A moment later, when disappointed hopes of frontier farms were swelling the ranks of the Trekkers, they had it—of the criticisms which caused this upset—on Governor D'Urban's authority (below, p. 160), '*This is all Philip.*' From that day to this the troubles of South Africa have continued to be 'all Philip'.

This book is thus the record of the failure of the attempt to save South Africa from itself by a wide early application of the principles Philip strove for. Why he failed his own evidence will best, or can alone fully, show—how, for example, the bitter hate already aroused by his work on behalf of the Cape Hottentots caused the Governor to shroud his own dealings with Philip on frontier matters in misleading mystery, and how the abandonment of the newly annexed 'Kaffirland' was pressed upon the Governor by the Colonial Office *against* Philip's advice.

Students of the Great Trek will be well advised to give attention to its effects rather than to sterile analysis of its causes. The concluding chapter should demonstrate how these were almost wholly disastrous. The hope must be that sharp gleams of new light from the lost Philip Papers may dispel some of the darkness which has so long obscured the frontier story. The evidence is that Philip was unusually well informed and that, in spite of this, his counsel went almost wholly to waste. The charge of 'outside interference' which has always clouded the minds both of the older frontiersmen and of their present-day heirs and successors cannot lie against Philip who was in fact an old-established and widely travelled Cape citizen—one who spoke for many more than himself and was even bound to express his opinions. Many of these opinions were unpopular and the offence they gave has lived on. The outraged frontiersmen, his contemporaries, denounced Philip and all his works and the descendants dutifully cherished the tradition of the fathers. The view that Philip is responsible for all that went awry in the country's history has thus become a national dogma and, perhaps more than anything else, blinded later generations to the true significance of the events of those decisive early years.

II

THE BANTU TRIBES—CUSTOMS AND
INSTITUTIONS—CHAKA AND OTHERS

In the days of the Dutch East India Company the only people
of colour in the Colony, other than the scattered Bushmen and
imported slaves, were the Hottentots. The Bantu tribes first
compelled attention only towards the end of the Company's
days and remained an increasing but still a frontier and external
distraction till some years after the Great Trek. It was not till
after 1846 that the colonial Government assumed direct responsibility for whole communities of *subjects* of Bantu race.

The unsatisfactory term *Bantu* was first applied to a group of
languages apparently derived from some common ancestor.
Many of the peoples now so named may have common physical
features; the black curly hair and thick lips of the negroid
persist, and similar social customs; but the name connotes no
single political group. History knows only scattered tribes,
loosely connected with one another like those of ancient Germany and Gaul, the very multitude of names indicating that
the tribes were constantly breaking up and new combinations
forming. Those most prominent in South African history fall
into four groups, Ama-Xhosa, Ama-Zulu, Bechuana, and
Basuto.[1] The Ama-Xhosa ('Kaffirs') held the old Cape Frontier, the Ama-Zulu (Angoni) the coastal belt farther east in
Natal and beyond; the Bechuana inhabited the country east of
the Kalahari and much of what is now the western Transvaal;
the Basuto, on the eastern High Veld, on the upper waters of the
Orange River and the Caledon, were the scattered remnants
gathered together and organized after the Chaka wars (below,
p. 31) by the great chief Moshesh in the South African Switzer-
land still known as Basutoland. The term 'Kaffir', now barred
(see Note on Nomenclature, p. xv), stands as a reminder of an

---

[1] The Bantu languages make use of prefixes—e.g. *ama*, or *ba*, denotes the whole
tribe, as in *Ama*-Xhosa, *Ba*suto; an individual is a *Mo*suto, *Mo*chuana; the
language, *Se*chuana or *Se*suto; the country *Le*suto.

east coast origin and of early contact with Islam; by long
association the name served to distinguish those of the eastern
frontier of the Cape Colony who were long the only Bantu
known to the Europeans.

The Bantu first figured in history in south-east Africa;
whether merely from the internal pressure of population or
from a combination of causes they had in the centuries preceding European settlement at the Cape of Good Hope gradually
penetrated far to the south. For the most part they avoided the
high open plateau; like the earliest Europeans they tended to
hug the sheltered *middle veld* below the escarpment, settling in
the congenial warmth of Natal and the eastern Cape, on the
well-watered slopes of the Drakensberg, and at least in the Low
or Bush Veld of the Transvaal. The extent of Bantu settlement
on the so-called *high veld*, the very heart of modern South
Africa, is uncertain (below, Ch. XIII). In spite of unmatched
summer grazing the rigour of the winter and perhaps the lack
of cover from enemies must have discouraged extensive Bantu
settlement; but the tradition that it was 'empty' ignores evidence
of the effects of the Boer invasion which clearly drove a wedge
between the Basuto of the east and the closely related Bechuana
who are numerous yet in the western Transvaal. For those
driven out the west may have been more tempting than the
alternative, the *low veld*, which was highly malarial. The
Kalahari is not a *desert*. The country north-west of the *High Veld*,
being arid, is healthy and good for cattle-rearing, even the
Kalahari having some good springs,[1] or at worst water-holes,
besides very considerable vegetation which affords the herds
(and still abundant game) both sustenance and beneficent
shade.

By the eighteenth century the Bantu were firmly established
as the only effective occupants of territory stretching from far
away in the north at least to the Kei. In the course of their
expansion they doubtless displaced or vanquished earlier inhabitants; that the coal black of the original Negro type is
noticeably unusual in the south is visual evidence that they
absorbed many Koranna, Hottentots, and others, including
even Bushmen. The theory that they are no more South African

---

[1] The spring at Kuruman, for example, is estimated to yield four or five million
gallons of water daily.

'aboriginals' than their own European conquerors probably owes its vogue to the fact that the Bantu became a serious factor so late in the history of the old Colony, as if they too were really only new-comers. Their conquests had, in fact, absorbed more of southern Africa than is usually admitted, including especially the tract from the Fish River to the Kei which the Bantu, like the Boers, coveted for the sake of the attractive districts from Bedford to King William's Town,[1] not because the arid Fish River bush might sometimes afford cover for thieving.

The earliest recorded conflict was in 1702 when a cattle 'bartering' expedition in the time of the younger van der Stel (Governor 1699–1707) had a serious skirmish 'three or four days' west of the Gamtoos.[2] The first time the Government was obliged to take cognizance of this new factor was more than seventy years later, in the so-called 'First Kaffir War', when the Fish River was made a dividing line between advancing colonists and the African tribes. Following petty 'wars' in 1789 and 1799, the British Government were in 1812 still attempting to 'clear the Zuurveld' (the country *west* of the Fish River), and Grahamstown was established as an outlying frontier post to hold the Fish River line. Undoubtedly the tribes were in effective occupation down to the Fish River long before the Europeans. Williams, of the L.M.S., the first missionary to the 'Kaffirs', took up residence at the 'great place' of the paramount chief, Gaika, in 1816. The 'great place' of a chief is not an outpost, and Williams's grave remains to show that Gaika was within three miles of the later Fort Beaufort, very near the Fish River. Even the outposts still farther west in the Zuurveld must have been fairly strongly held. The Fish River, so far from being an affair of outposts, became, in the language of 1914–18, the 'Western Front' of the long struggle, and European supremacy was not finally established over this much coveted and long

---

[1] 'The Kat and Koonap rivers are the finest part of the Colony', wrote the settler Thomas Pringle to Philip, July 1821, 'and still unoccupied . . . and highly eligible for a missionary settlement.' This belt had been newly cleared to form a 'Neutral Territory'.

[2] The 'Kaffirs' were probably also a scouting party, some days from their own 'land'; documents make no mention of any river east of the Gamtoos, but it seems likely that the Bantu front was far to the west of the Kei—some distance west of the Fish, and possibly even of the Sundays River. Annexures M ff. in the *Defence of W. A. van der Stel*, ed. Leibbrandt, Cape Town, 1897. See also below, pp. 43 and 75 n.

disputed area for fully eighty years. A 'last' war in 1878 made
it in truth a Hundred Years War. The territory from the Kei to
the Natal border is still almost wholly Bantu; and to this day
the fearful congestion of the African population from the Fish
River, indeed from Bathurst, to the Kei, in the area where the
struggle began, bears witness, not to any new or recent influx,
but to the thoroughness, and heedlessness, with which the older
population was not only conquered, but dispossessed. The first
phase in the history of Bantu relations with Europeans is this
long struggle, and there is overwhelming evidence to show how
it was not a lust for colonial cattle, but a passion to defend their
own land which kept chiefs like Maqomo, the most 'turbulent'
of the Xhosa leaders, in chronic unrest till their final disaster in
the 1850's.

The Bantu, being comparatively advanced, were a formidable obstacle in the way of advancing colonists. Unlike the
Hottentots, they had some skill in metal work and were armed
with assegais. Like Caesar's Germans, whom in fact they much
resembled, they did not specially devote themselves to agriculture, living rather on milk—that is, nutritious curdled milk[1]
preserved in gourds known as *kalabashes*—on beef, and to some
extent on the game they took. Yet even their rough and superficial cultivation of maize and 'Kaffir corn' (millet)—the latter
used especially to make their native beer—raised them many
stages above the merely nomadic Hottentots. Their tillage was,
and is, wretched, but in older, roomier days they had a shrewd
eye for the best patches of soil; they habitually settled in one
spot from five to seven years; then, even if the ground was not
exhausted, their huts needed to be renewed for hygienic reasons
and they moved slowly on, 'picking out the eyes' of the country
in their no doubt highly wasteful progress. The Bantu were
tribally rather than territorially organized, and so long as land
was plentiful their ideas of boundaries were as vague and
rudimentary as their notions of land ownership. Yet they were
definitely attached to their own 'country', and the traditional
reverence for the graves of their great chiefs suggests that they
were no mere nomads. Thanks to their agriculture, and to the

---

[1] Cf. Song of Deborah: 'He asked water, and she gave him milk; she brought
forth *butter* in a lordly dish' (Judges v. 25).

fact that in winter, or in time of drought, their cattle got some sustenance from the stubble of the fields, their food supply was far more regular than that of the Hottentots. The physique of these Bantu peoples was generally good; whatever their actual numbers they were relatively closely settled, and for that reason more formidable. The Hottentot mode of life could at best hardly support as many as three to the square mile, whereas the Bantu system could probably, without undue pressure, maintain a population of ten or more anywhere in the important Cape–Natal area.[1] Conditions in the north-west or Bechuana area were less favourable and there the rather scanty population lived in relatively large villages in the immediate neighbourhood of the stronger springs; in the east, except where they clumped together for defensive reasons, the *kraals* (huts belonging to a family unit) tended to be scattered broadcast.

This comparatively settled life made in its turn for a well-developed social organization. The possibility of accumulating cattle for cattle's sake—they sell or slaughter their 'wealth' but sparingly—raised individuals above the dead level of poverty that marked the Hottentots; and though to this day the communal life and instincts of the Bantu are very strong, they are by no means equalitarian. Their stronger men being relieved from the pressure of immediate want could leave most of the necessary tillage to the women and were free to follow the pleasures of hunting or, perhaps even, the 'predatory instincts' with which historians have too liberally endowed them. No doubt, as with others similarly placed, the first rise above the pressure of grinding want stimulated their fighting and acquisitive instincts; but the leaders of their marauding bands were seldom to be classed as mighty warlike chiefs. There is no reason to believe that military despotism was anything but a startling exception to the rude democracy that prevailed among them. The normal Bantu tribe, to this day, has its body of Custom, now usually recognized by European administrators as Law. It has also its *Pitso* (folk-moot), and the chief his *likhotla* (witan), an inner council of wise men and advisers. In practice, no doubt,

[1] Estimates place the population of the rather more favourable plains of western Europe at anything up to 30 to the square mile in the times of the very similar early Celts and Teutons. At the present day several Transkeian districts have about 100 persons to the square mile, but these depend largely on supplementary wages earned on the mines and elsewhere.

the measure of democracy would vary with the strength or weakness of the chief, and the composition of the *likhotla* would be as elastic as that of the early English witan. But there seems little doubt also that as a free people the Bantu had strong political instincts; drastic decisions would not normally be taken by a chief except on the advice of the *likhotla*, and with something like the general consent of the tribe as a whole. The way of dissenters was (and is) hard; an official opposition is not in tune with their custom; but even on their 'Western Front', the scene of the long series of 'Kaffir Wars', there was no effective paramount chief. Governor Somerset, for example, for official convenience made a paramount of Gaika. But Gaika was neither acknowledged by the tribes generally nor capable of making effective the greatness thrust upon him. Many difficulties arose after 1819 from the attempt to enforce recognition of the cession of territory which had been wrung from this chief.

In later times the disciplined military prowess of the Zulu made so great an impression on their neighbours in Natal and the Transvaal that many now generalize about the military instincts and warrior chiefs of the Bantu; when called upon to interpret Native Custom even courts of law tend to ascribe to ordinary Bantu chiefs absolute powers that were in fact enjoyed only by a few outstanding 'kings'[1]—the *amapakati* (counsellors) of old Kaffirland being confused with the *indunas* (military captains) of the Zulus. The almost constitutional chief with his body of councillors, not the despot, was more generally true to type, however the type may have been modified by the revolution forced upon the Bantu in the last 150 years.

The tribal life of the Bantu was clearly uncertain and insecure before ever they came to feel acutely the pressure of the civilized races. No doubt they were cattle-reivers, and highly dangerous and troublesome neighbours. Doubtless also their own military tradition made war an inevitable preliminary to equilibrium on frontiers where they and European colonists

[1] e.g. the Zulu kings, Chaka and Dingaan, their pupil Moselekatze of the Matabele, and possibly some pale imitators in Swaziland. On these points I was indebted to suggestions in a paper lent me by Mr. J. W. Honey, late Resident Commissioner of Swaziland, whose impressions were confirmed independently by informed Europeans and Africans like the late Mr. Aston Key, then of Herschel, and Mr. R. W. Selope Thema, a Johannesburg editor.

clashed. But the natural life of the Bantu, and their chief interests, centred not in 'thieving' but in land. Their primitive methods, and the droughts and other troubles that hinder South African production, can have left little margin of safety; their own population stresses evidently account for many of their internal dissensions. Since they have no records of their own on which to draw we are dependent for knowledge of their old conditions either on random travellers, or on colonists to whom they were a cause for alarm, if not a menace. The evidence of missionaries resident among them is, therefore, of special value, e.g. that of the French missionary Casalis, who, writing from the scene of disorders on the Basuto border, comments significantly:

I fear much confusion arises from the very limited and erroneous ideas generally entertained respecting the statistics of the Bantu country. The population is under-rated, the actual and future wants of the tribe are not taken into consideration. It is no childish debate about the useless waste that takes place at this moment. The present lamentable war of the Basutos and the Mantatees, *which originated in nothing else than a land question*, shows sufficiently how keen and deep are the feelings of the natives on the subject.[1]

The Bantu tribes did not 'always' fall out with each other merely from innate quarrelsomeness and love of fighting.[2] The Bantu as a people are long-suffering and law-abiding; a mere handful of European police[3] was formerly (c. 1920) enough to keep order in the wide area of the Transkei with its million inhabitants. In their own territories—though not necessarily in the artificial European-made conditions of mining camps and towns—all experience shows that white women, for example, are as safe as, or safer than, in a European capital. Indeed, history and administrators agree that the Bantu are singularly amenable to just government. They have never known slavery. Even in defeat which left them powerless and without status their leaders put their case not only with eloquence and logic

---

[1] Casalis to Philip, Feb. 1848.

[2] Even in the war of 1835 there is evidence that while they discriminated against traders—some of whom were not above suspicion—they habitually spared women and children (Cory, iii, pp. 72, 73). Though missionaries were repeatedly cut off by war, and completely in their hands, one of them was unmolested though all but an eyewitness of the Retief massacre. There is hardly a recorded instance of a martyr missionary to the Bantu.

[3] Apparently about 250 all told, including a 'mobile squadron' of over 100.

but with amazing good humour and tact. They are kindly and
cheerful and, as in the famous story of the last days of Dr.
Livingstone, faithful—a people most suitably summed up in the
untranslatable German word, *gemüthlich*. Dr. Theal—following
tradition rather than interpreting it—sweepingly suggests that
in their primitive condition the Bantu when they were not
stealing colonial cattle were 'slaughtering each other'.[1] But the
measured judgement of Bishop Stubbs on Caesar's account of
the early Germanic tribes is a corrective to exaggerations of
this kind:

The features remarked on by Caesar—the perpetual state of war,
the neglect of agriculture for pastoral pursuits and hunting, the
annual migrations of tribes—are, it is true, commonly viewed as
characteristic of the first steps out of barbarism into civilization; but
the first two are extremely liable to exaggeration by rumour, and
the prominence of the whole three in this description is owing to the
generally unsettled state of all tribes bordering on the Roman
conquests.[2]

The first quarter of the nineteenth century, when the European onset first became serious, was just such a period of unsettlement and of 'perpetual war' among the Bantu tribes
behind the western or European front. Some years after 1783, on
the banks of the Umfolosi in what is still called Zululand, a
'younger son' of the then undistinguished Ama-Zulu tribe provoked the jealousy of the chief his father by his athletic and
warlike prowess.[3] This lad, named Chaka, ran away from home
and took refuge and service with a rather greater chief, his own
tribe's overlord, Dingiswayo—himself a man out of the ordinary.
In his own youth Dingiswayo too had fled from his father. In his
wanderings he saw a little of the European military system and
was impressed by the value of discipline. Returning at last to
the chieftainship, he applied the lessons he had learnt to the
refurbishing of the traditional military methods of his own
people, laying the foundations of the military system afterwards
developed by Chaka and associated with the Zulu name. The

---

[1] Theal, v, p. 254 and elsewhere.   [2] *Select Charters*, 8th ed., p. 52.
[3] There are many recent examples. In 1925 the heir of the well-known Khama
had had about twenty years in exile, and about the same time a common labourer,
as it seemed, was recalled from the farm of a European to succeed his father
Mpefu as chief of the Zoutpansberg Bavenda.

unit was the regiment (*impi*), subject to an iron and, if reports be true, a bloody discipline. As in some other savage armies the braves were taught to regard marriage as a reward reserved for those who had worthily 'washed their spears' and had their baptism of blood. The usual Bantu weapon was the assegai hurled from a distance or, when it came to 'push of pike', broken off short and used as a dagger. The Zulus were more formidably equipped with a short stabbing spear; their regular formation in attack was the crescent, backed by reserves kept ready to be pushed forward to any point that was specially threatened. At the very outset Dingiswayo's manifestation of Bantu militarism reflected European example.

Chaka himself first came into prominence while still in the service of Dingiswayo, rising by the patronage of his master to the chieftainship of his own Zulu tribe. Finally, when Dingiswayo himself died without direct heir, he was thrust by the army, of which he was now the most distinguished leader, into the position of supreme power. Then, by all accounts, there began ten years or more of storm and stress for the whole of the Bantu people of southern Africa. Though dates, detailed facts, and estimates of the numbers involved are alike doubtful, it seems fairly certain, by unanimous Bantu tradition, that from a little before 1820 Chaka entered on the career of a Timurlane, attacking, murdering, or putting to flight, over an area wider than modern Natal and Zululand. In September 1828 he met the common fate of tyrants, being murdered in his own kraal in a 'palace conspiracy' by his two brothers; one of these, Dingaan by name, succeeded him as king of the Zulus and was to crown his career by the murder of Retief and his fellow-trekkers in the February of 1838.

The actual course of the Chaka wars is uncertain, but their effects, reaching far beyond Natal and the coastal strip in which they originated, largely determined the redistribution of tribes and set the stage for developments in the age of the Great Trek (below, Chs. XII ff.); thus the High Veld itself probably owed some increase of its comparatively small Bantu population to the dispersal of tribes by the wars of the 1820's. The carrying of war on to the High Veld was not the work of Chaka himself. One of his early victims was a certain Matiwana who, as Sir

George Cory puts it, 'unable to oppose the Great King, carried on the process of extermination on his own account' and, crossing the Drakensberg, sent wave upon wave of refugees flying or plundering over the plains beyond. Of these the best known are the bearded Mantatees who, in the middle of 1823, began to fall upon the unwarlike Bechuana of the west. These Bechuana were now under the influence of the London missionaries, and Robert Moffat at this point stood them in good stead, calling in the help of the Griquas (or Bastards), mounted and armed with guns (see Ch. IV), who met and defeated in the neighbourhood of Kuruman a party of raiders whom Moffat himself long supposed to have been Mantatees; they were in fact certain Bafokeng who had themselves been displaced by this so-called *horde*. The epithet was probably just, for the Mantatees soon broke up; one section, the Makololo, came to rest near the Zambezi and became protégés of David Livingstone; others, under Sikonyela, we hear of in the forties contending for land, the perennial quest, but this time on the Caledon River, and with Moshesh. Even the Griquas' own feuds were aggravated by disturbances among the Bantu. Bands of them rejected the government-favoured authority of chiefs like Waterboer and took to the 'mountains',[1] whence the name *Bergenaars*—whence also they carried on illicit trade with the Colony, and themselves kept the north in confusion by their plundering raids upon the unlucky Bechuana.

The Chaka wars also first forced the Bantu in considerable numbers across the mountain barrier of the Amatolas and the Katberg into country one remove from the influence of the sea-breezes, hitherto left to clans of Bushmen.[2] Round about 1820 the remnants of a royal tribe, the Tembus, began to occupy the country near what is now Queenstown, figuring in the frontier history of that time as the 'Tambookies', to the further considerable complication of the troubles of both tribes and colonists on the eastern frontier. About 1824 numbers of Bechuana refugees, flying both from Mantatees and from *Bergenaars*, made their appearance inside the Cape Colony and were readily 'apprenticed' or '*ingeboekt*' to farm labour. A little later, about 1828,

[1] *Cape Col. Qn.*, pp. 252 ff.
[2] As late as 1843 the Rev. James Read was exerting himself in these parts on behalf of a Bushman chief described as 'King' Madoor.

refugees from Chaka himself began either to disturb the uneasy peace of the eastern frontier, or to appear, as 'Fingos', in the Colony itself; and so for the first time the farmers began to draw on men of Bantu race for the supply of farm-labour of which they were so short.[1]

Not all the victims of the wars were mere refugees destined to become detribalized labourers dependent on white farmers. The troubles of these days gave his great opportunity above all to one of the most sagacious and statesmanlike of Bantu chiefs, one who was no mere bloodthirsty warrior. The Basuto chief, Moshesh, not only used his geographical advantages to make an impregnable fortress of his famous capital, Thaba Bosigo, but more than once was able to show both British and Boers that he knew something also of the arts of peace, and when to make or keep peace. He it was who, in 1832, sent an embassy to 'buy' a missionary from Dr. Philip, then on tour at Philippolis;[2] the price, 1,000 head of cattle, was carried off by border robbers (Korannas) and never reached its destination, but Dr. Philip was directly instrumental very shortly afterwards in diverting French Protestant missionaries from their disturbed first station among the Bechuana, to Basutoland with which their Society has been identified ever since. Moshesh's great feat was to bind the broken tribes of the broad valleys of the Drakensberg into a homogeneous people, the Basuto. This chief was yet to play a highly important part in the history of the country (see Ch. XVII), and Basutoland[3] remains, like the Transkei, a crowded but compact island of Bantu in the mixed and troubled South African scene.

The important influence farther north was an offshoot of the Zulu army itself, a 'Matabele' division which broke away under Moselekatze (Mzilikazi). This almost equally famous warrior fell out with Chaka and, being threatened with vengeance, took his army off to the north-west through parts of the northern

---

[1] *Cape Col. Qn.*, pp. 252 ff.

[2] Moshesh was so determined to have a teacher that he seems to have urged the local chief Adam Kok to come himself if no one else was available.

[3] It is significant that in the eastern Transvaal, in parts separated from 'Basutoland' by a large stretch of High Veld with only detribalized fragments of a farm-native population, the most widely spoken Bantu dialect is still *Sesuto*. The Boer Republics, therefore, must have driven a wedge into these Sesuto-speaking tribes; Moshesh's claim to more land than the Free State was willing to concede was justified.

Free State and western Transvaal; he followed this new route, it would seem (see p. 36, and note), to escape the raids of slave-traders in the north. Moselekatze no doubt modelled his rule on that of his master, Chaka, and practised a similar despotism. It is possible, however, that tradition is none too reliable, ex-aggerating, if not his savagery, then at least his power and its effective organization. Evidence suggests strongly that this potentate often went more like a fugitive in terror of enemies than like an all-conquering tyrant.[1] In 1829 Moselekatze was visited by Robert Moffat and in 1832 by some of the newly arrived French missionaries; a M. Lemue reported to Dr. Philip that Moselekatze was anxious to detain one of these forcibly, 'for himself'—rather a bear's embrace, no doubt, for the mere proximity of the Matabele soon drove the Frenchmen to abandon work they had begun in the later Transvaal among the 'Bahurutsi'.

This desire for a missionary was, perhaps, political rather than spiritual. 'Moselekatze', Moffat wrote to Philip on 15 August 1832.

appears ever since Berends' commando to entertain some doubts as to the real character and motives of missionaries, well knowing that the Banditti who treacherously assailed his territories and murdered his subjects emanated from the Missionary Station. . . . Notwithstanding his apparent attachment and confidence in me, he has some fears that I am a powerful chief, and had some part in the nefarious proceedings of old Berend.[2]

At all events little came of his overtures,[3] and Moselekatze's

---

[1] One Jan Viljoen, a well-known elephant hunter, who in later years was inti-mate with the chief, tells how Moselekatze himself claimed that his wholesale massacres were 'an act of policy': 'I was like a blind man', he is reported to have said, 'feeling my way with a stick. We had heard tales of great *impis* that suddenly popped up from underground, or swept down on you from high mountains' (referring, it seems, to cave-dwelling tribes with mountain strongholds in the Zoutpansberg) 'and we had a dread of the Korannas, mounted and armed with rifles. I had to keep open veld around me.' (Quoted in the *Star*, 17 Oct. 1925, by Adv. Eugene Marais, who adds a remarkable story of the privileges allowed to a certain Barolong who had guided Moselekatze from before the Boers on the Marico to safety in his later home in 'Matabeleland'.)

[2] Presumably Barend Barends, who, with one Hendriks, made a raid on the Matabele in April or May 1832, and seized some cattle. The raiders seem to have been ambushed, with loss of guns and horses, on their return journey.

[3] As late as Apr. 1834 Rolland, one of the French missionaries, wrote urging upon his colleagues, who had gone from Bechuanaland to Moshesh in Basutoland, the need for someone to 'propitiate' Moselekatze, even 'for the protection of Moshesh'.

'country' (if any such there was) never had the same settled attractions as that of Moshesh for missionary work. In 1832 he had the far north-west in terror, and Dr. Philip, returning from one of his tours of inspection in January 1833, warned the authorities at Graaff-Reinet of possible danger to the Colony itself. As a matter of fact this unrest, which prevented Dr. Philip from visiting the tyrant's kraal, was perhaps due to the lawlessness of some of the Griquas who at that very time, by Moffat's account, suffered chastisement at the hands of Moselekatze himself. As late as August 1835 Moffat appears again to have paid him a visit. In his Journal of that year he reported that Moselekatze was still wanting a missionary; he would have 'only Mosheti' (Moffat), and wished 'to throw away his spears and live in peace'. For a short time American missionaries settled with him, but about 1837, when the Voortrekkers came to blows with his *impis* at Vechtkop and Mosega, in the centre and west of the High Veld, they seem to have removed to Natal.

Fortunately the Matabele, as they came to be called, left the Colony alone. For some years they engaged in a struggle with the Boers for ownership of the Vaal country, and though not all their fights were against the Matabele, the Boers of the early Transvaal were almost annually on 'commando' and the country knew little peace or settlement. In the more open country of the north-west there was no natural fortress like Thaba Bosigo to make the rallying centre of a second Basutoland even had Moselekatze learned like Moshesh to make his military power merely defensive, and the Matabele were soon driven out. The ruins of their kraals are plentiful in the western Transvaal, and fragments of the Matabele themselves remain in that province. But the main body withdrew far to the north; Moselekatze's son was the Lobengula who was finally conquered in the nineties, near the site of Bulawayo, by the Chartered Company.

How far this great upheaval among the Bantu must be attributed, in Bishop Stubbs's words, to the 'generally unsettled state of all tribes bordering' on European conquests can never be fully known. From the nature of the case the effects of the frontier wars on the remoter tribes are not directly evident, but clearly there was a connexion. It is significant that the rise of

Chaka came at the very moment when things were moving towards a climax on the Cape frontier, and that his wars synchronize with those of Gaika and Ndhlambi on the borders of the Colony (see p. 51). The check to their vanguard on the Fish River, in the severe set-back which began in 1812, could not be without its influence on the Bantu in Natal and Zululand.

The slave-trade as a factor in producing so much war and tumult cannot be passed over. For a hundred years past traders had not only raided on their own account but set tribe against tribe in such fashion as leaves no reason to suppose the southern part of Africa unaffected. In 1823 Governor Somerset was discussing the desirability of annexing Delagoa Bay, significantly near the scene of Chaka's devastations, as a check on the slave-trade. Not long afterwards, Dr. Philip, writing from Bechuanaland in the end of 1832,[1] quoted hitherto unnoticed evidence that even South African Bantu tribes had direct cause to fear the ravages of the slave-trade. The tyrant warrior Moselekatze, it appears, when he fled before Chaka, first went to the north; but there he encountered 'brown-skinned men armed with guns', slave-raiders from Portuguese ports; which serves to explain, what is in itself surprising, the westward route followed by the Matabele in the devastating raid that carried them at last across mountains and open plains towards Bechuanaland. To his friend, Rev. J. Campbell, Philip wrote at the same time:

The people of Moselekatze have for ages past had to maintain an incessant struggle against the Portuguese slave-traders, and war has become their element.

The Chaka wars, whatever their origin, were contemporaneous with the growing impact of the European colonists upon the African people and had incalculable consequences for

---

[1] Dr. Philip's evidence is important, resting as it does on that of Mr. Moffat and of the French missionaries who had visited Moselekatze in person in 1829 and 1832 respectively—as reflecting perhaps also current native gossip. In 1830 he writes, sweepingly, from Kaffirland: 'Farewell and others (i.e. pioneers at Port Natal) have stirred up war wherever they have gone. To Farewell's establishment at Port Natal we are to trace the devastations of Chaka.' Moffat's own comment (15 Aug. 1832) suggests at least how the doings of the earliest Natal settlers appeared to their neighbours: 'Moselekatze knows well how many white men live with Dingaan, and how far they have assisted him in his sanguinary expeditions.'

the European population. Sooner or later delicate and difficult problems of frontier and legal relationships were bound to arise from the contact of races. But the devastation caused by the wars made the Boers believe that the land they coveted now lay empty before them. The feeble resistance of the Bantu gave the impression that they had been all but wiped out by their own wars, and so much of the land seemed to lie open that the Great Trek presently became in effect a Grand Dispersal. The Colonists were growing in number, and mere pressure of population heightened their land-hunger and drove them more and more upon the war-ravaged Bantu. Their own hard life and pioneering achievements have too largely filled the picture. Even at the time they were not without warning of the consequences of their heedless encroachment upon Bantu land. As early as 1824 Dr. Philip was writing:

I consider it highly impolitic to drive the Caffres to desperation by depriving them of their cattle, by illicit trade, or by encroachment on their grazing land. . . . Deprive a commercial people of their property, their ingenuity is still left, and may be turned to advantage; deprive an agricultural people of the produce of their fields and they will continue to sow for themselves in the hope of obtaining some return; but if you deprive a pastoral people of their herds, you instantly convert them into banditti . . . they have no resources left and they inevitably betake themselves to the thickets and attempt to live by plunder.[1]

This warning fell on deaf ears, for the sufficient reason that the encroaching colonists saw the indigenous peoples only as an obstacle to be overcome, or removed.

[1] Dr. Philip's *Memo. on Settlers*, written in 1824. *Cape Col. Qn.*, p. 114.

III

THE FRONTIER BOERS AND THE FIRST GREAT TREK—FIRST CONTACT WITH THE BANTU

For a hundred years after 1652, before the Bantu tribes began to affect the course of events, the very monotony of life in the European settlement helped to mould Boer character and habits and determine the general attitude of the colonists to later developments. Geographical conditions in the first instance decided the course of South African colonization—the scanty rainfall, the distance from one water-hole or fountain to the next, the lack of roads or transport, and the almost total want of markets for produce, most of all, the vast extent of the country itself. The Company Government's policy far from counteracting geographical influences rather reinforced them. Officially, indeed, its face was set against any extension of its responsibilities by colonial expansion—it was interested only to make the Cape serviceable as a port of call—but by cutting the prices offered for produce and by the restrictions laid on private trade of any kind the Company made Cape Town a place to be avoided and itself drove colonists to that dispersal over the country which it was utterly powerless either to prevent or control.

Only the Western Province had a natural agricultural potential, and a market, and there alone a solid nucleus, with Huguenot settlers as its core, established itself. At most 100 miles east of Cape Town, and considerably less to the north, the rainfall becomes increasingly uncertain and only grazing was possible. The economic consequence was a decline of living standards which is evident from the almost total absence east of Swellendam of specimens of the fine domestic architecture still to be seen nearer Cape Town. The arid interior bred a race of hardy pioneers of whom a growing proportion were content with lean-to houses, or even became more than *semi*-nomadic *trek-Boere*. The Company's land laws positively encouraged dispersal. The normal tenure was the *leenings-plaats*, or one year lease, for which the uniform charge was 24 rix-dollars[1] per annum, regardless of the value of the land. On the death of the owner the *opstal* (buildings and permanent improvements) was put up to auction (fees being an important source of revenue) and the proceeds of sale were, as common law required, divided equally among the heirs.[2] The purchase of the *opstal* carried with it the right to take over the lease and neighbours eager to acquire land for their sons nearby appear to have been ready buyers.

Except in the agricultural west all depended on cattle breeding and recurrent droughts made large farms inevitable; fencing and camping as a means of husbanding the pasture still commonly require costly imported materials, and till our own day winter-feeding of stock by the use of hay or ensilage was never practised. In the eighteenth century it became almost normal to move ever farther on and start afresh on the same easy leasehold terms. The old Boers, indeed, can hardly be blamed—the total absence of markets made intensive cultivation futile, and to subdivide a mere grazing farm was to reduce what little value it had. A formidable enemy might have compelled the colonists to dig themselves in round their base at Cape Town, but the Hottentot aborigines were utterly incapable of resistance. So long, therefore, as land was plentiful families trekked, the trek outspanned, the more favourable outspans became settlements, the Hottentot aboriginals moving on or else sinking into dependence as servants. Confronted at last with a *fait accompli* the Government could hardly refuse to recognize effective and almost entirely peaceful occupation; thus, step by step, the official boundary of the Cape Colony was pushed out far beyond the original 'Hottentots' Holland', in sight of Cape Town, to the distant Orange River.[3]

This unresisted colonial expansion, and the habit of mind

[1] The rix-dollar was once worth about 4*s*. 6*d*. I have often heard Cape produce-sellers ask for a *dollar* (*thaler*), meaning 1*s*. 6*d*., the nominal value of the depreciated rix-dollar of the 1820's.

[2] The desire of the settler-farmer to keep a family home intact would explain how in the West the extremes of the Roman-Dutch tradition of equal inheritance were modified by some of the sons taking their 'share' out of the estate in education or training instead of in land—thus preventing subdivision going to such disastrous lengths in the West as farther inland.

[3] E. A. Walker, *Historical Atlas*, O.U.P., Maps 7 and 10.

which it induced, ought to have been sharply checked in the
1770's when contact with the great Bantu people about the
Fish River put some term to the direct advance. It was no
longer safe for families to push out into 'Kaffirland'; the Fish
River, in truth, first indicated as the boundary as early as 1774,
and definitively so about 1780, remained the eastern boundary
for over fifty years—till 1847. This check was prolonged, but
only a partial barrier to Boer penetration. The urgency of
eastern frontier affairs has obscured the significance of the
advance that continued uninterruptedly in the north. As early
as 1778 the erection of Plettenberg's Beacon (near Colesberg)
to mark the northern boundary of the Colony was a sign that
the 'first Great Trek', as Dr. Gie[1] rightly calls the expansion
of the eighteenth century, was being diverted at last away from
the coastal belt; a few years later, in 1786, Graaff-Reinet was
established as a *'landdrostdy'* (magistracy) to serve the population of a large new district. Gradually this new northern area
filled up; in 1826, even while the direct eastward advance was
stayed, the Government by simple proclamation acknowledged
the Orange River as the boundary. Thus, in spite of the Bantu,
and in mere extent if not in its capacity to support a large
population, the expansion of the Colony went on as before.
Even Bantu opposition did little to break what was now settled
habit, or to mitigate the land-hunger that remained the great
characteristic of South African rural life.

In the north, where there were no 'Kaffirs', the old isolation
of the days before 1779 was even intensified. The early trek-
Boers, by whose efforts and for whose benefit Graaff-Reinet was
established in 1786, now found themselves in country with a
rainfall ever smaller and less regular; but there were springs in
fair abundance and, for a small population, highly desirable
farms in the kloofs and valleys about the great mountain knot
of the Sneeuwberg, behind Graaff-Reinet. Even along the base
of the Camdeboo Mountains, in the arid neighbourhood of the
later hamlets of Willowmore and Aberdeen, there are many
delectable farms. Mountains were no real barrier and before
long the Graaff-Reinet district had a ward or field-cornetcy
significantly known as *Achter*-Sneeuwberg. Here at last the Boers
began to touch the great inland plateau of the High Veld

---

[1] *Geskiedenis vir Zuid Afrika*, i, by S. F. N. Gie.

which figures so largely in later history. The dry western, or 'Karoo', portion of this plateau had on the whole been left unoccupied except in the neighbourhood of Graaff-Reinet itself. Beyond the Sneeuwberg the Boers came within range for the first time of country with rather more reliable summer rains, the *grass veld*, where in spite of droughts and locusts there was in those days little danger of over-stocking; there being comparatively little grass-burning the *vleis*, with their sponge of vegetation, retained their moisture, and the drought-resisting powers of the country were greater than now. The superabundance of game also made mere living comparatively easy, incidentally sparing farmers the need to slaughter cattle for food. Yet farms were inevitably more and more scattered. The isolation and self-dependence of the Boers were, if anything, intensified in these northern districts from which the bulk of the Trekkers of 1836 were destined to come. But conditions were very similar even on the troubled and insecure eastern frontier where land-hunger was less easily assuaged.[1] Writing from near the Koonap on 11 April 1830, one constant traveller, Dr. Philip, comments:

This morning about 5 o'clock some farmers passed us going to Beaufort to meet Mr. Stockenström to solicit farms in this country formerly belonging to the Caffres, and now to be divided among the colonists [i.e. land from which chief Maqomo had been expelled in 1829]. This craving for grants of land on the part of the Boers, and the means taken by Governments to gratify (it) call for some strictures in this place.

The habits of a great proportion of the Boers belonging to this colony are perfectly Scythian in their character. Accustomed to large grants of land when land was abundant and colonists few, they still think that they cannot subsist unless a farm includes the same range of country which it did in the days of their ancestors. Their habits are pastoral, they seldom cultivate more ground than is necessary for their own use, and their wealth is in their cattle. Having extensive herds they not only require much pasture, but are not satisfied if they have not different places to resort to at different seasons of the year. On these occasions, when they change their residences, their families generally accompany them, and they live in their wagons. Besides what they require for their herds, to save

---

[1] In 1796, for example, Graaff-Reinet burghers were petitioning the newly arrived General Craig for land 'unto the Konab, or it may be unto the Kat River'. They were put off with vague promises of 'later' (*C.C. Records*, vol. i).

them, they must have game also, and each farmer living in this manner, instead of a moderate sized farm, must have a district for himself. Their children are brought up with the ideas of their parents; (they seldom learn trades) unless it be as much knowledge of smith and carpenter work as may enable them to do something for themselves or their neighbours. Anything done by slaves or Hottentots is quite beneath them and it is very seldom indeed that you meet with the son of a farmer following a trade or serving another for wages (unless perhaps in rare instances confined to the neighbourhood of Cape Town) . . . from infancy their first thoughts, and those of their parents, to provide new places for them. (Occasionally) you will find a married son and a married daughter as permanent, nor are they contemplated as desirable longer than till they can be provided with establishments of their own. The practice along the whole extended frontier has been for many years to appropriate for the children the spots occupied by the Natives in their immediate neighbourhood. All they can see they consider their own, and when needed, the Natives are obliged to remove (to make room for) their cattle or their children. By this means they first take possession and afterwards get the Government to sanction the deed. (Nor is this practice) confined to those on the colonial boundary. Like the breaking out of water, although that nearest the break runs out first, that behind, even to the extremity of the dam, soon follows. Allured by the prospects of an estate in the new territory, such as have interest with those that have it in their gift soon swell the tide of emigration, and others who are poor sell their estates to their next neighbours who want them for their sons and daughters, and with the price they receive stock their new farms.

Supposing things to proceed in this order, it is obvious, considering the large families generally found among the Boers, that the colony must *double its extent* every thirty or thirty-five years. This is not mere theory, it is what has happened, and must happen, while the system which has hitherto been acted upon continues. . . . (Dr. Philip goes on to instance the northern expansion between 1802 and 1825.)

Under these easy-going and yet arduous conditions Dutch and Huguenots, with possibly a dash of Germans, were welded into Boers—with a predominantly Calvinistic religious tradition and, for the rest, a love of sun and open spaces, hardy self-reliance, consummate skill in handling a gun, and withal a kindly if robust sense of humour. On the other hand the Boer's self-reliance and love of independence tended to harden not only into an impatience of Government control, but into an incapacity for co-operation even with his own fellows. The Boers, Dr. Philip commented later, 'are gregarious but not social'. The habits fostered by the life of the eighteenth century go far to explain how it was that these sturdy sons of nature became a little contemptuous or merely regardless of the coloured population.

The natural tendency has been to interpret the course of history almost exclusively as it affected the fortunes of the white colonists. Just because the community was so small and dispersed it was fifty years before the effects of the check on the Fish River were generally felt. Life was dangerous for those of them who chose to farm on the frontier, but their troubles and difficulties were not matter of life and death for the Colony as a whole; as late as the twenties even frontier Grahamstown was almost more concerned about the Cape struggle for political rights than with the Bantu in their near neighbourhood.[1] Only after 1825 when expansion northward as well as eastward was checked, and the population rather larger, the issue was no longer to be deferred. By the thirties the stage was fairly set for the inevitable trial of strength between the European colonists and their Bantu rivals for possession of the land, and in the twenty years that followed all other questions tended to take second place.

The definite clash with the Bantu was only the final stage in a gradual development. The skirmish of 1702 did nothing to discourage further 'cattle-trading' expeditions—if indeed the discovery of Bantu wealth in cattle did not serve as a positive inducement to the more venturesome of the colonists to improve their fortunes. The Company, however, having no stomach for new responsibilities, habitually set its face against intercourse between its burghers and the natives, repeatedly issuing *Placaats* against such trade;[2] but as the *Placaats* had no administrative force behind them there were continual comings and goings between the Colony and Kaffirland, not without occasional appeals, on either side, to *Faust Recht*, the rule of the strong arm. It was in an attempt to put some limit to increasing disorders that in 1778, following 'non-intercourse' edicts in 1770 and

---

[1] *Cape Col. Qn.*, chs. ix and xiv.
[2] About 1700 the restraints on the cattle-trade were temporarily lifted.

1774, Governor van Plettenberg undertook something in the nature of a Grand Tour of the frontier districts. On the 'Kaffir' frontier he seems to have concluded a 'treaty', solemnly ratified by his Council of Policy, fixing the Great Fish River as the dividing line between the Colony and the Bantu territories.

Van Plettenberg's concern, after all, was not so much to fix carefully defined *territorial* boundaries[1] as to strengthen the colonial jurisdiction in a danger zone which was also the principal scene of illicit barter between colonists and Xhosa; he had an eye, that is to say, for general policy rather than for troublesome local details, or even for topography. In the first place the 'treaty' seems to have been concluded without reference to any of the greater chiefs west of the Kei—like Rarabe, the reputed Paramount, of blood royal; and while it is very doubtful if even a paramount had power to cede territory, it is quite certain that lesser chiefs had neither power nor authority to bind any but themselves. Indeed, it is clear that Governor and Bantu thought in different languages and little attempt was made to arrive at a real mutual understanding. Europeans are apt to read into such treaties the assumptions of 'civilization', without being at any pains to understand Bantu ways of thinking. To European minds the fixing of the colonial boundary at the Fish River carried with it the idea of annexation, with exclusive rights of control up to that point. Bantu custom, on the other hand, like that even of late medieval Europe, knew only *usufructuary* rights in land; Bantu chiefs habitually granted the use of land, in return for cattle, to men who virtually became their vassals; but the idea of title and private *ownership* in land was as foreign to their ways of thinking as to those of feudal Europe. This fundamental difference in standards would account for much of the friction which ensued. The Bantu treaty-makers of 1778 probably did no more than agree to anything the Governor proposed in order to rid themselves of an embarrassingly formidable visitor.

But neither was the Governor at pains to be precise in his definitions. 'The Fish River', for example, may sound a definitive term but was in all its long history as the boundary

---

[1] Sir Charles Lucas's suggestion, *Historical Geography*, vol. iv, pt. i, p. 82 n. 'The Dutch would presumably not have admitted the right of other Europeans to settle beyond them.'

of the Colony the endless source of disputes. Except in occasional seasonal floods the 'great' river is, in fact, no barrier at all, but fordable almost dry-shod along the greater part of its course. Even more serious, there was always a certain vagueness about what was meant by the Fish River line; for a matter of fifty miles, from near the later Fort Beaufort to the sea, the impressive valley of the river might well serve as a *line*, and this is probably as much as the Governor saw and had in mind. But above that point the river runs almost parallel to the sea and at right angles to any natural dividing line between Colony and Bantu. In later years it was habitually assumed that the Governor must have intended his line to follow the roughly straight north–south line of the tributary Kat River, an (always tacit) assumption which meant excluding the tribes from the valuable, well-watered foothills of the Katberg and Winterberg on *their own* side of the alleged Fish River line. This unusually beautiful country, not cover for thieves in the Fish River bush, was the prize so hotly contested for fifty years. The 'Treaty' of 1778 was unsatisfactory from beginning to end. If, as is doubtful, there was any chief capable of binding the whole of the Xhosa tribes, he had no hand in the bargain. It was no doubt impossible to make clear to the chiefs concerned the European conception of a boundary or of land-ownership, but in the last resort the boundary line itself was vague and indefinite. Thomas Pringle comments in manuscripts of the 1820's:

Nominally, the Governor had the consent of some of the Caffres, but not of the chiefs. The Ghonaquas (Hottentots) who inhabited the land between the Gamtoos and the Fish were never even considered. The Boers were left to deal with them as they had dealt with their brethren already extinct.

Hence, he concludes, the 'wars' of 1781 and 1789—and, he might have added, the unusually active part played by remnants of the Hottentots in the troubles of 1799–1803.[1]

The result was as might have been expected. It has never been suggested that the Fish River was a boundary of 'effective occupation', or that in 1778 there were no Bantu west of the Fish River, that is to say—in the new language—within the Colony. Even if white colonists now for the most part confined

[1] *Cape Col. Qn.*, p. 144.

their enterprises to the country west of the line they observed the colonial limits in a new spirit of assertive ownership. The very next year one of the Xhosa treaty-makers was forcibly driven across the Fish River 'out of the colony'[1]— and when the Xhosa made very natural reprisals upon colonists' cattle, the farmers, who were now fairly numerous in the neighbourhood of the later Somerset East, formed themselves into a 'commando' and the 'First Kaffir War' followed. The Government itself, however unwillingly, sanctioned action by the burghers, and by 1781 'the Kaffirs', we are told, had been driven across the Fish River, a fair share of their cattle being divided among the triumphant victors by way of compensation for their sufferings.

'The Kaffirs were expelled', so invariable tradition has it, but presently 'crept back'—as often on later occasions, and in other parts of the country. But in a wide, almost trackless bush country, with a very sparse and scattered population, no expulsion could have been so thorough as to necessitate any stealthy 'creeping' back. Even in 1921 the density of the population in the Somerset–Cradock–Bedford–Albany area was no more than from 4 or 5 to 12 to the square mile; in those days it must have been even less. The adventures of General Christiaan de Wet in the war of 1899–1902 are sufficient proof of the extreme difficulty, even with much better facilities—roads, railways, and the telegraph or even the heliograph—of making a clean sweep of (or by) columns operating in wide African spaces. It is obvious that while in this first war the Xhosa were sharply punished, the Zuurveld must have been only temporarily and very partially 'cleared' of its Xhosa population. The Company Government, indeed, was in no position to take strong, firm action for the holding of its new boundary, and in 1789 a 'second' war had begun, still for the most part *west* of the Fish River. This time the Government in making peace agreed to allow the Xhosa to remain in the Zuurveld, 'without prejudice to the ownership of Europeans'.[2]

In 1793 again there were both Xhosa attacks and a formidable counter-attack. The Government for its part was inclined to regard the encroachment of its own Boers as the prime cause of the trouble, and in 1793 General Sluysken, the last of the

---

[1] Theal, *History Before 1795*, iii. 128.
[2] Ibid. 181.

Company Governors, showed his disapprobation of the warring commandos of that year by a formidable proclamation which recapitulated all the penalties threatened by earlier edicts and forbade trade and all intercourse with the tribes beyond the Baviaans River (a tributary this time slightly *east* of the Fish River proper). Five years later, in 1798, the British Governor, Earl Macartney, followed this up with a proclamation defining the Fish River boundary a little more precisely and forbidding 'elephant-hunters' or others to cross the line except with an express permit. Neither the Company nor its immediate successors (British after 1795) were disposed to take the steps necessary for the security of frontier colonists but, in spite of Government frowns, the struggle had fairly begun for possession of the country 'unto the Konab, or it may be even unto the Kat'[1]—and beyond it, indeed, to the Kei. The time was not far distant when, as one General Vandeleur prophesied, 'either the Boers and British together must drive the Kafirs from the Zuurveld or the British must build a fort and watch the Boers and the Natives fight it out'.[2] The frontier Boers, that is to say, though they suffered constant raids and losses—more than once farms east of Uitenhage were left deserted—never dreamt of abandoning all hope of potentially fat farms for fear of a parcel of Ama-Xhosa barbarians.

The failure of the old Dutch Government to afford the frontiersmen the protection and security which they thought their unquestionable right, together with the practical humanitarianism of a Dutch official, the Landdrost Maynier of Graaff-Reinet, had consequences of permanent significance. In 1795 a party of malcontents took forcible possession of the *drostdy* (residency) at Graaff-Reinet, expelled the unpopular Maynier, who had done his best to restrain them from dealing with Natives and Native opposition in their own way, and proceeded to elect officials of their own. A few months later, Boers at Swellendam following this example established their own 'republic'. Both Graaff-Reinet and Swellendam were apparently far from the frontier, but in those days they were also the most distant outposts of Government, and the double outbreak was in large part due to the Company's utter failure to govern its

---

[1] Petition of the Burghers for land, to General Craig, in 1796.
[2] Quoted by Walker, p. 138.

dependency. In the seven years immediately following, 1795–
1803, the time of the first British Occupation, years of fair
progress and prosperity in the west, the interior and the eastern
frontier continued disturbed and the cleavage between the
Colony and the frontier deepened. In Graaff-Reinet there was
still overt rebellion; farther east, Xhosa and even Hottentots
raided and plundered and learnt the art of war from their
white masters—the Xhosa by 1803 being probably more firmly
established than ever in the Zuurveld from the Fish to the
Sundays River. The continuing state of insecurity, due as it
seemed to the weakness of Cape Town, confirmed a section of
the frontier Boers in a lasting tradition that the only remedy for
grievances was to take the law into their own hands and
establish a 'republic'; and so separatism was the last of the
legacies of the Dutch East India Company. That it was bound
up from its earliest beginnings with a peculiarly self-confident
view of the only way to deal with the weaker races may in part
account for the sometimes merely petulant aloofness of latter-
day republicanism.

After a few more years the authorities of the second British
Occupation (1806) really awoke to the state of the frontier. The
pressure of the farmers clamouring for land, and the insecurity
of legally occupied farms to the east of Uitenhage, led Earl
Caledon to send a certain Colonel Collins round the borders,
like van Plettenberg before him, to report; and in 1809
Collins recommended[1] that the best hope of peace was to extend the border to the Koonap, to increase the number of the
magistrates, to strengthen the European population, and, more
immediately, to drive the chief Ndhlambi and his people out of
the Zuurveld. Earl Caledon seems to have hesitated to use force
—fearing the disapproval of Whitehall; on 16 October 1809 he
reported to Lord Castlereagh against the proposal to clear the
Zuurveld, and in June 1810 that the frontier was 'quiet'. But in
1811 his successor, Sir John Cradock, inclining to more vigorous
measures, first deplored to Lord Liverpool the abandonment of
farms near Algoa Bay, then on 8 October ordered the landdrosts to call out the burghers, and finally on 18 October gave
Colonel Graham, the frontier commandant, a free hand to deal
with the situation—using 'persuasion if possible'. In the early

---

[1] *C.C. Records*, vii. 101 ff.

months of 1812 Colonel Graham came to blows with Ndhlambi near Coega on the Sundays River, and Ndhlambi and many followers were forcibly driven across the Fish River. In March, according to Dr. Theal, 'the war was over'; but in spite of the foundation of Grahamstown and lesser strong places to hold the line of the new–old Fish River frontier, there was very little difference between peace and war in those parts. The burghers called up in October 1811 were disbanded only in the July of 1814.[1]

The significance of all this is perpetually missed. It is preposterous to pronounce as if it were the righting of a wrong that '20,000 Ndhlambis and Gunakwebis' were 'driven out of the Zuurveld across the Fish River'. Ndhlambi's protest was reported from the Sundays River in 1811—'This land is mine. I won it in war, and intend to keep it';[2] land and not cattle-stealing was always the first concern. Any boundary that banishes and excludes all the original inhabitants of a district is an anomaly; annexation of the country carried with it an obligation towards existing occupiers. But now the Ndhlambis, who had obviously been in occupation of the Zuurveld for many years and had no other home, were only driven on top of their rivals, the Gaikas, who were neither able nor willing forthwith to make room for 20,000 immigrants. This long-deferred and strong-handed clearing of the Zuurveld could do nothing to bring peace and security to the frontier.

It was not as though the Bantu at this time lacked troubles of their own, other even than almost normal economic stress. It can only be imagined what wild news, and wilder rumours, were carried by the drums or 'bush telegraph' through all the regions between the Fish River and the scenes of war and tumult farther north. At any time, moreover, their tribal system was liable to such dissensions as rent even an empire like that of Charlemagne in ninth-century Europe. The chiefs were a royal family, but neither were the chiefs 'absolute' nor was there any salutary rule of primogeniture or direct hereditary succession. The heir was the son of the 'great' wife, not of the 'right hand' wife nor of the 'left' and, as the 'great' wife was commonly married late in life, this heir was often an infant whose elder

---

[1] C.C. Records, vii. 101 ff.   [2] C.C. Records, viii. 235.

821620   E

brothers were themselves the leaders of a strong interest or 'clan' of their own, possibly even regents during the 'paramount's' minority. The resulting multitude of chiefs of the blood royal explains the bewildering number of 'tribes'. On the Cape frontier, for example, the Ama-Xhosa were an imperfectly united tribal group who, till about 1775, recognized a common allegiance to one Palo. Early in the period of contact, however, two groups emerged, one, east of the Kei, adhering to Palo's 'great' son Gcaleka, the other, or western branch, following Rarabe. It was now the turn of the 'Rarabes' (as the western Xhosa are sometimes called) to break up; even in the 1790's there are ominous signs of divisions and of rivalry in their own ranks, some clans adhering to Gaika, others to his uncle Ndhlambi—Gaika being the heir and grandson, by the 'great' wife, of the widely acknowledged chief Rarabe, while Ndhlambi was the 'wicked uncle', an older and more experienced man, the son by a less important wife of Rarabe himself.[1] When to their own domestic quarrels (and faction fights and 'beer' fights are still common) there was added the struggle for land about the Fish River and the driving in of tribe upon tribe, the disturbance was manifestly increased. European intrigues for Xhosa support[2]—even if it was only by adventurers like one notorious Coenrad Buijs, with his Xhosa wives, in the Graaff-Reinet troubles following 1795—must still further have stimulated and intensified tribal divisions.

The internal dissensions of the Bantu soon reached a climax which materially affected the unity and disposition of the tribes in the Fish River area. The irruption of the Zuurveld refugees caused a great sharpening of the old feud between Gaika and Ndhlambi—and Ndhlambi, the chief of the newly conquered Zuurveld, was the source of disturbance. The more distant Gaika, who was less directly involved in the colonial advance and had, as it chanced also, the better hereditary title, was the recognized ally of the white man—who found it convenient to recognize his paramountcy in spite of his practical inability to answer for Ndhlambi and the western clans whose interests were primarily concerned. As early as 1803 he agreed with General

---

[1] For genealogy see Theal, iii. 93. In later times the chief Maqomo played a somewhat similar part by his younger brother, Gaika's 'great' son, Sandile.
[2] *C.C. Records*, ii, pp. 148, 333, 349, 364.

Janssens to acknowledge the Fish River as the boundary. In 1815 again Gaika found recognition of another sort, flattering no doubt to his sense of dignity; twice over he was approached with requests for help by Boer malcontents then engaged in the episode known as the Slagter's Nek rebellion—a protest against the legal countenance now being given to Hottentot servants.[1] In later years this was not forgotten by Gaika's son, Maqomo, who complained in 1835 that despite his loyalty in 1815 Gaika, when his turn came, like Ndhlambi before him lost his country.[2]

At the time, because of Gaika's seeming partiality for the white man and his failure to rally the Xhosa peoples for the defence of their Fish River borderlands, the leadership of the Bantu in what was unmistakably a primitive nationalist movement passed into other hands; between 1812 and 1819 an Elisha, at once soldier and prophet, by name Makana,[3] became their hero, evidently a remarkable personality. Makana's aim seems to have been to restore Xhosa unity—and the danger from the white man, who had already 'cleared the Zuurveld', gave him his rallying cry. In 1818 Makana's influence thrown on to the side of the fighter Ndhlambi was decisive in the overthrow of the waverer, Gaika, in a large-scale battle on the Amalinde Flats, near the later King William's Town. When, moreover, Gaika's appeal for Government help brought a European force raiding beyond the Fish, it was Makana who, on 22 April 1819, led a counter-attack and from an eminence still known as Makana's Kop, at close quarters, directed wave upon wave of warriors against the very gates of the barracks at Fort England in Grahamstown. The attack failed; Makana soon after was compelled to surrender[4] and it was left for Lord Charles Somerset to patch up with the restored Gaika a continuance of the *pax bellicosa;* his establishment of a 'Neutral Belt' was a vain attempt to place a vacant strip of land, 'from the Fish to the Keiskama', as a bar to the mutual encroachments of European and Bantu. The wide open spaces of the northern districts, where

[1] *Cape Col. Qn.*, p. 91.
[2] Journal of Capt. Stretch, Sept. 1835.
[3] For details see Theal, i. 269 ff. The missionary Williams writes of the prophet as *McKannah*, his bellicosity perhaps suggesting a Hibernian connexion!
[4] He died by drowning in attempting to escape from his prison on Robben Island; but for long years, according to Dr. Theal, his people looked for Makana's return—like that of a hero of the Middle Ages.

the ways and doings of the colonial farmers were little inhibited by fear of active opposition, better reveal the general pattern. A survey of contemporary happenings in that area may thus helpfully precede further consideration of how events in the east moved to their climax.

IV

THE NORTHERN FRONTIER—THE GRIQUA 'STATES'—EXPANSION CHECKED, 1834

THE Boers who joined the so-called first Great Trek to the non-Bantu North for many years found their occupation of land and fountains disputed only by remnants of the helpless Bushmen, as at Tooverberg (Colesberg).[1] But certain mixed-breeds, refugees from the Colony, mattered more. In numbers and organization they were weak, but having an admixture of European blood they were more sophisticated than the Cape Hottentots and even venturesome; also, they were not without cattle; but above all, as protégés of the L.M.S. they had champions to defend their rights as the first occupants of land about the Orange River, and of the not so numerous fountains in that neighbourhood. By the 1820's Boers looking for farms even on this secondary front no longer went unchallenged.

These mixed-breeds, themselves comparative new-comers, owed any little coherence they had to the organization and discipline of missionaries of the L.M.S. According to a fragment of missionary history Messrs. William Anderson and Kramer—two of the missionaries who arrived soon after Dr. van der Kemp, about 1800—directed their attention to Bushmen on the Zak River (north of Beaufort West). There they soon 'collected a number of people belonging to different tribes, Korannas, Namaquas, Hottentots, Bastard Hottentots, and Bushmen, who ultimately formed what is now called the *Griqua* people'.[2] For six years or more Mr. Anderson and his colleague lived a semi-nomadic life with this 'motley group of scattered remnants till they were able to induce their flock to settle in villages'. By about 1820 there seem to have been three such village centres,

---

[1] *Cape Col. Qn.*, pp. 128 ff.

[2] (Fragment in handwriting of Mrs. Philip.) These tribes were all closely allied—none of them Bantu. Colonists significantly tended to rank them all together as 'Bastards'; though at least one missionary distinguishes between 'Bastards' and 'Griquas'.

at Klaarwater (Griquatown), Campbell, and, a little later, at
Philippolis, with Andries Waterboer, Cornelius Kok, and Adam
Kok respectively as 'captains', appointed under missionary
influence and vaguely recognized by the Cape Government. It
must have been heart-breaking work for the missionaries to
build up the so-called Griqua 'states'; that there were three—in
a population estimated in 1823 at no more than 3,000 in all—is
the measure of their ultimate insignificance.

The difficulties were, indeed, immense. The nature of the
country made close settlement impossible. The Griquas retained some of the primitive nomadic traditions of the aborigin-
al Koranna or Hottentot tribes, while the more sophisticated
'Bastards', cherishing resentment against the labour conditions in the Colony from which they had fled, were likely to be
intractable. Even the advent of white colonists brought neither
agricultural development nor such local demand for labour as
would have provided wages, however poor, to supplement the
bareness of life in these arid districts where, even in later times,
only the diamonds of Kimberley have made some progress
possible. In those early times the Griquas easily fell into bad
ways, not without prompting from runagate Europeans.[1] A
very old Bechuana once assured me there were in his early days
'only lions and Bushmen' in that country! The Griquas seem to
have thought in these terms of the unfortunate Bushmen as
there to be harried, and not infrequently pursued them with
'commandos'.

The presence on the frontier of an even rudely organized
body of coloured people closely related to the 'free' coloured
inhabitants of the Colony would have seemed to necessitate
some attempt to define their official and legal relations with the
Colony. The Government was not anxious to incur new responsibilities, but from time to time it stepped in to remind the
Griquas of their obligations. The first instance of interference,
however, was not calculated to promote harmony, or to give the
Griquas confidence in the benevolence of the Government.
When in 1814 it was proposed to strengthen the Cape Corps (of
'Hottentots') for the defence of the eastern frontier, the colonial
origin of the 'Bastards' was the warranty for ordering Mr.
Anderson to furnish twenty recruits from Griquatown to make

up the quota to be 'commandeered' from the nearest (yet far distant) *drostdy* of Tulbagh. The missionary not unnaturally failed, or refused, to make himself responsible for doing duty as recruiting sergeant.

As a direct consequence the official view now came to be that it was undesirable to have such communities of coloured people, near or beyond the frontiers, imperfectly controlled by missionaries; they would only serve, it was alleged, as 'rendez-vous' for runaway servants. Two Bushman stations of the L.M.S. were actually suppressed in 1818; their fate was the burning question in the first two years of Dr. Philip's superintendency. The Rev. John Campbell, a visiting Director of the L.M.S., agreed, in 1820, that there was need for firm 'control'; meantime, in 1819, Governor Somerset had gone so far as to complain to London that the mission stations 'subtracted that useful class of labourers from those useful occupations to which they were best suited', and told Dr. Philip that 'Griquatown should be broke up'.[1] Griquatown, in fact, was not so treated; but the threat did much mischief. For when in 1822 its chief was so far recognized as to have Mr. John Melville sent to him as a resident Government Agent, Waterboer and the Agent were continually hampered by the people's natural fear that the Government's main object was to draw on the military resources of the Griquas and 'make them soldiers'.

In the early twenties anarchy in the Griqua country was intensified by the reactions of the Chaka wars. While three chiefs contested the supremacy in the villages, malcontents broke away altogether and took to the 'mountains', whence there came and went small bands of *Bergenaars*,[2] obtaining all the guns and powder they needed by illicit traffic with white colonists, and too often paying for them with cattle stolen from neighbours like the Bechuana. In 1822 Dr. Philip wrote:

---

[1] *Cape Col. Qn.*, ch. x.
[2] 'The spirit of independence among the Griquas, with the strong prejudice in the minds of some against the Colony, appears to me to be occasioned in great measure by their connexion with the "Bastards" of the Colony, who live all along the Orange River, and in different parts of the country, and who seem at present to acknowledge no authority whatever. . . . The obstruction to the introduction of suitable regulations and the preservation of good order is the want of power in the chiefs. . . . That the banditti (e.g. plunderers of the Bechuana) should have such facilities in trading with the farmers on the frontier favours their independence and is an inducement to others to join them' (Melville to Col. Bird, 22 Jan. 1824).

The Boers began to visit the Griquas and trade with them in guns, gunpowder and brandy; whereupon they soon got tired of depending on their own efforts to increase their herds, (and, becoming more daring went further afield and) attacked the herds of the more helpless Bechuanas with guns.

One influence alone promised to check Griqua dissensions. Early in 1823 Robert Moffat reported from Lattakoo, or Kuruman, the menacing advance of the Mantatees—a 'fierce nation from the south-east, who lay everything low before them'. 'Kureechane', where in 1820 John Campbell had attended a vast *Pitso*, or folk-moot, of 16,000 or 20,000 Bechuana (so he estimated), was said to be a heap of ruins. Three months later, in June, Mr. Moffat found it necessary to ride post-haste to Griquatown for help and, towards the end of the month, a body of Griquas, 200 of them with only fifteen rounds of ammunition apiece, broke the attack near Lattakoo. The raiders, it seems, were a remnant fleeing from the real Mantatees, who were themselves disorganized fugitives; but the unwarlike character of the Bechuana, and at any rate their dependence on widely scattered water-holes or fountains, made any interference highly disturbing. The confusion, and the opportunities of plunder afforded for many years by the comings and goings both of Mantatees and of Bechuana fugitives, also gravely disturbed the unity and coherence of the unstable Griquas.

The importance of these small and inherently weak Griqua states arose from their strategical position. Dry and difficult as it was, their country commanded two main lines of advance into the centre of Africa and was, therefore, directly and vitally involved in the developments of the next twenty or thirty years. Griquatown was early recognized by travellers like the Rev. John Campbell, and after him by his colleague, Dr. Philip, as the 'gate' to the far interior. The chief of Griquatown was from the beginning in close touch with the Bechuana tribes;[1] these reached as far south as Taungs and Kuruman, and occupied also a great part of what is now the western Transvaal. Later, Griquatown and Kuruman became the recognized starting-points of the 'Missionary Road' into the interior—a road favoured as at once more central, and a way of avoiding the ups

---

[1] e.g. tribes such as the Batlapin, Barolong, Bapedi, Bahurutsi, Bamangwato, Bakwena, Bangwaketsi.

and downs of any route that had to climb the High Veld ridge
of the Transvaal only to descend again to the malarial valley of
the Limpopo. This was the road, first followed by Moffat and
Livingstone, which ultimately figured largely in the Cape-to-
Cairo plans and dreams of Cecil Rhodes.

Immediately, however, these continental considerations
mattered less than others of only local import. While Waterboer
held the gate to the interior, the Kok family round Philippolis
were at the point of convergence of four of the main *drifts* or
fords across the great Orange River, right across the main or
High Veld line of advance, first of the old colonial Boers and
ultimately of the Great Trek itself. The Griquas, therefore, who
had fled from the Colony with ideas of 'independence' not unlike those of later Boers, were destined not long to remain
undisturbed; in 1826 the Colonial boundary was extended to
the Orange River and, before many more years had passed,
their claims to the land and the fountains they had occupied on
its northern bank were sharply challenged. In the late twenties
Philippolis was already torn by dissensions due to the close
approach of the Boers. In the thirties and forties Philippolis
became even more acutely the storm centre of disputes between
Boers and missionaries, the latter seeking to defend the prior
rights of the coloured people. The greater part of the Griqua
country was soon so completely absorbed by the dominant
Europeans that the important part it once played is apt to be
forgotten. The virtual disappearance of the Griquas followed
but, however feeble, they obstructed the way to the north at a
moment when the Bantu threatened to close the road to the
east and thus had significance out of all proportion to their
numbers and quality.

As early as 1820 Dr. Philip had begun to plan for political
reform and general reconstruction in Griqualand. He proposed
to strengthen the missionary personnel, urging also that 'by
increasing their artificial wants, you increase the dependence
of the Griquas on the colony, and make for the preservation of
peace'.[1] In criticizing Mr. Melville's appointment as Agent in
1822 he put his finger on the weak spot of frontier policy, of
that as of a later day, when he insisted that 'such an Agent

---

[1] Dr. Philip to Sir Rufane Donkin, 12 May 1820.

should have effective Government power behind him, and Government ought to *accompany the appointment with sufficient power to enforce its authority*.[1] But the pre-1828 disabilities of the Hottentots[2] within the Colony brought Nemesis in their reactions even on trans-frontier problems; the semi-civilized Griquas had fled from insecure, unrewarding service in the Colony, and such stout champions of the Rule of Law as Dr. Philip himself were, just at first, chary of bringing them too directly under the control of the Colonial Government. To Robert Moffat he wrote on 31 January 1822 (a letter of which the then newly appointed Mr. Melville was the bearer):

The present situation of our stations within the Colony gives us very little to hope from the extension of the Colony. . . . Look at Bethelsdorp, Theopolis and Zuurbraak. While the greater part of the able-bodied men are serving the Government, and receiving nothing but rations, the women and children are perishing at home for want of the necessaries of life, and the missionaries are teased to death about every trifle the local authorities think proper to impose upon them.

As it was, Mr. Melville's letters, both to the Governor and to Dr. Philip, make it clear that with little or no effective support behind him, the more Waterboer tried to get control and to keep order in the country in a natural and evidently sincere desire to stand well with the Government, the more the *Bergenaars* continued to attract recruits by trading on the general 'fear of being made soldiers'.[3] Waterboer's reward, indeed, was to have Andries Stockenström, Landdrost of Graaff-Reinet, writing to warn and advise the Governor against assisting him on the ground that he 'is unpopular with his own people'.[4] If he was unpopular it was undoubtedly because of his attempt to suppress gun-running and lawlessness.

'After four years' discouraging work'[5] the Government Agent resigned in despair in April 1826. The depredations of the *Bergenaars* continued, though they do not seem to have been so serious as to prevent a good deal of coming and going by solitary

[1] Letter from Griquatown, to some unnamed official, in Sept. 1825, when Philip reviewed the whole history of the Griqua frontier from which he had just returned.   [2] *Cape Col. Qn., passim.*
[3] Letter of J. Melville to Colonial Secretary, Dec. 1824.
[4] Report from Landdrost of Graaff-Reinet, 22 Oct. 1824.
[5] Cory, ii. 229.

travellers.[1] Under the guidance of a new and capable missionary (Mr. P. Wright), Waterboer seems gradually to have
established order in his own immediate neighbourhood; when,
about 1832, a new and serious danger arose through the advent
of the formidable Zulu (or Matabele) Moselekatze, Waterboer
was one comparatively stable protection to those whom Dr.
Philip described (after a tour in 1832) as the 'peaceful and unwarlike Frontier Boers'.[2] All this time partial Government
recognition had continued; a note survives, dated 7 August
1827, in which Captain Stockenström requests 'Captain' Waterboer to apprehend a burgher called Karel Kruger who had
crossed the border with a false pass, and to 'hand him over, a
prisoner', to any one of the field-cornets on the frontier. Many
later difficulties, both in the days of the Trek and at the time
when diamonds were discovered, might have been prevented
had the highly elastic boundaries of the Cape Colony been extended at that early time to include definitely this Griqua
country.

So long as intercourse between the Colony and Griqualand
was so slight the failure of the Government to follow any
strong or consistent policy in the north was hardly to be
wondered at. The population was so scanty that fifteen or
twenty horsemen constituted a 'robber band' and the advance
of such a party against Griquatown a 'battle'. But now, just
when the anarchy of the Griqua bands was beginning to yield
in some small measure to discipline and missionary organization, the economic distress of the colonial farmers, and their
chronic land-hunger intensified by droughts, brought increasingly large numbers of Boers to sow fresh discord.

The 'First Greak Trek' which had gone on almost uninterruptedly through the later eighteenth century now pressed in upon
the Philippolis Griquas. Actual annexation, though hitherto it

[1] Mr. Miles, Dr. Philip's substitute, visited Griquatown on the eve of a *Bergenaar*
'attack' in Dec. 1827, and Messrs. Moffat, Hamilton, and Hughes seem to have
moved freely between Griquatown and Kuruman.

[2] In face of Moselekatze, Waterboer kept his head better than his neighbours. To
one panic-stricken appeal from a Bechuana chief, he replied, with characteristic
shrewdness, advising the chief not to show his alarm, but '*blij dood stil*' (keep perfectly quiet); his own preparedness, and comparative efficiency, kept him and his
immediate neighbours from suffering any serious interference.

had never been long delayed, tended to linger behind occupation, and the years following the 'Orange River' boundary
proclamation of 1825 were marked by great activity on the part
of trekking Boers along the newly defined boundary. Unlike
earlier movements the trek in this part of the country had eye-
witnesses and is described, especially in reports to their superintendent, Dr. Philip, by the London missionary champions of
the Griquas who, with remnants of the Bushmen, were now in
danger of being dispossessed and, in the classical sense of the
word, 'exterminated'. Not only was the eighteenth-century
'trek' prolonged into the nineteenth century without any pause,
but the Greak Trek itself was taking fairly definite shape for
some years before 1836.

As early as 1825 a missionary artisan named James Clark,
who had the Bushmen as his special charge, wrote from Philippolis describing a journey he had made 'to the east'; he had
difficulty, he said, in getting into touch with the wild Bushmen;
they fled at the approach of his party; one old man, however,
explained that 'they thought we were Boers, that their native
kraals were near the boundary of the Colony, but that in consequence of Boers coming over the boundary . . . they had left
their kraals and gone farther into the country'. At a station
well beyond the Colony, that is to say, 'Boers who come over the
Cradock (i.e. Orange) to pasture' (Mr. Clark's words) were a
matter of course and no new phenomenon. Throughout the
year 1826 Mr. Clark's Journal is full of complaints that the
Bushmen were leaving him in consequence of the numbers of
Boers pressing into the district, apparently with Government
permits, and that Boers were petitioning the Government for
leave to occupy the (Bushman) fountains *beyond* the Orange
River which had been fixed as the boundary one year before. In
December 1828 he writes:

I beg to mention that in consequence of *hundreds* of the Boers
having been over the boundary this, *as in former years*, with their
cattle, (they have been since last June in the Bushman country),
they are not only driving the Bushmen from their fountains, and the
wild game, their principal support, but they have thus reduced them
to the necessity either to steal the farmers' cattle, or perish of hunger.

About this time, indeed, the pressure became too great for the
shy Bushmen and Mr. Clark was obliged to remove to a new

'Bushman Station' (at or near the later Bethulie), leaving Philippolis entirely to the Griquas whose numbers, it seems, were being recruited from among the newly freed Hottentots of the Cape Colony.[1]

While it must be said that the Griquas themselves were as likely as the Boers to harry the unfortunate Bushmen—even in 1833 Dr. Philip was still censuring Kok for the behaviour of his people towards them—Mr. Clark's Journal is illuminating as evidence that as early as 1826 the Boers had made their presence felt. Mr. Clark mentions also attacks by 'Caffres', presumably remnants of the Mantatees, and refers to the Boer habit of leaving cattle and 'cattle places' (farms used for grazing only) in charge of 'Caffre' herdsmen. This practice, remarked on also by Captain Stockenström, was complained of by Mr. Clark as depriving the Bushmen of their only hope of employment, and tending, therefore, to drive them to live by theft. But the 'Trek' was as yet primarily a search for grazing rather than a wholesale migration of families. Mr. Clark, indeed, attributed some of the Boer unsettlement to the new quit-rent tenure of farms,[2] as if the increased Government charge for land forced a choice between over-stocking the farms and a trek; habitually, he added, they spared and increased their herds by living on the game which still abounded.

The Boers had in fact come to stay. 'Captain' Adam Kok's solemn restrictions on the sale or exchange of the farms he 'granted' to his burghers were utterly futile.[3] Repeated references by missionaries clearly indicate that in return for wagons, oxen, or possibly brandy, the unstable Griquas readily gave the encroaching Boers extensive rights to lease or occupy both lands and fountains. Their leaders appealed in vain to the people to put ultimate security before the chance of immediate profit. In the end of 1829 a copy of a petition signed by Adam Kok, Hendriks, and others begging the Governor to deal with

[1] 'Hottentots were glad to leave the Colony because the Boers left no land for them there' (Clark to Philip, 2 Apr. 1830).

[2] The quit-rent introduced after 1813 was a charge that varied according to the quality of the land—the charge for the older *leeningsplaats* had been an invariable annual amount (Walker, p. 204).

[3] Philippolis, 5 May 1828. 'By this the place called Witkrans is given to the Burgher Manels as lawful property to him and his heirs, under this condition that the said Manels shall not sell or exchange this place to any colonial Burgher. Given by Captain Adam Kok and his council.' (Signed Capt. Adam Kok.) (Translation.)

Boer encroachments on 'land that belonged to their fore-fathers' was sent to Dr. Philip by Mr. Melville, now turned missionary, and confidential secretary to Adam Kok.[1] The petition urged that the Griquas had always been a defence to the Colony, recalled with alarm the 'oppression' their fathers had suffered, and begged that the farmers be forbidden to cross the frontier. Significantly, they also asked for a ban on 'hawkers' who supplied Korannas and others with ammunition (this be-ing a hint that they were not responsible for alleged robberies); some eighteen months later, May 1831, Kok was writing to Philip still protesting rather lamely against a charge that his Griquas had attacked the Bechuana. Mr. Wright had some reason to fear (in August 1833) that 'it is so easy to steal cattle, and then to exchange cattle for ammunition from traders and horses from Boers, that it is difficult for "good men" to remain "good" in that country'. Griqua depredations, however, were without terrors for the Boers; in the letter of 1831 Kok protests that his people are about to move, since they 'love freedom and fear the Boers'; the Boers are too strong to be resisted and, though they encroach on their lands and fountains, the Government does not protect them; they mean to go, there-fore, they 'know not whither', but 'will take a missionary with them'.

Of the steady Boer encroachment there is no doubt and, being wholly without government, the country was thrown into greater confusion than ever by disputes between masterful, land-hungry Boer colonists and feeble Griquas who, first in the field, had taken possession of the most eligible farm-sites. In 1831 Kok was thinking of removing 'he knew not whither'. In October 1832 Dr. Philip wrote from Cradock: 'there are 1,500 Boers (the numbers are probably travellers' guess-work) across that boundary, depasturing the Bushman country and contending with the Griquas'. Two years later—in what were really the initial moves in the 'Great Trek'—there were said to be 1,600 Boers beyond the Orange River, half of them on the 'grounds of the Philippolis mission station' (a 60- or 70-mile stretch). They

[1] At first, 31 Dec. 1828, Mr. Melville remarked that he was received with hostil-ity or suspicion at Philippolis because he brought no supply of the gunpowder which as Agent he secured for Waterboer, and also because of his previous holding of a Government position. In Oct. 1830 he had settled down, and tells Dr. Philip he 'will see that the chief writes nothing but what will bear examination'.

were at this time only so much 'of' the Colony that they came to Colesberg annually to pay their taxes.[1]

In face of this now permanent complication in what was still sometimes called Bushmanland, the Government like its predecessors was inconsistent in its attitude. Economic forces were in any case too strong. On 25 April 1828 Major Dundas, Civil Commissioner of Albany, suggested to the Government the expediency of relieving the distress of farmers then suffering from drought by granting them permission to pass the frontier. This was refused, the letter being endorsed with the Governor's minute in pencil: 'Acquaint the Civil Commissioner that His Honour cannot approve of this suggestion. It would lead to the unlimited extension of the Colony.'[2] Notwithstanding the Acting Governor's disapproval, however, or before it had reached him, Major Dundas seems to have acted on his own responsibility, issuing the following notice,[3] which was freely acted on for years to come in spite of a long series of earlier prohibitive proclamations:

The inhabitants of the sub-division of Tarka are hereby informed that the undersigned has been apprised by the Field Cornet, J. H. Steenkamp, that the cattle belonging to the inhabitants of his division suffer much by the drought for want of good pasturage.

The Field Cornet is, therefore, hereby empowered to allow the cattle to be sent to graze beyond the boundary, in such places as are not occupied by Tambookies, or other natives.

He will also be vigilant to prevent as much as possible all intercourse with the said natives.

Civil Commissioner's Office, Cradock,
April 14th, 1828.
(Sgd.) W. B. DUNDAS,
Civil Commissioner for Albany and Somerset.

There is an undated copy of another Government notice

---

[1] Dispatch No. 40, 1 June 1834, and Chase, *History of South Africa*, ii. 35, 255. In Oct. 1834 Philip wrote to Miss Buxton: 'When I was on my Northern Tour in 1832 there were not 15 Boers, where there are now 1,100. I was then apprised to their intentions, and warned the Government of the danger, but nothing was done.'

[2] *Cape Town Archives*, vol. Albany, No. 588.

[3] There is a doubt about the date, but none about the fact of this notice. Sir B. D'Urban, in the discussions of Sept. or Oct. 1834, refers specifically to Dundas's notice of 14 Apr. 1828, annulled in *Gazette* of 12 Sept. 1834 which also recapitulated earlier prohibitions, now to be enforced, against trekking.

bound up with Mr. Clark's letters, which obviously belongs to this period:

(Griqua Country): And whereas many memorials have been presented, praying for grants of land situated beyond the boundaries of the Colony, and even beyond the Great Orange River, it is hereby notified that no attention will be paid to such Memorials.

In spite of the frowns of the Government memorials persisted,[1] or land was occupied even without regular legal sanction. Dr. Philip, when discussing later frontier questions with Sir Benjamin D'Urban, blamed 'the imbecile administration of Sir Lowry Cole'[2] for much of the trouble in the north and hinted that the contradictions were deliberately designed, the prohibitions and restrictions for the consumption and solace of uneasy Secretaries of State, and possibly of humanitarians—the concessions, like that of Major Dundas, as expedients to meet the local situation. But the weakness lay rather in the Government's inability to cope with the situation. With no legal authority, few troops, and no police, the Government was nearly helpless even to maintain order beyond the frontiers where, as Earl Goderich (Colonial Secretary) reminded Governor Sir Lowry Cole on 3 December 1831, colonial judges had no jurisdiction unless with express Parliamentary sanction.[3] Only a strong administration could really have availed. But now, in spite of the confusion across the frontier, the Government which so lately as 1825 had extended the Colony to the Orange River refused any further responsibility. It neither attempted to limit Boer expansion nor brought the Griquas under its protection and control.

The Colony and Governor, had they chosen to attend, might have been guided by the good sense and moderation of one travelled and well informed statesman, their bugbear Dr. Philip. On his first trip to the north, back in 1825, he summed up the position in a sentence: 'The Landdrosts of the Frontier districts are too far removed from the scene of action. What would

[1] See, for example, reference by the Trekker, Sarel Celliers, Bird, i. 252.
[2] Letter to Miss Buxton, 7 Oct. 1834.
[3] Such powers were sanctioned only in terms of the Cape of Good Hope Punishment Act of 1836, extending jurisdiction to Latitude 25 degrees S., and even then proved so unsatisfactory in practice that the Act was seldom applied, and did nothing to control the Trek (see below, Ch. XII).

Scotland be like were there no magistrate north of Edinburgh?'
Returned from England in 1829, Dr. Philip was on tour again
in 1830 though on this occasion he did not go north of Kaffirland. Armed with frontier impressions, however, and letters
from the spot, in his report for 1830 he wrote:

Things cannot remain long as they are now. The farmers have *for
some years past* been in the habit of crossing the Colonial Boundary
and oppressing the Griquas in their own country. The Griquas have
hitherto borne all this with admirable patience, waiting for the
Colonial Government to put a stop to the cause of their grievances....
The Griquas are to a man attached to the English Government, and
are willing to make sacrifices to remain in connexion with it.

And again:

... such has been the beneficial influence of missionary institutions among them that the Griquas might be more formidable than
the Caffres, but it has not been necessary to have *one* soldier on the
more extended Frontier of the Griquas, to defend that part of the
Colony.

To this Philip added a note on the trekking habits of the
Boers. Their numbers, he says, it is impossible to calculate, for
at eleven fords they are continually passing and repassing,
some of them coming 'even from within an hour of Graaff-
Reinet':

Last year ('29) a Veld Cornet had only one old man left, and asked
permission to recall some farmers for the protection of the Colony.
Farmers generally go with three, five, or ten, or even more, waggons
to a great distance up the Caledon, Orange, Riet and Modder
Rivers. ... Each brings nearly his whole stock of cattle, including
often the herds of one or two friends who have remained at home. ...
In return to the Bushmen for a little tobacco and garbage, the
farmers fatten more cattle, get a better price, and large quantities of
game. ... They organize shooting parties; one farmer and son went
for ten long days to the source of the Modder, got eighteen hippos,
sold for skins a load of sjamboks level with the sides of their waggons,
the large at 3 R.D.s., the smaller at 4 skillings, besides 180 lbs. of
bacon at 4s. per lb.; and besides all this, wood for building. In
three weeks, seven waggons passed at one spot, and returned almost
immediately well laden.

Again in 1832 Dr. Philip set off on tour, spending the whole
summer (September to February) in the interior, November

and December in the far north—returning to Cape Town by Graaff-Reinet, the Kat River, and Bethelsdorp, the road he had gone. By this time, for his share in freeing the Hottentots and pressing for the (now imminent) emancipation of the slaves, Dr. Philip's name was a hissing to the colonists. His travels were not without anxiety: the Governor thought he was 'mad' to make the venture. Sometimes to the Boers he met he was merely 'a *sendeling*' (missionary), for when known to be 'Dr. Philip' he was repeatedly refused leave even to 'out-span'; 'On some occasions, I believe the Boers came together to do me injury, but the moment I went up to them in a friendly manner, offered them a pinch of snuff, and talked with them a little, I had them all as civil as possible'. Even so, by the end of October, he was relieved to reach peace and security . . . 'amid savages . . . in the lion country' at Philippolis.

After a long tour Dr. Philip returned to Cape Town in March 1833 and began to press upon the Government the importance of a settled policy on this frontier.[1] In Griqualand he had seen the firstfruits of ordered missionary instruction, so that a people who, as he said, were till at least 1811 mere nomads completely ignorant of tillage had made most notable progress even since the time of his first visit to them in 1825. Now by the efforts of Mr. Wright, aided by one of themselves, Willem Fortuin by name, the Orange River had been utilized for irrigation. This suggested the practical comment:

In a country like this the mechanic may do as much for the Kingdom of God as the missionary, and the man who subscribes money to purchase a pump to raise the water of a river at a missionary station does a service as truly acceptable to God as the man who lays out his money sending missionaries and Bibles to the heathen; for what can a missionary do for the salvation of such people if he has no means of bringing them together to receive the first elements of Christian instruction or of keeping them together till those instructions give rise to the formation of a society which will give a permanent footing for the Gospel, with all the apparatus of printing and schools that must follow in the train of the missionary before he can have any security for the effects of his labours?

---

[1] The Civil Commissioner of Graaff-Reinet got little encouragement in trying to take a serious view of the situation. Early in 1832 he was informed by the Colonial Secretary: 'The Governor laments the continuance of atrocities by Griquas. . . . *In calling the attention of the chiefs to these outrages you have already done all that can be done* in such distressing cases' (Col. Bell to van Rynveld, 16 Jan. 1832).

Both by letter and in conversation Dr. Philip pointed to the economic consequences of unrestrained trekking, 'with no villages forming', and no markets. 'The system is ruinous to the Colony. The extension of the boundary adds greatly to the expense of defending it.' Yet there is no expansion of the colonial revenues, 'since all are producers and there are no consumers'. To stop all trekking would have been to run counter to natural forces and attempt to change the essential character of the country, but the Trek need not have gone all unheeded. Dr. Philip pressed two alternatives on the Governor.[1] By this time the reforming Ordinance 50 of 1828 had secured the legal position of the free people of colour in the Colony and he now came down definitely in favour of closer relations between Colony and Griquas. Failing 'incorporation' of the Griquas in the Colony—'on the same footing as the Kat River Settlement'—he suggested that they arm the one capable ruler, Waterboer, with effective authority, and supersede the weaker Koks (who owed their position to the L.M.S.). The Koks, he agreed, failed to restrain, if they did not even encourage freebooters and banditti, like one Stuurman who was then raiding northern farmers from his base on islands of the Orange River. To incorporate the Griquas might be a strengthening of the frontier; with a small garrison of thirty men at Philippolis to represent the colonial authority, and with regular salaries for the chiefs, the Griquas might serve as a defence against both the Matabele and the Orange River banditti along the whole of a 300- or 400-, if not a 700-mile, frontier. Unless some such action was taken the country would fall to the Boers who even then were 'casting their eyes on the territories of the Griquas'; these territories, however, 'would not satisfy fifty families of Boers' who would, moreover, be 'unable to protect either themselves or the Colony against Moselekatze'. As in many other instances, Dr. Philip was too far-seeing for his contemporaries, but on this occasion he was too late. There were difficulties in placing Boers indefinitely under the jurisdiction even of Waterboer—his ultimate survival was due less to his authority than to the fact that the Griquatown area offered fewer attractions to settlers than the country behind Philippolis.

[1] These suggestions, the substance of conversations, were embodied, apparently by request, in a long letter to Col. Wade in Oct. 1833.

'Incorporation', therefore, Dr. Philip's first alternative, would
have been wiser, for the first essential was to establish a strong
civilized government capable of dealing with land and other
disputes by ordinary legal process.

The authorities, thanks not a little to Dr. Philip's prompting,
were not ill-informed. They were apt, however, to stress the
incidental lawlessness rather than the need for systematic legal
control. Thus Colonel Wade, the Acting Governor, reported to
Mr. Stanley on 14 January 1834:

> It is not pretended that there has been of late years any increased
> demand for powder, for the usual purposes within the Colony itself,
> and there is not the slightest doubt, that, from these places, it finds
> its way across to Bastards or Korannas, and other native tribes. . . .
> Having sought information on this important subject from the
> magistrates, missionaries, and all others who could best inform me, I
> cannot hesitate to assert that to the hourly traffic in arms and
> ammunition must mainly be attributed the increased boldness of the
> banditti. . . . But besides these there are the farmers, who in defiance
> of the law and the severity of its penalties [sic], emigrate beyond the
> boundaries, and at the same time that they supply the natives with
> the means of attacking the Colony, unfortunately furnish them also
> with something of a reasonable pretext for doing so, by dispossessing
> the weak and unarmed, and occupying all the fertile spots and springs.
> In my opinion, there is no part of the frontier affairs that requires
> more decided and prompt measures than this one. In the country
> between the frontier line and the upper Orange River, there are at
> this moment upwards of a hundred families. . . having seized upon
> the district that best suited them without any regard whatever to the
> rights of the natives. . . . But to oppose the banditti, measures of a
> more decided nature must at length be had recourse to. They are
> ever increasing in number and in daring, and yet, strange to say,
> whilst a regiment of British Infantry, &c., are permanently posted on
> the Eastern frontier, there is not one soldier or any organized means
> of defence . . . that can be depended upon to oppose the merciless
> invaders of the districts of Somerset, Graaff-Reinet, Beaufort and
> Clanwilliam.

Immediately after this Colonel Wade was superseded by Sir
Benjamin D'Urban who, as later events were to show, was not
distinguished for prompt and courageous decisions. When at
last he roused himself to action, in the end of 1834, he was, no
doubt, forced by the attitude of Downing Street to lean towards

Dr. Philip's second alternative. In December Waterboer came
to Cape Town and returned fortified by a 'Treaty'.¹ Had only
Waterboer and Griquatown been concerned, all might have
been well; the treaty with Waterboer might have been a preliminary to ultimate incorporation. But by this time the centre
of interest had shifted to Philippolis, which was on the line of
the main Boer advance, and in such dire confusion as was far
beyond the power of any petty local chief to order. About this
time Adam Kok of Philippolis set out independently in the
hope of concluding a treaty with the Governor on the eastern
frontier where he was expected in September 1834. Shortly
afterwards Adam Kok died and was succeeded by a son Abram
(who indeed seems to have belied the faith the missionaries put
in his powers as a ruler). The Government, failing entirely to
grasp that the situation in Philippolis was the crux of the matter,
'recognized' Waterboer who had no authority in Philippolis,
leaving Kok to be dealt with separately; in October 1834 the
Civil Commissioner of Graaff-Reinet was writing to:

afford His Excellency opportunity to judge how far Adam Kok is to
be depended on. Almost all the representations and complaints about
illicit traffic in gunpowder &c., have come through Philippolis, and
notwithstanding all possible exertions on the part of the Clerk of the
Peace, he has never been able to succeed in getting Captain Adam
Kok to co-operate with him in trying to prevent it.

The result was that, on the very eve of more compellingly
serious complications on the Xhosa frontier, there was no treaty
with Philippolis; chaotic disorder was official warrant for leaving
well alone and doing just nothing.

Even the incorporation of the Griquas in the Colony (which
was obviously right) might at most have delayed that swallowing up of their land which economic pressure soon effected in

¹ Waterboer was pledged to keep order in his district and to send back fugitives
and criminals to the Colony; he was to protect the frontiers from invaders or
marauders, and generally to co-operate with the Colonial Government. In return he
was to receive a salary of £150 per annum, and adequate supplies of ammunition.
Mr. Wright, moreover, by a letter from the Governor, dated 15 Dec. 1834, was
appointed *confidential organ* of communication between Governor and Chief, being
required to obtain all possible information about surrounding tribes, and to make a
report at least once monthly through the Field Commandant of Graaff-Reinet. In
Mr. Wright's absence, Waterboer was to report direct, £50 being set aside for
expenses.

any case: the plan of establishing 'reserves' and making them inalienable had not yet been evolved. As it was, these people were left as before without any effective government, but 'recognized' to the extent that in the north, as formerly only in the east, Boer appeals for grants of land were now firmly refused. So long as there was room for comparatively unchecked expansion to the north the check in the east mattered less; but now land-hunger became really acute. The Government's utterly ineffective efforts to protect the Griquas' interests only engendered violent Boer antagonism. It was thus that the stage was set for an explosion against the scruples or fears of a Government that, having failed to maintain 'proper' relations between masters and servants, refused either itself to take a firm hand with Griquas and Bantu, or to allow the colonists to take the law into their own hands and expel such Amalekites from their possession of the land. For some years longer the Griqua territories remained as a feeble barrier, whose only effect was to force the Great Trek further afield more rapidly and super-ficially than need have been. From the end of 1834 only the Xhosa seemed to matter. By the time any Governor felt able to spare another thought for Griqua affairs they had become part of a far more complex whole. Boer colonists pushing into Griqualand, and far beyond it to the north, had completely out-flanked the Bantu front, flattened out the Griqua 'salient', and made the disturbed frontier line run continuously from the Fish River to the Orange, the Vaal, and beyond these, into Natal.

V

THE *MOVING* FRONTIER IN THE EAST—A NEUTRAL BELT?

HAPPENINGS in the northern districts (outlined in Ch. IV) may seem to be only by-play; but they bring out with unusual clarity at least two major reasons for the poor success of the long struggle to achieve stability on the more important Bantu frontier in the east. One of these was the form the colonists' challenge took, the other the weakness of the official response. The doings or achievements of the participants in the so-called 'first' Great Trek are no measure of their decisive influence on the future course of their country's history; the spacious and leisurely life of the Boers of those *flat* northern plains (reverently spoken of as *die platteland*) soon became very many Afrikaners' idea of the perfect life. Those first trekkers clearly had no room in their scheme of things even for Griquas who were a product, born and bred, of their own Cape Colony. The Boers of the east, and certainly their manner of land usage, were essentially the same, but the unlooked-for cattle-lifting resistance of the tribesmen checked their advance. This was intolerable but gave rise only to ever-increasing demands for the Government to take stern or sterner measures for the restraint of these thieving infidels.

The official response to the colonists' demand was no less in character. The infirmity of purpose manifest in a succession of Governors' handling of the comparatively simple stresses arising on the Griqua front is a measure of the weakness shown in dealing with the much more complex situation on the borders of Bantuland. From first to last it was the invariable official rule that responsibilities likely to involve new and foreseeable expense must always be deferred, and if possible evaded altogether. Nor was this official policy only in the very impecunious Cape of those days; Dr. C. W. de Kiewiet once wrote of the British Treasury as making it 'almost a rule to pay only for disasters', never, that is, in order to forestall such.

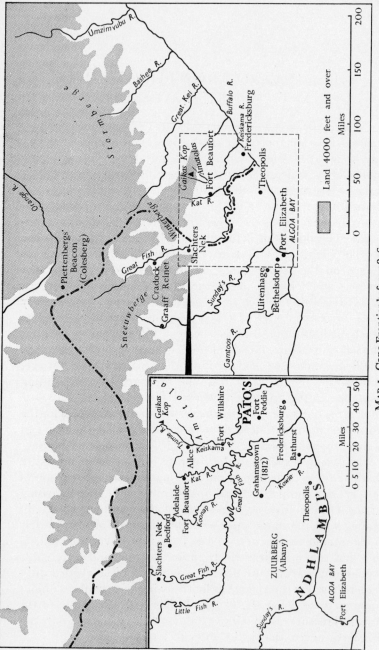

MAP I. Cape Frontier before 1826.

The blundering authorities, it may be said, had no precedent to guide them; North American example, in a parallel situation, was emphatically only to be avoided. The American parallel was at any rate far from close: the number of the Cape colonists was perhaps 30,000 when the Americans were about 2½ millions; at the Cape a widely scattered handful depended on one distant seaport when America was thirteen states, each with its own independent base; and whereas the American Indians were open to pressure at almost any point, the Bantu for many years, having one flank on the sea-coast, the other resting on a massive mountain escarpment, pinned their rivals to a line no more than 100 miles long. This bastion was widely circumvented at last almost by accident; the Great Trek in its desperate effort to get clear of the Ama-Xhosa destroyed this advantage and in doing so completely outflanked the position of the whole mass of the Bantu tribes of southern Africa. Modern South Africans are still not to be encouraged (above, p. 5) to think of their 'problem' as unique—for the consequence was that, piecemeal, these tribes were no less completely conquered even than the American Indians. There is one vital difference. To the credit of all the South African races, white and black, the long struggle never degenerated into an indiscriminate slaughter. It is the crux of the whole matter that the Bantu survive, in massive numbers if in less favourable conditions than might have been, as a social factor in all the country's affairs.

The Bantu tribes, far more for example than the Griquas, were always a *society*—fragmented no doubt, like that of pre-feudal Europe, yet with established customs which were the ready-made basis on which to build a legal system. When European farmers made their appearance on the borders of Bantuland friction with those in possession arose inevitably from the wide difference between European and Bantu ideas of what constituted a just law, above all of property in *land*. Occupation, so far as it was effective, gave the Bantu a respectable right, even at law, to be where they were, but no land was fenced and even tribal boundaries were vague; it was to no one's advantage to claim exclusive rights to *property* in land in a subsistence economy like theirs. Colonial farmers, on the other hand, were individualists and readily planted themselves on unoccupied sites where there seemed to be room, without stopping to ask about the grazing or hunting or any other rights of such as might have been there before them; but they were themselves widely dispersed and isolated and their cattle, at least, became fair game for tribesmen who not unnaturally felt they were being dispossessed and had the advantage, at least, of being much more closely grouped together. The inevitable result was the period of unsettlement marked by cattle-thieving raids, and counter-raids, which drove Governor van Plettenberg (above, Ch. II) to try the plan of fixing a line of boundary, the Fish River, to keep the rivals apart. The actual 'war' which soon followed proved the new boundary to be, at once, ineffective, and provocative of increased unrest; cattle-thieving went on as before, giving occasion for such strong pressure as displaced whole tribes or hurled tribe back upon tribe. When, in consequence, the Bantu were driven to still more cattle-thieving, to war among themselves (Amalinde, 1818), or even to an attack on Grahamstown (1819), the logic of the policy required the fixing of a boundary still farther east; but the forces at the Government's disposal were unequal even to the task of holding the Fish River and could not begin the process all over again from that point.

The rulers of the Cape, soldiers most of them, steadily made it their first duty to *hold a line*; but they were really called on to harmonize the claims of rival societies spread out over a wide region—what the American historian F. J. Turner long afterwards defined as a *moving frontier*. Unlike their American fellows the Boer colonists were too well-ordered, and at any rate in the eighteenth century too weakly organized, to enforce their own will when their governments inevitably failed in their effort to establish peace and security even up to their (imperfectly defined) boundary. But in addition, both the rulers and the much harassed colonists utterly failed to see how the increasing disorders arose directly from the devastating effects of the colonial advance on the social and economic life of the dispossessed Bantu. The prime need of both groups was grazing land; and the more the colonists, who had higher standards, seized of this scarce commodity at Bantu expense, the more the tribes were forced into the straitened conditions their rivals were striving to escape. As time went on the military inclination to punish lawless wrongdoing by seizing cattle, or land, was reinforced by a widespread assumption that if the tribes had less land to spoil by their wasteful methods, more would be free to ensure a plentiful supply of farm labour. In spite not only of missionary but of many administrative officials' warnings[1] the pressure on the Bantu never relaxed; and yet the 'authorized version' of all this history will still have it—in spite of admitted exceptions[2]—that here was no more than an unending series of raids by 'thieving Kafirs' on the herds of hard-working, unoffending white farmers.

The truth is rather that the continuous growth of the Colony at the expense of the Bantu, instead of stimulating better land usage by the white farmers, intensified rather the disposition to never-ending trek and the superficial agricultural methods that so long persisted. It was not only that a steady process of depression and mutual impoverishment at last brought untrained, undisciplined 'poor whites' into direct competition with landless and overcrowded poor blacks (see below, Ch. XVIII). In the latest phase of all the spirit of 'the frontier', ineffective though it had been in the beginning, swept back triumphantly in the 1950's and 1960's to apply to the tortured body of South Africa remedies of its own devising, for disorders for which its own devotees were largely responsible. The situation on the old Cape frontier undoubtedly gave those who had to cope with it much excuse for being absorbed by the mere task of trying to keep the peace; the country being unproductive the force at their disposal was meagre, besides which their distant Home Government was always watchful and impatient of expense. It is to be remembered, too, not only that slavery was still an unchallenged feature of the established order, but also that the Bantu were the close cousins of those who furnished the main

[1] Administrative officials, bound as they were to secrecy, could not always express themselves openly, but their letters and journals, now available, make it clear that they gave many warnings to the authorities. Capt. Charles Lennox Stretch, for example, frequently cited below, who had long served as a Resident Agent among the Xhosa tribes and was later a member of the Cape Parliament, was typical of many who have done more than can ever be known to foster a lasting belief in the white man's justice.

[2] It has a certain significance that the earliest conflict of Europeans with Bantu in 1702 was due to a cattle 'trading' expedition of colonists, who may or may not have been attacked 'without provocation' by the 'Kaffirs', but were admittedly guilty of 'plundering' the weaker Hottentots. Fouche's *Adam Tas*, p. 335. See also pp. 25 n., 43.

body of the world supply of slaves; it was unlikely, if only for this reason, that officers responsible for order on the frontier would have either eye or mind to weigh the ultimate social consequences of their actions. The East India Company government, which had consistently refused to recognize so much as the legal existence of the less formidable Hottentots, would fain have kept altogether clear of the Bantu; but before ever these became a force to reckon with the petulant resistance put up by the Bushmen (and its own care for economy) had won its approval for a famous, frontier-born system; the Bushmen thus early taught the Boers the need to unite for their own defence by forming *commandos*. The wars the Company became involved in (above, p. 45) were small affairs conducted almost entirely by such commandos, either with or without instructions from Cape Town.[1]

The Company's most important action was its well-meant but very casual 'treaty' in 1778 giving the Colony a legal (if not rather legalistic) claim to the country up to the Fish River. Eleven years later, it is true, when the Bantu proved themselves still a factor on the colonial side of this boundary, the Company forbore to expel the culprits, and 'allowed' them to remain where they were—'without prejudice to the *ownership* of Europeans'. But after 1806, when the stronger British Government turned its attention to the eastern frontier its officers, without over-scrupulous inquiry into all the circumstances, were readily persuaded that the Bantu responsible for disorders in the Zuurveld were *within* the Colony—where they had no right to be. In extending the boundary to the Fish River the Government had never extended its administrative functions to include the Bantu as subjects within the sphere of its jurisdiction and protection; and even now, instead of adhering to this first principle of government, Sir John Cradock all too faithfully imitated his Company predecessors in refusing to think of the Bantu people as an integral part of the colonial society, took a short-cut, and forcibly 'cleared' the Zuurveld of its Bantu population. This much-commended 'strong' action merely transferred the clash to the region of the Fish River and beyond. Since some tribesmen had lost land, and others went in fear for theirs, the operation served rather to provoke further and increased 'depredations'.

The continuing disorders gave occasion at least for an appeal to 'native custom'—an early experiment in this field. In 1817 Lord Charles Somerset made an agreement with Gaika to apply to the disease of cattle-stealing a primitive practice, familiar to the early English,[1] and known in South Africa as the Spoor Law. This required owners, accompanied by 'patrols' of troops, to follow the 'spoor' of stolen cattle to the kraal at which it ended, and there 'either to retake the cattle or recoup themselves at the expense of the kraal'.[2] Sometimes an equivalent number of beasts sufficed, sometimes an equivalent (and arbitrary) value;[3] further, if one visit obtained satisfaction, good and well, but this, says Dr. Theal, 'seldom happened'; whereupon a 'reprisal' was deemed necessary—that is to say, 'a joint force of burghers and soldiers marched to the kraal *suspected* of being most deeply implicated in the robberies, and *secured* compensation'.[4] Any supposed check on the number of beasts alleged to be stolen was ineffective and, without doubt, as Theopolis Hottentots once complained, 'the sins of jackals, wolves and tigers were often laid on the backs of the Kafirs'.[5] The Spoor Law was thus, very clearly, Bantu custom applied without the qualifications or safeguards observed in Bantu practice. For example, the Bantu, like the Anglo-Saxons, were expected to halt on the border and send for the nearest headman (as it were the English 'hundredman') and throw on him the onus of proving that the 'spoor' led through or away from his area, it being accepted that 'any attempt to obliterate the spoor would be sufficient proof of guilt'. Once guilt was reasonably established there was a further all-important safeguard—the nearest kraals were made *collectively* responsible over an 'area taken according to the value of the property stolen'. 'The usual course is to include a sufficient number of kraals for the number of cattle paid not to exceed one or two

---

[1] Stubbs's Charters: 'We have ordained,' says Edgar's *Ordinance of the Hundred* (959–75), 'concerning unknown cattle, that no one should possess it without the testimonial of the men of the hundred, or of the tithing men . . . also if the hundred pursue a track into another hundred, that notice be given to the hundred man and then he shall go with him. If he neglects this let him pay xxx shillings to the king', &c., &c.

[2] Walker, p. 161.

[3] Cory, iii. 55 n., for a glaring example of frontier 'valuation'.

[4] Theal, ii. 3.

[5] *Cape Col. Qn.*, p. 239.

for each kraal' (i.e. household). In the last resort 'the tribe as a whole is responsible'.[1]

The difficulty of applying Bantu law from the outside is obvious. It was, for example, permissible for those following the spoor to question men, women, or children, and information might easily be given in order to save the 'nearest kraal' from the penalty. But where the theft was one of tribe from tribe, still more of a tribe from the Colony, the patrols were likely to meet a conspiracy of silence. Cautionary rules, therefore, got little attention from the colonial authorities, distracted as no doubt they often were by the vagaries of the Bantu on one side, and the complaints of farmers on the other. The 'Kaffirs' were undoubtedly awkward neighbours, but an experienced missionary commented in 1830:

It is highly desirable that a better understanding should be established between the Colony and the Caffre nation. The custom is still maintained by some colonists of making reprisals for cattle stolen from the Colony by sending armed patrols into Caffre-land, attacking and plundering different sections of the country for the supposed guilt of one or more kraals. *In most cases the guilty escape with impunity, while the innocent are deprived of the means of support and reduced to want and misery.*[2]

The frontier system, Dr. Theal agrees, was 'not free of abuses'[3] and from time to time working rules were amended. General Bourke, for example, decreed in 1828 that patrols must not enter Kaffirland unless cattle were actually in sight; but Sir Lowry Cole made an apparent increase of cattle-stealing (for which there were special causes, below, p. 89) the occasion for tightening up again and allowing patrols to follow the spoor wherever it led, but 'not to seize Kafir cattle in compensation'. The inevitable result of such incessant 'patrols', varied as these were by more intensive 'commandos' or 'reprisals',[4] was the tale

---

[1] Quotations are from a memo. 'The Spoor Law', drafted by Mr. (later Sir) W. E. Stanford in 1882, shown me by the late Mr. W. Carmichael among the records of Tsolo where he was Resident Magistrate.

[2] J. Brownlee's report to L.M.S. for 1830.

[3] Dr. Theal (ii. 4 n.) qualifies this admission, suggesting from his own personal experience in 1877 that old men who had lived on the frontiers in the twenties entertained no grievance about the activities of patrols. 'Taking the district between the Keiskama and Fish River from Gaika was regarded very differently, and in their view real injustice.' In other words, surely, cattle-stealing was a mere incident in the war for possession of the *land.*

[4] Contemporary accounts distinguish between 'patrols' (where the owner, accompanied by troops, tried to follow the spoor of his own stolen beasts) and the

of storm and stress that is the history, as usually detailed, of the frontier throughout the twenties and thirties, the official policy of these years in particular being castigated as 'vacillating'. But examination reveals no real variation in principle or method; the vacillation was only in the degree of vigour with which successive Governors applied the rule of force. The stresses which the Spoor Law was in 1817 designed to relieve reached a crisis very shortly afterwards (above, p. 51), which was the occasion for Governor Somerset's forlorn experiment in 'seg-regation', a neutral belt to keep the rivals apart.

A clear-cut plan of separation must have its attractions as a means of avoiding the complexities that arise where advanced and backward peoples are thrown together in one community. In the twentieth century (below, Ch. XVIII) orthodox Afri-kaner Nationalists go so far as to claim that the *apartheid* they stand for was the invariable policy of their own *voortrekkers*. A self-denying policy adopted by these predecessors might indeed have made the plan Somerset adumbrated in 1819 possible then, or even later. But, as his modern imitators were to do, Somerset left out of account the need to order such relationships as were already established, or becoming so; even in that day of small things thieving raids were not the whole picture. Many points of contact were developing. The beginnings of Grahams-town reinforced the hitherto only slightly represented trading class, and in 1817 the Governor himself had instituted a system of 'passes' to allow natives to visit a *fair* to be held twice a year, first in Grahamstown, later at Fort Willshire on the Keiskama. In the twenties also, as colonial development in-creased the demand for cheap labour, frontier officials found farmers torn between fear of the 'thieving propensities' of the Bantu and a desire to make use of them as servants. The eco-nomic need tended to prevail to bring more and more into the Colony and keep them there.[1]

more elaborate expeditions where troops combined with a burgher 'commando' to make 'reprisals'—possibly for a series of alleged thefts. Frontier tradition suggests that the theoretically less objectionable 'patrol' was liable to abuse, since in practice the farmer's friends joined together to hunt the spoor without waiting for the troops, and virtually levied private war. See also p. 108 n.

[1] As early as Oct. 1823 the missionary Brownlee wrote to Mrs. Williams of how natives were being 'induced into the service of Boers', sometimes, he says, 'with threats of Robben Island' (the convict station) if they refused. See also Cory, ii. 382, and *Cape Col. Qn.*, pp. 252–3.

Those same years saw the beginning, too, of regular missionary work in Kaffirland. The L.M.S. here, as elsewhere, was first in the field, and Mr. Joseph Williams, their pioneer, who settled with Gaika near the later Fort Beaufort in 1816, has left a journal which throws light on frontier conditions. His missionary venture, it may be believed, met with some opposition, and probably more ridicule—the 'general opinion', so he writes, 'both of Boers and of officers being that nothing but powder and ball would do to bring such savages to their senses'. The Xhosa, too, had their suspicions, he says, 'because Boers had circulated the report that the missionaries had come for the Caffres' destruction'. Little was really known about the Bantu and Williams's first impressions were not good. 'The chiefs are very anxious and greedy over presents—they continually ask for them.' Witchcraft, he found, was a serious factor in native life. Just then a certain 'prophetess' was active in 'smelling out' culprits, and he describes how 'they think nothing of murder if the prophetess ascribes any calamity to the poison of a particular individual'. Gaika and Makana, both of whom 'are anxious to profess Christianity', were remonstrated with; 'but they do not see the wrong of committing murder when a person is accused, for example of withholding rain. . . . In fact life is of little value. One human life is reckoned as equal to three beasts.' When at last the attempt was made to bring the Bantu under European law (and even in Anglo-Saxon England the *wer-gild* of a *ceorl* was doubtfully more than the value of 'three beasts') not many administrators had the wisdom to explain their innovations with the care used by Theophilus Shepstone when in 1850 he introduced a new code into Natal with the preamble: 'Know ye, therefore, all Chiefs, Petty Chieftains, Heads of Kraals and Common People, *a man's life has no price; no cattle can pay for it.*'[1]

Questions of men and of cattle were constantly being thrust upon the attention of the earliest missionary; one of Williams's great worries was that the colonial authorities could see little justification for any missionary who was not also at least a semi-official Government Agent in Kaffirland. Colonel Cuyler, for example, the Landdrost of Uitenhage, had written demanding information about thefts by Xhosa, expressing at the same

---

[1] Quoted by Professor E. Brookes, p. 52.

time his willingness to hear complaints against colonists; he
even suggested a weekly letter; whereupon Williams protested
that he had no secular authority, and could not afford the expense of such regular communications. In the end Cuyler, losing patience, seems to have written saying that he could not see
that Williams was serving any useful purpose if he did not help
to 'control' thefts, and reported him to the Governor as 'har-
bouring' runaway Hottentots from the Colony: 'He is not to be
allowed to do as Mr. Read and Mr. Anderson do.' About the
time of his death, therefore, in 1818, Mr. Williams's station was
included in the criticism then being levelled against all missions
'beyond the Colony'[1] and for two or three years new stations
were prohibited altogether. Yet, in the hope of keeping missions
under control, Mr. J. Brownlee was appointed by Lord Charles
Somerset to succeed Williams as a 'Government' missionary and
remained in official service till 1825 when he returned to the
L.M.S. Meantime Dr. Philip, whose experience led him to
oppose the tying of missionaries to the Government, had won
his battle for the removal of the embargo on extra-colonial
stations, and in the early twenties representatives of the Wesleyan, Glasgow, and London Societies established themselves
throughout Kaffirland. The missionaries were one more link
in the chain of influences that were fast binding together the
interests of the Bantu and the Colony.

It was thus at a time when interdependence was growing that
Lord Charles Somerset chose to make his designed attempt to
put a definite barrier between the Colony and the Bantu
peoples beyond the frontier. Official opinion traditionally
strove to reduce intercourse to a minimum; the Company
having set the fashion of running away from the difficulties, the
Report of the Circuit Commission in 1813, together with many
of the letters of frontier officers about the same time, show that
for some years before its deliberate adoption in 1819 the plan
of a neutral belt was taking shape. The experiment may have
been worth a trial. Even Dr. Philip remarked at first on the
'impossibility of promiscuous intercourse [and of] Kafirs coming
freely into the Colony'.[2] The war of 1819 seems to have moved

---

[1] *Cape Col. Qn.*, p. 128.
[2] Quoted from a 'Review' of South African Missions by Dr. Philip, a document
intended 'for publication' but cancelled at the end of 1821 (*Cape Col. Qn.*, p. 134).

Lord Charles Somerset to think of setting patrols to keep the
land between the Fish and the Keiskama empty of both black
and white. But his settlement was almost unplanned, besides
being cavalierly executed. From the nature of the case a 'treaty'
with a barbarian chief rests on an insecure foundation. The
agreement should, therefore, have been drafted in very clear
and definite terms; but the Governor obviously acted on the
contrary assumption, that any form of words would suffice for
a savage. In spite of Gaika's overwhelming defeat at the hands
of Ndhlambi in 1818 the Governor persisted, as he had done
previously, in refusing to treat with any but Gaika who himself
protested that he could not speak for other chiefs. It was thus
not even a peace dictated to a vanquished enemy; it was a peace
dictated to a potentate of straw set up for the occasion by the
victor and then not even a written bond but a verbal arrangement. Somerset's own account is highly disingenuous. On the
day of the treaty Somerset announced in the *Cape Gazette* that
by a bargain with Gaika the country between the Fish and
Keiskama was to be thoroughly cleared, and expressed the hope
that 'as the boundary is completely freed from Kaffirs, repose
and security will be the results of the late operations'. *On the
same day* he reported to London by way of comment on the
treaty—what he had not said to Gaika—'The country thus
ceded is as fine a portion of ground as is to be found, and, together with the still unappropriated lands in the Zuurveld, it
might perhaps be worthy of consideration with a view to systematic colonization.'[1]

The definition of boundaries remained vague. Gaika indeed,
having given away land belonging to tribes whom he did not
control, was 'allowed' to remain where he was, in the Chumie
Valley. But before very long, in spite of the alleged stipulation
that it 'was to be occupied only by soldiers',[2] the 'neutral'

Dr. Philip, whose first trip to Grahamstown and Theopolis was made within
three months of the Battle of Grahamstown, in July 1819, was impressed by the
havoc wrought by war. On his return journey he 'saw no Caffres and did not wish
to see any'. 'The farmers,' he wrote on his return to Bethelsdorp, 'have been
stripped of everything, and unless the commando shall recover their cattle they
must be ruined.'

[1] *C.C. Records*, vol. xii, 15 Oct. 1819. In 1824 the Commissioners of Inquiry sent
out to review the whole state of the Cape Colony found conflict of opinion about
the terms of the treaty even between Somerset and the Colonial Secretary, Col.
Bird.   [2] Theal, i. 283.

territory filled up with farmers and came to be described, almost habitually, as the Ceded Territory. As early as 1820 the Acting Governor, Sir Rufane Donkin, having gone to the trouble of getting Gaika's consent—as if to a departure from the bargain of 1819—supported a short-lived scheme for a military settlement at Fredericksburg, near the Keiskama.[1] About the same time a party of Highland settlers was destined for the Kat River Valley and, as they failed to come, Thomas Pringle, then settled near the frontier and enthusiastic about the quality of the land, made suggestions for the strengthening of the frontier by planting a settlement of Hottentots there.[2] His proposal shows how little people on the frontier itself were even aware of the plan for a neutral belt. Next, with Donkin's encroachment for precedent, the chief Maqomo, elder son of Gaika, 'crept back' into the upper part of the Kat River Valley, to be followed by his brother Tyali, and it was felt politic to leave them alone so long as they behaved themselves.[3] In 1822 a blockhouse, the nucleus of the later Fort Beaufort, was established on the lower Kat River a little north of its junction with the Fish, 'to act as a check upon Maqomo'.[4] Three years later the missionary Brownlee,[5] casting about for a sphere of work on his return to the L.M.S., reported mournfully that the site of Williams's former station was now 'for ever separated from Caffre Territory'; the reason was that in the years before 1826 the Colonial Government had systematically been making grants of farms between the Fish River and the Koonap 'not only to British Settlers, but to colonial Boers'. In 1825 the Governor had expressed an intention 'not to permit the Territory to be inhabited until our endeavours to civilize the Kafirs had been successful',[6] Somerset for once showing himself a more incorrigible optimist than any of the missionaries. But the clamour of the colonists for farms, and more farms, made short work of his intention and an important part of the country was soon broken up to supply their demand. In 1825 the district of Somerset was extended to include the modern Bedford; in 1827

---

[1] Cf. evidence of Stockenström, *C.C. Records*, 8 Aug. 1825.
[2] Letter to Philip, 15 Jan. 1821. On the Kat River project see also p. 93 and note.   [3] Cory, ii. 343.
[4] Ibid., 147.   [5] To Philip, from the Chumie, 3 July 1825.
[6] Somerset's second thoughts in reply to Crown Commissioners, *C.C. Records*, 4 Jan. 1825.

the only point at issue seems to have been whether or not the regulations which forbade British settlers in Albany to keep slaves ought to be enforced upon Boers in the Ceded Territory. It never crossed the mind of those responsible for law and order that the Xhosa had as good right to return to their own homes in the neutral belt as colonists to have it portioned out to them in farms. It is true that in 1829 the Kat River Settlement was established for Hottentots, whose usefulness Pringle had earlier suggested, and whose claims had been pressed by Brownlee in 1825;[1] the chiefs Pato and Congo, too, were given permission to graze west of the Keiskama by Proclamation of 17 April; but in that very year, 1829, the colonial boundary was definitely extended to the 'heights west of the Chumie'.[2] This was in effect the end of the 'neutral' belt, but by no means of the stresses it was meant to relieve.

[1] 'From the late arrangements in enlarging the colonial boundary by colonizing a portion of the Neutral Territory between the Fish River and the Gonappe, I think the Hottentots have a strong claim.' He therefore urges 'a new Institution in those parts as a better buffer than white men who cross the boundary and traffic with Kaffirs more than the Hottentots do (Brownlee to Philip, 28 Mar. 1825).

On 29 Sept. 1828 the Commissioner-General was given authority to inspect the Kat River lands for this purpose (*Cape Archives, Sundry Letters*, vol. 261). Dr. Philip at this time was away in England, but missionary letters suggest that the establishment of the Kat River was a move in the war for Hottentot rights, and deliberately designed to weaken the 'dangerous' influence of the L.M.S. See Theal, ii. 10, and *Cape Col. Qn.*, p. 241, also below pp. 92 and 93, n. 2.

[2] Walker's *Atlas*, Map 10.

FRONTIER UNREST AFTER 1829—
TRADE AND LABOUR

THE steady growth of intercourse across the frontier in the years of comparative peace after 1819 was wholly natural—as more historians must have recognized but for their cattle-thieving obsession. All over Africa in our own generation even minor economic activities, so long as they are *new*, have had an irresistible attraction for unsophisticated tribesmen, drawing them, some perhaps, like moths to the flame. *Ex Africa semper aliquid novi* is at best only a half-truth; the insatiable passion of the African peoples themselves for novelty has had its effect on the political awakening of their continent—the tense situation in many parts comes of sharp disappointment that the new and better living conditions of which they now have ample evidence are less easily attained than in their impatience they had fondly hoped.

In the Cape of long ago the attractions of the Grahamstown fairs set up in 1817 proved to be so great that in the twenties they were moved to Fort Willshire, a frontier post on the Keiskama. In 1827 General Bourke made these more frequent and then, plucking up courage, gave a few traders permission to enter through the more open country north of the Winterberg where, also, the tribes were supposed to be more peaceably disposed. Presently, in 1830, the fairs were judged unnecessary, restrictions lifted, and persons of assured good character[1] permitted to pass and trade freely anywhere, and carry their wares far into the heart of this early Bantustan. In itself, no doubt, the trade was small; the Bantu could offer, besides domestic basketware, only hides and skins and a diminishing quantity of ivory (this last the original cause of a 'boom' on the eastern frontier[2] in the twenties). Yet, small as it was, this trade was something wholly new and likely to grow, to the benefit of all parties; in the five years 1831–5 the value of hides and skins exported

[1] Cory, ii. 342.   [2] Ibid., ii. 174.

from the Colony doubled in value till they accounted for fully
one-quarter of the country's total exports; and it is evidence
of the growing importance of the native trade, as well as of
settler activities, that 19 per cent. of this total was now from
the open roadstead of Port Elizabeth.[1] The traders concerned
probably found their free and adventurous life as great an
attraction as any hope of making large profits; yet in the 1835
war the Xhosa are surprisingly said to have made a dead set
against them, as against a class they hated.[2] It certainly was
not long till the traders came to play a regular and established
part in the life of every tribal community. In many of the
territories today much of the trade seems to be still in the hands
of families who have succeeded to the business of fathers and
grandfathers. The calling probably offers a good living rather
than a great fortune, but a strong mutual attachment has often
grown up when the trader is at pains to understand the life and
ways of the customers among whom he makes his home.[3] It has
usually been easy for Europeans who choose to live among them
to maintain good relations with the naturally patient and
friendly Bantu.

Isolated traders, like missionaries, readily enough adapted
themselves to life among the Bantu, but in the 1820's, as in our
own day, it was a very different matter for members of the Bantu
race to fit into the much more complex structure of colonial
society. The 'neutral belt' policy, had it been given a proper
trial, might have kept the Bantu at a distance from the Colony
and by reducing the pressure upon them ensured that, so far as
they came to better their fortunes in European areas, they came
in more easily manageable numbers. Officials and missionaries
perhaps continued to look askance at the growth of intercourse,
as appears from the hesitant encouragement given even to trade,
but the colonists themselves were in two minds. These 'Kaffirs'
were still 'incorrigible thieves'—a charge, incidentally, in flat

---

[1] Theal, ii. 43, gives the annual value of hides and skins and of total exports as
£37,454 and £218,412 respectively from 1826 to 1830, and £62,829 and £243,646
from 1831 to 1835.

[2] Cory, iii. 73. Many traders were murdered, and Read's letters especially
emphasize their misdeeds and their unpopularity.

[3] There is reason to add that the steady impoverishment of the Bantu generally
added considerably to the difficulties of traders, and that this, rather than keener
competition, latterly adversely affected the traders' prosperity. (Articles in *Cape
Times*, 12 Apr. 1926 ff.)

contradiction of wide later experience of Africans as domestic servants—it was dangerous to have many of them (at any rate on the farms of one's neighbours!). In the twenties, however, the new slave laws, and the prohibition of slaves in Albany and in the Ceded Territory, made the labour shortage acute. In spite of the risks, therefore, colonists often met their needs by the employment of Xhosa, as well as refugees (Bechuana or Fingos). These Bantu were cheaper even than Hottentots and the demand for their services grew steadily. Wiseacres might shake their heads, or write to the papers about it;[1] but it was not only the weak-kneed humanitarianism of the Acting Governor, General Bourke, that was responsible for an Ordinance (No. 49 of 1828) definitely providing for the admission of Africans to the Colony; this law authorized the nearest border field-cornet to grant 'passes' to any who desired to enter the service of colonial farmers.

The traditional South African history still tends to classify its governors after the fashion of *Kings* and *Chronicles* in old Bibles; poor General Bourke's term, for his share in the emancipation of the Hottentots by the 50th Ordinance, and for the evils supposed to flow from this new frontier law (No. 49), tends to rank almost as 'Bourke's wicked reign'; his very uninspired successors, on the contrary, Sir Lowry Cole and Sir Benjamin D'Urban, did what pleased colonial opinion—and were, therefore, 'good'. On this principle we are given to understand that the 49th Ordinance was never more than a wrong-headed law, chiefly notable for its effect in facilitating 'thieving'.

The later history of this Ordinance is on any showing extraordinary. Immediately after its promulgation the outcry against increased thieving was so lusty[2] that on 25 August 1829 the Ordinance was 'suspended', by Dr. Theal's account, or 're-pealed', according to Sir George Cory; Dr. Theal explains that at this date Sir Lowry Cole 'instructed officials to apprehend all who were wandering about without *proper* passes', recognizing, in fact, that the object was to facilitate the employment of Bantu natives. How their engagement was regulated thereafter is not

[1] Among many examples, 'W.G.' in the *Grahamstown Journal*, 14 Feb. 1833, describes the 'scarcity of labour' as the 'cause of all our troubles'. 'Yet,' he adds, 'Kafirs are not to be trusted as servants in the Colony.'

[2] Theal, ii. 11; Cory, ii. 341, 350–61, 367–82. Other letters cited are in Cape Town Archives.

so clear. For a time the question lapsed. At the end of 1836 the Ordinance was sometimes referred to—on 13 February 1837 Stockenström acknowledged a letter from Sir B. D'Urban assuring him of the legality of Ordinance 49. By the forties the use of African labour was established custom; on 20 September 1844, for example, H. Fynn, Government Agent with the Tambookies under the treaty of 1836, complained of the conflict between the terms of the treaty which he had to administer and the 49th Ordinance, pointing out that when he, as Agent, refused passes, his Tambookies were able to get them freely from frontier officials *under Ordinance 49*. On 27 September 1849 Colonel Mackinnon complained in the same terms from the newly created British Kaffraria—passes were being given by missionaries and traders 'apparently under Ordinance 49, though regulations under that Ordinance were never made'. Thereupon, on 3 October 1849, Attorney-General Porter minuted that a new Proclamation could only be made under the 49th Ordinance which, though marked in 'Harding's *Ordinances*' as 'allowed' by the Home Government, had not really been so allowed. It therefore fell under a clause of the Royal Instructions and *lapsed after three years*. But, he concludes, 'The cessation of the 49th Ordinance it is not desirable to proclaim.'

There could hardly be a better illustration of the slackness of colonial frontier administration. The interpretation of the 49th Ordinance as a mere humanitarian blunder altogether misses its social significance. Like the relaxation of trade restrictions about the same time the Ordinance was prima facie evidence of increasing 'normalcy' on the frontier. It was first and last a labour law, intended to meet a need that was especially acute at the moment if loudly voiced complaints of shortage due to the emancipation of the Hottentots are to be taken at face value;[1] the Ordinance was an attempt to regulate the flow of labour. Africans had been coming in almost by stealth but the Government seems to have forgotten the reason for this unwonted excursion into the field of labour legislation. By 1829 or soon after, well before the war climax of 1835 or the upheaval that followed, officials and colonists alike had eyes for nothing but the physical disorder prevailing. The half-hearted frontier experiment in total separation was dead and conditions much the same as before 1819.

---

[1] *Cape Col. Qn.*, pp. 219 ff.

The lull which followed the collapse of Makana's attack in that year (p. 51) had at least allowed time for the British Settlers planted in Albany, about Grahamstown, in 1820 to get over their first troubles.[1] This infusion of new blood, and perhaps also the cash circulated in their modest effort to establish themselves, much strengthened the Colony's hold on its eastern districts; but to create and to maintain the proposed vacuum in the belt of country beyond the Fish River was an impossible task never seriously attempted. Certain Xhosa chiefs are said to have 'crept back' into the Kat River area but this attractive country could never be really cleared; it was not a confined river valley but a wide *strath*, with numerous *kloofs* (glens) running off it and affording ample cover. From these, no doubt, occasional Xhosa raids were made on the cattle of farmers who were actually granted farms in other good country nearer base, on the Koonap; so by 1822 patrols were again in full cry and, before long, commandos and reprisals as well. The farmers must have had reason to feel anxious, but 'Colonel Somerset's blundering commando' is also to be remembered which in 1825 twice 'burnt the *wrong* village', with loss of life.[2]

In 1829 the definitive annexation of an important part of the so-called Ceded Territory not unnaturally gave rise to new and extensive 'depredations' and brought a climax of unrest; thereupon any reconstructive measures that may have been contemplated gave way to others more strictly military and defensive. In the new phase the chief Maqomo, regent for Gaika's heir Sandile, appears as the arch-troublemaker—and the principal sufferer. After the fall of Ndhlambi, Maqomo and his people were the Colony's nearest neighbours and, as such, exposed to heavy pressure. Even if he, and they, were just at first left unmolested in the Kat River country the tradition is at fault which has it that the new European farms, together with General Bourke's milder laws, tempted these Xhosa to 'indulge' their passion for cattle-stealing and general lawlessness. Of themselves the new annexations were enough to confirm all tribes alike in the judgement a later missionary reported, that 'the white man conquered only in order to dispossess'. At this time, moreover, the Ama-Xhosa were caught between two fires, being directly involved in the disorder caused by the irruption among them of refugees fleeing from Chaka (above, Ch. II) who had all the country to the north in a ferment. Between 1826 and 1828 colonial troops penetrated far beyond the Keiskama, to the Kei and the Umtata, against raids supposed to be led by Chaka himself.[1] The immediate occasion of decisive action against Maqomo, who had earned grace to be left unmolested for nine years, was, significantly, a raid he made not on the Colony itself but on certain new-comers, the Tambookies. It was no doubt inconvenient to have the Bantu fighting each other so near the colonial frontier, but this clearly was an internal feud; doubtful as his tenure was in face of the Colony, it was natural for Maqomo to seize on quarrels among the refugee Tembu, or Tambookies, to strike a blow against these fresh invaders of his shrinking pasturelands.[2] But in 1828, when the colonial expeditions entered Kaffirland to forestall the danger of attack by the Zulus, the unfortunate Tambookies,[3] in flight before the 'Fetcani', who in turn were victims of Chaka himself, had thrown themselves upon their protection. The dignity of the Government being involved, the Colonial Secretary, on 6 February 1829, instructed Colonel Somerset to punish the 'atrocity and insolence of Maqomo's proceedings, the well-grounded conviction that he has long forfeited any claim to favourable consideration having at length determined His Excellency to take steps for ridding the Colony of the neighbourhood of this most troublesome and dishonest chief'.[4] Early in May the necessary steps were taken, with the inevitable kraal-burnings and impounding of cattle, and Maqomo was driven out to find new homes for his people as best he might among his friends and neighbours farther east.

This chief Maqomo, who figures largely in frontier history for many years, was by all the evidence one of 'nature's gentlemen' and had a great faculty for gaining goodwill, if not respect and esteem. In his misfortunes his first stalwart champion was the nearest missionary, the Rev. John Ross of the Glasgow Missionary Society, some of whose pleadings were extant.[5] In

[1] Cory, ii. 344–63.
[2] 'The Tambookie chief had planted some kraals near the sources of the Koonap' (Cory, ii. 380).
[3] In July 1825 the missionary Brownlee writes of a 'third' attack on the Tambookies, either by Mantatees or 'Fetcani'.   [4] Cory, ii. 380.
[5] Copies of notes and letters in Philip MSS.

1832 he returned for a time to his old haunts, with the surprising but express permission of Colonel Somerset 'who had always been indulgent towards Maqomo'.[1] In later years bluff and good-hearted Harry Smith agreed for once with Somerset and was obviously fond of this 'most troublesome and dishonest chief' and, we are told, could 'refuse him nothing'![2] When in 1835 Sir B. D'Urban pronounced Maqomo and many more to be 'irreclaimable savages', one of the missionaries' ladies protested: 'If only he could meet Maqomo!' Still later, even after Maqomo, like so many of the chiefs, had taken badly to the white man's fire-water, Captain Stretch was known in the Cape Parliament for his devoted attempts to redress some of his wrongs. Among his own people his memory is still green[3] and Xhosa bards make invocation, to this day, 'By Maqomo!'

Whatever his personal qualities, Maqomo's star was an unlucky one, and it is clear that the cause of all his trouble was his natural desire to keep his land. It may well be that it was from his senior, Maqomo, that the younger Paramount Sandile learnt to pronounce: 'The patrimony of a chief is not cattle. It is land and men.'[4] Though his plea on the eve of ejection in 1829, to be taken under colonial orders, need not be taken seriously,[5] Maqomo clearly had reason for desperation like that which drove Gaika before him to beg, quaintly, to be given lands—and peace—*in England*.[6] As his missionary, Mr. Ross, pointed out in an interview with Sir Lowry Cole, colonial commandos often 'recovered' more cattle than they had lost, and by making one tribe pay for the theft of another set tribe against tribe. The Government constantly demanded that the chiefs should punish raiders but Maqomo was chastised for punishing the raiding Tambookies; with Bantu logic he retorted that magistrates were not punished when colonial wrong-doers escaped.

---

[1] Cory, ii. 451.

[2] e.g. Cory, iii. 228. Captain Stretch in 1836 once wrote, 'Smith can refuse Maqomo nothing.'

[3] The blue flowering plumbago is known as *umthi ka Maqomo*, 'the shrub of Maqomo' (*Drawn in Colour*, by Noni Jabavu, John Murray, 1960).

[4] Quoted by Walker, p. 119.

[5] Mr. Ross wrote on 23 Apr. 1829 to Col. Somerset, on Maqomo's behalf, requesting 'a section of land where he may be under your hand and receive orders in all affairs from yourself'.

[6] Cory, ii. 350.

The disingenuous treaty of 1819, which the Government observed only when it suited itself, was now the pretext for the chief's total expulsion from an especially vaguely defined part of the territory in question.[1] To add to Maqomo's very real sense of grievance the clearing of this area was made the occasion for acting on the plan (above, p. 83, also p. 93, n. 2, below, of filling up the vacant Kat River lands with Hottentots—thus doing a tardy measure of justice to the Hottentots at Xhosa expense, while at the same time making them a 'buffer' against them. The idea of three thousand Hottentots exhausting the carrying capacity of the district must have seemed extravagant to the overcrowded tribes beyond; and since, according to Mr. Ross, those expelled included fragments also of Gaika's people, and Gaika had in 1819 been the ally of the Colony, Maqomo had further reason to complain that, if indeed this land was forfeit—which he refused to understand—then, 'though his father Gaika, and his chiefs, had accompanied the colonial forces against Ndhlambi, after Ndhlambi was defeated they deprived them of their country as if they had been the offenders'.[2] A missionary sums up: 'We used Gaika as long as he served us. When he failed to conquer Ndhlambi we did so ourselves and *then took Gaika's* country.'[3] With the sanction of Colonel Somerset Maqomo returned once more to a corner of the Kat River Valley, only to be finally ejected in 1833; yet it was admitted that his faithful dealing with thieves 'gave no ground for complaint'. Not without reason, 'Maqomo's heart was very sore about the land; the subject always set him on fire.'[4]

The expulsion of Maqomo did little to bring peace—as how could it? On 2 January 1830 Sir Lowry Cole, writing to Sir

[1] Of the establishment of Fort Beaufort to guard the 'frontier' (and to 'watch' Maqomo) Dr. Philip writes from the spot in 1830, that it is as much use to protect the alleged frontier 'as Perth would be as a fort to protect Blair in Atholl from invasions from the north'. Following the definition which annexed a large part of the 'neutral' territory in 1829, Col. Wade in 1833 made a further 'rectification' which 'cut off from Kafirland the beautiful site of the present Lovedale missionary institution, and several square miles of fertile land now in possession of the Fingos' (Theal, ii. 55). It was not only Maqomo who suited himself about the line of the boundary.

[2] Manuscript report by J. Fairbairn of an interview with Maqomo, 1830.

[3] Manuscript notes on Ross's negotiations.

[4] Evidence of chief Botman in 1836, quoted by Cory, ii. 398 n.; also Cory, ii. 451, and iii. 52.

George Murray in Downing Street, regretted that Xhosa were ever allowed to re-enter the Ceded Territory; having been allowed back, they have 'gradually occupied the best part of it', and 'have claimed the occupation more as a matter of right than of sufferance'. In recent months, moreover, of 5,000 cattle stolen not more than 1,500 were recovered by patrols.[1] Hence, to bar further encroachments, the Government had tried the experiment of planting Hottentots in the 'vacant' land.[2] To this Murray replied on 6 May 1830 regretting the presence of the Xhosa but definitely discountenancing forceful expulsion, though 'misconduct' was 'to be punished immediately'. Lord Goderich added (26 May 1831) a suggestion that the territory be used 'for the general purposes of settlement'; farms were to be *sold* not granted, and only to Englishmen and Hottentots, on no account 'to the boers of the Colony'.

Measures and precautions were equally vain. Depredations continued, and lost nothing in the telling by frontiersmen. Firmer action occasioned indeed some bad attacks of nerves; in September 1829 the Governor made a dash to the frontier, only to reach the conclusion that 'a coalition to invade the Colony never entered into the contemplation of the chiefs'.[3] On New Year's Day 1832, a Sunday, Colonel Somerset rode hurriedly to the Kat River, to find the Hottentots quietly at church whereas the Boers, hearing that the Hottentots were

---

[1] These allegations of numbers stolen must be taken *cum grano salis*. In an unfenced country, full of wild beasts, all losses were habitually ascribed to 'Kaffirs'. See also p. 275.

[2] The Kat River Settlement was at last a Government venture, unprompted by missionaries. In this connexion, indeed, Cole made his well-known attack on Dr. Philip, who was to be 'kept out' of the Kat River as, 'it is to be feared, more a politician than a missionary'. As a constituted congregation the Hottentots themselves, however, 'called' and brought in James Read and the L.M.S., obliging the Governor to send his own nominee as an afterthought. Mr. Read's appointment was confirmed by Philip on his return from England, on the ground that 'the hatred of the colonists against him was not from the moral obliquity into which he had been led [before his suspension ten years earlier], but for his uncompromising stand against Oppression'. Read, on this account, was *persona grata* also with the Xhosa—an important consideration in a settlement planted in 'Kaffir' land. The Hottentots, thus 'reinstated to the rights of British subjects, and to a place of residence denied them within the limits of the old colonial boundary' (Brownlee's report, Dec. 1830), for a time did very well. Missionaries described the foundation of the Settlement not only as a blow aimed against the L.M.S. but also as a 'popular' act to disarm critics of the Government for its treatment of Maqomo. It was at any rate accepted by the Xhosa, and also helped to keep the Hottentots loyal to the Colony in 1835 (*Cape Col. Qn.*, pp. 239–42).   [3] Cory, ii. 393.

about to attack them, were mobilizing and preparing to 'get in first'.[1] The position of the tribes themselves was pitiable. In their unsettled state, one chief complained, they 'had no security that the place they were in today would be theirs to-morrow'.[2] In 1832 an L.M.S. missionary, Kayser, was 'sent to be near Maqomo, though the way Maqomo is moved from pillar to post by the Government makes it impossible yet to establish a regular mission in his country, as he desires'[3]—and impossible, it may be added, to make any serious advance in the task of education and of civilization. A year later, 2 November 1833, the missionary James Clark, now moved to the Keiskama, wrote of the effect of the expulsions from the Ceded Territory:

There is no doubt they will be quarrelling among themselves about the want of pasture; as they are now thronged upon each other, their cattle will be in such great numbers that the first drought they will find themselves poor and dying with hunger.[4]

In all these years there is growing tension but no hint of measures calculated in any way to meet the essential problems of this frontier. Patrols, commandos, and the 'clearing' of any number of Zuurvelds did nothing whatever to establish the authority of law and ordinary civil government. All this time officials were at any rate preoccupied; the Cape was feeling the full force of humanitarian sentiment—and old-fashioned Boer farmers, who unwillingly submitted to the 'reform' and eventual abolition of slavery, might even resist laws that threatened to make Hottentots their legal equals.[5] The Bantu on their side had reason to go in fear that they would be 'broke up as the Hottentots were'.

---

[1] Read to Philip, 3 Jan. 1832.
[2] Philip's notes on conversation with 'one of Gaika's sons' in 1830.
[3] Philip's report to L.M.S., Sept. 1832.
[4] It has some significance that this extract is from the mass of evidence, much of it from the L.M.S., that reached the Colonial Office in 1835 (P.R.O. *Papers Relating to the Kafir War*, 1835). There is evidence, not sufficiently complete to detail, that years of unusual, perhaps despairing, unrest on the frontier were often also years of drought—1834 for one.   [5] *Cape Col. Qn.*, chs. xv, xvi.

VII

HOW JOHN PHILIP CAME TO TAKE A HAND

At the eleventh hour an attempt was made to avert the impending disaster. The drive towards some real policy for a settlement on the frontier came originally not from governors, nor from the more enlightened of the colonists, but above all from Dr. John Philip. The missionaries on the frontier had good reason to fear that the Bantu would be reduced, like the Hottentots before them, to landless serfdom; Fingos and other refugees were already competing with their Hottentot converts and 'under-cutting' wages.[1] The missionaries knew also that the restlessness of the tribes was due to the pressure they were suffering. After his first journey through 'Kaffirland' proper in 1830, Dr. Philip wrote advising the Paris Missionary Society against venturing there:

The Caffre frontier has been for some years in a very troublous state. Since 1812, three districts have been taken from that nation and added to the Colony (the last not later than 1828). In consequence of these curtailments the Caffres have been driven back upon the territory that is still left to them, and several of the chiefs, with their people, are without any fixed residence; and while they profess themselves willing to receive missionaries they profess they cannot protect them nor afford them the opportunity of instructing their children by settling in any one place.[2]

More generally Philip commented later:

Individually, savages may be as rational (as far as their observation goes) as Europeans, but it is in union and government that they lack the justice and lawfulness of civilized nations. The power of the chief . . . tends to express force rather than justice. But without a religious basis for their civilization they use their knowledge only to

[1] *Cape Col. Qn.*, p. 253.
[2] In the first instance the Frenchmen went to the Bechuana, but on the advent of Moselekatze transferred to Basutoland. In 1833 Dr. Philip was similarly called upon to advise the American Board of Missions, and it was on his suggestion that the Americans shortly after settled in Natal.

rob their neighbours and then lose all again in marauding expeditions. *When men have no settled homes* . . . it is easy for them to desert the means of instruction on any provocation.

The first hint that Dr. Philip was to transfer his vigilance to Bantu affairs came very soon after his long visit to England; he had gone there in 1826 to put the case for the legal protection of the Hottentots before British rulers and people. Returning to Cape Town on 7 September 1829 he found news awaiting him from the inland stations which led him, on 4 January 1830, to set off on a five months' journey to the interior. He was no longer *persona grata* in the Colony; his published *Researches* had involved him in a trial for libel and to Fowell Buxton he wrote confidentially (5 January) noting the change in public feeling from the days when he had been an accepted protagonist in the fight with Lord Charles Somerset.[1] About the same time he wrote to Mrs. Buxton (24 December): 'Our great people here know that everything is not yet just as it should be on that [eastern] frontier and have some dread of an exposure. My journey, however, is purely missionary, and beyond the duties of a missionary it is not my intention to go.' Certainly he adhered to his intention of moving cautiously. Two years later, in September 1832, he set out once more, to spend a long hot summer travelling, this time both east and north; it was only after his return to Cape Town in March 1833 that, armed with fuller knowledge, he entered the fray in real earnest.

Even on the earlier journey, in 1830, his observations are more than a mere tourist's impressions; four times already he had been in Albany (in 1819, 1821, 1823, and 1825), and in 1825 far beyond it to the north. Very few officials or colonists, and no Governor of them all, had seen as much of South Africa, and few had a wider range of correspondents. Entering Kaffirland, his experiences elsewhere made him at once appreciate the significance and the beauty of the land itself—the country towards the Katberg and the Amatolas.

Since I left Fort Willshire I have been travelling in the finest country I have ever seen. I do not know how to describe it better than by requesting you to fancy to yourself all the riches and beauty of the finest English scenery spread over the barren mountains, deep

---

[1] *Cape Col. Qn.*, chs. xiv, xv.

valleys and picturesque ravines of the Scotch Highlands. I do not
wonder that the Caffres are a cheerful people, their mountains and
valleys are quite inspiring. Everything in this country is divine,
except the habitations of the human race.

Of the Bantu themselves he wrote:

The Caffres are not the savages one reads about in books. They
are intelligent and are not afraid of conversing with strangers; they
are, moreover, well acquainted with their own history and study
mankind, if not books; at ten years old, they are politicians! ... They
have humour and are clever at giving characteristic nicknames;
they are not generous, but they say they are poor. They acknowledge
the white man's superiority in science and arts, but do not individually feel inferior to those they meet; though they despise the contempt of the colonists, yet it rankles in their minds and degrades
them in their own estimation.

Like the Victorians after him, Dr. Philip attached a deal of
importance to dress, going so far as to make the adoption of
European clothing a mark and test of civilization. The men in
general, he finds, go almost naked, but 'they have their points
of delicacy'. Of the many chiefs he saw, he remarks: 'They do
not all adopt European dress entirely, because all their people
could not afford to do so, and they would alienate their sympathy. It is customary for them', he notes, 'to dress when they
dine with British officers or people. Then they are immaculate.
At interviews they wear skins.' Referring to the first missionary
and to Dr. van der Kemp's having 'gone amongst the Caffres,
wearing their clothes and eating their food', Philip thinks this did
'great good'. 'You might expect criticism of this practice from
colonists', but he is surprised at Lichtenstein in the *Quarterly
Review* being so 'unphilosophical'. Van der Kemp's 'successor',
he adds, 'made a fool of himself by wearing skins when the
Caffre chiefs themselves would have worn black coats'.

The 'romantics', Dr. Philip admits, may have 'exaggerated
Caffre virtues', and 'between the world of the European and
the world of the Caffre there is a great gulf', which neither can
cross without a thorough knowledge of the other's language.
Yet Philip and his party go unarmed, and 'the Caffres have
made no attempt to steal our oxen though they were left un-
tied'. This suggests the missionary's comment:

The Caffres have not only gained nothing by their intercourse with

the colony but they have greatly deteriorated. In the earliest contact
in the Zuurveld there were no commandos to rescue stolen cattle . . .
only petty thefts. They have acquired no arts from us, they have
borrowed none of our agricultural processes. . . . The farmers have
done nothing for them. . . . Their manner of life and their super-
stitions are the same. But stealing is more common. . . . Many of them,
particularly their chiefs, have been ruined by violent spirits. They
have had the vices of civilization grafted on. . . . Only the missionaries
have done them any good, trying to civilize them by understanding
them . . . and they have so far been limited. The value of missionary
labour begins to be appreciated. The missionaries are respected, but
they have been more useful as a protection than as seminaries. . . .
On the other hand, nine-tenths of the settlers are opposed to the
civilization of the Caffres.

Dr. Philip was an observant traveller; but there are glimpses
in his 'Journal'[1] also of the missionary statesman who applied
what he saw to his judgement of official policy. As he travelled
he interviewed a large number of chiefs including the Queen
Mother, Sutu, with her minor heir Sandile, and the big brothers
(or wicked uncles) Maqomo and Tyali. The burden of their
complaint was almost exclusively of the loss of their lands, of the
wrong done by the treaty of 1819, and of faulty or corrupt interpreters; Gaika neither had the power, nor dared, to give
away the land of other chiefs—no more right, Philip comments,
than the King of England to cede the property of his subjects—
and in the end he was bereft of his own land. 'At the end of the
conversation Maqomo and Tyali told us they hoped the missionaries would help them by representing their grievances to
the Government, but we refused to interfere.' Dr. Philip, however, drew his own conclusions. Gaika had been a mere tool in
the hands of the Government. 'The borders[2] were modified at
the caprice of military men. . . . What Boer would stand it?'
Though the chiefs seem to have said little, he was moved by the
evidence of his own eyes to indignant condemnation of the effect
of commandos, in which 'the love of enterprise among the
soldiers who would otherwise die of ennui has found an outlet':

[1] Dr. Philip's custom on tours was to write a full account of his doings and
impressions and send these to Mrs. Philip to be kept for future use and reference.
From stations in the Colony he posted instalments as letters; when he left posts
behind him he kept a 'Journal'.
[2] He seems to vouch for one official by whom the Kat River was 'discovered' to
flow into the Fish, not, as was supposed, into the Keiskama.

The thieves on the borders have been represented as those who
have been robbed in the interior and brought down to the frontier
by their necessities. This is not the fact. The people who infest the
Bush on the frontier are those who have been robbed by the colonial
commandos. This was the case with the Bechuanas I met at the
Cradock (Orange) in 1825, and it is now the case on the Eastern
frontier. . . . Some of these commandos have taken ten or sixteen
thousand head of cattle from the Caffres. . . . Nineteen out of twenty
who have been plundered were innocent. . . .

Stockenström stated[1] that he could mention fifty cases when Boers
had gone on commando *having lost no cattle* . . . says, too, it is exceedingly difficult to trace spoors, but Somerset and others can do it in
any quantity when they lead to a *kraal* that has good cattle in it.

This statement is taken from a private letter and was never
submitted as a public charge. Making allowance for some exaggeration it is still a heavy, not easily refuted indictment.
Two years later, in September 1832, while Dr. Philip was himself once more at the Kat River Settlement, some horses were
reported 'stolen by Caffres'. Spoor-finders followed into
Kaffirland without success. Three or four days later the animals
were found grazing in a corner of the location—not stolen at all.
'What', he asks, 'if Boers had made the same mistake? . . . All
losses', he continues, 'tend to be made good at the expense of
the first Caffre cattle met with' . . . but 'Caffres thus losing
property have no remedy at all'—and, as he had pointed out
many years earlier, in 1824,[2] a pastoral people, deprived of their
herds, 'have no resources left and inevitably betake themselves
to the thickets and attempt to live by plunder'. Summarizing the
impressions left by the tour in 1830, Dr. Philip is unusually
captious:

Such is the system that is now followed, that I can see nothing
before the Caffres but slavery or extermination [meaning, as usual,
extrusion from their lands] if they are not educated. Education would
teach them that their true interest is to be at peace with the colony
and the folly of resistance, raise them above stealing, and fit them
for coming under the colonial Government. Such as have been at the
mission stations prefer the Government of the colony to that of their
chiefs. Many are now leaving Lovedale and the Chumie to settle in
the neutral territory and among the farmers. . . . Their country is

---

[1] Cf. Cory, ii. 398.   [2] *Cape Col. Qn.*, p. 114.

already courted. There are numbers of rapacious individuals who
have set their hearts upon it.

Slander and defamation, and the injuries done them by the
colonists, have already done their work, and their slanderers are
now waiting an opportunity to excite a quarrel that will furnish a
pretext to the Government to drive them from their lands, when they
hope to share their cattle and their land. In such a colony there are
numbers of toadeaters, civil servants who want estates. These men
are on the very borders, from them the Government secures all its
information respecting the Caffres, and they are incessant in their
exertions to accomplish their objects. Frontier Boers, Field Cornets,
magistrates, friends of magistrates want new grants of land, and these
grants must be taken from the Caffres.

'The English', he remarks further, 'have never pursued a wise
and liberal policy in their colonies. They have been too much
guided by "monopolists".' As for the Bantu:

Why not leave them? Let the military come to the Keiskama and
no farther. . . . Were there but one man in Caffreland to tell the
wrongs these people have suffered for the last thirty years from the
British Government, he would rouse a spirit in England which
would do more for them than all the assegais of their country from
the Keiskama to Port Natal. . . .

This outburst is unusual, and far from being Philip's last
word on the needs of the Bantu. An active supporter of the
movement which in 1829 led to the opening of the South
African College, the nucleus of the later University of Cape
Town, he was also thoroughly modern in his consistent advocacy of what he called a 'native agency' of fully trained
Coloured and African teachers. (This was one of many themes
left over for fuller study which the loss of the Philip Papers now
makes impossible.) Immediately after his 1830 tour Philip in
fact kept his observations on the state of the frontier very much
to himself; as became a good citizen, who was also mission
superintendent, his prime concern was to equip himself with
first-hand knowledge of the situation as a whole. For two years
after this first really close look at the Xhosa districts his trial for
libel (above, p. 16) and a disputed claim to land on the Theopolis mission-station kept him preoccupied.[1] Occasionally, in
private letters, he made some allusion to 'the bloody com-

[1] *Cape Col. Qn.*, ch. xv.

mandos' (as to his friend Thomas Pringle in January 1831); but till his next tour at the end of 1832 there is little more about the frontier. By this time (September 1832) the Hottentots on the Kat River had learned to attribute their new-found freedom to Dr. Philip's championship; now the chiefs also looked to him 'to *get land* and redress of grievances for us'.[1] Dr. Philip for his part kept to safer topics in his interview with Maqomo, Botman, and others, taking the occasion of their visit to an Infant School to read them a lesson on the importance of knowledge as the 'true source of English power and greatness'. 'The Gospel', he comments, 'is the same', but in England it has a thousand years of growth and development behind it.

On 11 October 1832, in a letter to Miss Priscilla Buxton[2] from 'Buxton', a village on the Kat River, Dr. Philip returned at last to the 'horrors' of the commando system:

The pretence is the predatory habits of the Caffres, stealing the cattle of the colonists. Any lying Boer has only to go to a military post and say he has lost so many cattle. A commando is immediately got up. No affidavit is required, no proof as to the number said to be stolen. . . . The first Caffre cattle the commando comes to, upon the *spoor* of the cattle, are seized. . . . If the Caffres resist they are shot dead upon the spot, as if they were dogs. On such *evidence* they have been declared to be a nation of thieves, robbed of their cattle, their only means of support, and from time to time of their country.

Continuing, he points the contrast with the Hottentots, settled on the most exposed part of the frontier to protect the Colony from the Xhosa, who have no difficulty in recovering stolen cattle through and by the chiefs themselves:

This is a fact which speaks volumes, which will fill the Government with astonishment . . . but to which *no* reply can be made. The Government at Home, after this *fact* is known will be wholly without excuse if a stop is not immediately put to the nefarious system of commandos.

Indignation breaks out in this still quite private letter at the blatant one-sidedness with which frontier happenings were continually regarded. Dr. Philip had been one of the first to stress for European farmers the economic evils of dispersion, and was

---

[1] Maqomo, Philip says, wanted 'a missionary, but not a fool or a child'.

[2] Most of Dr. Philip's correspondence with Fowell Buxton was made through other members of the family.

never lacking in sympathy for their losses and sufferings. The fierceness of his criticism was directed against the only remedy hitherto attempted, and its disregard of elementary safeguards of justice,[1] the failure, for example, to require reasonable proof of losses sustained. There was neither civil control nor legal check upon the exclusively military treatment of what was in essence a social disorder. Events were soon to prove that it needed no outside interference to give the Bantu a sense of grievance.

Even after the tour of 1832 the humanitarian protest was first made public, not by Dr. Philip himself, but by an eager though inexperienced fellow-traveller who knew less how to walk warily. Early in 1833 Dr. Philip returned from the far north to find the heather set on fire by articles contributed to the *Commercial Advertiser* by the Honourable Alex Bruce (a 'descendant of the Kings of Scotland') who had returned to the Colony from the Kat River some months earlier. Dr. Philip had learned in his struggle on behalf of the Hottentots that the case must rest 'on generals rather than on particulars',[2] but his aristocratic colleague, 'a stranger who had merely galloped round the country for three weeks', plunged straight into controversy and was at once discounted as a 'maligner' of the colonists. In Grahamstown on his way back in January, Dr. Philip supported the *Grahamstown Journal* in its demand for a 'full investigation' of Bruce's charges; he would have evidence from missionaries on the spot, as well as from discharged soldiers of the Cape Corps (Hottentots), on the 'whole trend of policy since 1819'. Sir Lowry Cole decided that 'the case scarcely called for an investigation'; 'it had been refuted' already, and coming from such a source could command no serious attention.[3]

Dr. Philip's moves are not clear in detail; when he was thinking hardest he seems to have written least[4]—but of the

---

[1] Philip's Journal for Oct. 1832 vouches for a story that in 1828 a commando under Col. Somerset, finding three branded cattle with one of the chiefs, confiscated the whole herd. The 'three' were afterwards 'proved' to have been obtained by an exchange with a trader.   [2] *Cape Col. Qn.*, p. 163.   [3] Cory, ii. 424.
[4] Cf. *Cape Col. Qn.*, p. 138, for a similar lull in correspondence after Philip's Bethelsdorp discoveries at the end of 1821. The Philip MSS. normally included the rough drafts if not actual *copies* of his more important letters.

trend of his activities there is no doubt. There was obviously little to be done with or through Sir Lowry Cole and, as frontier policy was the special concern rather of the Secretary of State, Philip made his appeal to Fowell Buxton. In any case a change of Governor was in the wind,[1] and now was the time to get the ear of Downing Street. On 7 March 1833 Andries Stockenström[2] sailed for England, taking with him letters and an introduction to Buxton. In June and July 1833 there was some excitement in Cape Town about Cole's new *Commando Ordinance* (the 99th); on 10 July Miss Buxton is promised more documents bearing on the commando system; and in a letter begun on 21 September, but finished only on 5 December, Miss Buxton replied to Philip:

My father has been very well this year, and gained twelve pounds weight in the first twelve weeks after the Abolition of Slavery. He has taken a great holiday, I must say, but is now turning his mind a little to your part of the world, and your horrid commandos. *He has been with Mr. Stanley several times about them,* but begins to fear that little will be done without open war, and public opinion. Therefore, he is very anxious to make himself master of the subject before another session, and begs you to send him all the facts and authentic documents you can, without any delay.

The Governor's 99th Ordinance was designed to deal with raids and disorders on the scattered northern front of the Colony; distances there were so great that farmers proved unwilling to serve on commando and Cole felt it necessary to stiffen the law with penalties. Though it had been designed less

---

[1] Philip writes to Stockenström as early as 13 Jan. 1833 hoping for fuller cooperation with the 'next governor'.

[2] The relations of Philip and Stockenström at this stage are curious. In 1825 the two had made friends and come to an 'understanding' on general policy (*Cape Col. Qn.*, p. 213). After Philip's return from England he seems to make only one, unkind, reference to Stockenström—warning Pringle against him (Jan. 1831). Now Stockenström was thinking of resigning and of a trip to England, and in Oct. 1832 Philip wrote indicating that 'an introduction to Mr. Buxton would be undesirable. In England he should be independent.' Stockenström was quick to take a hint, and in November replied agreeing that as he and Buxton might be in agreement it would be well to avoid the appearance of 'collusion' for the defeat of those who differed from them. On his northern trip Philip seems to have mellowed, and on 13 Jan. 1833 wrote cordially hoping to be in time to talk things over before he sailed. Finally on 7 Mar. Stockenström sailed, armed both with his introduction from Philip to Buxton, and with a bundle of letters 'for 55 Devonshire Street', the Buxtons' London house.

for the east than for the north, the Ordinance alarmed the
critics of the eastern commandos especially by its second clause,
which authorized any official from the Civil Commissioner
down to the provisional field-cornet 'at all times of actual or
threatened invasion, or for the protection of the colonists or
their property, or when they shall otherwise deem it absolutely
necessary', to summon or, in effect, 'commandeer' men for
military service. It may be that Cole, who by the time the
Ordinance reached London was himself in England, failed to
distinguish between the needs of the eastern and northern
frontiers. The evidence, however, with which Dr. Philip armed
Mr. Buxton was sufficient to warn Lord Stanley of the danger of
increasing the efficiency of the military machine.

In a memorandum, undated, but from its references obviously belonging to 1833, Dr. Philip reviewed the situation. The
farmers' requests for the help of patrols, he pointed out, were
unchecked by any need to make affidavit or furnish proof of the
extent of their losses: the frequent patrols were impoverishing
the Xhosa and therefore had the effect of provoking more of the
thefts so much complained of. The experience of the Kat River
showed the system to be as 'unnecessary as it is impolitic and
unjust'. Indian parallels do not hold: 'From what parts of our
Indian territory have the Indians been exterminated? . . . The
friends of humanity will have no objection to the annexation of
the Caffre country to-morrow, provided the people are not
robbed of their cattle and deprived of their country.' He remarked further that there were many traders (up to two hundred) in Kaffirland, and that these went unprotected without
suffering harm. Finally, a point forgotten by Sir B. D'Urban
and others who complained that missionaries failed to give any
warning of the outbreak a year later, Dr. Philip clearly fore-
shadowed ultimate resistance by the Bantu, and inevitable war,
'since they will feel they may as well fall by the sword if the
present system is to continue'.

These arguments seem to have prevailed. Commando service
might be unpopular in the north, but the patrols on the eastern
frontier were always active. On 9 November Stanley informed
the Governor that the Commando Ordinance 'has been reserved for further consideration'.[1] On 15 November Sir Lowry

[1] The Secretary of State also asks for more information about Crown Lands,

Cole submitted his defence and explanation, but on 27 November the point was decided against him and the Ordinance disallowed as from 1 August 1834. This was not all. In his dispatch of 27 November to the new Governor, Sir Benjamin D'Urban, Stanley expressed the view 'that there may be something in the allegations' against the commando system, which he considered 'brutal'. In consequence: 'It will now, of course, be incumbent upon you to devise such other measures as may appear calculated to protect colonists against unprovoked aggression.' To this end—and here Dr. Philip's constructive proposals are in evidence[1]—D'Urban was instructed to consider the propriety of stationing Government 'agents' on the frontier, also the practicability of annual presents, or salaries, for the chiefs as a means to regulate and improve intercourse with the Bantu tribes as a first step towards reform.

The onus was now upon Sir Benjamin D'Urban. The system was inherently vicious and already almost beyond reasonable control. The humanitarian contention which had moved Stanley was eminently sound; it was not that innocent 'Kaffirs' were habitually wronged by cruel and vindictive reprisals, but that the whole policy of the frontier was stupid. Exclusively military control could not in any case attain the only real end, a well ordered, settled *society*.

'more particularly those in the Ceded Territory, which are understood to be better adapted for cultivation than the unappropriated land within the limits of the colony'.

[1] Cf. letter of 19 July (below, p. 110, n. 2) and also D'Urban's dispatch of '9 June 1836', referring to the idea of 'an establishment', as suggested in Stanley's dispatch of 27 Nov. 1833, and discussed with Dr. Philip 'as one versed in the subject of that dispatch and of its bearings and intentions'.

VIII

THE NEGOTIATIONS OF PHILIP AND D'URBAN IN 1834

Sir Benjamin D'Urban began his fateful term of office on 16 January 1834, and by no means with the plaudits of the philanthropists[1] who cannot have known that his instructions (8 November) expressly enjoined him 'not to propose or assent to any Ordinance whatever' imposing on non-Europeans 'any disabilities or restrictions' not equally applying to Europeans. Dr. Philip may have been slow to move but was industrious in following up what had been gained by Buxton's intervention, and he laboured throughout the critical year 1834 to keep the new Governor to the task of reconstruction assigned to him. On 20 January, within four days of D'Urban's landing, Philip wrote to ask favourable considerations for the Griquas who 'with scarcely any exceptions are desirous of being included within the limits of the colony'. He respectfully asked D'Urban to give his attention to the full *memorandum* which he had submitted to the Acting Governor Colonel Wade in October 1833 (Ch. IV above). On 17 February he wrote to the L.M.S.:

> I am busy preparing notes for the governor, to assist him in coming to an opinion on the frontier system. He proposes to leave Cape Town next April to see and hear with his own eyes and ears, and to form a plan to remedy the evils so much deprecated. I sincerely hope he will be kept free of any colonial bias. All our hopes depend on the introduction of a different frontier system.

A month later, on 13 March, Dr. Philip's eastern notes were completed and submitted to the Governor in a memorandum of great length, recapitulating and elaborating, with detail, the arguments already outlined in his letters to Mr. Buxton. The

---

[1] Dr. Philip wrote in dismay to Buxton: 'I see by the papers to-day (1 Sept. 1833) that our new Governor has left Demerara amidst the regrets of the colonists. I am almost in despair at this circumstance. Had they had public rejoicings on the occasion, I should have had more hope of him. "Oh, Lord! how long" are we to have such men sent us as governors?'

effect of commandos and of patrols as hitherto practised was, in short, to create a constant state of alarm in the villages; instead of putting down thieving, it made fresh robbers. At the same time the system was a temptation to unscrupulous colonists and bad men were attracted to the frontier by the opportunities of plunder; worthless horses were sometimes purposely lost, and the indemnity for stolen animals was oppressively heavy. Tribes in the immediate neighbourhood might be the first to suffer, but the repercussions reached far into the interior—adding to the commotion already caused among the tribes generally by the ravages of the slave-trade. Having detailed, further, the disputes about the lands beyond the Fish River, Philip argued that these arose inevitably out of Somerset's treaty with Gaika in 1819; the suggested remedies included a proposal to require an affidavit or other certificate of the number of animals alleged to be stolen, and of their value—with a penalty for deception.[1] More Hottentots might be placed 'on land that would not satisfy 50 Boers', so that a strong force of Hottentots might easily be rushed to any point of disturbance. Finally, whatever was done should be reduced to 'something written'—that chiefs might know to what they were committed and that there might be an end to the 'fluctuations' of frontier policy universally complained of;[2] the tribes never knew from one Governor to another what was the policy of the day.

To this long statement the Governor replied promptly; but with an apparent desire for secrecy in his dealings with Dr. Philip, the now bitterly unpopular champion of 'vagrants', this note like the whole of a series of seven was written with his own hand:

Sir Benjamin D'Urban presents his compliments to Dr. Philip, and is very much obliged by his communication of to-day.

Sir Benjamin D'Urban has for some time been grieved at the drought, which has occasioned such distress along the frontier line; but he has to-day more favourable news—and he hopes that the

---

[1] In a letter to D'Urban in July Philip maintains that 'depredations' were 'much exaggerated'. Many farmers even then were 'in Kafirland itself' and one, he instances, 'claimed double the number of cattle he ever possessed', as was 'proved by a reference to the landdrost's book: when detected, the man confessed his mistake, without appearing in the slightest degree ashamed of his conduct.'

[2] Cf. Theal and Cory, *passim*: Philip elaborated this point in a letter of 27 Oct. 1834.

rains which have hitherto been but partial may have been more general.

To the Rev. Dr. Philip.   *Thursday, 20th March*

A long pause followed of which Philip took advantage to prepare a further formidable series of documents for Mr. Buxton who, for his part, made a fruitless endeavour in the same year to secure a Select Committee to investigate the policy pursued towards the native races of the Cape frontier.[1] Then at last the Governor woke up to remember the charge laid upon him by Lord Stanley in the previous November:

Private   GOVERNMENT HOUSE
                                        Saturday, 31 May 1834
Sir,
The time is now come for me to take into my most serious consideration the whole of the frontier system, and I have accordingly been for some days past devoting it to that important subject. In the process of this, the Memoir with which you had the kindness to favour me, has demanded my careful attention; and thereupon I will request you (if it be not inconvenient to you) to call upon me on Monday next at half past one o'clock.

The enclosed was addressed to me the day after I had had the honour of an interview with Mr. Stanley and Mr. Ellis immediately before I left England.

In your Memoir you advert to a Paper which had been published in the 'Commercial Advertiser', as deserving notice. I have not seen it; if you can readily lay your hands on it, perhaps you will take the trouble to send it me for perusal.

Believe me to remain,
With great respect and esteem,
Sir,
Your very faithful, humble servant,
B. D'URBAN

[1] A mass of documents including Ross's evidence on Maqomo, a letter ascribed to the chief Tzatzoe, and a long letter of his own to the American Board of Missions, was posted apparently on 5 May, the postal charge being originally no less than £5 (*Cape Col. Qn.*, p. 58). Mr. Buxton got his Committee in 1835, and several of these papers are printed in the volume of *Evidence* (1836). In his own letter Philip distinguishes between 'patrols' and 'commandos'. The patrol is purely military, with possibly a farmer guide, the commando is primarily a much larger mixed force of soldiers and burghers, bent usually on reprisals; the term commando, however, is also used for small expeditions, seemingly well known and common, where farmers themselves acted together, without the formality of getting military help. And cf. p. 78, n. 4.

The interview that followed this letter was the first of a good many, and for two or three months relations between D'Urban and Philip were intimate, with much passing to and fro of letters and even of private official documents. But the period of intimacy was short—it was interrupted when Dr. Philip set out for the frontier on 13 August, to return only after Christmas within a few days of D'Urban's own departure to conduct the war. It is clear that the two men never reached any real understanding. Discussion began on the question of the proposed new frontier 'system'. D'Urban's instructions (from Stanley, November 1833) had not only suggested the propriety of establishing 'agents' on the frontier, but had authorized expenditure for the purpose—the rather inadequate sum of £600 for the payment of 'prudent and intelligent men'. Further consideration of the names of the proposed agents passed between the Governor and Philip.

Private and Confidential

My dear Sir,   *18th June 1834*
    I am very much obliged by your letter of the 12th which I should earlier have acknowledged, but for much pressing public business.
    Your remarks are, I am certain, very valuable, and you may rest assured that they are not—and will not be lost upon me.
    You mentioned, the other day, the Name of a Person on the Eastern (or North Eastern) side of the Colony, whom you thought eligible for a *resident agent*, in Kafirland, and I made a note of his name at the time, but I cannot lay my hand upon it now, and it has escaped my memory. Be so good to inform me of his name and description. It was a person who you said was likely to have applied for some grant of land?
    I shall go to the Frontier (many thanks for your anxiety about me personally) as soon as I have disposed of two or three very important matters of business here, which I *must* see to myself before I quit the seat of Government. When that is done, the Weather and the Rains will be but secondary considerations (as such things ought to be where duty is to be done).
    In the meantime, I think I have instructed the authorities in that quarter cautiously, but effectually, so that they can get on for the present without me.   Very faithfully,
                                            My dear Sir,
                                                Yours,
                                                    B. D'URBAN

In his reply next day Dr. Philip suggested that the new plan would meet with opposition not only from the colonists but from 'higher quarters' (meaning probably Colonel Somerset and the military authorities). An agent, he says, to gain the necessary respect, must be 'broad, educated, and a gentleman'. The Governor, Philip tells Mrs. Buxton about this time, 'has received my suggestions favourably, but nothing can be done till the Governor visits the frontier',[1] action being delayed till the Governor should see conditions for himself.[2]

In these months of 1834 D'Urban freely consulted Dr. Philip about other points of the highest importance that were now forcing themselves upon his attention. One of these was the threatened modification of the Hottentot reforms of 1828 by a 'Vagrant Law' which was introduced in the Council in May. In June Dr. Philip had an opportunity of calling the Governor's attention to a great influx of alarmed farm Hottentots to the Kat River. D'Urban on 22 June was able to report a favourable intervention on their behalf.[3] It is significant also

---

[1] Undated letter in J. G. Gubbins collection.

[2] A month later (19 July)—when wider issues had been opened—Dr. Philip returned to this point and suggested in detail that in Kaffirland there would be *three* agents, one with the Pato-Congo tribes in the south, one with the Gaikas (Maqomo) in the centre, and one with the Tambookies in the north. Of these, one should be chief, with a salary of £500, two of them subordinates with £250 each; £154 suggested by the Commandant is inadequate, but a total expenditure even of £3,000 would cost much less than 'armies'. The essentials of this plan were adopted a year or two later when Dr. Philip's own name had become anathema to the Governor.

[3] A letter written by D'Urban, 22 June 1834:

Private   *22 June 1834*

My dear Sir,

The circumstances of the Hottentot families of Rudolff van Ender, Andries Andries and Hans Battercense (I ... [words illegible] ... Rennie of Hans Hans) who had migrated from Graaf Reynet to the Kat River in consequence of orders, real or supposed, attributed to two Field Cornets of the former district, were brought under my notice in the end of April by Capt. Campbell and Capt. Armstrong—and a strict Inquiry into this alleged proceeding which had caused so much distress to these unfortunate People, was immediately directed to be instituted, the result of which I am every post expecting, from the Civil Commissioner Mr. van Ryneveld.

Capt. Campbell and Capt. Armstrong stated at that time that 'the whole of the land at the sources of the Kat River, intended for the free Coloured Inhabitants, had been already appropriated to them, and generally in small allotments, so that the whole Population was as dense as could be admitted'.

He has, however, doubtless suffered these families to remain, and, as they do not seem to have been followed by others (which was at the time to be apprehended) I dare say there will be no difficulty about their being located.

that on 31 July D'Urban took an opportunity of delaying the 'Vagrant Law' by asking for the opinions of the judges.[1] In the end he decided against the law, probably as a result of Dr. Philip's representations;[2] it was an inestimable advantage to 'have the ear of the Governor', as he put it, at this crisis in the fortunes of his particular protégés, the Hottentots.

The most engrossing subject at this time was, however, the increasingly serious discontent among the frontier Boers. Not only were they full of natural complaint about the insecurity of the frontier but now, on top of the (alleged) 'vagrancy' of the lately emancipated Hottentots and the Governor's hesitation about the 'Vagrant Law', came the announcement that on 31 December 1834 all slaves were to be set free. As early as February the resident J.P. at Cradock reported 'ferment' in his district, and that farmers were leaving the Colony, taking slaves with them.[3] Hardly had D'Urban and Philip parted after their first interview when D'Urban followed it up with a note:

Private and Confidential

Thurs. Mg., 12 June 1834

My dear Sir,

You will have in recollection my conversation of the other day with you?

With reference to it, be so good to read this, and afterwards send it to me again.

Very sincerely yours,

B. D'URBAN

'This' was a letter of 7 June from Colonel Somerset, Commandant on the frontier. Its purport seems to have been the insecurity of the frontier, the 'contempt' inspired in the Boers by the failure of the British Government to give protection, the imperative need to strengthen the Cape Corps, and the threat

I shall write about it immediately, as well as about relief being afforded them. But I expect to hear in the interim that all this has been already done under the orders of Capt. Campbell, and the Justice of Peace on the Kat River. I am much obliged to you for this, as I shall always be for any information which you give, or may give me, and you may be assured that it will be held confidential.

Believe me,

Very sincerely yours,

B. D'URBAN

To the Rev. John Philip, D.D.

[1] Theal, ii. 81.   [2] *Cape Col. Qn.*, p. 243.   [3] Cory, ii. 461.

of the Boers that they 'would be obliged to leave that part of the Colony unless they are protected'.

The same day (12 June) Philip returned Somerset's letter, commenting that the complaints were not supported by detailed evidence, pointing out also that Maqomo, already punished for interfering with the Tambookies, could not in any case be concerned in troubles on the upper Koonap. The frontier is so ill defined that 'excuse me saying I have my suspicions that they (complainants) are themselves in the Caffre country'; there are 'disaffected' Boers, he adds, 'occupying farms on the Kye'. The tail of Philip's letter had a sting—His Excellency should warn colonists that a stranger was already on the frontier collecting information for a Select Committee of the House of Commons.[1]

The very day after he received this reply D'Urban wrote off post-haste to Somerset and to others on the borders. He does not want, he says, to go himself to the frontier till August. 'There appears to exist a great alarm and excitement for which I am at a loss to account.' He hopes it is not 'got up by the Boers or others interested' in discussions in the British Parliament for which, he hears, *agents* are *now* collecting information. 'Be sure', he concluded, 'that alleged robberies are *within the proper and well-understood boundary of the colony.*' Inside a month, which was prompt for those days of no roads, reports came back from the frontier, and D'Urban wrote to Philip:

Private and Confidential

My dear Sir,   *14th July 1834*
I told you the other day that I had some papers to send for your perusal. They are herewith, and I will request you to return them to me as soon as you shall have read them, because I want to have reference to them in the course of the week (indeed on Wednesday).

No. 1 has reference to the subject of Mr. Read's letter to you of 10 June, returned herewith, being in original, and contains the result of an investigation which I had directed to be made in April as to the causes of the removal of Hottentot families from Graaf Reynet to the Kat River.

No. 2 has reference to Mr. Read's other letter of which you were so good to send me an extract, upon the 'emigration of inhabitants beyond the border carrying with them slaves'.

---

[1] Who this was does not appear.

The papers marked (*a*) in this packet will give you the result of the inquiries set on foot by the Civil Commissioner thereon. (*b*) will show you that this subject had my early consideration after my arrival. I am at a loss to conceive the cause of the alarm expressed by the Rev. Mr. Munro and the Rev. Mr. Read in the extracts sent to me in your letter of the 27th June. There is no official measure pending inimical to the Caffres. A formal communication was made to their assembled chiefs on 17th June from me, which I trust may have a good effect—and the instructions which I have sent to the Civil Commissioner, Commandant and Magistrates, are assuredly of a nature not at all to warrant any such alarm, the tenour of them being to repress all violence on the part of our own inhabitants, while, at the same time, due and *legal* protection must be afforded to the persons and property of His Majesty's un . . . and unoffending subjects living *within the proper boundary* of the colony.

I must, however, apprise you that the amount of stolen cattle from farmers in the districts of Albany and Somerset within the six months preceding the middle of June has been in round numbers 900 head, and of horses 100, and that by my last month's (?) reports I see that the robberies have been latterly attended with more than one attempt at murder and great ill-usage of women.

I have not failed to avail myself of several of the suggestions in your letters, where they have been applicable to the existing state of things and you will always oblige me very much by giving me the advantage of your future views.

> Believe me ever, dear Sir,
> Very sincerely yours,
> B. D'URBAN

To the Rev. John Philip, D.D.

The enclosures included a report from a Mr. Rennie, a farmer on the Baviaans River, who had just returned (29 June) from the White Kei, and a letter of 27 June from the Civil Commissioner (Campbell) of Albany. From these, certain facts stand out clearly. There were 'depredations, especially in Albany and Lower Somerset,' and, says Campbell, 'the idea that these are fabricated for any purpose is absurd; they are increasing if anything', and extend to Grahamstown and Lower Albany, 'both of which have been free for some years'. On the other hand, possibly as a result of the combined effect of these depredations, of shortage of farms in the Colony, and of Hottentot and slave legislation, a good many farmers had undoubtedly taken the risk of the 'Kaffirs' and gone 'beyond the border'. Mr. Rennie had heard that '1,200' Boers had crossed the Orange River owing to severe drought in the Tarka; more definitely, he had found 31 families between the Swart and Wit Kei, and 21, he gathered, had crossed the boundary for pasture—'eleven of them to form a permanent settlement'.[1] These Boers, moreover, had 15 slaves with them, and one, to 'mak siccar', had put his slaves in irons.

In more general terms this state of affairs is confirmed by the Civil Commissioner. There is and has been 'trekking' and farmers could not survive the dry season without it—nor *will* they when the land beyond is taken up; therefore the authorities wink at it, and in any case could not prevent it because on the border there are neither troops nor field-cornets—the latter being chosen for their central position in the wards—and 'because' (for what mad reason does not appear) notices warning farmers against trekking 'had to be sent in English which very few read or understand'. In the last two years, he adds, permanent emigrants have been filtering out from *western* districts—whether to evade the slave law he does not know.

The Governor's communication, which shows that even at this time he was not 'in Philip's pocket', at once had Philip busy writing—obviously with great care; so many drafts survive of letters dated between 15 and 22 July that it is not clear which or how many of them reached Government House; but the trend of his argument is quite clear. On 15 July Philip thanked the Governor for the opportunity given him of supplying information 'on the important matters now engaging Your Excellency's attention', and asked for another day 'to look up his files'. Then he got to work, and at once seized on essentials commonly missed by both colonists and their historians: he puts no reliance on exact numbers, such as the '1,200' trekkers beyond the Orange River, but quotes a letter from the missionary Kolbe (from Philippolis on 13 May) in support of the view that their numbers are certainly relatively large. In the north, he points out, the Griquas are peaceable and inoffensive, whatever the 'Caffres' may be, and the troubles and difficulties are due 'solely to the advance of the Boers'. The only thing needed is to 'secure to the Griquas the possession of their

[1] Obviously the 'trekker' Louis Trigardt and his friends. Cf. Cory, ii. 461.

country, freed from the annoyance and injuries they are now suffering'. 'Drought', he holds, is no warrant or excuse for the Boer exodus; 'I know of no *unoccupied* country on the borders of our Colony', and drought hits the native inhabitants just as hard as the colonists; farmers, in any case, 'have no business to keep 2,500 beasts while they pay the *opgaaf* tax on only 250'. Let them, if they must habitually overstock, provide themselves with reserves '*behind them*'; but 'for this they must have *paid*, and this is the sole reason for their present unjust and disgraceful practice—avarice is the motive. . . .' Farms said now to be inadequate were granted quite recently, many of them only in 1828. A draft of 18 July continues:

The invasion of peaceable countries and the progressive extermination of their inhabitants cannot be connived at, much less sanctioned.
Britain which has extinguished her Slave Trade and recently given
twenty millions to procure freedom for her slaves, will no longer suffer
her national honour to be tarnished, as it has been, by the system
which has been so long pursued in this colony to gratify the avarice of
the Frontier Boers. . . .

In 1809, and 1810, the Boers complained of the Caffres as they are
now doing, and to gratify them the Zuurveld or Albany was taken
from the Caffres. . . . In a few years the Caffres became as troublesome on the Fish River as they had been on the Zondag River. . . .
It was next found that the Keiskama [was as bad] . . . and Maqomo
and Gaika's Caffres were driven in 1829 from the Kat River and from
behind the Gonap. All these invasions and those also on the Northern
frontier were in the first instance preceded by permitting the Boers
to cross the colonial boundary under the pretext that it was necessary
to preserve their cattle from perishing. . . . After being allowed to
roam about in the country of our neighbours for a few years—to
make room for their children they found the actual possession of those
countries necessary, and they were gratified in their wishes. . . .

When I was at the Caco (Gaga) Post in 1830 some hundreds of
Boers had been applying for land in that district. Scarcely had they
settled but they must have liberty to cross the boundary in dry
seasons . . . that is, every season; and if the Key was the boundary
to-morrow, in seven years they would be on the Umtata.

From the whole of the Civil Commissioner's letter your Excellency
must perceive that the laws are not enforced. One cannot, therefore,
wonder at the contempt into which the British Government is
said to have fallen among the Boers. That having sent a Government
Order on so important a subject in the English language only, to

men whom we *know to be ignorant of that language*, is no extraordinary instance of Frontier management. . . .

When your Excellency shall have time to settle the affairs of the Frontier on an equitable basis and when it shall be known that faithful men will be appointed over them, and supported in the discharge of their duty . . . when proper agents shall be appointed and proper relations entered into with the Frontier nations . . . and your Excellency already perceives what is to be done to remedy the evils of the old system . . . every difficulty will be overcome. . . .

The Boers, like all ignorant people, just take as much as is given them. They acknowledge no other limit. When Government assumes a commanding aspect, no people on earth are more submissive. And it is lamentable to observe how for so many years their ruinous encroachments have been winked at, and even encouraged by the Frontier authorities. It is to this we are to look as to the spring of all the mischief. Your Excellency has a great work upon your hands, a work which involves, in it, the prosperity of the Colony and the preservation of the Tribes to a great extent beyond it, and I sincerely hope that Your Excellency, under the blessing of God, will be instrumental in effecting both.

This analysis of the fundamental causes of frontier troubles defies serious challenge. It may be that Dr. Philip tended to be more right in what he affirmed than in what he denied, and that at least he did not gauge the strength of the farmers' absorption in their own grievances. In picking out flaws and discrepancies in the reports from the frontier Philip may have been dialectically over-subtle. For example, he reiterated that figures of losses went all unchecked, taking no account of strays or of restored animals; and that Somerset put the thieving in Upper Somerset, while Campbell put it in Lower Somerset or Albany. Yet the very discrepancies were evidence of sorts that there was general stealing and unrest; long-established European farmers justly complained that life on the frontier generally was intolerably difficult and dangerous. It remains that in seeing further and deeper into the causes of the unrest, and in his consistent emphasis on the need for civil administration rather than military (and militarist) 'handling' of the frontier, Dr. Philip was a lonely prophet and pioneer. Most of the trouble, he insisted, arose from one weakness: the distant Government in Cape Town could not hope to control efficiently a frontier where there was scarcely any civil administration at all.

The case for a constructive policy broke down before the opposition of men who could not see beyond their own very real sufferings. Discontent was already so great that their movements were no mere casual migrations of a semi-nomadic people but the beginnings of a deliberate and voluntary exile. As Philip himself wrote a little later:[1] 'When I was on the Frontier in August and September all the talk was about *Boers leaving the Colony*'—with the addition, certainly, that they had hopes that 'the Governor would come and give them new farms beyond the Frontier'. This was the time of the so-called *Commissie* Treks (below, p. 197); the most promising excursion was that of Piet Uys who in 1834 spied out the land towards Natal and brought back favourable reports. Other famous leaders of 1836, like Piet Retief, were known to be even then contemplating their great removal.[2] Dr. Philip's representations[3] clearly disturbed the Governor; on 5 September he himself drafted a memorandum, and on the 10th got from the Attorney-General a list of the laws nominally in force imposing penalties for emigration, together with an opinion (which was unhopeful) on their efficacy. On the 12th a Proclamation in the *Gazette* called attention to these old laws and expressly cancelled the temporary permission granted by Dundas (above, p. 63) in his Notice of April 1828.[4] The upheaval caused by the outbreak of the 'Sixth Kafir War' in the following December has totally obscured the significance of events that were clearly the first moves in the *Great* Trek.

The emotional storm raised by that unhappy war and its immediate sequel has, it is not too much to say, been a dominant force in the country's history ever since. One article of the faith will have it, in particular, that that war, *a fortiori* the Great Trek and all the fatal divisions it caused, were due not to the ineptitudes of frontier policy but to the 'interference' of certain missionaries and other wicked persons. The result is too often an almost congenital blindness to the possibility that the Bantu can have grievances other than such as misguided Europeans discover for them. Words written by Colonel

---

[1] To Buxton, 1 Jan. 1835.

[2] Walker, p. 181. Letters of Stockenström and others in 1836 and 1837.

[3] In a letter of July 1834, and *via* Buxton as early as 1832 or 1833.

[4] See references in Eybers, p. 145. The actual documents of 1834 were not available in Cape Town Archives.

Somerset in the end of 1834 were quoted with unction to clinch an article denouncing the critics of a Nationalist 'Colour Bar' Bill in 1926 as 'A New Philip Party':[1]

> As a result of the pains taken lately by evilly disposed persons to put into the minds of the Kafir chiefs the idea that they are oppressed by the Government, a feeling of enmity has been aroused in them which must be seen to be believed.

Colonel Somerset, Commandant on the Frontier and virtually second in command in the Colony, assuredly ought to have been in the Governor's confidence about his plans for reform. Owing, however, to the extraordinary secretiveness of D'Urban in his intercourse with Dr. Philip in these fateful months, neither Somerset nor anyone else knew that Philip's expedition was a definite 'mission' authorized by the Governor himself to prepare the way for his own coming: 'My proposal' (to go ahead of the Governor to gather fuller information), Dr. Philip wrote in a later 'Narrative', 'was warmly embraced, and being told that the Governor would certainly leave Cape Town by mid-September, according to agreement I left Cape Town on 13 August 1834.' Philip, therefore, far from 'interfering', was so much in the Governor's confidence that on 12 August, 'in the bustle of leaving', he was still receiving highly confidential documents to keep him apprised of what was going on.[2] News of an alarming murder in Hintza's country having reached him, D'Urban at once wrote on Tuesday, 12 August:

> My dear Sir,
> I send these for your persual, when you have read them be so good as to return them, for I have not (as I intended) second copies of them.
> Very sincerely yours,
B. D'URBAN

Dr. Philip himself was highly reserved about the important part he played, letting himself go only to those at a safe distance. To the L.M.S. on 13 August, very near if not on the day of his departure (and to a Director in the same words), he wrote:

---

[1] *Die Burger*, May 1926.

[2] The L.M.S. in London got impatient at times. On 21 July 1834 Philip was told by Ellis the Secretary: 'You will not allow your correspondence with that respectable individual [T. F. Buxton!] to interfere with your communications with the Directors.'

I am setting off [early] that I may meet the Governor on the Kat River, to try, if possible, to introduce a new system. . . . I am the only person in the Colony who knows the Governor's mind on this subject, but this is a circumstance that *must not be known here*, and I must not anticipate too much till I see how he will be able to stand in the midst of all his civil and military authorities, who will do all in their power to shake his personal resolution and . . . do everything to defeat us in our object.

Even James Read was unaware of Philip's role as adviser to the Governor. Knowing as early as April of D'Urban's intended visit, Read wrote both on 5 and 13 August welcoming Philip to Kaffirland, but utterly preoccupied with the question of Hottentot 'vagrancy' and never mentioning the Xhosa—as he must have done had he had reason to imagine that Philip was coming on a semi-official embassy.

Philip's letters from the frontier, both to D'Urban himself and to Buxton, Pringle,[1] and others in England, show that while there he was conscientiously gleaning information about frontier conditions but keeping very dark about any 'mission'. 'If the missionaries were left in ignorance on the subject' (of any agreement with the Governor), he writes later, when D'Urban himself was taking credit that the chiefs knew, through Philip, of his 'favourable intentions', 'I could not have made it known to the chiefs, as the missionaries were my interpreters.' Philip was hopeful that reform was to come; but except that the Governor contemplated, or even recognized, the need for a 'new system' there was, of course, nothing definite for him to communicate. It may well be that he travelled with a consequential air; and the chiefs, being full of real grievances, may have concluded that it was not for nothing that an important visitor of this kind came talking, as he was bidden, of the prospects of a changed frontier system. They naturally welcomed him, and were for some time after his visit on their very best behaviour. Perhaps Dr. Philip himself underestimated rather than exceeded his warrant; from first to last he regarded his mission as an informal attempt to 'prepare a way' for the Governor by getting more complete information. D'Urban's own later account[2]

---

[1] Thomas Pringle was now Secretary of the Anti-Slavery Society. Even to him Philip says only that 'the present Governor appears to be willing to do what is right'.　　　　[2] P.R.O., C.O. 48/49, Dispatches of 5 Jan. 1835.

gives the journey more official significance than Philip ever attached to it:

I had in the middle of last year caused communications to be made to the chiefs . . .[1] expressive of my disposition to enter into a new order of relations with them, upon a footing which could not but be advantageous to them . . . [though] its carrying out must mainly depend on themselves. . . . I afterwards availed myself of a tour which Dr. Philip, the Head of the London Mission, made through those tribes later in the year—to explain to them more fully, and in detail, the nature of the agreements which I should be prepared to enter with them, provided that meantime they abided by the line of conduct suggested.

This January dispatch must have been inspired by the prickings of a bad conscience; the 'detail' of the new order depended on his own constantly deferred visit—'to see for himself'.

Sir Benjamin proved to have a faculty for delay. In January 1834 he arrived with definite instructions to attend to the frontier, the condition of which was obviously of vital importance to the life of the Colony. By April his impending visit had been announced to the Xhosa chiefs; but only on 31 May (above, p. 108) 'the time has *now* come' to give the matter his august attention. Then, indeed, he hoped to go in August. In August Mrs. Philip was given a definite date, 15 September. On 12 September he tells Somerset that he is coming 'early next month'; the same day Lady D'Urban called on Mrs. Philip, for the third time in three weeks, to ask for 'news from the frontier' for the Governor, who is 'certainly going' early next month. By 3 October Mrs. Philip began at last to despair; 'I really hope Sir Benjamin means to go', she writes to her husband. 'Lady D'Urban says now about the middle of the month, although the Town report is that he is not going at all.' At that very minute a note arrived from Government House announcing the appointment to be Resident Magistrate, Uitenhage, of Mr. Houghton Hudson who is 'to meet us on the frontier when I go thither'. Another note followed immediately telling Philip, through her, of his plans for meeting the Griqua Waterboer who, it had been intended, was to meet him at Graaff-Reinet but was now to await his 'return' to Cape Town. Mrs. Philip then adds:

[1] Cf. D'Urban's letter of 14 July 1834, above, pp. 112–13.

I shall say nothing about it in town, for it seems to be a secret that he is going at all, and perhaps he wishes to come upon the people in the interior unexpectedly. I find that the people here are quite annoyed at him, he is so particular, so close. . . . For my part I think there is a great deal more in him than many are willing to allow and from experience we see that he is very attentive to business.

On 17 October, and again on the 20th, Mrs. Philip has 'no certain news' of the Governor's plans. She now 'hears it may be 15 November', but he has to be back for 'Emancipation Day' on 1 December. Unfortunately, she thinks, Colonel Wade (ex-Acting Governor, and hero of the 'Vagrant Law') will be his forerunner on the frontier. Finally, on 31 October, Lady D'Urban says 'about the 10th. I shall believe when he is off!'

An enclosure to R. W. Hay of the Colonial Office in a dispatch of 10 November gives D'Urban's own explanation—one Philip himself was to accept (below, p. 139, and note). 'Communications which I caused to be made' to chiefs both east and north have, he thinks, had a good effect—and he hopes for still better results from a personal visit to the frontier *where he would have gone two months ago* but for his waiting for instructions about the regulation of slave-apprentices (due to be freed on 1 December). Meantime, he had reason to believe that good had been done by the visit of an (unnamed) 'resident of fourteen years standing'. The unnamed resident's reports from Kaffirland had also made their impression;[1] the discontent of chiefs like Maqomo, the Governor explained, arose from their expulsion from the Ceded Territory. The tribes were at present quiet and friendly,[2] and the prospects good for the conclusion of a 'political and commercial treaty', with regular agents to represent the Government in Kaffirland. He thinks also that he will need probably £1,800 rather than £600 for the new frontier agents and goes on to suggest that Colonel Wade, who 'has ill endured the loss of consequence' in his new position of subordination, 'had better not come back from his leave'—especially as 'there are certain points in the system that preceded

[1] About 22 Sept. Philip began to 'report', and with the secrecy preferred by D'Urban, sent this and later letters under cover to Mrs. Philip, 'lest a letter addressed to Your Excellency from this place (Philipton, Kat River) should cause "surmises" '.

[2] All accounts agree that 'thieving' was less prevalent during the time of Philip's visit. Cf. Cory, iii. 47.

me which I have not been disposed to adopt'.[1] In November, when Philip was on his way back, D'Urban had Waterboer to dinner[2] and concluded a treaty with him; after this, Mrs. Philip wrote again on 21 November: 'Wade is coming by sea and will get the first word of the Governor . . .' but the Governor, who is now 'waiting for important dispatches', will 'probably make up his own mind *when he visits the frontier*'.

The Governor's delays made all Philip's efforts on the frontier vain. On his visits to the chiefs in September Philip was accompanied apparently by the Reads, father and son, and by a Hottentot, Stoffles, but there was no written record of their doings. In October, however, he settled down on the Kat River to sort out his impressions while he waited for D'Urban; and seldom in his busy life did he do more writing. So far was he from having 'details' of the Governor's scheme that his own ideas were just beginning to mature; for example, to T. Pringle (7 October) he writes of having a tentative plan now clearer in his own mind, and this he will submit to the Governor; and to Mrs. Philip (14th) he is 'not sorry the Governor is delayed as I am now ready for him with a grip of the whole situation'.[3] To D'Urban himself he wrote at frequent intervals. Sometimes it was on points of detail; on 22 September, for example, he anticipated later practice by suggesting the Chumie Post as headquarters for the agent, who 'could not very suitably live in a Kafir Kraal'. Another letter, on 9 October, is a recital of 'cases', but goes on to describe how—in spite of 'thieving'— 'where on my tour in 1832 there were not 15 Boers, there are now 1,100'. Confirming this statement by a reference to evidence from the mission station at Philippolis, he takes occasion to emphasize the oneness of the frontier; in the much simpler north a 'treaty' might give the essential 'protection' needed for the Griquas against the encroachments of the Boers.[4] For the

---

[1] Wade had offended in particular by acting in Council (on 'Vagrant Law') so as to 'place the Governor in the position of explaining and justifying his official acts at the bar of the Legislative Council'.

[2] On this episode Mrs. Philip comments: 'Well may the Dutch people say the world is at an end, and the Bible not true', adding, however, 'I hope the poor man's head (Waterboer) will not be turned.'

[3] His Kat River experience also inspired another vigorous letter in denunciation of Col. Wade's Hottentot 'Vagrant Law'.

[4] 'A fortnight ago,' he had told Pringle on 7 Oct., a 'Proclamation appeared prohibiting Boers from crossing the boundaries of the Colony under a penalty of

Bantu frontier he remarkably anticipates the best later practice;
the very foundation of his plan was, he told Pringle, to *substitute political commissioners for military officials*. To D'Urban himself (14 October) he emphasized how he would find that the
'exceptional difficulties were due to the neglect by his predecessors of any *system of Justice*'.

Philip at this time took no offence or alarm at the Governor's
delays but he presently bethought him also of Fowell Buxton,
who for the moment was only a second string to his bow; as in
the twenties he had resort to British political aid only when
direct dealings with the Colonial Government seemed hopeless.[1] About this time, however, there was some prospect of a
Select Committee of the House, and in August Pringle, agitat-
ing in London, had sent Philip a reminder: 'By the way, you
should stir up Buxton. . . . He is a most excellent man, but
dilatory, and somewhat irresolute when he has to deal with
civil men like Spring-Rice (then Colonial Secretary), trusting to
their good *intentions*.' Mrs. Philip also reported Pringle as saying
that Buxton had to speak 'as members were leaving in shoals',
and that he was lucky to get a quorum for an 'Address'. Buxton,
in consequence, began to get very full letters from the Kat
River,[2] important evidence which he used with effect in the
following year when he came to move, successfully at last, for
the well-known 'Aborigines' Select Committee; by that time its
functions included an inquiry into the causes of the frontier war
which had broken out in December 1834.

At length, about 27 October, Dr. Philip began to think of
returning. Finding 'suspicion' arising about his long visit, he
told Colonel Wade he was waiting in the hope of seeing Adam
Kok. But he had also come to think the Governor had 'better
see the chiefs *alone*' and sent a statement on frontier policy to
meet D'Urban in Grahamstown. In this document he avowedly
paid more attention to existing evils than to the possible remedy.
Colonel Somerset, for example, had just demanded from

---

ten pounds. In face of that, twelve Boers have passed through this Settlement, in
front of the chain of posts, into Caffreland. Another party crossed last week behind
the Winterberg, refusing to obey the Field Cornet who ordered them to return.'
   [1] Cf. *Cape Col. Qn.*, p. 185.
   [2] One was drafted on a huge closely written folio sheet. Then remembering that
this had to serve to congratulate Miss Buxton on her marriage, he 'took a smaller
sheet' and began again!

Maqomo 480 cattle—more than the chief had already returned—and more, the chief protested, than were ever taken by
Xhosa. Philip urged investigation of this claim: 'First ascertain the *facts* before Somerset carries out his threat of an expedition into Caffreland.' The patrol system, he insisted once
again, was 'unjust and indiscriminate'. There must, further, be
written agreements about boundaries. 'Passes' for traders were
too freely given; Maqomo, on the other hand, was lately
arrested at a missionary meeting for having no 'pass'. In this
connexion (diagnosing an evil that has persisted) he urged that
Africans should be treated by officials 'with ordinary civility and
respect'. Any new system, finally, would require a strong hand
to restrain the prejudice of the colonists and, 'as in India', it
must be *civil* administration. Without military help from Europe
the colonists, he said, would find themselves compelled to live
closer together and amicably with their neighbours. As it was,
he reiterated, 'even on the Eastern frontier you will find many
Boers living in Caffre territory'—1,500 by some accounts he
had heard. Thefts, therefore, could not be so bad as alleged, but
the present method of dealing with them was demoralizing the
people. Following this, in a private letter:

Having done this [i.e. drafted what he calls an appeal, based on
'justice', and sent it to meet the Governor] I consider my work in
this place done. Nothing is now left to accident. I can leave the
frontier, should the Governor not come at this time, without caring
whether I am at a public meeting of the chiefs or not. The principle
of my scheme (and that is all I care for) is now no longer an experiment that may fail, but a law that must be enforced. God commands it. The thing is practicable. . . . I stand as on a rock.

Then, indeed, in a moment of misgiving (showing again that he
was not blind to the losses of the farmers) Philip wrote to Miss
Buxton (now Mrs. Johnston) on 21 October: 'What is to happen if the Caffres shall continue to steal from the Colony, and
if lies and perjury shall be employed as they have been to ag-
gravate the evil, and if the colonial spirit shall again prevail?'
Shortly afterwards (24 November), Philip's friend, Sir John
Herschel, the astronomer, wrote welcoming news from Philip
of a probable restriction of commandos; he was pleased with
Waterboer (who 'dined' and was shown the stars), and concluded by emphasizing the 'ill effect of the increasing *bellum*

ad internecionem on the colonists themselves, who presumably approve, *thinking by long use that it is essential to their welfare and safety*. In their zeal for the material welfare of the colonists such humanitarians forgot how little any people like what is 'for their good'; but their fault was that in the essentials of frontier policy they were too enlightened and advanced for their time.

Philip's last memorandum from the frontier seems to have reached D'Urban only in the middle of January, when his preoccupation with the new sufferings of the frontier farmers blinded him finally to the constructive and more important part of Philip's work and writing. While Philip was on his way back, travelling, in face of colonial hostility, with the escort of a friendly field-cornet, D'Urban tarried in Cape Town. The frontier, therefore, remained in the unrestricted control of Colonel Somerset, who chose this moment to step up 'reprisals'; Somerset's action, following on D'Urban's delay, precipitated the crisis. After the event many on the frontier spoke wisely of the comings and goings of (drought-stricken) Xhosa, and a great 'meeting' of Gaikas and Ndhlambis in August,[1] as having foreboded a 'long premeditated onslaught'. The Governor at least had been repeatedly warned of danger ahead; though relative peace and quiet prevailed at the time Philip made his communication in September, nearly thirty years of border 'law', culminating in such a month of harrying as Sir George Cory graphically describes,[2] sufficiently account for the outbreak of resistance with violence. On 20 November, while Somerset was contemplating action for the recovery of his '480 cattle from Maqomo', a farmer named Joubert was robbed in the bush near the Koonap of 'three horses and a foal'.[3] The farmer and his friends set out and tracked the spoor to a kraal on the Keiskama where, presently, they got the chief Eno to admit the liability of his people, and to promise redress. 'After waiting five days and nights' nothing happened; so the farmers applied to Fort Willshire, whence on 2 December Ensign Sparks, an 'inexperienced youth' ('spectacled, and fond of mathematics', says Dr. Theal), set out with an orthodox 'patrol' to investigate. Arrived at the alleged guilty kraal, and getting no reply from

<hr />

[1] Cory, iii. 47.   [2] Ibid. 54 ff.   [3] Ibid. 54.

the 'sullen' occupant, 'they dismounted and seized *forty head of cattle*'. Here Sir George Cory hesitates, and explains[1] in a note that the relative market price of (any?) horse and native cattle being what they were, 'no injustice was done in this reprisal'. But now—as if the chief more than agreed about market prices— the culprit told Sparks that 'Eno had already taken sixty from him for his offence'. This certainly suggests a very wealthy kraal, if the number is to be believed; but without any investigation, 'Sparks advised him to get them back from Eno'. After this exploit it is hardly surprising that the patrol was sharply challenged within a mile, being saved from attack only by the intervention of Eno's son, called Stock. Near Fort Willshire, however, they were attacked again, and this time Spark was wounded in the arm by an assegai. 'Thus the Kafirs drew first blood', comments Sir George Cory.

In all the previous years of patrols there is little or no evidence of forcible resistance and, before taking the action such unwonted violence seemed to demand, Colonel Somerset might well have looked to the state of his armaments. 'Ammunition in the Government magazine' was, however, 'at its lowest ebb', and the troops 'barely sufficient for the defence of the outposts of Grahamstown'.[2] Unconsidering, or nothing daunted, Somerset set out with a stronger force. One day, though he 'scoured the bush', 'not a kafir was to be found'. On the next, Eno arrived with a large retinue for a parley. Eno was then told that he 'had forfeited the indulgence of residing west of the Keiskama', and was required also to 'restore' 150 head of cattle 'and the horses already stolen' (and paid for by the cattle?). Eno proved submissive. In two days 137 cattle and 13 horses were 'captured'; and within a week the number 'sent in' by him was 237 cattle and 18 horses.[3] 'Stealing', however, continued, as did reprisals—cattle were taken for more stolen horses and, 'some other cattle' being seen to emerge into the open, men were 'sent to take them also'. Somerset, in fact, was out to 'drive the last man over the Keiskama'. It was war, and inevitably serious incidents followed. The cattle 'seen to emerge', and 'seized', proved to be the personal property of a chief; and to seize the cattle of a chief was by Bantu custom to declare war upon him. A tribesman slightly wounded in a skirmish turned

[1] Cory, iii. 55 n.   [2] Ibid. 64.   [3] Ibid. 57.

out to be a petty chief, Xoxo, and this was 'an insult to the
memory of their ancestor Rarabe'.[1] Sir George Cory comments:
'The continued stealing of cattle and horses had long, too long,
been a regular feature of the life of a frontier farmer, and
in this respect there was *nothing particularly exceptional* in the
fateful month of December 1834'—nor, it is to be feared, was
the manner of treating the disease unusual.

From a different angle James Read looked on in despair. On
9 December he wrote from the Kat River to Dr. Philip:

Somerset is now clearing the country from Willshire to the sea,
all Eno's people and Congo's people. The old thing over again; for
the act of one man punish hundreds, and now again just in the
time of harvest while the corn is in the fields. Can this be Sir Benjamin's order? or would they dare take such a step without orders? I
am sorry for the case at the moment, as the chiefs will think we have
deceived them.[2]

It needs no elaborate theory of 'long premeditation' and
preparation to account for the explosion that followed. Before
Christmas the Xhosa tribes had hurled themselves upon the
Colony, devastating whole districts, up to Grahamstown and
beyond, with fire and assegai.[3] The organization of the Bantu
was far too loose for long and secret planning, even under
stress of a common feeling of reckless desperation. Twice,
early in the year, D'Urban himself had 'caused communications to be made' to the chiefs, promising them changes—so
that it did not need Philip to suggest to them that reform was
due. Instead of a friendly visit from D'Urban to hear what
they had to say, and to originate a new order, Colonel Somerset followed hard upon Dr. Philip's embassy with almost un-
precedentedly violent application of the old.

The Governor's reforming zeal evaporated finally the moment he reached the frontier in January and saw the havoc
wrought by its Xhosa invaders. Suffering a violent revulsion of
feeling he threw his weight, like the soldier he was, on the side
of those whose faith was in the sovereign efficacy of 'powder
and ball'. Turning almost with venom against all that was
wisest in the counsel of his former adviser, Dr. Philip, D'Urban

---

[1] Cory, iii. 57–59.   [2] P.R.O., 1835, 'Papers'.
[3] Even then the evidence is that women and children were uniformly gently
treated. Theal, ii. 91, and Cory, iii. 73.

himself led an outcry against him which was never to die down. The clamour understandably raised by both Boer and Settler sufferers not surprisingly drowned for the moment Philip's more sober warnings,[1] and the 'mystery'[2] enshrouding the dealings detailed in this chapter may excuse these being so long obscure. But Philip's later writings and doings (below, Chs. IX ff.) are no less grossly misrepresented; his 'interference' on behalf of Hottentots had already won for him his fixed place as the very *diabolus ex machina* of South African history.

[1] D'Urban complained, 5 Jan. 1835, that missionaries gave no 'warning' of an outbreak.   [2] Theal, ii. 50.

IX

THE WAR OF 1835—D'URBAN AND HIS PHILANTHROPIST CRITICS

On the Christmas Eve of 1834 the storm broke, and for several days the scattered and undefended farms and homesteads of the frontier colonists were plundered and ravished over a wide area. The toll taken of European lives was relatively small, but so far from the Ama-Xhosa being driven, according to plan, beyond the Keiskama, the hard lessons of 1819 were not lost on them now. This time there was no massed attack on Grahamstown; instead, by operating in small bands they were able to take advantage of the physical features of the country and almost completely evade any decisive conflict with the strong columns presently sent out against them. The final conquest of the Bantu was not to come yet.

In the last days of the year news of the invasion reached Cape Town. Early on the morning of New Year's Day Colonel Harry Smith set off alone on a famous six-day ride of six hundred miles to bring order out of chaos in the east. This breezy soldier was to have a long experience of the Cape frontier. Impetuous he always was—he had saved and won a young Spanish bride at the sack of Badajoz in 1812—and always theatrical, whether storming at the City Fathers of Grahamstown, or dressing up Xhosa chiefs, or firing off charges of gunpowder to impress them. Almost sentimentally pious, he was at the same time essentially kind and human. Smith's slow-going, slow-thinking superior, Sir Benjamin D'Urban, was a complete contrast and followed, as befitted his dignity, more at leisure. Smith got busy putting the Grahamstown Committee of Safety in its place as early as 6 January, but D'Urban had to arrange his affairs in the capital and only set sail from Simonstown on the 8th, arriving in Grahamstown on the 20th.

The Governor's long-deferred visit to the eastern districts had now come about under very difficult circumstances. Sir Benjamin was, naturally enough, 'horrified' at the ruin he found in

Albany. But, with little power of fitting policy to the facts for himself, he was not slow, like some other responsible but muddled men of affairs, to take impressions ready-made from those nearest at the moment; throwing to the wind all promises of reform, and forgetting all he had learned in 1834, he was at once satisfied that the war was 'the result of long combination'; 'so well have the wily savages masqued their purposes that neither missionaries nor traders suspected anything.'[1] Missionaries, at least, had given him ample warning that things could not long continue as they were; and even now, had he stopped to consider which of the chiefs were most implicated, he might have drawn some significant conclusions for himself. By all accounts the most truculent of the chiefs was Tyali, whose cattle had been seized during Colonel Somerset's recent clearing of the country; his brother Xoxo it was, too, who had been wounded in December. Another was Eno, the hero of the Sparks episode (above, p. 125). By some accounts Maqomo, more important than either of these, at first hung back; but he was in it too, and had his own very real grievances; according to a missionary version of a comment by one Major Cox, he was indeed 'a much wronged man'. Pato, on the other hand, was quiet—a testimony, it may be, to the pacific influence of the Wesleyan missionaries. But Pato had also been for years in peaceable occupation of the lower and less attractive part of the Ceded Territory, in Peddie, and being little troubled by commandos had less cause for complaint.[2] The same Pato (below, p. 134) was out fighting to the last ditch in the later war of 1847.[3]

Farther afield there was a greater chief than any of these, the Transkeian Xhosa Paramount, Hintza. That he sympathized with his western kinsmen's troubles there need be no doubt; nor that when either tribal or colonial cattle were to be had he received them gladly, for 'safe keeping', beyond the Kei; but the assertion that he was the 'chief instigator of all the mischief'[4] rests on the flimsiest evidence of panic-stricken traders, and is at any rate of only academic interest. D'Urban, however, took the charge seriously; one of his first actions seems to have been to

[1] Letter of 21 Jan. to his Secretary, Col. Bell, who was left in charge in Cape Town.
[2] Evidence of Rev. W. Shaw and Rev. S. Young. Cory, iii. 304, 307.
[3] Ibid. iv. 514.
[4] Ibid. iii. 116.

authorize a 'mission' to Hintza to obtain his 'neutrality or co-operation'—in effect to compel his co-operation. This almost wanton extending of the scope of military operations for the not very adequate colonial forces, within a week of his arrival in Grahamstown, shows how soon Sir Benjamin absorbed the traditional precepts of the frontier. Discarding all ideas of a constructive policy for the *control* of black and white relations, he seems at once to have inclined towards the demarcation of a new and more distant line of frontier, an enterprise that must infallibly reproduce all the successive troubles of past years. As early as 28 January D'Urban had begun to toy with the idea of pushing the colonial boundary back from the Fish River to the, possibly, shorter and more easily defended line of the Kei.[1] To this plan he adhered consistently in the months that followed, though never making it quite clear how he proposed to deal with the immediate problem presented by the Gaika tribes between the Keiskama and the Kei.

The course of the short campaign—it was virtually over by the beginning of May—confirms the view that the Governor was concentrating on the military needs of the moment and had little eye for the troublesome details of the administrative system that could alone have established permanent peace. The first task was to re-occupy Fort Willshire and other posts abandoned in the rush of war. After some delay caused by the flooding of the rivers by the summer rains, this was done; and in February and March the troops carried the war into the enemy's country. The tribes, knowing they had merited punishment, were still careful never to show themselves in force; it was not Colonel Smith's fault that, as he complained, the only possible warfare was a kind of 'Smithfield Market cattle-driving'. 'You gallop in', he said, 'and half by force, half by stratagem, pounce upon [the 'Kaffirs'] wherever you find them, frighten their wives, burn their homes, lift their cattle, and then return home in triumph.'[2] The country lent itself to guerrilla tactics; in June, and even in September the Xhosa were still active in

---

[1] D'Urban has noted and marked a memo. by one Campbell, dated 28 Jan. 1835, which claims that the Kei is safer and shorter, and argues also for the occupation of Natal. Rough notes indicate that the Surveyor-General who was called in questioned the 80-mile estimate of the length of the line. D'Urban, however, advocated the Kei line as being 'considerably less than 100 miles' (Cape Town Archives).

[2] Quoted, Cory, iii. 130.

their 'old haunts' in Albany and on the Koonap,[1] in spite of the 'conquest' of the country up to the Kei. Certainly Maqomo and his friends were by no means broken and the essential frontier was still unpacified when D'Urban, about the end of March, started his greater enterprise against the distant Hintza.

Throughout April the troops pushed forward, collecting much cattle, but still with little serious resistance. At last, at the end of the month, after repeated 'summons', Hintza himself arrived in D'Urban's camp in the neighbourhood of Butterworth, having come of his own free will to negotiate. The *Diktat* which followed was more drastic than Lord Charles Somerset's peace in 1819. A new Province of Queen Adelaide embracing all the land from the Keiskama to the Kei was formally proclaimed on Sunday, 10 May, and Hintza, the Paramount, was required to initiate the new régime by 'ordering' Tyali, Maqomo, Eno, and the rest to make peace, while himself finding surety in some 50,000 head of cattle and 1,000 horses. The Xhosa ambassador, now hostage and prisoner, was royally and kindly entertained by his 'father', Harry Smith, but could hardly be called a consenting party. Tragedy followed quickly. The very next day the troops set out to take possession—Hintza, full of suspicions and fears, being taken along with them to guide them to the cattle he was to restore. On a difficult part of the road, Hintza, like an ill-fated Rob Roy, made a dash for freedom but was quickly pursued and shot; unhappily also, his body was mutilated. The circumstances of this tragedy gained immediate notoriety and became the occasion of a formal inquiry which honourably absolved all the officers immediately concerned; yet the episode remains a mystery.[2] As early as 2 June Sir John Herschel wrote to Dr. Philip, who seems to have agreed: 'As I now view it, Hintza's death is a most untoward event, but a mere chance-medley affair brought about by his own conduct.' It was indeed highly 'untoward', and had a profound and unfortunate influence on African opinion. According to frontier tradition it was a long time before chiefs would again willingly trust them-

[1] Cory, iii. 175, 216.
[2] Sensational evidence was collected by one Dr. Ambrose Campbell, a somewhat eccentric or 'cranky' Grahamstown doctor, and sent by him to Dr. Philip, who forwarded the letters, with little comment, to the L.M.S., whence they reached Lord Glenelg.

selves to British officers.[1] It is significant, moreover, that among themselves the war of 1835 came to be known as the 'War of Hintza'; his share in or responsibility for the outbreak was only remote and indirect but its tragic denouement has made him a national hero.

The death of Hintza was an event of the kind highly conducive to the build-up of national self-consciousness in the people it affected; but this could not come about for many years if only because their internal dissensions were already acute and, as things turned out, the conflict on the Cape frontier was to make these even worse. These so-called 'Nguni' Bantu tribes of the south-east, Xhosa and Zulu, were close kin; Xhosa and Zulu can still make more of each other's speech than is usual where such kin groups have become geographically separated. But the pressure productive of so much earlier migration was now sharp. The territorial expansion natural and even necessary to pastoralists like the Bantu had at this time reached a geographical or 'rainfall' limit; the High Veld to the right of their presumed 'advance' was uncongenially cold, and the Karoo, which lay ahead, must make their normal way of life almost impossible. A struggle for *lebensraum* was inevitable, and cannot be ruled out as at any rate contributory to the Chaka upheaval which was pouring successive waves of displaced persons, from the Natal region, in upon the Xhosa; not surprisingly, it was more than these could do to make room for their own people, Ndhlambis and Gaikas, thrown back upon them from the Colony. Roaming bands, like the Mantatees farther north but with fewer witnesses to record their moves, added much to the prevailing confusion. From about 1820 various groups appeared, traditionally as 'destroyers'. Some, notably the Baca, survive in the Transkei as a distinct tribe. In 1828 the 'Fetcani' drove the Tambookies (Tembu) upon Maqomo, greatly adding to that worthy's troubles (see Ch. VI). Undoubted 'remnants' including Fetcani, making the best of the name given them by unwelcoming Xhosa, coalesced very well and made their mark as the *Fingos* ('dogs!').

The early sufferings of these Fingos as refugees came to be charged indiscriminately against Hintza's people who, by some

---

[1] The incident is also said to account for the quite unusual mutilation of European victims of the war of 1850 (Theal, iii. 89).

accounts, treated them as 'slaves'. Doubtless they were still too newly arrived to be fully absorbed as good Xhosa and had many disabilities in their new home, but these came a good deal short of 'slavery'.[1] The mere fact of their being where they were shows that they had enjoyed protection of a sort; some were apparently even able to acquire cattle of their own.[2] The advent of the powerful white man, however, seems to have suggested to them either the possibility of escape from thraldom, if such it was, or else the advisability of being on the side of the big battalions. Sir Benjamin D'Urban now found the Fingos so anxious to secure protection as to be ready allies. Tempted by the prospect of making use of them as a buffer to protect the frontier he was very willing to apply the principle *divide et impera* and take them under his wing. So it was that on 24 April, before Hintza's surrender, D'Urban gave the Fingos their wish and proclaimed them British subjects. Thereupon these new subjects, some 16,000 all told,[3] having collected much cattle—their own and Hintza's—set off in a long procession to seek asylum nearer the Colony. Their defection was a sore blow to the Xhosa, and sorer still when Xhosa violence against Hintza's 'dogs' was made a warrant for keeping Hintza himself under closer surveillance, at the same time that the cattle lifted by the Fingos from Hintza were ignored in the reckoning of the 50,000 for which the chief was held responsible.[4] This was far from being the end. In the months and years following the Xhosa had the mortification of seeing these 'deserters' planted on Xhosa land, comparatively rich, and basking in the sunshine of official favour. This it was that provoked the chief Pato, who was loyal in 1834, to try in 1846 to drive the Fingos out of 'his' country.[5] In later times the Fingos increased far beyond their original 16,000 or 17,000 and became an important factor in frontier life. Originally, perhaps, a less warlike people, they showed themselves both shrewd and

---

[1] Stretch writes to Fairbairn on 22 Mar. 1836: 'Ayliff (a Wesleyan missionary) is returning to Hintza's counrty to collect more Fingos seeing that many have gone back to their oppressors.'

[2] Frontier tradition, from a Fingo source, boasts of a Fingo who, being trusted by a Xhosa chief as 'milkman' (in effect King's cup-bearer), betrayed his benefactor and slew him, fled to Col. Smith, and persuaded the good Colonel that the Xhosa were the aggressors. Smith, without inquiry, is said to have taken this man's story as a warrant for threatening Hintza and his people with dire penalties for their alleged ill-treatment of the Fingos.

[3] Cory, iii. 145.   [4] Ibid. iii. 141, 148.   [5] Ibid. iv. 437.

capable, and among the best schoolgoers. Their prolonged feud with the Xhosa kept them distinct, and served also to hold their loyalty. Over and over again willing Fingos were brought in to act as a protection or buffer against warring or rebel tribes and rewarded for their services with 'rebel' lands—in the first place the former Gaika lands about Alice and Peddie in 1836.[1] In 1835, with the unfortunate death of Hintza also rankling in the minds of the Xhosa, the Fingos thus brought in were a new complication of the frontier situation, an embarrassment rather than a source of strength.

The formal peace, as announced by Proclamation, with some pomp and ceremony, in the presence of the unhappy Hintza on 10 May, was gazetted on the 29th; its text said that Tyali, Maqomo, and others, having 'without provocation or declaration of war' invaded and plundered the Colony, having now been 'defeated, chastised and dispersed', were sentenced, as 'treacherous and irreclaimable savages', to be 'for ever expelled' from the country west of the Kei River. All this was in terms of agreement with Hintza as the 'paramount chief of Kafirland', with whose 'concurrence and countenance' these crimes were committed, who had now been 'compelled to sue for peace and accept the terms of it'. Poor Hintza's unlooked-for death made little real difference. It was not as if this got rid of an astute, still less of a powerful enemy; even Hintza had little control over Maqomo, and his minor heir, Kreli, can have had none whatever. Any professing 'settlement' was in truth meaningless so long as Maqomo, Tyali, and the rest, though they may have been dispersed, were roaming at large. These, the effective chiefs, were certainly not yet 'expelled' from their country; driven by hunger,[2] they were still making occasional raids on colonial farms and property. There being as yet neither peace nor order, 'conquest' held out the prospect only of a prolonged campaign in difficult, wooded country against an embittered and desperate enemy. Total expulsion was a task far beyond the power of the

---

[1] The feud with the Xhosa persisted; in days when outside pressure was obliterating tribal distinctions, at least among the more educated Africans, discussions about Bantu leadership used occasionally to reveal the latent rivalry of Ama-Xhosa and Fingo (cf. articles and correspondence in the Johannesburg newspaper *Umteteli wa Bantu*, 1928).

[2] Missionary letters, e.g. from Mr. Munro, Grahamstown, emphasize the distress.

forces the Governor had available. He was giving away the skin before he had shot his lion.

The stilted phrases of the Governor's May Proclamation were clearly such as came spontaneously from a not highly imaginative official at a moment when his feelings were still deeply shocked, not only by the ruin he had himself seen around him, but also by what he heard from those who had suffered, and from their neighbours; his proposals (they were no more) were the equally spontaneous expression of his idea of the punishment the perpetrators of such ruin had merited. Had he stopped to consider how his plans were to be executed he must have known, none better, how little there had been to check the horror of which so many colonists had lived in almost hourly dread—a mad rush by hordes of plundering barbarians, perhaps nearly to Cape Town. But the anxious colonists were not well placed to assess the merits of D'Urban's plans. Some idea of the state of mind of people in Grahamstown in the first months of 1835 was to be inferred from eyewitness tales (still occasionally heard not very long ago) of the panic that seized Natal on the morrow of the disaster suffered by British troops at Isandhlwana in 1879. Thus D'Urban's *words* passed for deeds and were heard with relief, or even rapturously, as promising the tardy fulfilment of long-cherished hopes. When these hopes came to be rudely dashed, disappointment quickly turned to unreasoning rage. So it is (above, p. 128) that D'Urban has remained the hero whose wise and beneficent frontier policy was rendered void, with disastrous consequences, by the 'machinations' of Dr. John Philip. D'Urban's opening move clearly settled nothing. The belated (and short-lived) emergence of the Philip Papers made it possible, and necessary, to re-examine the story of the break-down of the D'Urban policy in some detail.

The earliest criticism came chiefly from the *Commercial Advertiser*, edited in Cape Town by Dr. Philip's son-in-law, John Fairbairn; Dr. Philip personally had nothing to do with the newspaper, his communications being only to his own Society in London, and to Fowell Buxton. The *Commercial Advertiser* made an unlucky beginning. On 24 December 1834, when only the news of Colonel Somerset's earlier activities could have reached Cape Town, the paper made unfavourable but not unjustified comments on the high-handed treatment the frontier tribes had been receiving. But this issue of the paper reached Grahamstown on 2 January at the height of the worst panic of actual war. Thereupon 479 infuriated frontiersmen signed their names to a declaration denouncing these and former 'false statements'; this cited 'the visit of its Editor to the frontier as among the causes of a confederacy among the Caffre chiefs which threatens the total ruin of a large portion of the Colony', and vowed a severe boycott.[1] The colonists were in no mood to distinguish nicely between the criticism of a faulty system of frontier administration and personal attacks on themselves and their interests. Fairbairn, for his part, did little to mollify their wounded feelings and, in their continuing rage, they could thereafter see in him and his like only a clique of bemused fanatics.

Grahamstown even went one better and began to elaborate counter-accusations. There was, for example, the preposterous charge, embodied in this January declaration, that Fairbairn's tour of Kaffirland in 1830 had inflamed the chiefs with such a sense of grievance that it was responsible for their outbreak four and a half years later. And had not the arch-plotter, Dr. Philip, been intriguing with the chiefs even in the last months of 1834? In the light of after events the agitation against the Hottentot Vagrant Law, and a 'missionary meeting' on the Kat River in September, assumed new and sinister significance; though the Hottentots had already proved their loyalty, 'An English Settler' wrote to the *Grahamstown Journal* on 13 February to say how the chiefs had been impressed at that September meeting by this important visitor who 'had the ear of the Governor', and an ear also for their grievances.[2]

---

[1] Cory, iii. 90.

[2] In July 1835 Dr. Philip's friend, Capt. Alexander, then an officer on D'Urban's staff, better known later as the traveller Sir James Alexander, having absorbed on the frontier D'Urban's official view of events, suggested that the chiefs had 'deceived Philip when he went among them as a negotiator', and that severe measures were now necessary against them. On 21 Aug. Dr. Philip replied insisting that he went in 1834 merely to 'collect information' for the Governor, with no authority whatever to 'negotiate'. He was all the more 'secret' about his hopes of a 'change' of policy for fear of rousing frontier opposition; even James Read, he claims, knew nothing of the Governor's direct interest in the inquiries that Philip directed Read to make, till Read heard of it in Grahamstown in 1835 from the Governor himself.

Further, 'I am perfectly sensible of the truth of all you say about the Governor's urbanity . . . and the readiness he always manifested to hear everything I had to tell him. . . . The affection I bear to him gives poignancy to the grief I feel at the

The outbreak of war brought a lull between two distinct phases in Dr. Philip's campaign. Originally he had tried to persuade D'Urban of the impolicy and crudity of the old frontier system, as practised, *in excelsis*, by Colonel Somerset at the end of 1834: later he directed his criticism against the unwisdom of D'Urban's *May* policy (not the proposal to annex Kaffirland, only the project of driving the offending chiefs out of their homes). In the interval between January and May, when and so long as the colony was in actual danger, he refrained completely from any kind of opposition. On 1 January, the very day the news of the invasion reached Cape Town, Dr. Philip wrote and signed a circular to all the L.M.S. stations calling on the missionaries to see that the Hottentots 'obey His Excellency's summons, as no doubt they will', and give all the service required of them in the 'dreadful state' to which the Colony has been reduced in this sudden crisis. This injunction the Hottentots fully obeyed. But the outbreak itself was no surprise; D'Urban twice remarked on the 'extraordinary fact'[1] that the outbreak befell 'without arousing the suspicion' either of missionaries or of traders, but Philip at once wrote to London, on 2 January: 'The irruption of the Kafirs has not come upon us without warning. The Government has been told for years that this crisis was unavoidable if the old system should be persisted in.'

The philanthropists generally, having had such a clear anticipation of the dangers of the old policy,[2] could not now share the common feelings of the Colony. To Philip it was 'this catastrophe', as contrasted with 'what might have been' had the Governor's visit not been deferred.[3] At great length on 9 January Dr. Philip wrote to Buxton excusing D'Urban for staying in Cape Town:

difficulties in which I now see him involved in the attempt he is making to expel the hostile tribes from their native soil. If their expulsion is just and absolutely necessary you are correct as to the necessity of shooting the Caffres, burning their corn, and taking from their women even their milch goats; but the necessity and policy of the first measure must be determined before the second can be defended.' (See also *Cape Col. Qn.*, p. 240.)

    [1] To the Secretary of State on 5 Jan. and again to Col. Bell from Grahamstown on 21 Jan.
    [2] e.g. as early as 12 Apr. 1834, Read wrote to Fairbairn: 'It is a wonder that under all provocation during the last eight months the Kafirs have not attempted to retaliate.'   [3] To T. Fowell Buxton, 19 and 23 Jan.

Had he, for example, left Cape Town while the Vagrant Law was pending in the Council, with Colonel Wade, the father of that Act in his chair, our situation might have been worse than it is . . . with the whole coloured population alienated. . . . Thousands of Hottentots would have left the Colony. . . . [There were also] the foolish fears of the Cape Town people about the 1st December, the day on which slavery was to cease. . . .

Till late in 1835 there is no suggestion of censure on D'Urban even for his fatal delay, though more than once Philip hints somewhat wildly that the war was not unwelcome to those who were determined to get Kaffirland given out as sheep farms— or even that had Colonel Somerset desired war he could not have gone a better way about it. Not without reason he was angered by the boast of an eastern official that 'powder and lead' would now 'put an end to the march of humbug' in frontier policy. These months' most despairing (and characteristic) comment comes on 16 February from Mrs. Philip:

The Caffre War has put an end to cheering hopes that another nation might have been saved from extermination by their Christian neighbours. Alas, I fear the poor infatuated wretches, goaded by oppression, appear to have put it out of the power of the missionaries to plead their cause.

For the rest, in letters to Fowell Buxton at this period Dr. Philip was content to 'point out the cause of this catastrophe and to give you suggestions as to the course to be followed at home to close the wounds . . . and to gain the object we have had so long in contemplation'. He quotes a letter from a Mr. Fleming of Uitenhage[4] as expressing his own sentiments:

I have come to these conclusions about this disastrous state of things . . . that the *system* has engendered a bad feeling, that the recent patrols caused it to burst forth, that the Caffres—'all the tribes'— have not combined, and if they had they might, if guided by an intelligent person, have destroyed every town from this to Cape Town and ravished the country at the same time. It required but boldness and celerity during the *Panic*. . . . No one ever seems to have apprehended that the power of the Caffres to blast the Colony was hanging over our heads like a drawn sword suspended by a thread. . . . I must confess this fact is alarming. Our contiguity to such formidable enemies shows the necessity of basing our intercourse on principles of

¹ To T. Fowell Buxton, 23 Jan. 1835.

justice if we wish to avoid future causes of war, as well as maintaining a strong attitude on the frontier line to defend the Colony. We must be the masters, but rule as we do in India, making the interests of the natives the grand policy of our conduct. Our very existence in India is a miracle of God for that object, and when we neglect it the Kingdom will depart from us—and it is such views I am inclined to take of our rule and of our duty in this quarter of the world.

Thus nearly a century earlier an unknown Uitenhage merchant used language—preserved by chance in this letter from the best-hated South African humanitarian of his day—prophetic of the 'sacred trust of civilization' doctrine of the Covenant of the League of Nations. This doctrine, startling even in 1923 when echoed in the famous Kenya Declaration of the Duke of Devonshire, was too much for the suffering Cape Colony of 1835, and served only to bring upon its chief sponsor the charge laid against Jeremiah of old: 'This man weakeneth the hands of the men of war that remain in the city, and the hands of all the people; but this man seeketh not the welfare of his people, but the hurt.'

Abuse was the natural weapon of the more extreme of those who could see no further than that the Colony was in mortal danger. 'We have all manner of stories', Dr. Philip writes on 5 February, 'about the missionaries being the cause of the war, and how they got out whole boxes of assegais from Austin Friars [L.M.S. headquarters] to distribute among the Caffres before war commenced.' Again, to James Read on 13 February: 'The Grahamstown people are throwing much dust, but it blinds no one but themselves.' His chief concern with this dust was its possible effect on the Governor:

With his conduct, so far as it is yet known, I am satisfied, but as he is now upon his trial we must be reserved in what we say about the future. No man who ever came to the Colony had to encounter one-tenth of his difficulties. . . . If he is not supported from home, he may make the same complaint as General Janssens made to van der Kemp, that he was required to 'break iron with wood'. He has not now on the frontier a single man about him who has any other notion of settling the affairs of the Caffres but by powder and lead. The frontier colonists have long set their hearts upon Caffreland—they already calculate upon having it given them for sheep-farms and the general cry is 'blood! blood!' . . . . The war is ascribed to Pringle's poem 'Makanna's Gathering' (which no Caffre ever saw), or to

Fairbairn and his paper: we are told by the *Zuid Afrikaan* of yesterday
that 'as for Dr. Philip and his crew, the inhabitants ought to extir-
pate them forthwith'. Here we have all the venom engendered by the
Slave Question, the Hottentot Question, the Vagrant Act, and their
fear of having their expectations with regard to Caffraria disappointed, concentrated and pouring out all its energies like the
lava from the crater of an active volcano. . . . But my object is not to
fix your attention upon Fairbairn and myself, but to show you what
the Governor will have to contend against. . . . It is obvious that he
can do nothing efficiently to effect the introduction of a mild and
equitable system on the Caffre frontier unless he is supported from
Home.[1]

Even if the Governor was 'on his trial', Dr. Philip was still loyal
to him. 'There is a party here hoping that the Governor will
fall, but we have put the saddle on the right horse', he writes on
27 February, 'and Sir Benjamin has nothing to fear from what
has yet taken place.' His letters, therefore, deal with general
questions. To his view of the causes of the war he adds a warning
against the expansion of the Colony:

The Colony is nearly all just farms and families, no villages are
forming and the distant Boers, having no markets, never think of
producing more than for their own consumption. Therefore, they
contribute nothing towards defraying the expenses of defence. . . .
The Colony, since the British got possession, is already doubled in
its extent. The English Government has robbed the natives of a
territory as large in thirty years as was taken by the Dutch in 150
years. . . .

Expansion is actually dangerous:

since it may drive the Kafirs back into the more savage interior, from
the frontier where they have been in contact with more humane
standards. The Cape will then have Dingaan and Moselekatze as
still worse neighbours.

A few months later Philip was to press the need to extend at
least colonial law and institutions; and now, in urging the
return of Stockenström, a capable civilian whose removal in
1833 he held to be a main cause of the war, he again stressed the
essential of all reform: 'The affairs of the frontier must be
consigned entirely to a *civil* agency; exclude the military in all

[1] To T. Fowell Buxton, 23 Jan. 1835.

ordinary circumstances from meddling with the affairs of the Caffres.'[1] This was the burden of all Dr. Philip's letters to Fowell Buxton, but he added one definite proposal: 'In any case there should be a Committee of the House of Commons to take into consideration the whole of the frontier system.' By 12 March the January news had reached England, and Priscilla Buxton wrote at once to say that her father had given notice to move on 19 May for such an inquiry; by that time he hoped to have facts 'to go upon'. This time Mr. Buxton 'got a capital good Committee', the so-called 'Aborigines' Committee of 1835–7.

After 10 May, when the war had drawn to an end of sorts and Sir Benjamin D'Urban made his great Proclamation, there is at once a new note in Philip's letters: 'The Kafirs have been subdued', he begins on 23 May:

In former communications I informed you I considered it my duty to support the Governor in what he had done and was doing in relation to the Kafirs, but that I then considered him upon his trial, and that we should be called upon to decide on his conduct in this affair by the manner in which the war might be carried on and concluded.

Dr. Philip now turned again to the general state of Kaffirland as he had seen it, taking as his text the terms of the Governor's Proclamation.[2] In view of his repeated warnings the initial suggestion that the invasion was 'without provocation in a time of undisturbed peace' moved him almost to scorn, driving him back to recapitulate—with fresh evidence—his view of the fundamental causes of the war. 'It is true', he says, that when he reached the frontier in the previous August the chief excitement was about 'Boers leaving the Colony', and 'the hope that the Governor when he came would give them all new farms beyond'. But things were also sufficiently settled for '200 traders' to pursue their activities in Kaffirland and, as the Scottish mission-

---

[1] To Buxton, 23 and 27 Jan. and 17 Feb. Col. Smith later reached the same conclusion.

[2] Between February and May Dr. Philip seems to have worked at a long memo. on 'The Causes of the War' which was still in preparation as late as 1 May. Quotations following are from this document and from a long series of letters written between 23 May and 15 July, dispatched apparently in two or three great bundles before the middle of July. These exist, some in draft manuscripts, some at the L.M.S. rooms in London. Long passages in the L.M.S. copies are marked in red, 'To be sent to Mr. Buxton and Lord Glenelg', and may be seen also in the volume *Papers on Kafir War of 1835* (C.O., 48/165).

ary Ross pointed out, the Xhosa had that spring planted 'immense gardens and cornfields'; 'what abundant crops' certain officers saw, as did Ross himself, and Read (above, p. 127), giving the prospect of a good harvest after the notoriously heavy drought of 1834. These signs of peace suggest not that the war was a 'long premeditated' onslaught but the very reverse; that, as Ross and others agree, all was calm with no serious excitement, till December. Then, instead of the Governor coming to make reforms, Somerset, Sparks, and Sutton (another patrol leader) were 'let loose' and their 'patrols', more active than ever, 'kindled the flame'.

'The harassing conduct of the frontier authorities', Dr. Philip himself continues, 'and the refusal to allow the Kafirs to occupy a small part of the country taken from them, and of which we made no use, was a constant source of irritation, [but] wherever this rule had been relaxed and grazing allowed, the colonists have been least molested and thefts by Kafirs checked.' The only chiefs left unmolested were Pato and others who had grazing in what the Governor himself had described as 'an uninhabited and worse than useless' part of the Ceded Territory. But, 'not only were the Kafirs driven from what no one could deny to have been part of the Neutral Territory; they had at the same time the mortification of seeing their kraals and huts burned on ground which had always been regarded as part of Caffreland'. Philip himself found only 'destruction'; 'for 20 miles west of the Chumie there were no huts standing', and below the junction of the Chumie and the Keiskama, on 5 November, he had 'seen kraals burning'. This destruction went on till December, and the wounding of Tyali's brother was the last straw. 'What an abuse' to term this a period of 'profound peace'! 'It was impossible for the Kafirs to see their country taken from them piecemeal for fifteen years, and not to ask how to save themselves. But there was no plan among them to attack the Colony before the Sparks and Sutton affairs.' 'Then indeed', writes Ross on 5 June, 'the Kafirs took fire, and the last communication I had with Sutu [the Queen-Mother] before leaving, was that they were stirred up and encouraged by Hottentots and some Boers to attack the Colony.' December, at least, when the storm broke, was 'no time of undisturbed peace and amity'.

A second phrase of D'Urban's roused Philip's ire—the suggestion that he had 'long and maturely' considered his change of plan from the 'new system' of 1834 promising civil law in the place of commandos, to the 'sentence of extermination' pronounced in the May Proclamation when he had been only a matter of weeks on the frontier. On 18 January Philip had written to him, still in the manner of a trusted adviser, calling his attention to the state of Hottentot families left without their soldier bread-winners, and begging him to 'discriminate between the innocent and the guilty' in Kaffirland. There is no evidence of any reply, or of any further exchanges between them, though at that time Philip clearly was still most willing to believe in the Governor's benevolent intentions.[1] As late as 17 April Captain Alexander had written to Philip from the Kei expressing the hope that 'you will shortly see a new and better order of things introduced on the borders of Ethopia'. But now, still without a word to Philip himself, D'Urban— having on 19 June brought himself after the usual delay to frame a dispatch to London reporting his 'long matured' May 'settlement'—seems to go out of his way to give warning that 'Dr. Philip and his party' are sure to attack 'this important measure of extension as unjust in itself, and very probably as severe in execution'; at the same time, as if by way of counter-blast, he expressly claims that he has the full support of the Wesleyans.[2] The emphatic change that took place in the Governor's attitude when he reached the frontier must indeed have been prompted as much by what he heard from colonists as by the light of his own judgement.

Philip and others ascribe it to the advent of the short-lived Tory ministry under Sir Robert Peel (November 1834 to April 1835).

[1] Philip begins to be a little guarded on 1 June: 'Fairbairn has not said all he might on the war on the ground that we think it desirable to leave a retreat open to the Governor.' It should be remembered that letters travelled slowly. Events on the Kei on 10 May were known in Cape Town only after the 20th, so that little Cape Town criticism can have been known to the Governor when he wrote on 19 June. Capt. Beresford, however, who left Cape Town with D'Urban's dispatches about 26 June, writes to the Governor on the 12th to say that his policy is welcomed by 'all except the Saints', whose influence soon came to be feared.

[2] Dr. Philip wrote a great deal about the attitude of the Wesleyans, pointing out to Buxton (20 June) that several leading Wesleyans were settled in European charges, shared the Albany panic, and 'knew nothing of the commando system which goaded the Caffres to desperation'.

'The news was conveyed to [D'Urban] before any change in his purpose was avowed. . . . Whatever the Tory ministers may do for England, it is indicated pretty clearly what he expected from the effects of their administration in the colonies.'

The Governor's use, chance and rhetorical as it probably was, of the phrase 'irreclaimable savages'[1] particularly galled 'the Saints' as they were nicknamed; it was like salt rubbed in the wound caused by the more important 'sentence of extermination'. The suggestion that the Bantu were 'irreclaimable' was a direct challenge to the missionaries and to the first principle of all their work. Even at that time Dr. Philip was able to point to a good deal of evidence of their progress. In twelve years, he claims, the frontier trade of Grahamstown had grown to as much as £35,000 per annum. In the war itself women and children were invariably spared.[2] One native carried a child to safety in Grahamstown, only to be made a prisoner for his pains; the missionaries, moreover, 'enjoyed almost absolute security'—Brownlee had made the journey *on foot* to Burns' Hill and the Colony, even interviewing Maqomo *en route*, and some stations were abandoned only by express command of the military authorities. He also contrasts the free movements of Major Cox and other officers who visited the chiefs in Kaffirland with the forcible detention and death of Hintza.

The humanitarian attitude to the decree of 'extermination' was quite straightforward, but the choice of that word has been widely misunderstood as implying a charge of wholesale massacre. Philip and his circle regularly used the word in its literal classical sense, meaning the banishment or extrusion of the tribes from their *land*. The earliest reference is, perhaps, on 29 May:

We have twelve missionaries in Grahamstown at this moment, and others of our Kafir missions in other places, and if things go on as they appear to be doing, and *if the Kafir country is to be given to white settlers*, all our labours in Kafirland must be lost.

[1] This phrase is echoed and denounced in the letters of the time by Philip and Fairbairn, by missionaries and their wives, as well as by Dr. Ambrose Campbell and also by Sir John Herschel. Mrs. Philip writes on 23 June: 'Oh! our Governor from whom we expected so much has preached us such a practical lesson from Isaiah ii. 22 ("Cease ye from man . . ."). The Caffres have been pronounced "irreclaimable savages" and are to be driven from their country.'

[2] Cory, iii. 72, 73.

As Dr. Philip had been urging all along, the problem was to *govern and administer* the frontier as it existed, not to create a new frontier and begin all over again on the old plan:

You will recollect [he continues on the same date] that I have said *I do not object to any of the countries beyond us becoming part of the Colony, provided the natives have their lands secured to them* and are governed as the Hindus are, and that it is the system of extermination to which I am opposed. . . . [No decision is yet announced, but] it is the opinion of the Colonists[1] that they are to have the territory divided among them, and the treatment of the Caffres [their 'expulsion'] gives but too much countenance to the supposition.

Again, on 4 June, still to Buxton:

Had the Governor taken Caffraria under British protection, or had he added it to the Colony, reserving at the same time the country to the Caffres, the result might have been in the end favourable to the success of our missionary labours. England, like the Romans, by spreading her institutions over such provinces as Caffraria, might have made her dominion a blessing to this ill-fated Continent.

This restrained statement of the only ultimately sound policy for such a frontier has been completely drowned in the torrent of abuse provoked by what Philip's antagonists took as unwarranted reflections on their own conduct, like the next sentences of the same letter, its strictures on 'the brutalizing effects of an unjust system':

England [he continues] has the abolition of the Slave Trade and of Slavery to her glory, but if the extermination of the natives is permitted . . . no credit can be given to the Government for abolishing the slavery of Africans while she leaves the natives, whom she makes it a felony to transport, to be massacred wholesale by her troops to gratify the cupidity of men who have been turned into monsters by the brutalizing effects of one of the most unjust and bloody systems that ever disgraced any country. The error into which Sir Benjamin D'Urban has been led by the ascendancy gained over him by those who have been long the abettors and the life of this system may to a certain extent be relieved; but if the sentence of expulsion be sanctioned by the British Government, our hope of saving and civilizing

[1] Cf. *Grahamstown Journal*, early in June: 'Anyone who ventured to predict at Christmas that before midsummer Sir D'Urban would seize as a colonial possession a larger tract of country than all the former encroachments, as they have been called, of all the former governors put together . . .' would have been 'a fit subject for a lunatic asylum'.

the nations from the border of our Colony to Delagoa Bay are at an end.

The dispute focuses some of the many issues the twentieth century habitually over-simplifies as one 'colonial question'. Dr. Philip saw more clearly than most the shortcomings and the needs of the Bantu peoples; in contemplating for Britain a 'civilizing mission' like that of Rome he was on common ground with historians who once freely acknowledged the debt the more advanced peoples have owed to Rome and to benevolent despots of their own. The Cape farmers had reason to know the weaknesses of neighbours from whom they had suffered in their own struggle for existence in untamed country (and generalizing 'anti-colonialists' are slow to see how much under-development comes of such peoples' inexperience and lack of training). But the farmers were also confident that they understood the situation, from bitter experience, better than anyone else could. They were intolerant even of informed inquirers from without as interfering busybodies. They were, moreover, the first genuine anti-colonialists, being resentful of what their modern successors stigmatize as 'remote control'. Their distant rulers, they judged, were turned off the straight path by evidence of those less well informed because not directly concerned; worse still, such evidence came to the authorities at second hand, therefore, without being fully understood, if not with a hostile bias. For this reason colonial resentment naturally concentrated on the principal outside observer, Dr. Philip.

Philip, for his part, was in one particular over-confident; the strong, impartial Imperial rule he hoped for was not to be expected from a Government whose working rule was to avoid burdening its taxpayers with new and costly responsibilities. He stressed less than perhaps he should the inescapable *necessity* of close administration. But at least he saw the likelihood that both official and unofficial anti-slavery enthusiasts, seeing that the Bantu were not slaves, would be content to leave them 'free'. Accordingly on 28 June, when he heard that Captain Beresford of the Governor's staff was to go to England that week 'to try to get sanction for the annexation of Caffreland to the Colony', he returned to the theme, concluding a thirty-six page letter to the L.M.S. with a postscript:

I wish it to be understood that I do not object to the extension of the colonial boundary to the Kei River *provided the lands are secured to the Caffres* as has been the case in all our conquests in India. It is to the extermination of the Caffres that I object, and that is a measure Parliament can never sanction. The people exempted from the exterminating decree form a very small part of the Caffre nation, and if Caffreland is given to the colonists they will not be allowed to enjoy long what may be left to them. Should the news of the change of Ministers lead the Governor to show mercy to the proscribed chiefs and peoples I shall write you immediately; in the meantime Mr. Buxton should be in direct communication with the Colonial Office to prevent, if possible, the plan proposed by the Governor of giving Caffreland to the colonists. Should that measure be approved at Home our hopes are at an end. Nothing [will remain] but a continuance and extension of the system of desolation so long carried on in South Africa. O that the wickedness of wicked men were come to an end.

A reiteration of the same evidence before the Select Committee a year later[1] still made no impression.

D'Urban's own action while these 1835 letters were on their way was such as to vindicate the contentions of the critics. On 4 June, within three weeks of the peace, Dr. Philip had heard of negotiations between Major Cox and the chief Maqomo.[2] When Cox said the war must continue, Maqomo replied: 'Very well, you may fight, but I will not.' Whereupon Philip comments:

But no! the submission of the chiefs would have spoiled the idea of the new order of things which had *long* been considered, and determined for *weighty* reasons. . . . The itching ears of the projectors of these measures of spoliation [must be] gratified with the magical sounds of 'Province of Queen Adelaide'.

In other words, the chiefs were ready to submit, but the 'decree of expulsion' meant prolonging the war indefinitely.

To make 'expulsion' effective, however, by 'clearing' the whole of the county up to the Kei River was at any rate impracticable. As soon as the May 'peace' was proclaimed the colonial burghers became impatient to get back to their farms and homes and were disbanded; though the services of the

---

[1] Aborigines Committee, evidence, p. 625.
[2] Maqomo, it seems, protested that he had no confidence in the English people as Hintza was a prisoner and two of his men (Hintza's) had told him to be on his guard.

Hottentots were retained, apparently to the distress of their dependants in the Grahamstown location and on the mission stations, the Governor seems to have taken no steps to secure reinforcements for his garrison of regular troops. Nor had he really counted the cost of the task he had set himself.[1] There was considerable delay in getting the Fingos whom he had taken under his wing placed in a 'location', and they dispersed themselves in disorderly groups over the eastern districts. The mere fact of their presence on the frontier—some of them on old Xhosa lands—was a chronic irritant, not only provoking Xhosa attacks and cattle-raiding under the very guns of the frontier posts,[2] but also strengthening the will to resistance; in the middle of August some of the burgher forces had to be recalled to arms.

The Governor now protested that 'the fire was nearly extinquished when it was lighted again by the unnatural invectives . . . of Dr. Philip and his party'.[3] Dr. Philip had some word of what was going on, and for the first time gave vent to mild personal criticism of D'Urban in a letter of 14 August. 'Poor man, if his head were but as good as his feelings. He is just like some good-natured parent who, having lost authority in his family, works himself into a frenzy.' But in fact D'Urban's difficulties, the counsels of his new advisers the Wesleyan missionaries, and probably also the military experience and the humanity of Colonel Smith, were bringing about a modification of his views and a will to a less Carthaginian peace.[4] On 18 August Colonel Smith told the Governor in a 'confidential P.S.' he thought that if he could get hold of Maqomo he could get the chief to agree to, and to recommend, a British occupation, which would 'protect and provide for them [the Xhosa] by equitable laws and just magistrates'—adding, 'with no Moultries or Bowkers'.[5] D'Urban in reply, on the 21st, speaks

---

[1] Cory, iii. 272.

[2] Cory, iii. 194 ff. In later peace negotiations the chiefs 'protested' against bringing Fingos 'across the Kye'. Capt. C. L. Stretch's 'Journal', 15 Aug.

[3] To Mr. Borcherds, 16 Aug. (D'Urban MSS. copied in South African Library).

[4] These new influences are reflected in a note from young Theophilus Shepstone suggesting, as early as 28 July, that hints of the Governor's intended clemency be circulated stealthily by the agency of Xhosa women. Shepstone was the son of a Wesleyan missionary, at this stage an interpreter, one of the first of a long and honourable line of administrators born and brought up on frontier mission stations among the people themselves.   [5] i.e. Settler magistrates (D'Urban MSS.).

of 'overtures' from Maqomo, who begged that he be not 'sent beyond the Kei'. After another month of cautious and delicate negotiations, with Major Cox, Captain Stretch, and others seeking out and reasoning with Maqomo in his own haunts, a new peace was signed at Fort Willshire on 17 September. By the new treaty Maqomo and his friends, so far from being 'expelled for ever', were left to stay pretty much where they had been.

For the first time since the beginning of the contest in 1779 the neighbouring Bantu were made *subjects*, a recognized part of the frontier population under Government care, presumably, therefore, with the right to be protected in their lawful interests. Responsible opinion had slowly been converging to the view that the civilized government must take control of the frontier as a whole—an important advance. Within a few months D'Urban and Smith proceeded to the appointment of Resident Agents with each of the principal tribal groups, and recognized certain chiefs as 'magistrates'.[1] Colonel Smith and his colleagues had no experience to guide them in the task of administering justice with primitive chiefs as magistrates. It was a good many years before administrators hit upon the plan, now almost universal,[2] of recognizing the legal authority of Native Custom so far as it does not conflict with the 'general principles of humanity recognized throughout the civilized world'. In practice, Colonel Smith carried on with the utmost kindliness and goodwill, and considerable success, as '*Inkosinkulu*', or Great Chief. Smith might be fond of 'acting a passion', but he soon made friends with Maqomo, granting him the use of land he coveted on the Keiskama, and urging on him the sowing of corn. Were they not now 'our subjects', even 'our Kafirs'?[3] Maqomo, he says, wants schools, and teaching, and money, and 'missionaries, who do not pray more than one day in seven, but who teach us to be useful to each other'. Smith, indeed, was ardent for 'policy' and a 'new system' and, as was his wont, more single-hearted than the Governor. Smith could even learn to write: 'The old

---

[1] The tribes concerned were the Gaikas, the Ndhlambis, the Ama-gunukwebe (Pato and Co.), and later, the Tembu or Tambookies to the north. The Chief Magistrate was Hougton Hudson, whose name was suggested by Dr. Philip in 1834 (above, pp. 109, 120).

[2] Cf. Transvaal Law 4 of 1885, and Union Native Administration Act of 1927.

[3] To D'Urban on 27 Sept.

colonial system tended to promote plunder, the punishment was inefficient though most unjust.'[1]

D'Urban carried a heavier responsibility and, being worried, clung to the old ways. To Colonel Hare he wrote (19 September 1835) bidding him 'keep the country well scoured and shoot all Kafirs found in it. . . . The whole is an experiment never tried before and we must give it a fair trial. . . . But even if it succeeds it must be *bellum in pace* for some time.' To Armstrong a week later: 'Keep the district clear. You have still the right to shoot them; this is an absolute necessity.' On the other hand, on 6 October, there being 'now no more war', Smith deprecated making 'bandits' of the people by 'driving them across the Kei'. A few days later the Wesleyan missionary Boyce, who succeeded Dr. Philip as the Governor's confidential adviser, was urging strong measures for the 'security' of the colonists: Bantu custom, he pointed out, sanctioned a fine of ten head of cattle for every one stolen, and to exact only one might be taken by the Xhosa for weakness or stupidity; yet, as such severity might not be practicable on a large scale, the Government ought to make up the deficiency in the compensation paid to suffering colonists by grants of land between the Keiskama and the Kei. On this and other suggestions Colonel Smith expressed his disappointment with Boyce as 'more full of dragooning our new subjects than a hundred soldiers'. 'The Man of the Gospel is, after all, a worldly fellow.'[2]

D'Urban's original plans for his new Province were open to serious question on another important point. From the beginning he resolved to restrict and define the Xhosa's right to remain in occupation of their old homes. Maqomo is, indeed, 'to be a British subject'; but 'if this is so', D'Urban writes to Smith on 21 August,

he may be placed in a *location* in His Majesty's Colony, provided he becomes responsible for certain main points in his people's conduct. This location must be made with a careful limitation. There must be sufficient intermediate space, *to be filled as soon as practicable with British locations*, between the Gaika's Western boundaries and the Western banks of the Chumie and Keiskama.

This is one of the earliest appearances of the ill-omened term

[1] D'Urban MSS., Sept. 1836
[2] D'Urban MSS. in South African Library: Memo. of 12 Oct.

location which came to be normal usage, not for D'Urban's proposed tribal homelands, but for the squalid and overcrowded slum-quarters of every town and village in the country— quarters that were very many non-Europeans' only home, and the only 'Native areas' most Europeans ever saw. Like so many more in this field D'Urban was lacking in foresight, taking no account of how these people were to fare when natural growth increased their numbers. Far from being a pioneer of 'segregation', he pinned his faith to 'a judicious inter-mixture of farms and locations' in the confident belief that 'thus alone it must be, if by any device these savages are to be at length (at any rate the rising generation) assimilated with the mass of old colonists'.[1] It never appears how he proposed to devise a system of local administration capable of harmonizing the conflicting interests of farmers and natives, and so of serving the needs of any district as a whole.

Dr. Philip soon heard what was in the wind, probably from Captain Alexander of the Governor's staff to whom he wrote from Cape Town on 21 August 1835:

> I have always thought it would be a good thing to take the Caffres as subjects under the British Government provided their country is secured to them; but the dispersion of English or Dutch settlers among them in present circumstances is a scheme that cannot succeed, and one that the Home Government will never sanction.

In fifty years, he concludes, 'perhaps'.

As it turned out, D'Urban's plans miscarried and his white settlements were not begun. Some twelve years later the good Sir Harry Smith, guided in his turn by considerations of purely military expediency, was destined to begin the long process of planting settlers in among 'locations', and making Kaffraria a chess-board of black and white areas.

But that was not yet. Judge Menzies soon warned the Governor (in October 1835) that only the Crown could authorize him to naturalize aliens; the Bantu were aliens who could not legally own land; and chiefs could be made legal magistrates only by Charter. The treaties, in short, were of no effect till ratified by the Crown. In the last resort, therefore, Smith's authority as

---

[1] In dispatch of 9 June 1836 D'Urban again expressed his belief in the benefits of 'inter-mixture', from 'locations judiciously introduced'.

'Great Chief' depended on the bayonets of the troops and on martial law. Colonel Smith very well understood his position. When in August 1836 D'Urban finally took fright and de-proclaimed martial law, Smith protested: 'The sooner we march out of the Province the better, for how am I to "eat up" Kafirs, according to Blackstone?' The essential royal assent was never given. Why, and with what results, are another long story.

X

THE D'URBAN SETTLEMENT 1835-6

THE reversal of the D'Urban settlement synchronized with the Great Trek and is often taken to have been its main cause. But a revision of the 'authorized version' both of the settlement and of its reversal is long overdue. It goes almost unnoticed, for example, how in the year 1835 D'Urban himself made a complete *volte-face*; the plan he actually tried to carry out in September was fundamentally different from that which originally drew such severe criticism. Yet the radical change he made was hardly so much as reported to London. Such account as he sent of the September Settlement was not written till November and reached London only in January 1836. Lord Glenelg's famous dispatch of 26 December 1835, that is to say, was written in condemnation of the May policy which D'Urban himself had found impolitic, or merely impracticable. These May plans, and the causes of the war in which they had their origin, had set Lord Glenelg asking so many questions that he had ears for nothing else until his doubts were satisfied; but the weight and asperity of his dispatch so overwhelmed the Governor that he, for his part, left Glenelg's questions all unanswered in effect for more than a year.[1] All this time, therefore, because of the bad impression made by D'Urban's ill-considered first thoughts on how to deal with the frontier situation, the attitude of his superiors was stiffening.

In May, we know, D'Urban's plan had been to annex his new Province, to clear it entirely of the Xhosa clans responsible for the outbreak, and to replace the expelled Xhosa by white settlers. By August he had come to see that wholesale expulsion was impracticable and, in private at least, that this involved a radical change of policy. On 21 August, in the private letter in which he expounded to Colonel Smith his plan of interspersing

---

[1] Glenelg's dispatch was sent off in Dec. 1835. Its receipt was formally acknowledged on 23 Mar. 1836. But the full reply, dated June, was dispatched only in Dec. 1836, or even Jan. 1837, and received only in Mar. 1837. For at least a year, therefore, Glenelg had practically no news from the scene of war.

'locations' of Bantu with Europeans instead of expelling them altogether, he ends with the words: 'I have come to the conclusion, trampling underfoot my preconceived opinions, and sacrificing also some prejudices . . . to open a door to the course of proceedings above adverted to' (i.e. to make peace without driving the Xhosa beyond the Kei). But later, and in his official letters, D'Urban's cue seems to have been, for some reason, to minimize the importance of the change. Thus in a confidential note of 17 September which was presently embodied in his November report to Downing Street he writes of a 'new system, long and anxiously deliberated', whose terms were

in conformity with those I held out to them (the Xhosa) in my overtures of 12 May, but with a little extension as to the numbers to be entertained, arising from the supplication of these people, their expressed contrition, their professions and, however justly deserved, their sufferings.

It may have had its effect that ordinary colonial opinion undoubtedly wanted nothing more ardently than the May policy of total expulsion. Several times, in September and October, the *Grahamstown Journal* recorded its objection to having any of the Xhosa left in the Amatolas, a wooded mountainous country whence depredations (said to be more numerous than ever) might easily be made; on 8 October the paper knew of 'no solitary instance in which those (September) treaties have been spoken of with unqualified approbation'. The vocal displeasure of the Grahamstown people is proof enough of the difference they, at least, saw between the May plans and those of September, and it may be that it was to soothe these ruffled feelings that D'Urban now made light of the change, stressing the fact that while Xhosa would be 'settled in a portion of the land conquered from them', yet of this land *'large tracts are still left vacant for the occupation and speculations of Europeans'.*[1] As late as 17 March 1836 the *Grahamstown Journal* was protesting that it 'never admired' the Settlement of September; but this time it was alarmed—'the whole frontier is in a ferment at the news' that Downing Street was disapproving: 'Not that they want the lands for farms, but for protection . . . to give it to [the Xhosa]

[1] In a confidential Note on the Treaties, 17 Sept.; to Bell on 25 Sept.; and again in November to Glenelg.

would increase robbery and cause the frontier to be deserted';
for this reason they would not have *any part* of the land revert to
the aborigines. Two weeks later, on 31 March, alarm changed
to consternation at an 'incredible report' that Stockenström was
to be made Lieutenant-Governor, and even the modified September policy reversed. Only this dire threat—and a feeling
that the September treaties, even with their concessions to the
'Kaffirs', were at any rate better—gave D'Urban the whole-
hearted support of colonial opinion. In the end D'Urban hero-
worship became so ardent as to cover up his generally inefficient
conduct of the whole affair.

It was only after deliberate delay, meant to ensure that his
report 'might conclusively embrace this series of measures and
events', that D'Urban at last, on 7 November, dispatched
detailed (September) proposals, 'which appear satisfactory with
regard to present effects and future prospects—for which I
humbly trust to His Majesty's gracious approval'. Colonel Bell
at least, in Cape Town, realized that the Governor had made
concessions which, he trusted, would close the mouths of 'the
Saints'; but the light in which these were presented to Downing
Street was ill designed to allay uneasiness:

> Our losses [D'Urban reported] were under 1,000, theirs over
> 4,000 of their warriors. There have been taken from them also—
> besides the conquest and alienation of their country—about 60,000
> head of cattle, and almost all their goats; their habitations are every-
> where destroyed and their gardens and cornfields laid waste. They have
> been, therefore, chastised—not extremely but perhaps sufficiently,
> and will, I think, have such a salutary recollection of what they have
> suffered as to prevent a recurrence.

'The gentlemen to be selected as Resident Agents, in the spirit of
the Secretary of State's dispatch No. 13 of 17 November 1833',
will he hopes, prove efficient, at a cost 'somewhat less' than he
had estimated in his dispatch of 28 October 1834. 'It was indeed
high time to devise measures differing in character from those
after former wars' since these invariably 'left conditions on the
Border as bad as, or worse, than before. It is worth a trial'; but
'it is obvious that for a considerable time to come Law Martial
must continue in force. . . . The terms, in short, of becoming
His Majesty's subjects, settled by His Majesty's grace in a portion of the land conquered from them—of which, meanwhile,

large tracts are still left vacant for the occupation and speculations of Europeans—instead of expelling them beyond the Kye,
whence they might return', are such that 'their system of clan
chiefs will be at once broken up and its spirit rapidly subdued
and forgotten—and the whole will be brought under the power
of the general colonial laws'. These will be easily enforced as
'the military power is ever at hand'.

The original of this dispatch in the Public Record Office
betrays a little of the impression it made. Significant words are
scored and underlined in pencil: 'the Kafirs have been "*chastised—not extremely*"; to enforce the laws "*the military power is ever
at hand*" ': and as for the hint that 'large tracts of Kaffirland are
still left vacant', a pencilled marginal note exclaims, '*European
speculations!*' There is not much doubt that if D'Urban's language, emphasizing the chastisement of the Kaffirs and the hope of
planting settlers in the conquered territory, was designed to
allay colonial feeling, it could hardly have been more nicely
calculated to touch a sore spot in the conscience of Lord Glenelg
and his permanent advisers. The reference to No. 13 of 1833
was a reminder that D'Urban had gone out in the end of 1833
with express orders to devise a 'new system', and the report that
war had broken out followed hard on the dispatch of 28
October 1834 in which D'Urban himself, recognizing the defects
of the old order, was sketching plans of reform. Though the
Governor was 'taken by surprise', permanent officials did not
change so often as Governors or Secretaries of State and can
hardly have been astonished to hear that the bad old system had
produced an outbreak.

The part played by the Colonial Office in this truly 'colonial'
situation (above, p. 147) is necessarily hard to determine with
precision. Historians have traditionally blamed the almost sin-
ful weakness of the Minister, Lord Glenelg, for all they considered went wrong; they certainly needed to take stock, too, of
the influence of the advisers on whom Gibbon Wakefield and
Charles Buller were very soon to be heaping unmerited extremes
of abuse. These so-called 'Colonial Reformers' were so far right
that in the tiny colonial department of the Ministry of War and
the Colonies (where four juniors, two of them probationers,
seem to have sufficed for all the routine work and Ministers
seldom stayed long) two seniors, both of them outstanding

personalities, must virtually have *ruled*. At a time when West Indian slavery was the chief concern, R. W. Hay, Permanent Secretary till 1836, handled the affairs of a small African section but, having no strong views, left no mark. James Stephen, on the other hand (after 1847 Sir James), originally accepted part-time work as Counsel in 1813 hoping thus to be able to help the anti-slavery cause—as became a loyal Evangelical of the inner circle of the 'Clapham Sect'. A private letter of 1816 shows him closely watching the parliamentary moves of 'the enemy, i.e. the West Indians'. Stephen was thus almost a foundation member of the infant Colonial Department; by all accounts the organization of the Office was of his contriving and at least by 1825, when he became permanent Counsel, and before he was made permanent Head (1836-47), he was its moving spirit. In the early thirties Stephen was joined by a like-minded friend and admirer, Henry (later Sir Henry) Taylor who was eleven years younger, an intellectual who had a literary reputation in his own right, and continued at least within call of the Colonial Office till he finally retired only in 1872.

The Cape crisis of 1835 fell due for attention when Stephen and Taylor were still deeply immersed, as Stephen had long been, in a struggle to ease the transition from slavery to freedom in the West Indies by a system of 'apprenticeship'. But 'remote control' (above, p. 147) is inevitably defensive and negative rather than constructive, even when in the hands of such good and able men—the West Indian planters must *not* perpetuate relics of slavery, and the ex-slaves must be protected from local officials who might become petty tyrants by usurping royal prerogatives of which the Colonial Office was the careful guardian. A prompt and vigorous local executive was thus all but impossible, and yet the Office was ill-equipped to make good this deficiency. The 'apprenticeship' itself is an example, being all too largely of the Office's own contriving, and so rigid that islands as different as Jamaica and, say, Antigua and Montserrat, all received the same directions. In the event the ruin of the Island economies was least calamitous in Barbados where alone local opinion was able to play some part in the guidance of policy. Professor W. L. Burn's study of the apprenticeship[1] leads him to conclude that 'the administrative burden'

---

[1] W. L. Burn, *Emancipation and Apprenticeship in the British West Indies*, Cape, 1937.

THE D'URBAN SETTLEMENT 1835-6

(of their own scheme) 'crowded out the development of policy' by Stephen and Taylor, Glenelg himself doing little to help.

There was little chance, therefore, of the Cape's special needs getting the fresh consideration they demanded—the dominant anti-slavery cult almost forbade. Stephen heartily approved the Hottentot-emancipating 50th Ordinance. Just man that he was, he is on record also as deprecating a 'discriminatory' provision demanding a knowledge of English from Boers wishing to qualify as jurymen. But it was hard, from London, to appreciate the difference between Hottentots, or ex-slaves in the West Indies, and these Bantu; they were at any rate *free*, not slaves. The instinctive reaction was to insist that they remain free. The Governor did nothing at all to clear the issues.

Throughout 1835 D'Urban was quite extraordinarily reticent, giving London no hint of any need for reinforcements, or of the additional expenditure likely to be involved, omitting even to clear the ground by full and clear explanation of the causes of the war, and of the necessity for remedies so much more drastic than those contemplated in 1834. D'Urban was sparing even of ordinary news. In effect he was asking London to approve the annexation of a large new Province. Yet in the whole year the only detailed information he sent,[1] after almost formal intimation in January that it was war, and short notes in February and March, was the report of 19 June on the May dispositions; that of 19 November on the much amended September proposals reached London only in January 1836[2] just after Glenelg had made his large pronouncement on the May settlement. D'Urban's new dispatch in which he so unwisely made light of the great changes he was now proposing only further shocked his superiors, as we saw, and seemed to them to raise more new questions than it answered old. A carefully reasoned dispatch such as was due from the Governor, especially had it arrived, as it well might, only a few weeks earlier and compelled full reconsideration of the official reply, might have changed the course of South African history.

[1] Glenelg himself complained that, having heard in London early in 1835 of an invasion of the Colony, he got his next report six months later: 'I [then] for the first time became aware that the war was to end not in the repulse of the invaders, but in the acquisition of a new and extensive province.'
[2] See Cory, iii. 272. The June dispatch was carried, with verbal evidence to back it, by a staff officer, Capt. Beresford, son of Lord Beresford.

As things were, the dispatch on which the Colonial Office laboured in the last months of 1835 was to prove decisive. With such very scanty official information to work upon it was natural for the Office to welcome any available supplementary evidence. Mr. Fowell Buxton was, we have seen, 'well informed' by Dr. Philip of what was passing at the Cape; his representations about the 'commando' system on the frontier had already borne fruit in the instructions given to D'Urban when he was appointed Governor. As Chairman of the Select Committee appointed in May 1835 to inquire into the treatment of 'aborigines' in all the British Colonies, Mr. Buxton was now in close touch with the Colonial Office. From his own point of view, therefore, D'Urban would have been well advised to anticipate, and meet if he could, the criticisms he knew must reach London, rather than vent his spleen, as he did afterwards, in pencilled notes on unwelcome dispatches that presently reached him. On Glenelg's dispatch of 20 October 1835, a warning to go slow (below, p. 167), D'Urban's very first remark is: 'Philip's insinuations have been working their will here.' Many notes on that of 26 December are illegible, but one stands out: '*This is all Philip!*'

It is not to be supposed or suggested either that Buxton made precipitate use of Philip's evidence, or that the Colonial Office received it except with due caution. Buxton deferred even his motion for an inquiry from March till May (above, p. 142) till he should receive 'further information'. For some time longer he adopted Dr. Philip's waiting attitude—busying himself with his 'capital good Committee' which took the evidence of Stockenström (with this he was 'delighted') and of Mr. Shaw, Wesleyan missionary, 'who has given better evidence than we expected'.[1] According to a letter of 28 August from his Secretary, Miss Gurney, to Dr. Philip, Mr. Buxton

has spent much time over your letters though not in answering them, and he means during the recess to get the subject thoroughly up. He has a doubt whether it would not be advisable to summon yourself and Mr. Fairbairn to give your important evidence personally next session. On the subject he would be much obliged to you to write him *immediately* your own views and opinions. For the present he has thoughts of going to the Government and of urging them to

[1] Col. Wade also 'attended all the meetings' of the Committee, and letters suggest that it was through him that news leaked out to the Cape.

suspend the ratification of the arrangements with respect to the new Province of Caffreland till the origin and cause of the war be investigated.

Though news of events in May had thus reached England, Mr. Buxton, according to Thomas Pringle in 1834, continued to be slow to move. In the first months of the war Dr. Philip, it will be remembered, regarded D'Urban as still on trial and held back as long as the country was in danger. Even his weighty Memo. on the 'Causes of the War' was still in preparation about the time of the May Proclamation. Then, for the first time, he felt himself bound to strike at his old friend the Governor; and on 23 September, as an endorsement shows, a great mass of his communications arrived simultaneously at L.M.S. headquarters, supplying far more detailed information than D'Urban's official letter, and only three weeks after it, together with closely reasoned criticism of the course of policy the Governor was proposing to follow. These documents arrived opportunely, in time for one of the missionary society's regular Committee meetings, and at once made a profound impression. Mr. Ellis, Secretary of the L.M.S., got busy—possibly even without fully digesting Dr. Philip's letters. Mr. Buxton, whose 28 August 'thoughts of going to the Government' had not yet matured, now roused himself, and only three days later, on 26 September, Mr. W. A. Hankey, the retired treasurer of the Society, to whom the news quickly spread, reported: 'Ellis and Buxton are at this moment at the Colonial Office.' On the day of this first momentous interview Ellis himself still found time to write to Dr. Philip, officially, about Buxton's project of summoning him to England,[1] and 'privately', as follows:

LONDON, Sept. 26th, 1835
Private

My Dear Sir,

My official letter to you of this day's date will convey to you the views generally of the Directors on the question proposed to them by

---

[1] Letters passing between Buxton, Sir George Grey, Under-Secretary for the Colonies, and the Treasury show that the move to have Philip officially summoned to give evidence was too late for that session. The Treasury could meet the expenses of his visit only with express authority from House or Committee. The onus, therefore, was on himself, and shortly after receiving this and other letters of August and September, he sailed for England on his own responsibility (Jan. 1836), with only an implied promise that Buxton and others would help to defray expenses if official help was not forthcoming.

Mr. Buxton, viz. their inviting your return to give evidence before
the Committee of the House of Commons on the general question of
the treatment of the Aborigines of South Africa have received at the
hands of the Colonists, and the best means of preventing the recurrence of the evils complained of.

Since the interview with Mr. Buxton on 2nd Sept. all your letters
have come to hand, and all of them within the present week. Part of
them I had the opportunity of laying before the Committee on the
day of their arrival, and recieved instructions to see Mr. Buxton on
the following morning. On the next morning your long letter of 4
June came to hand, and without summoning a Committee, I took
them all to Mr. Buxton. He instantly wrote to Lord Glenelg requesting an interview on the subject of the seizure of Caffer Territory, the
expulsion of the Chiefs, death of Hintza, etc. To this interview he
requested me to accompany him, I having furnished him with copies
of your letters as far as the time would admit. I breakfasted with him
and Mr. Johnston this morning, and at 12 met with him and Lord
Glenelg at the Foreign Office. His Lordship's attention was called to
the origin of the War, the increase of the Commando System in the
close of 1834, the conduct of Sparks, the fine levied on account of his
being wounded, the assault of Lt. Sutton, the wounding of Macomo's
brother, the murder of the Caffers as having urged the people to
desperation, the honourable manner in which the Caffers had conducted the war: Macomo's conduct to Sparks, the Chiefs' conduct to
Major Cox and Lieut. Grant, the circumstances of the arrival of
Hintza, his detention as a prisoner and the savage manner of his
death, the subsequent proceedings of Col. Smith—especially his
dispatch as published in Fairbairn's Paper of the 1st. July; the injustice of expelling the people from the country and the inevitable
destruction that must follow: with a request that he would restore the
country to the Caffers, or if it must be part of the Colony, not to give
it to the Colonists, but preserve it for the Caffers, bringing them
under the laws of the Colony.

To this Lord Glenelg replied that he has a different version[1] of the
cause of the war, the conduct of the Caffers, the circumstances of
Hintza's death, and the necessity for extending the Colony to the
Kei. The cause of War, he said, was, secretly, Hintza's disaffection to
the English, the refusal of Macomo to restrain his cattle from prohibited territory, the frequent in-roads of the Caffers to the Colony,
their plunder and outrages, the increasing complaints of the Colonists of the loss of property and insecurity of life, which had rendered

---

[1] In addition to D'Urban's scant dispatches, there was the *verbal* evidence of
Capt. Beresford, the bearer of the dispatch of 19 June.

military protection necessary, and which led to the breaking out of the war at a time when it was evident no apprehension was entertained in any place of its taking place; as the Frontier had never been in a more unprepared and unprotected state. To meet this the evidence of Mr. Ross and others was adduced as to the extensive cultivation etc. and your own evidence as to what you saw of the vigour with which the Commando System was pursued when you were on the Frontiers: the statements of Macomo in his letter to the Governor, and his pointing you to the smoking huts, together with a full detail of the affair of Sparks and Lt. Sutton.

In regard to Hintza's coming to the British camp, and his death, the letter of Dr. Campbell of the Glasgow Mission Society, with the evidence of Glass, were read to his Lordship, and evidently, produced a deep impression. He inquired, 'Where is that Man?' and was told 'in Dr. C.'s keeping'. His Lordship then said that he understood the missionaries had been in great jeopardy until the arrival of the Governor. Our evidence of the kindness and protection of the Caffers was then fully brought under his notice, and also the treatment of the Caffer Chiefs; as to the necessity of extending the Frontier in order to protect the Colony—the good understanding between the Hottentots at the Kat River Settlement and the Caffers, until the former were brought under the Commando System, was adduced, together with Capt. Stockenström's evidence that for this purpose no extension of the boundary was necessary.

His Lordship then wished Mr. Buxton to furnish him with all the information he possessed, and Mr. Buxton is to forward to him your letters with a digest of their contents. He then expressed his wishes to receive any information the Directors might possess, as it was his desire to be fully acquainted with all the circumstances, and he promised to give the whole case his best attention. Here the matter rests for the present. What I have done in communicating with the Secretary for the Colonies has been on my own responsibility with the sanction of one or two of the Directors. I was most anxious to prevent any pledge being given to the party (which is) anxious to secure the sanction of the Government to the expulsion—or rather extermination—of the Caffers, and therefore, communicated instantly with Mr. Buxton and the Colonial Office. I shall bring the whole of the documents before the Board on Monday, and shall be able to write you more fully as to the views and proceedings the Directors may adopt, by the next conveyance. The conduct of Macomo in refusing to withdraw his cattle from the prohibited Territory, the great increase of the depredations of the Caffers, which occasioned the more urgent complaints of the Colonists, appeared to be regarded by Lord Glenelg as the causes of the War, not the increased aggressions of the Colonists. On this point and on Hintza's conduct, whether he secretly prompted the War, and as secretly urged the Chiefs to continue it, and not to comply with the terms or wishes of the Government, the fullest and strongest evidence should be supplied.

Lord Glenelg referred to a pamphlet which he had; it was entitled, I think, 'Narrative of events which preceeded the irruption of the Caffers'. It appeared about 60 pages, and was printed at Grahamstown. Neither Mr. Buxton nor myself had heard of it. Send copies if you can. We have not all Mr. Fairbairn's papers you mention. It would be well in cases of importance always to send duplicates, and then if one is lost, the other may come.

I mentioned to Mr. Buxton this morning the desirableness of you bringing over a sensible intelligent Caffer should you come,—he said it would be an excellent plan. Should you determine to come, you will think of this; it might be of the utmost benefit to his nation.

I have just returned from the Colonial Office—the time for the vessels' departure has arrived, and I must close with assurances of sincere sympathy with you and deep interest in the preservation of the people in whose behalf you have made such persevering exertions.

> Believe me,
> Yours very truly,
> W. ELLIS

The tone of this letter suggests what happened. Ellis clearly enjoyed a new sense of importance and closely maintained the touch with Lord Glenelg thus established. Finding that the Colonial Office was 'kept in surprising ignorance', his first step was to send copies of Philip's chief communications,[1] with others as they arrived, these being followed up by letters and requests, 'repeatedly enforced in personal audiences'—for example, on 25 November, 'I have just returned from the Colonial Office where I have been for *the last four hours*'. But Ellis had not Philip's grasp of affairs, and his emphasis tended to be on the wrongs suffered by the Xhosa for years past, on the tragedy of Hintza, and generally on the emotional side. He stressed the case for the restitution of forfeited lands, failing to

---

[1] Usually the names of writers were suppressed, Ellis explaining that the letters were so frank because they were obviously meant to be private. It seems to have weighed with Glenelg that Philip had been D'Urban's 'negotiator' with the tribes in 1834. Examination of the volume C.O. 48/165 shows that its greater part is of L.M.S. origin, including letters from missionaries like Read and Ross who wrote from the front to Philip.

understand as Philip did how necessary it was for the British Government to take full responsibility and control by acknowledging the offending tribesmen as British subjects. At this very time, on 19 October, far away at the Cape, Philip embodied his maturer views—more clearly and emphatically than in any letter that reached Glenelg—in a striking letter to the younger James Read at Bethelsdorp:

On the subject of it being desirable that the Caffres should be retained as British subjects, I have long made up my mind. The question is not with me what might be, had we such men as Governor as William Penn, but what kind of Governor we have to expect in the ordinary course of things, and as the affairs of our Colony have been managed, and will be managed for a long time to come. *The Caffres cannot otherwise be saved from annihilation.* Were the Colony surrounded by belts of Native Tribes under the British Government, nations would get time to form beyond us, but no Tribes will be allowed time to rise into civilization and independence on our borders, if they are in immediate contact with our colonists. We never could have done anything with the Griquas, if it had not been that our work had arrived at a certain point before the Colony was extended to the Great River, and even notwithstanding their distance from us, nothing but a peculiar combination of circumstances could have saved, or can even now save, them. . . .

Contiguous nations never can be independent of each other without a balance of power, and there can be no such balance betwixt this Colony and the uncivilized tribes upon our borders. This fact must be obvious to any man acquainted with the Philosophy of History, and may be seen with half an eye by any one who is accustomed to look at men and things in the Colony as they are. . . . Barbarous nations may rise to civilization and independence situated in the midst of nations in similar circumstances with themselves, and even in that case it must require long periods of time, and they must work their way to those points through great difficulties and much bloodshed; but in immediate contact with civilized nations—never! It may do very well to produce a momentary excitement on an English platform to talk of raising up civil Governments in Africa, as a man would light one candle by the gleam of another; but woe to the cause of missions and humanity in Africa if our missionaries beyond a certain point have no better light to guide them in their labours. When Mr. Campbell one day told me that Kok and the Griquas promised to keep his laws, and he wondered that they did not keep their promise, I asked him how long the

Israelites kept their promise made at the foot of Mount Sinai—'all these things will we do'. . . .

The more silent we are on the present state of things on the frontier the better; the question has become now so complicated that it will require more evidence than certain persons possess to know what should be done. Your wisdom now is to be careful to note down facts, and to avoid giving opinions. An experiment has been set up, and we must confine our attention to the results. . . .

Yours very truly,
JOHN PHILIP

Here, at least, Dr. Philip, far from 'unwarrantable interference', was unduly silent; his alternative to D'Urban's plan made no traceable impression in any quarter, official or unofficial. The Colonial Office was at all times insistent that the colonies in its care should pay their own way (however poor the way might be) and no less consistently set against assuming new responsibilities likely to be unremunerative and probably costly; Imperial ambitions had no place whatever in the Office tradition. Stephen and Taylor (above, p. 158) thought West Indian precedent proved enough about this very different situation to warrant them taking, as from Philip's letters, anything that confirmed their prepossessions, while ignoring all else. Philip's own supporters were equally unhelpful. His London spokesman, Ellis of the L.M.S., was a champion in the first place of that 'nonconformist conscience' which guides the judgement on public affairs even of many English men and women who are themselves of the Establishment. The emotional force generated in defence of 'right' action was effective in maintaining the long, but almost straightforward anti-slavery movement. The same spirit reawoke from time to time to effect redress of wrongs suffered by dependent peoples. But, as Philip wrote in this letter to young Read, the cult of 'momentary excitement on an English platform' was no proper basis for the hard thinking needed to evolve the constructive and reconstructive measures called for in the new lands. Above all where advanced and backward peoples clashed, the sentimental approach was inevitably one-sided and at times disastrously provocative. As early as 1843 Philip's promising son, William, was identifying this point of view by the name of the famous place of meeting off the Strand, '*Exeter Hall*'.[1]

---

[1] See *Cape Col. Qn.*, pp. 61–62. William Philip was accidently drowned at the

In face of the Colonial Office, and of 'Exeter Hall', the fate of D'Urban's experiment in annexation, which even Philip wanted on conditions, now depended on his stating a case to satisfy his critics, and this he never so much as attempted. Stockenström's evidence to the Aborigines Committee during the summer told against D'Urban's plans, his stress being all on the short-comings of the old frontier system and, generally, in favour of greater leniency; beyond this the Committee was not destined to have much influence, either now or later.[1] The immediately decisive evidence came through Mr. Ellis of the L.M.S.; though the Committee took evidence all the summer, Glenelg still had a 'different version' on 26 September; but by 20 October, after his talks with Ellis, his opinion about the justice of the annexation had decisively changed—a note was sent warning D'Urban, and two devastating sentences obviously reflect considered drafting by the best brains of the Colonial Office, James Stephen and Henry Taylor: 'His Majesty's Government, anxiously bestowing consideration' on the matter, are,

as yet unable to apprise you of their decision in regard to the territorial acquisition which has been the result of your aggression upon Caffreland. The present inclination is to doubt in some measure the justice, and in a larger degree the necessity, or the policy, of that acquisition.

D'Urban is not to 'anticipate the decision of His Majesty's Government upon the question of retaining or rejecting that acquisition, [but he is] *not to make a single grant of land*, build forts, or commit his Majesty's Government any further'. Then, after more 'anxious consideration', on 26 December Glenelg launched his bombshell.

opening of a unique water-supply he pioneered at the Hankey Mission Station in 1845.
    [1] The huge Blue book of 1836, containing the evidence taken by this Committee, together with earlier 'leakages', was a mine for Cape journalists at the time, and has been invaluable to historians since. This has obscured the fact that its Report (below, pp. 187 ff.) was in the end rather a damp squib. But the existence and composition of the Committee seriously offended the colonists and their private friends in England. Capt. Beresford, for example, D'Urban's dispatch-bearer, reported on 8 Dec. that the Committee would certainly meet again next session, commenting: 'It is disgraceful the way this Government truckles to the Radicals, Saints and agitators.' Col. Bell in Cape Town writes about the same time, on hearing that Philip was to proceed to England: 'He and Stockenström' with a 'packed' Committee, and 'with its president', 'will be heavy odds against the Colony'.

While the blow of 26 December was preparing D'Urban and his colleagues toiled on; Colonel Smith, in particular, was busy and enthusiastic in his efforts to discipline the frontier. There was still some word of mere repression; on 10 November Smith wrote from King William's Town of beautiful land reserved for settlers in the Amatolas, where, 'within the last three weeks I have burned 2,700 huts'. In the same breath, however, he adds: 'Again I say 100,000 men would not have kept the people over the Kye', and for the next three months he carefully and generously pushed on with plans for the 'location' of the Xhosa population, with some regard to facts as he found them. Three days later the Glasgow missionary, Ross, reported from Grahamstown to Dr. Philip:

> Everyone is beginning to *see* that the statements of a few missionaries, as to the ground or country given in the Treaty to the Kafirs being inadequate for the population, were true. The Commissioners are [now] urging grants permanent and inalienable.

The Gaikas alone were found to number over 55,000, and before February, Captain Stretch, one of the Commissioners, reported: 'as the ground defined in the treaty of peace is by far too limited, we have recommended most of their former territory being restored'.[1] On 4 February Smith 'thanks God the great subject *location* is now finally settled'; and on the 6th D'Urban himself dated a letter to Glenelg saying that he had taken a census of the Gaika and Ndhlambi tribes and 'enlarged their locations to their great satisfaction—they being *more numerous than he thought*'. 'All' is now 'peacable'—on the new borders and on the old.

An equitable land settlement, which incidentally left less room for the 'European speculations' feared of Glenelg, paved the way also for administrative measures calculated to establish the frontier on something more permanent than 'Martial Law according to Smith'. It would appear that Major Maclean, well known later as Commissioner of British Kaffraria, came very near at this early date to the plan which has often been successfully applied in later times. Writing 'with due deference' of Smith as 'Great Chief', he comments:

---

[1] This was to Fairbairn, who as editor of the *Commercial Advertiser* would seem to have arranged an authoritative news service. Stretch, and later Stockenström, were for long in the habit of sending him a fortnightly bulletin.

It is not a time for experiments. . . . Radical changes can only be effected by imperceptible degrees. . . . No, No! a spark could ignite the whole fevered body. With tact and firmness (by all means) in the interim all coercive measures necessary should appear at least to emanate from their own judges and tribunals. [In a particular case under discussion] I would advise a meeting of the Councillors of Sutu, submit to them the cause of complaint, let them decide and enforce the law, the 'Great Chief' reserving to himself the right supreme to approve, confirm or revise their proceedings and verdict.[1]

Colonel Smith himself had some grasp of the needs of the situation. 'That (the old) Border policy was insufficient, unjust and imperfect is well known', he writes to the Governor,[2] but it was unjust 'not alone to the Kafirs, but also to the colonists', who had 'embarked their capital' in expectation of protection and reasonable security. He would now have religious establishments, with schools and schoolmasters, to train the Bantu in 'mechanical arts', would prohibit 'ardent spirits', but encourage the use of money, and the growth of towns and villages as the 'nuclei of civilized life'. In the last days of the experiment, in July 1836, Smith drafted a simple Code of Laws—somewhat on the lines suggested by Major Maclean—which would make salaried chiefs, with Bantu police, primarily responsible for the maintenance of peace and order.[3]

Meantime a section of the Boer colonists were becoming restive; before ever Glenelg's dispatch arrived there was continuous outward pressure of the kind that culminated in the 'Great Trek'.[4] Yet, in Albany, in spite of occasional depredations, there were not wanting signs of prosperity. Military expenditure may have had something to do with this; Captain Stretch, for one, anticipated Stockenström in accusing Grahamstown merchants of 'profiteering'.[5] There is also less challengeable

---

[1] Copied in letter of Feb. 1836, from Stretch to Fairbairn (or Philip), apparently reaching Philip in London, and marked 'For Lord Glenelg'.

[2] On 10 Apr. 1836, and other letters in D'Urban MSS.

[3] Sir George Cory (iii. 330–1) suggests that this was on lines afterwards followed in the Stockenström treaties; but there was the essential difference that Smith's chiefs were to be 'British subjects'.

[4] Cory, iii. 259 ff. Cf. especially Col. Somerset's Memo. of Oct. 1835, and the Attorney-General's opinion in Aug. 1836.

[5] Capt. Stretch alleges in Jan. 1836 that 'in a few weeks' D'Urban was involved in heavier expenditure than the whole cost of Colonel Willshire's campaign in 1819, Grahamstown merchants contriving, for example, to get the Hottentot levies

evidence of prosperity in the columns of the *Grahamstown Jour-nal*[1] where, in March and April, discussion was renewed on the old question of shortage of labour. 'Much as we may want servants,' writes A. B. on 7 April, 'Kafirs cannot be safely employed'; and yet, though employers of 'passless Kaffirs' incur a fine of £5, the law is 'practically a dead letter'. In May, moreover, a 'Juvenile Emigration Ordinance' was introduced in the Legislative Council to help to 'meet the urgent need for labour'.

On the whole, therefore, 'the System'—as D'Urban and Smith called it—was promising well;[2] but an effective substitute for Martial Law had yet to be found. The credit for what success there was must be given rather to Smith; the Governor appears all this time to have been nervous and uncertain, as if his task was too heavy for him. Smith, though impulsive, could not have been a more loyal subordinate; yet D'Urban's trust even in him was by no means unqualified—he dallied in Port Elizabeth in November 1835 for fear of leaving Smith alone in the east with full discretionary power and was not above letting his doubts on the subject be known.[3]

It may be that the more vital Smith sometimes needed the Governor's restraining hand, but the senior man's interventions were not all happy—as when he pressed for greater stringency to

dressed in 'Caffre baize from Tom Wood's store'—'rubbish' costing 'thousands' instead of 'hundreds', which was recommended because it would be needed 'only for two or three months'. So much, he says, for this 'stricken people, where £. s. d. are concerned'. (For Stockenström see Cory, iii, pp. 370, 398, and *Cape Col. Qn.*, pp. 79, 80.)

[1] The *Journal's* suggestions at this time favoured treating the Hottentots as 'colonists', with ordinary 'title' to land; this being calculated, so critics objected, soon enough to disperse them among the farmers as servants. One R. M. Burnley, quoting the *Journal's* account of a Wesleyan meeting in Feb. 1836, breaks out against 'this Gazette of Methodism—the voice of a tiger-cat from behind the cowl of a monk!'

[2] Capt. Stretch gives favourable evidence to the Governor on 17 May, 'The new order is progressing with every prospect of success'. Even the 'new colonists (Xhosa)' say 'we cannot revert to the way we have lived. . . . To give up (the new Province) would be ruin both to Colonists and to Caffres, and this opinion prevails among the latter to a considerable degree.' On the other hand, in August, missionary Brownlee returned to King William's Town, but hesitated to 'show tacit approval' by building a new station. His old place was now Government headquarters, and, so he understood, 'nearly half the country was reserved and intended to be given to colonists'; therefore, for missionaries to accept such grants 'would prejudice the Caffres against them'.

[3] e.g. to Capt. Armstrong on 17 and to Col. Bell on 27 Nov. (D'Urban MSS.).

be used against the King's new subjects, the Xhosa. D'Urban also showed himself unjustly distrustful of those older subjects, the Hottentots, of whom Smith thought sufficiently well to write in August 1835 to their missionary, the Rev. G. Barker:

> It is evident the wily Kaffir built much on being joined by the Hottentot community in his late acts of perfidy . . . in which expectation he has not only been disappointed in a friend but has found a bitter and vigorous enemy.[1]

But in spite of this, when the Hottentot levies, and their missionaries on their behalf, were urging that, having lost a whole planting season, they should, like the burghers, be released from their prolonged military service, D'Urban wrote to Smith (8 January 1836): 'I have every reason to believe that the *Unnatural Party* (the London Mission) are straining every nerve to disaffect the Hottentots.' To this, Colonel Smith, who had more than once expressed his thanks for the loyal service rendered by the Hottentots, returned (on the 26th) a laconic 'I doubt it.'[2] D'Urban's hostility to the London Missionaries became an obsession and even led him to victimize James Read; he 'can't think' of Read's returning to his charge on the Kat River—'the demon is not to stalk again in the Settlement'.[3] Philip counselled Read to have patience—though himself at last impatient:

> Since his arrival on the Frontier the Governor appears to have no mind to keep him out of difficulties or to extricate himself when he gets into them, and he suffers no one to approach him who has any more mind than he has himself.

And for once Read had his revenge; forbidden to return to his station, he was left free in 1836 to make a British tour with Dr.

---

[1] Fairbairn explained in a letter to Philip (25 Oct. 1836): 'There is no doubt that the alarm and agitation caused by Wade's Vagrant Law induced the Kafirs to believe that the Hottentots would not be very hearty in the colony's defence.' In this instance D'Urban's action in vetoing the Vagrant Law saved the country from a Hottentot rebellion (*Cape Col. Qn.*, p. 240).

[2] Probably before receiving the Governor's note of 6 Jan., Smith wrote (or had written) to Capt. Stretch on 11 Jan.: 'If you will express your desire for those (Hottentots) who have faithfully and bravely served, I shall have pleasure in laying the same before the Government.' Some distress seems to have continued and in 1837 Stockenström planted Hottentot settlements on the Fish River; but the site chosen proved to be arid and totally unsuitable.

[3] To Col. Bell in Nov. 1835.

Philip. Neither his meetings, nor even his evidence before the Select Committee, were of any great significance except for their effect, not only on 'the colonists', but on D'Urban who had himself thus driven him from his regular mission work.

The lack of balance manifest in D'Urban's actions at this period is in keeping with the remissness of his dispatch writing. Such dispatches as he did send conform to one type—usually a somewhat perfunctory explanatory letter, always with scores (and even hundreds) of 'enclosures',[1] from which the Secretary of State and his officials were left to draw their own conclusions. D'Urban it would seem, had a mind only for details, with little or no grasp of the situation as a whole—what Fairbairn named as his real defect, 'no power of reaching a clear decision based on principle'.[2] In the early months of 1836 frequent rumours reached him[3] that his policy was little favoured, and presumably ill understood; but even when, in March, Glenelg's challenging December dispatch arrived to prove this, D'Urban was content to await a reply to his own November letter.

[1] 254 'enclosures' on 9 June 1836 (sent off only in Jan. 1837), 125 of Stockenström's letters in June 1837, followed by 120 in July. In the delayed dispatch of '9 June' the Governor actually seems to congratulate himself that he 'now' had the advantage of being able to forward Smith's report on the successful administration of the already abandoned Province.

[2] To Philip at the very time, 28 Mar. 1836, of the arrival of Glenelg's dispatch.

[3] Repeatedly from Capt. Beresford (e.g. about Nov. 1835) and from one of a leading Cape family, the Cloetes, then in London.

XI

LORD GLENELG AND THE REVERSAL
OF THE SETTLEMENT

THE mere length of the Glenelg Dispatch (150 folio pages) made it the more portentous for poor Sir Benjamin D'Urban; the often illegible, pencilled notes on the Cape Town copy show how for most of a year it had him floundering. Even the generalities with which the dispatch begins are mordant. D'Urban's military success is 'grateful', but 'success against such an enemy would bring little accession to the military distinction which you have acquired in other parts of the world'. Then comes the first point: 'I still find myself impeded (in my) anxious desire (to reach a decision) at a much earlier period by the want of official information for the guidance of His Majesty's Government (as to) the origin, progress and result of your hostility with the Kafirs. . . . With the most ample details of all your military operations you have not combined any clear and comprehensive[1] explanation of causes. . . .' (On this D'Urban notes: 'I thought it had been well enough known.') Glenelg began, he says, 'with a predisposition in favour of the measures adopted by yourself and deferred a decision to the latest possible moment'; but when D'Urban's dispatches never came he felt 'at last reluctantly compelled to draw many conclusions from less authentic sources of information'.[2]

Glenelg agrees with his predecessor, Lord Aberdeen, that it was D'Urban's duty to meet the necessities of the situation, namely: (a) to repel invasion, (b) to do so possibly even within Kaffirland itself by counter-invasion, and (c) to ensure against a recurrence. But, he adds, with an eye on the campaign against Hintza, 'hostilities might have been more limited in their range'. The Kaffirs, he goes on to observe, in words deeply

---

[1] The words 'clear and comprehensive' are set in and added to the original text.
[2] These documents 'from various sources' are 'carefully recorded in this office . . . to remain here in vindication of the opinions deduced from them'—presumably Colonial Office 48/165, 'Papers relating to the War of 1835'.

galling to colonial opinion, had '*ample justification*' in the 'conduct towards (them) through a long series of years, and which
the short period of your administration could not have enabled
you to correct . . .'—('I had begun and the Kafirs knew it,'
D'Urban comments).[1]

Glenelg then deals at length with the alleged 'ample justification' for Xhosa unrest and retaliation—[always, it should be
remembered, in the light of D'Urban's May Proclamation,
which threatened merely to reproduce on the new Kei boundary
the troubles of many years on the Fish and the Keiskama].
Going back to the treaty with Gaika in 1819, he criticizes the
attempt to repeat with Hintza the futility of trying to bind
other chiefs by an agreement with a paramount they did not
acknowledge. The occupation of 'neutral' territory involved the
dispossession of Xhosa who thereupon 'endeavoured to resume
possession of some part of their lost country . . . but were at
times driven back at the point of the bayonet'. The commando
system it is 'impossible to condemn too strongly or lament too
deeply as productive of calamitous results', including 'extremities' like 'the burning of huts' and the punishment, as by
Sutton and Sparks in 1834, of resistance made by Xhosa in
defence of their 'ancient and lawful possessions'. D'Urban's
comments on all these points show touchiness, but little grasp
of the situation as a whole. Of Xhosa in the Neutral Territory
he notes: 'They lived in it by sufferance': expulsion by bayonet
was 'Not in my time': of commandos, 'What have I to do with
this?' 'Burning of huts' was 'not latterly'. As to Ama-Xhosa
rights of possession, D'Urban refused to acknowledge that not
only were they in effective occupation, but that Kaffirland was
their only possible 'home'—his final retort was a well-seasoned
'red herring': 'I differ. They were not their ancient possession.
They had taken them from the Hottentots ... (the rest illegible).'

The 'irreclaimable savages' passage in the Proclamation
gave Glenelg 'pain'; as did a Wesleyan Memo. of 10 January,
which went farther 'than you' in severity. Even the smallness of
the casualties was evidence against the charge of 'savagery'.—

---

[1] Glenelg disputes, apparently, that Dr. Philip in 1834 ever negotiated or
delivered any message 'from D'Urban to the chiefs'. On this D'Urban who, like
Philip, had hitherto rather minimized the formal significance of this embassy, now
retorts: 'He did both. Fortunately I have his own handwriting to prove it.'

'Is this a reproach?' D'Urban asks, 'There seems to be no feeling for the losses and wrongs of the colonists.' D'Urban had indeed begun to realize by September that the only Government capable of maintaining the equal justice, or the 'equal punishment' of black and white so eagerly desired by Glenelg, was one that made the Bantu British subjects, but this advance was completely overlaid by his unlucky emphasis on the acquisition of land for 'European speculations'. Glenelg's instructions, tentative as they were, undoubtedly by-passed the crucial matter of *control*. Crediting tribal institutions with the permanence and stability of a settled government, he laid it down as a first guiding principle that on grounds both of 'justice' to the Bantu, and of 'expense', 'any extension of His Majesty's dominions by conquest or cession is diligently and anxiously to be avoided'. None but Xhosa (and Fingos) were to be settled east of the great Fish River. D'Urban had already suggested that 'this accession of territory will be some indemnity against the expense of the war'. Glenelg agrees that it contrasts with the 'prevailing sterility of our own possessions', but inveighs against the already excessive extension and expense of the Colony. To keep the peace there should be a local militia, a 'wise Border policy' (D'Urban: 'What is that?'), with a Lieutenant-Governor, a 'Protector of Native Tribes', 'Agents' in Kaffirland, and 'Treaties'. Finally, though sovereignty between the Fish and Keiskama rested on no foundation of International Law, its relinquishment was impossible; but the claims of sovereignty over the new Province must be renounced—'right being on the side of the invaded'.

D'Urban was given till the end of 1836 'to prepare the public mind' for abandonment, but it has been questioned whether this allowed him any real discretion. 'All deductions', Glenelg expressly states,

are based on a view of the Origins which must be disproved. . . . I cannot, I repeat, hazard the experiment of laying upon you peremptory and inflexible instructions for your guidance in these affairs. . . . It will become your duty to assume to yourself the responsibility of suspending, until further directions, the execution of any part of the following instructions which you may be convinced had its origin in any such misconception. . . . (And at the end) His Majesty's Government will await with solicitude the report you will transmit to me in answer to this dispatch. That (report) will contain as full explanation as you can on every topic on which I have stated doubts and difficulties. After deliberate consideration of (the reply) . . . final instructions.

On the other hand, the evidence of Lord Howick, a member of the Cabinet, suggests that this discretion, rather curiously at variance as it was with the peremptory order to abandon the new province, was only a Cabinet gesture to mollify King William IV:

It appears that the King has most strenuously objected to that part of it which peremptorily orders the relinquishment of the newly acquired territory. Lord Glenelg obviously thought that this altera- tion would be decidedly wrong. Spring-Rice concurred with him. . . . I said that I was willing for the sake of soothing His Majesty to con- sent to the Governor's being allowed some latitude as to the time and mode of surrendering the territory, but that nothing should induce me to agree to the dispatch being delayed or to the orders for the surrender of the territory so unjustly acquired being rendered even a degree less peremptory.[1]

D'Urban's marginal comments show that he was thrown into some pardonable confusion about the discretion left to him. His first remark is: 'From p. 102 I am authorized to suspend until further directions . . . the case was so widely different when I reported in June . . . (remainder of sentence illegible). His Lordship seems to have written at any rate in ignorance of the peace and the terms of (?) the treaties.' But D'Urban himself had failed to make this essential change clear, and one episode suggests that Glenelg was not immovable; in March 1936, on representations made by Stockenström, now Lieutenant- Governor designate, he at once modified his ban on settlement beyond the Fish River in favour of colonists already established there. [Later, according to Stockenström, Glenelg himself was to speak of 'this premature abandonment'.] But D'Urban delayed incredibly to answer this March letter. For a time, indeed, even while thus dallying, he used the discretion to carry on his 'system'. To Smith he wrote in May: 'If I do not err, he (Glenelg) is not at present prepared to order me to withdraw from the Province.' Yet at the point where Glenelg

---

[1] From Howick's *Journal*: an excerpt sent to me by Professor W. P. Morrell, of Balliol College, now of New Zealand.

closes the dispatch with His Majesty's *personal* demand for proofs of the establishment of a 'Border System advantageous alike for Kafirs and for Colony', D'Urban's comment seems to suggest that he regarded the issue as settled: 'I have done this. What those may do who alter it, time will show.'

In spite of the discretion wrung from him 'for the soothing of His Majesty', Lord Glenelg himself proceeded to act as if 'abandonment' was fixed policy. On 5 February he appointed Andries Stockenström to be Lieutenant-Governor of the Eastern Districts, with express authority to make 'treaties' with the Xhosa chiefs. In this matter Dr. Philip's advice did not affect the issue, except possibly that, in several of the letters which had reached Glenelg, Stockenström was mentioned as the only man capable of carrying through a more enlightened frontier policy. In a letter on 17 December, which can have arrived only when the appointment was settled, he wrote:

The proposal of Philips (a 'Settler') to send out a Lieutenant-Governor is a Grahamstown opinion and one that should not be acted upon, which is likely to make things worse. The people on the Frontier want a little Court among themselves, and a man whom they hope to influence by having him in their midst. The only public man fit for the introduction of the New System that I know personally is Stockenström, and it would be sufficient in the meantime to send him back as Commissioner-General with full and well-defined powers to introduce the new system and watch over its workings for a time.

In the same letter he says once more:

I believe I formerly intimated to the Directors that as matters stand it would be well to retain the Kei River as the boundary of the Colony—but no English or Dutch should be allowed to settle or have land among the Caffres.

The Governor, in spite of the innovation, remained the supreme power and the only channel of communication with London; but the new officer was to be primarily responsible for the Bantu, it being felt that, with the Governor so far distant at Cape Town, 'the tribes were almost permanently under martial law, the administration of justice being left to the Commandant and his soldiers,' and the latter 'sheltered from all real control'. Even so, though Stockenström received a copy of the 26 December dispatch showing 'H.M.'s strong disposition to abandon the conquest', he was also told, 'final decision is suspended. . . . You are not to proceed to treat with the Kafirs till the Governor's final report is received; meantime it is your duty to administer the law as it actually stands.'

Glenelg, that is to say, continued under the influence of the impressions that went to the drafting of the December dispatch. This had cost him much effort and till its wide general questions were answered there was—he felt—no more to be said. When therefore D'Urban's November dispatch reporting his modified plans arrived these received short shrift. The treaties 'scarcely demand a very studious consideration', wrote Glenelg on 17 February, since 'the King is not disposed to accept the allegiance of the Kafirs. I regret that His Majesty's ratification was not declared essential to their validity.' 'It remains to be seen what will be their fate', he concludes,[1] and, cutting out polite phrases like 'confidence in your humanity' (which appears in the original draft), asks bluntly for 'further explanations'. Thus far Glenelg; he had made up his mind according to the light he had, and got no more material for his 'final decision' for over a year. Long before that time D'Urban himself, with the help of Glenelg's deputy, Stockenström, had taken the final steps and abandoned the conquests of 1835. On 23 March, indeed, D'Urban briefly acknowledged Glenelg's outburst, speaking unrepentantly but without elaboration of the importance of the newly acquired territory to the 'colony in a position so improving'. In April he was in correspondence with Smith about it, Smith sympathizing: 'It is evident Lord Glenelg is shuffling every responsibility upon Your Excellency', and adding: 'That canting crouching jesuitical dispatch is really (for) the House of Commons.' On 13 May the lion roused himself: 'I am now in a condition to overthrow every assumption and every argument and inference put forth by Lord Glenelg by the stubborn power of facts and *I shall send off my dispatch in a few days*.'[2] Though notes went in the interval, this essential reply, dated 9 June (and see below, p. 185) reached London only on 15 March 1837.[3]

---

[1] The original draft, thus modified reads: 'They will probably be abrogated' (Public Record Office Copy).

[2] D'Urban MSS. to Smith, 13 May.

[3] What minor dispatches reached Glenelg is not quite clear. On 13 Nov. 1837 Glenelg complained to Napier that he was 'nearly 18 months in office without news'.

One initial excuse for this astounding delay was that Captain Stockenström, the new Lieutenant-Governor, was expected to arrive very shortly after the dispatch, bringing with him fuller and later instructions from the Secretary of State. His arrival was further delayed by three weeks in quarantine, till 23 July. It cannot be said that Stockenström was welcome. D'Urban, indeed, agreed with Smith (1 May) that 'His Majesty's Commission must be respected', whether or not with Smith's further remark that Stockenström possessed 'a very considerable share of common understanding'. But there was never any real hope of friendly co-operation by Sir Benjamin D'Urban with a man of such strongly marked and independent character expressly commissioned to carry out a reversal of his own frontier policy. The appointment indeed was unwise. Lord Glenelg had almost better have anticipated his dismissal of D'Urban and made an entirely fresh start.

Captain Stockenström has been spoken of as an enigma. His twenty years' previous service, however, when he was in virtually unchecked control of the immense lonely frontier district of Graaff-Reinet, largely explains his later attitude and conduct. Stockenström was in origin a colonial frontiersman, latterly, and even more particularly, a keen and zealous official. His official duties brought him an increasingly strong conviction that the interests of Bantu, Hottentots, and even Bushmen, did not get full justice where they clashed with those of their conquerors, the white colonists. Keenly interested in his work, he was, like other officials thus placed on the frontier, delighted to get rare opportunities of 'talking shop' with intelligent visitors. But he was never an Evangelical philanthropist, and may well have wondered to find how much he had in common, even in 1820, with a new-comer like Dr. Philip.[1] An intimacy thus begun slowly developed; Stockenström was glad to talk things over when he got a chance of doing so, and Philip and others were much impressed both by Stockenström's inside knowledge and by his sympathy with measures for the common good alike of colonists and of natives. Stockenström's latest term of office, as Commissioner-General on the eastern frontier, had been unfortunate; his authority had conflicted with that especially of the military commandant and, rather than continue as the

---

[1] As in 1820 and again five years later (*Cape Col. Qn.*, pp. 129, 214).

'fifth wheel to a waggon', he had thrown up his post early in
1833; he left the Colony, as if for good, possibly embittered and,
it would seem, full of contempt for the methods of the frontier
administration. When news of the Kaffir War reached London
in 1835, absolute confidence in his own capacity as an administrator made him even too ready, when consulted, to support
Glenelg in the view that for the control of frontier relations
annexation of Bantu territory was at any rate superfluous. He
seems to have believed, not unwarrantably, that while in the
end annexation was desirable, it might, if applied without
such a period of preparation as 'treaties' would make, lead to
opposition and open resistance.[1] Confident in his own ability,
given a free hand, to bring order out of chaos, and going out
again with the more emphatic title of Lieutenant-Governor, he
believed that his new commission was sufficiently clearly defined to save him from his earlier embarrassments. His confidence was doomed to early disappointment. Sir Benjamin
D'Urban was of a no more yielding disposition than Stockenström himself and, starting with a prejudice against the man
deputed to undo his own work, consulted him no more than he
was compelled to do, kept him in the dark about at least one
vital decision (the repeal of Martial Law), and in the last resort
held up his communications with London.

The Lieutenant-Governor had other trials which were of his
own making. In the summer of 1835, before ever his new
appointment had been mooted, Captain Stockenström had
been called to give evidence before the Aborigines Committee; and there, free from the cares of office, but with an
official's consciousness of having inside information for an
important audience—probably also nursing a grievance that he
was an official no longer—he certainly 'let himself go'. His
main evidence was a critical review of frontier policy, but his
hint that the prevalence of cattle-stealing was largely due to the
carelessness of the farmers themselves, and that 'punishment in
ninety-nine cases out of a hundred falls upon the innocent', led
him in the end to a round condemnation of the commando
system. Frontier life being anything but safe or easy, a young
colonial community was naturally sensitive to such blunt
criticism. In 1835 the Eastern Province was smarting under the

---

[1] See also pp. 211 ff., and Ch. XIII, below.

fresh wounds of a war that cost it more than cattle. Before ever it was known that this culprit critic was to be Lieutenant-Governor there was a howl of rage at the evidence he gave in London. Ignoring Stockenström's comprehensive criticisms of the frontier system, and fastening on incidentals, the leaders in Grahamstown furnished Colonel Wade, before March 1836, with affidavits to prove that he had exaggerated or misrepresented the details of one particular episode[1] of five years back.

When this maligner of the good name of the frontier colonists arrived to be their Lieutenant-Governor Grahamstown was up in arms and 'welcomed' him with a 'loyal' address[2] challenging him, in Sir George Cory's words, 'to say to their faces what he had said behind their backs'. The civic rage was such that though Stockenström was only a Captain, and an irregular at that, the officers of the garrison indignantly went out of their way to do him honour. Sir Benjamin D'Urban quite truthfully reported to Glenelg on 23 August that while, officially, Stockenström was 'studiously' paid every attention and honour, he had 'as Your Lordship is aware, from some circumstances past, come out under the disadvantage of being personally unacceptable to a large proportion of the inhabitants of the districts he is destined to govern'. The 'address' was but a foretaste of what he was to suffer during some twenty-three months of personal wrangling and strife which left him too little time or mind to turn his constructive administrative abilities to the work he had taken in hand.[3]

It had needed something more than 'studious' attentions and honour to keep Governor and Lieutenant-Governor on good terms. On 12 July, reporting that the Lieutenant-Governor was delayed in quarantine, D'Urban had protested once more, still without any detailed supporting argument, that his own frontier system 'even surpasses my expectations'; it was, he wrote, 'calculated to ensure the security of the frontier and the speedy civilization and happiness of the Native tribes beyond it'.

Nevertheless [he continued] it is my duty to obey your Lordship's commands, and I shall proceed to do so with as little mischief to the Colony as may be compatible with that obedience unless I shall find

---

[1] Cory, iii. 286 ff.   [2] Ibid., 341 ff.
[3] This is strikingly suggested by a series of almost fortnightly letters of 1837–8 to Fairbairn, in the J. G. Gubbins Collection (below, Ch. XVI).

on conference with the Lieut. Governor (who may have a later opinion than 28th March) that there remain any reasonable grounds for my continuing to take upon myself the heavy responsibility of further delay.

On 23 August he noted the 'excitement caused by the prospect of renunciation' of a 'system whose efficiency has proved it equally beneficial to colonists and tribes', and added that after a 'confidential conference' the Lieutenant-Governor had agreed to their taking 'the still remaining chance of Your Lordship's determination having undergone a change'. Meantime, on 5 August, the Governor had sent Colonel Smith detailed in- structions for the abandonment of the new province[1] but— presumably as the result of this consultation with Stockenström, who 'seems a straightforward man of business enough'—he added a note suspending these orders: 'Although I have scant ground I am decided to continue to hold the Province upon my own responsibility . . . (till) further positive orders.'[2] On 17 August Stockenström left for the frontier, apparently under the impression that for the present 'the system' was to continue.

D'Urban's next action gives the measure of his would-be co- operation with Stockenström. By general consent the efficiency of 'the system', however hopeful it might seem, depended in the last resort on the power of the frontier authorities to enforce their decisions under Martial Law without the inconvenient interference of the ordinary courts. But the Law Courts of those days were more jealous than they have always been since of the executive's use of emergency powers; at the very outset (in October 1835) Judge Menzies had warned D'Urban of legal difficulties, suggesting that the new territory should be treated as a conquered province, 'to be ruled as the Crown should think fit' rather than as an integral part of the Cape Colony. Now, as the upshot of discussions with the Judges, on 18 August, the very day after Stockenström's departure, like a bolt from the blue, came the Governor's Proclamation that as 'peace, order and good government' prevail in Queen Adelaide, *Martial Law should cease*[3].

[1] Detailed in Cory, iii. 327 ff.

[2] 'Although', also, 'by waiting I may forfeit the advantage of their execution under your able auspices.' The 'instructions' were apparently intended to draw Smith's comments.

[3] The debate with the Judges had been known, to Col. Smith at least, fully a

Stockenström, that is to say, in spite of his private 'conference' with the Governor, had had no warning of a step that made 'the system' finally impossible. D'Urban's action in this matter was either disingenuous or, according to Fairbairn, merely 'stupid'.[1] To Stockenström he wrote on 19 August that he had deproclaimed martial law 'rather reluctantly', having 'no alternative'; on 7 September he was not above boasting to Lord Glenelg that his 'system' had brought such 'tranquillity' as to make this deproclamation of martial law possible. As 'all agreed' that without martial law the 'system' was impossible, the Governor's conduct in this matter was some warrant for Stockenström to claim in later years that the decisive step in the policy of retrocession was D'Urban's own.

Stockenström could now (5 September) only protest that his advice had not been asked. A week later he took over from Smith and as soon as he faced the hard facts of the Frontier he seems to have come down decisively in favour of Lord Glenelg's policy. On 22 September he wrote to Fairbairn:

As for keeping this territory, it is quite out of the question. Even Smith and his party admit that it cannot be done without Martial Law, and I even believe they feel that it can neither be done with or *without*. I only wish we had Lord Glenelg's final decision.

And again:

If Dr. Philip succeed in keeping the new territory we shall be in a pretty scrape unless he can get Joseph Hume [a leading Radical M.P.] to allow us a few extra regiments.[2]

month before; in August he had expressed concern at Sir John Wylde's opinion that the jurisdiction of the Colonial Courts ran in 'Adelaide' as in the Colony.

[1] (To Philip on 10 Sept.): 'When will they spare us a man with intellect—who can comprehend a thing and know his own thoughts?'

[2] This is quoted in a letter to Dr. Philip from his daughter, Mrs. Fairbairn, who adds: '*Supposing that you approve of keeping it.*' From a letter of the same date (Capt. Stretch to Fairbairn) it appears that Stockenström and Fairbairn favoured evacuation, while Stretch, like Dr. Philip, thought: 'More can be done for the happiness of the Caffres if they remain under the British Government than is possible under their own.' Mrs. Philip writes of the end, on 22 Dec.: 'Mr. Fairbairn feels rather troubled at your letter to him about the giving back of the Caffre territory to them as it is actually done and proclaimed last week. How it will answer I know not. I confess I should have been glad for the people to be under equal laws with ourselves, but Stockenström wrote to Fairbairn that he found it would be impossible to retain the country without a much greater force than he could command, so he thought it would be better to give it to them than to have it wrenched from us by another overwhelming war.' Later, the letter from Mrs. Johnston (Priscilla Buxton)

Stockenström, the Governor wrote on 13 October, having seen conditions for himself was satisfied that abandonment was expedient. There was 'nothing left for the Governor to do but to issue the necessary instructions'.[1] In October accordingly D'Urban took the law into his own hands and resolved to 'put an end to the suspense' by ordering the evacuations to begin forthwith.

From this point the two men were hopelessly at loggerheads,[2] and Stockenström for his part, having made up his mind, did not stick at half measures. Even Lord Glenelg, in his December dispatch, had contemplated treating the old Ceded Territory, from the Fish to Keiskama, as part of the Colony. Stockenström decided that a strong line of forts on the Fish River itself would give more efficient control of the dense bush on the Fish River than smaller posts scattered amongst the tribes beyond it. To this end he used his wide discretion as Lieutenant-Governor to abandon forts which D'Urban would fain have maintained and, ultimately, in the treaties he concluded on 5 December, to make over the Ceded Territory, as a 'loan in perpetuity' to certain Bantu chiefs—*quamdiu se bene gesserint*. These treaties, indeed, were Stockenström's work entirely since, as D'Urban himself had reminded him (13 October), Lord Glenelg had laid on him the responsibility for 'framing, consolidating and carrying into effect such a system as may ensure the maintenance of peace, good order and strict justice' in frontier relations. Following Glenelg's instructions to the letter Stockenström went the length of withdrawing completely from Kaffirland. Abrogating

in Aug. 1837 (see below, p. 188) seemed to assume that Dr. Philip in England gave way on annexation in the belief that Stockenström was capable of carrying through a 'new system'.

  [1] Cory, iii. 366.

  [2] Stockenström (to D'Urban on 18 Jan. 1837) 'regrets that he is seldom able to make his acts intelligible to or to get them approved by His Excellency'. To Glenelg on 15 Mar. D'Urban complained of the division of powers 'when there is a Lieutenant-Governor like the present one, self-confident, impatient of control and jealous to a degree' of his own authority. His independent military power, in particular, is 'an encroachment on the duties of the General Officer Commanding, who cannot honestly be held responsible'. D'Urban of course had a case, but the methods he chose to remedy the position were dubious. Presently, in June, he sent home Stockenström's dispatches 'for a year' to show the difficulty of their relations. Later, a 'confidential' letter of 11 Aug. to Bowker, a frontier official, asks him to 'keep me acquainted immediately and directly with all that may occur under your observation . . . by every post'—suggesting that the Governor was not above dealing with and through subordinates.

anything resembling the old 'commando system', the treaties threw on the chiefs the onus of keeping the peace and of checking cattle-thieving; British authority in Kaffirland was no longer to be represented by magistrates, but by mere Agents with only 'diplomatic' powers. On 2 February 1837 a Proclamation formally renounced British sovereignty in Kaffirland.

Now that the issue was settled Sir Benjamin D'Urban turned at last to his long-deferred reply to Lord Glenelg. On 3 November he had resumed the dispatch officially dated 9 June:

This delay can be of little consequence as in my dispatches from 7th November to June and July the position would have been shown to be so changed that my answer (to 26th Dec.) could no longer have been necessary to Your Lordship's decision. . . .

On 2 December he starts off once more:

The time has at length arrived when I may no longer delay the execution of Your Lordship's will.

He is very sore that 'even after six months' practical experience of the system' adopted in September 1835 that decision should remain unchanged. 'The determination to renounce the Province of Adelaide', he continues,

had been made known long before *I* had given it publicity, and in truth the state of uncertainty on both sides of the border had at length assumed a dangerous aspect and could have been endured no longer. . . . Hence the execution of Your Lordship's deliberately projected renunciation of the acquired territory admitted of no longer delay and it will thus have been effected (as you designed) by the end of the present year.

D'Urban had made no use of the interval of discretion allowed him to explain himself and get a more favourable verdict. Now the deed was done he still harped on the excellences of his 'system', a closed issue; but the main concern of the dispatch still dated '9 June'[1] was to fix the responsibility for its abandonment on Lord Glenelg and his 'anonymous' advisers, and, to this end, to explode 'assumptions, arguments and inferences, the same as those which appeared here during the last year in a colonial paper, the organ of Dr. Philip of the L.M.S., whose relative is the editor'. Various dark allusions gave colour to the

---

[1] For a detailed summary see Cory, iii. 315 ff.

picture of Philip's 'machinations' in London during the sittings
of the Aborigines Committee. Like Lord Charles Somerset in
1824[1] D'Urban put the blame for all his troubles on the doughty
Dr. Philip, and to this day D'Urban's allegations pass for definitive history.

By D'Urban's example an extended British tour, which was
more than anything else a missionary campaign, has been given
a political importance it never merited. Philip and his party
reached England in the spring of 1836 on a visit urged upon him
by Fowell Buxton. The suggestion that he should bring 'a
Caffer' came from the L.M.S. and was designed for purely
missionary propagandist purposes. Dr. Philip seems to have
thought for a moment of getting the chief Maqomo. In the end
he took Jan Tzatzoe, a lesser chief who was also a mission teacher,
not without friction due to Martial Law restrictions, and to
the fact that Tzatzoe was one of Colonel Smith's 'magistrates'.[2]
The common theory that all England was roused to indignation
by 'horrid tales' of the wickedness of the colonists rests on a very
frail foundation. 'Exeter Hall' has never been more than a well-
organized body of enthusiasts, influential out of proportion to
their numbers just because so few people were likely to bother
their heads seriously about happenings in a remote and rather
insignificant Colony. In the country generally 'Exeter Hall'
depended for support on those who were enthusiastic for
'foreign missions', especially the keener Nonconformists. It was
to these—and primarily to raise funds for mission work—that
Dr. Philip and his companions addressed themselves at meetings
in all three kingdoms. Philip's unique experience was wasted.
The moment he arrived, in May, Ellis of the L.M.S. had
begged him a talk with Glenelg but Stephen refused it as '*not
desirable* . . . so avowed an enemy of the Governor is scarcely
entitled to any peculiar attention from the Secretary of State'.[3]
After that Philip could act only through Buxton, and even
here he never had the success he looked for. Buxton's first
concern, throughout, was with the more general question of
West African and West Indian slavery; his *Memoirs* make
singularly little reference to the Cape in the most critical years

---

[1] *Cape Col. Qn.*, p. xiv.
[2] An unverifiable recollection persists of a (burnt) Philip letter in which, after
delays, he peremptorily bid James Read 'Fetch Tzatzoe!'   [3] C.O. 48/169.

of its history. His services to the humanitarian movement which is supposed to have stirred public opinion so deeply did not suffice to save his seat at Weymouth in the election of July 1837.

In 1836, however, and part of 1837, Dr. Philip undoubtedly hoped for great things from Buxton's Committee. In the early summer of 1836 he crossed swords with his old acquaintance, Sir Rufane Donkin (now an M.P. and a minority member of the Committee), as well as with Colonel Wade (Acting Governor in 1833), and flattered himself that he had 'blown their evidence to pieces'. Dr. Philip was not above 'diplomacy'. To Fairbairn, June 1836, he describes how, on Mr. Buxton's advice, he 'out-generalled' Wade and Co.: 'I wrote an introduction to my papers on the Kafir affairs, and I made it long to tire them, and when it had done as I anticipated, to avoid hearing the whole they agreed to print all before they were read.' For his own part he adhered (above, p. 183, n. 2) to the advice that 'the recent treaty (annexing Kaffirland), with such modifications as may be deemed necessary, should be confirmed by the British Government'. In the winter his hopes and his activity mounted even higher. 'I can do here what I can't do at the Cape', he writes in February. Mrs. Philip, indeed, sent him a 'scolding' for neglecting his home letters, and began to insist quite strongly on his return—he even protests at her urging a friend to send him back, 'as if I were a little boy playing truant!' Throughout the winter, especially in January at Northrepps Hall, Buxton's home near Cromer, he was excited and preoccupied, helping the Chairman to draft—or even himself drafting—the 'Aborigines Report'. By April the draft was completed and Dr. Philip set off in high spirits on another missionary tour —satisfied, among other things, that 'the Tories and the King must give way to the Report, and D'Urban's recall must follow as a matter of course'.

But D'Urban, whom Philip now regarded as impossible, was not yet finished with. Apparently only in August the bad news reached Philip on his return from Scotland that D'Urban's belated reply—'a bundle of papers a yard high', says Miss Gurney later—had at last arrived; certain Buxton letters in the Philip MSS. only now clear up the mystery of the really rather colourless and innocuous Report which issued from the famous

Aborigines Committee. A letter to Philip from Priscilla Johnston (Buxton) explains its history:

We have been longing for some communication with you. . . . Surely the events of the last few weeks have been matter of common and deep interest—and then *the report*! Our dear report, alas! you will have to behold *sore* gashes in it and especially in *your* part—I mean the Caffre War. Anna Gurney says it is like a table without a leg—and I feel for you when you first have to look upon it. As to us, we have become by this time tolerably reconciled considering *how much* is gained, and that after all, if words are restrained, *deeds* have not been—Adelaide restored and the Government apparently enforcing the right system. I have just been looking over the letters which passed at the time between the Cottage ladies and ourselves, and as I believe I should have been faithful to my old correspondent had you been in Africa, I think I will copy a few extracts from them which will interest you.

My father wrote to Anna Gurney June 17th thus: 'At the last meeting on Wednesday week, when I began in a good audible voice to read our South Africa, Gladstone and Bagshaw proposed to omit the whole of it. This did not disturb me. I had no fear that my troops would consent to such slaughter and it proved on a division that they had but their own two votes. But then Sir George Grey did alarm me, he said they had received and answered a Dispatch from Sir Benjamin D'Urban, that it was absolutely necessary for the Committee to read it before they agreed on their report—and that it was gigantic in size. He was pleased to think, however, that if we were lucky and the printers industrious, it might be in print in two months! At the same time we received intelligence that the King was dying—and I was told on authority that immediately on his death there would be a Dissolution. So the least toil was postponement for the Session—to which, very probably, was to be added my being turned out. No wonder I was alarmed and took to being sulky. I went, however, soon to Grey and after a good deal of poking at his conscience, we agreed that I should consent to hack away at South Africa, all that related to the late War, and that then he should not insist on the destruction of the whole. I have given him leave to mark all offensive passages for suppression—subject to my approval. These I hope to get on Monday, and I mean to sacrifice much rather than lose the Session—but it is hard work—it would have made you laugh or cry or both, to have watched the coolness with which he set his mark against our tit-bits. I bore it well at first, but when I saw him put his ugly scratch against our most stinging morsels, I almost fainted with horror. Still, I think we shall retain *almost all that is necessary*—though the ornamental will surely perish. Such gashes and ghastly wounds as he had the heart to make!. . . . While I am writing, down comes a packet from Andrews containing Grey's alterations—tho' dreadful, they are bearable, even if we have to submit to them all. . . . But South Africa, shorn of its beams, and dull as an advertisement as he has made it, will do the *main job*.'

On June 24th he writes: 'Dearest ladies, I thank God the Report is through the Committee—and I report it on Monday to the House—that is but form, the thing is done.'

June 28th, my mother writes from Weymouth whither she had accompanied him: 'Monday saw the happy conclusion of this dear Report—presented and done with. We waited, though very anxious to go to Weymouth. I persuaded him to wait and do it himself— and it was well—for the clerk said it could not be printed, it was so much interlined—but he made him get over the difficulty, one which might have been a sad obstruction, by saying he would him-self correct the press. He was next told it was impossible to have it presented till after the private business, which would last for hours, but he mastered this too, went to the Speaker and said his sick wife was waiting at the door of the House, all packed for Weymouth, if he would allow him to come on *first*;—and by his pathetic pleading he obtained leave, was instantly called, in one minute his precious report was carried up, presented, and ordered to be printed—he was out of the House—and we drove off in Triumph.'

I am sure I need make no apologies for sending you these letters for I am certain they will interest you. They must be kept private of course. We have never seen the report, they corrected the proof of the parliamentary copy, but it is not yet printed; you cannot, how-ever, expect too much devastation of the Caffre War, Hintza's death, etc., for you will find scarcely a trace of it.[1]

Belatedly, Anna Gurney writes on 15 October 1837, with many underlinings:

He (Buxton) thinks after all he *forgot* to explain to you *the* point on which the great omission turned. The fact was this. In the very last

[1] This letter (Priscilla Johnston to Philip, 25 Aug. 1837) throws an illuminating sidelight on how the cheap penny postage of 1840 was so long delayed; expensive postal charges mattered little to those who, having friends at Court or in Parlia-ment, used 'franks' as a matter of course. Mr. Buxton having lost his seat—'Now we have no franks it is rare to me to write so much, but I must beg one from a friend, the first frank I have asked for almost in my life.'

Dr. Philip seems to have got the Aborigines Protection Society to publish an 'edition, with comments', which probably embodies some of the discarded 'Report' (London, 1838).

days of the session Sir George Grey brought down to the Committee
a heap of fresh documents—papers from Sir Benjamin D'Urban, etc.
—a pile standing a yard in height. It was a physical impossibility
that these should have been *printed* within four months—and yet, as
they *were* given in, it would have been manifestly unjust to give the
summons of the case, without the other members of the Committee
examining, or at least having the *power* of examining them. Mr.
Buxton *did*, I believe, turn them over—and saw *nothing* to invalidate
our statement—but that would not have been done for all the Committee—and to have delayed for the sake of *completing the* Report
would at that late period have lost the whole of it—and he thought
the '*principles*' were worth preserving, though the hiatus is *terrible*. *I*
said at the time it was like tearing the *heart out* of our creature!

Mrs. Johnston remarked tartly, 'Sir Benjamin D'Urban's
reply to Lord Glenelg's dispatch was *pert* to an excess, no other
word describes it,' and as if in agreement, Glenelg himself
objected to 'passages which I must be permitted to regard as of
a declamatory nature and upon which it can scarcely be incumbent on me to dwell'; on 1 May in a letter received by
D'Urban on 26 August 1837, he wrote that it was clear they
could not work together and he was 'left no alternative' but
to announce the Governor's recall. In a personal letter of 16
August Henry Taylor, of the Colonial Office, agreed that the
King had no option but to consent to the recall because of
'expressions you used, not in a hasty effusion, but as the result
of deliberate reflection'.[1] Without needing Philip's 'machinations', D'Urban's recall took effect in January 1838 on the
arrival of Sir George Napier.

While this order was pending, D'Urban and Stockenström
were left to get on each other's nerves for the whole of one unhappy year, 1837. Never was a new experiment for the control
of the difficult Cape frontier launched under conditions more
unfavourable. The relations between the two officials went
steadily from bad to worse. One cause of dispute was D'Urban's
legacy of special obligations to the Fingos whom he had accepted as British subjects, back in April 1835. Being a homeless
people, the Fingos had to be provided with land; but when all
land east of the Fish River reverted to the Xhosa chiefs they
were little disposed to tolerate 'traitors'. Even in the old Ceded

---

[1] D'Urban MSS., Cape Town.

Territory the Fingos were a constant source of annoyance to the Xhosa to whose cattle they had liberally helped themselves. It was largely for fear that they would be unprotected that D'Urban had taken alarm in the beginning (October 1836) at Stockenström's plans for withdrawing to the back line of the Fish River. When the treaties took effect, Xhosa attacks on them were a continual embarrassment to Stockenström and Stretch on the frontier; far away in Cape Town the Governor felt his honour to be involved in giving the Fingos ample protection.

It made for conflict that while the Lieutenant-Governor was responsible for the welfare of the Eastern Province, the Governor remained Commander-in-Chief of the forces. In a wordy war between the two principals throughout the year the colonists were overwhelmingly on the side of the Governor; Grahamstown, seething with discontent and disappointment, was convinced that no good could possibly come of Stockenström's administration. Stockenström and his officials were equally emphatic that Grahamstown alarm was the work of a 'war' party and not borne out by the facts of 'depredations'; they even contrasted the existing 'tranquillity' of the frontier with the conditions prevailing before August under Colonel Smith's Martial Law[1]—to the further annoyance of D'Urban who, on 12 August, went so far as to write to Glenelg: 'The treaties are nothing but waste paper.' The truth would seem to be that the strong feeling of resentment at the policy of 'abandonment' was intensified by war losses, and found vent in personal attacks on Stockenström[2]—who himself consistently favoured compensation for 'real' losses. Since D'Urban, even as late as his reply of '9 June', not only urged effective protection and security but suggested that the grant of 'farms', presumably in Kaffirland, might help to meet the need, the abandonment was a double disappointment to frontiersmen.

[1] e.g. in letters of 15 Jan., 13 Feb., 24 Feb., 18 May, and Frontier reports generally. Stockenström on occasion took the offensive, as when he hinted that all was peace except so far as D'Urban himself had set 'Kaffirs' and Fingos against each other, whereas under Hintza there was no feud.

[2] Cf. Cory, loc. cit. These attacks, culminating in the publication of highly offensive cartoons, led to his unsuccessful libel action. *Stockenström* v. *Campbell*. A charge against Stockenström of misconduct in an early frontier campaign persisted till at last an official inquiry cleared him.

The storm on the eastern frontier died down gradually, but
the plan Stockenström proposed to work to never really got a
fair trial. In August 1838 his personal trials proved too severe
and he took long leave. In 1839 Glenelg's successor, Lord
Normanby, concluded that the Lieutenant-Governor's unpopularity made it unwise to retain him in office; at the same
time he rewarded his services, and consoled him for his sufferings, with a baronetcy. The removal of the man they knew as a
friend by no means reassured the Xhosa; but the unsettlement
which persisted throughout the following years of comparative
quiet was at the time, and has remained, overshadowed by the
pressure of dramatic events elsewhere—D'Urban in his last year,
1837, which was also that of major developments in the Great
Trek, was rightly much exercised about the Boer exodus. It was
one more count, in his view, against Stockenström (who was
doubtless never a model of tact) that he mismanaged and offended his important frontier parishioner, the Boer leader Piet
Retief (below, p. 198); yet, failing permission to make grants
to the malcontents of trans-frontier farms, there was little the
Governor himself could do to discourage the movement. By
common consent the abandonment of the new Province of
Queen Adelaide precipitated the large-scale emigration of
1837; but such a vigorous body of pastoral farmers as these
Boers must sooner or later have resolved to test the quality of
the land beyond which, by this time they had good reason to
believe, was far superior to anything they had yet found anywhere east of the zone near Cape Town; the distance they must
go to reach it made it obviously an advantage to move in a body
rather than as units; but to treat the events which were the
occasion of the first mass movement as also its main cause disastrously obscures the truth. For many years the mass of the
frontiersmen had been watching with mounting concern, if
not with indignation, the tenderness of successive governments
for Hottentot and 'Kaffir' rights where these clashed with their
own. The disappointment of the hopes raised of farms in the
Province of Queen Adelaide was the last straw. This it was that
gave the more venturesome among them the opportunity of
winning recruits for a mass movement—and the mass continued
to cherish its grievances even in exile.

Much analysis of the causes and more tracing of the fortunes of the Great Trek has too much diverted attention from significant developments on or near the old eastern front. There the first effect of the removal of so many farmers must have been to ease some of the tension; it was a year or two before big events in the Xhosa rear, or even the wild rumours spread by 'bush telegraph' about these, could begin to be disturbing. It made for calm, too, that in spite of frontier troubles the economic prospects of the Cape Colony, as far east as Albany, were being much brightened by the growing success of wool-farming. Besides its frontier hides and skins (above, p. 86 n.) the Cape in 1834 exported 114,000 lb. of wool; by 1841 the total was over 1 million lb., in 1851 $5\frac{1}{2}$ millions and wool the largest revenue producer of them all. One palpable result was a steep rise in farm prices, in spite of the number thrown on the market by the Boer exodus. Stockenström, now himself an Albany farmer, even claimed the booming prices in 1842 as evidence of the success of *his* 'system'.[1] The 'authorized version' of this history is again at fault here, and distracting; while stressing the claim that the trekkers, who were few if any of them slave owners, were indifferent to slave emancipation, it makes the elaborate 'method' of paying the compensation, as it was, an undoubted 'grievance'. But whatever the losses suffered by individuals, the flow of compensation money in such a poor country contributed materially to a modest 'boom' and so long as this lasted, or till the next drought, Xhosa frontier policy merely drifted. The consequences were fatal; for in this interval of nearly ten years the potential area of conflict was enormously widened. Everywhere the fundamental issue was the same; the presence of the Bantu was the supreme challenge to the statesmanship of Boer and Briton alike, requiring the leaders of the stronger peoples to shoulder the responsibility of working out a durable *modus vivendi* with their weaker neighbours. The sudden widening of the field, before any sort of settlement had been effected in the east where the challenge originated, was the supreme disaster of the country's history. The lull in the east could not survive the strain of renewed, very severe drought (see Ch. XV). The crisis which ensued was prolonged, and this time (see Chs. XVI, XVII) nation-wide.

[1] *Cape Col. Qn.*, pp. 79–81.

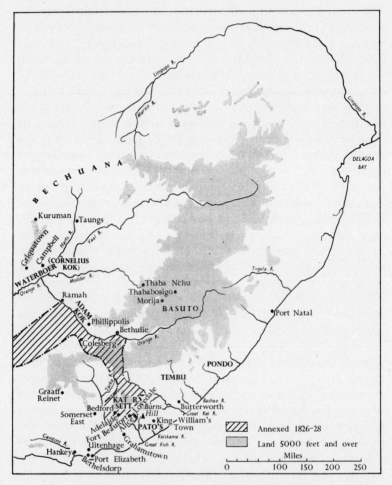

Map 2. Frontier on eve of the Great Trek 1836

XII

THE GREAT TREK AND THE TURNING OF THE BANTU FLANK, 1836–42—BRITISH INTERVENTION IN NATAL

THE Great Trek was an essentially conservative movement, a chance seized by men bent on preserving a way of life, and the manner of thought of an age which elsewhere was dying or already dead. By perpetuating and accentuating the dispersal of the population the move not only made Boer isolation more extreme than ever, thus prolonging and deepening the backwardness that became typical of the *back veld*. The consequence for national policy was in the end the undoing of the enlightened liberalism which by its successful freeing of the Hottentots in 1828 and of the slaves in 1833 provoked the movement. The withdrawal of the die-hards may have cleared the way for the legal and political equality written into the Cape constitution of 1853. But the even more far-reaching result was that the great scattered mass of the Bantu tribes—those hitherto screened by the Ama-Xhosa who had so long held the narrow front between the Winterberg and the sea—began and continued to be dealt with, not in the spirit of liberalism, but on principles that look backwards to the days before 1828 and now make the word *liberal* a term of abuse.

The Great Trek was, in the first place, a good deal less sudden and cataclysmic than is sometimes suggested. The year 1836 is invariably given as its starting-point, but the movement was in being as early as 1834. Earlier emigration was prompted by natural land-hunger; in the early thirties the settlers on the Griqua border still regarded themselves as Cape Colonists and even rode from Philippolis to Colesberg to pay their taxes.[1] But the 1836 trekkers at once showed themselves determined to escape altogether from British control.

[1] Walker, p. 186, and above, Ch. VI.

Yet this separatism was no new phenomenon—Boer republicanism had broken out at Swellendam and Graaff-
Reinet in the last days of the Dutch East India Company. With
undoubted grievances to feed on, this deeply rooted intolerance
of authority[1] was growing vigorously for many years before
Lord Glenelg was heard of, in protest against the Cape Government's heretical innovations. Few frontiersmen owned slaves to
be troubled about, but the anti-slavery movement's nagging
fight to improve the status of all these southern African children
of Ham gravely affected their authority over their own servants.
Legal protection by Circuit Courts, the 50th Ordinance of
1828, and the refusal of Sir Benjamin D'Urban and of Downing
Street to go back upon the Ordinance by passing a Vagrancy
Law sufficiently stringent to secure 'proper' relations between
masters and servants[2]—these were only the highlights of a prolonged fight on behalf of the so-called 'free' persons of colour.
This Hottentot legislation was bitterly resented—possibly all
the more because weak administration may have made these
measures fully more irritating than they were effective. Only a
few frontiersmen were slave-owners, but none was so poor as to
be without coloured servants; the idea of subjecting the authority of the master to the sovereignty of the law thus brought
dismay to almost every farm-house. The maintenance of elementary discipline seemed impossible under such conditions, and
the insistence, forsooth, on the 'rights' of coloured persons laid
the train for an explosion. In a more confined country there
might well have been a general rebellion. The wide spaces of
South Africa suggested the obvious alternative and the leading
malcontents resolved rather to leave the Colony altogether. In
new states of their own they would be free to pursue a policy
more in harmony with their own traditions and prejudices.
Their repudiation of British allegiance, first in Natal, and later
in the north, very soon conclusively showed the Trek to be in
fact a rebellion.

Before there was any question of a Glenelg policy one Louis
Trigardt, the greatest die-hard of them all, elected to brave the
terrors of 'Kaffirland' itself and settled, with the permission of
Hintza, on or about the upper reaches of the Kei River.
Trigardt, the son of a Graaff-Reinet republican of 1796, was

[1] *Cape Col. Qn.*, pp. 84-86.   [2] Op. cit., *passim.*

leader of a band of the virtual nomads known as *trek-boere*. Towards the end of 1834 he came into collision with the law by carrying slaves across the border. Most of the slaves escaped, but he himself presently came under even graver suspicion of intriguing with the enemy Xhosa[1]—a charge which, to the colour prejudice of later times, seems wellnigh incredible. Thereupon, about April 1835, he finally betook himself across the Orange River to pursue his adventures in the Zoutpansberg and beyond. In the north he was soon joined by kindred spirits, notably the van Rensburg party who moved to the region of the Limpopo but were never heard of again. The outstanding bravery and resource with which such men endured hardship and danger in the wilds command their meed of admiration, but are after all the marks of the individualist frontiersman in many other lands.

Meantime the idea of an escape from the restrictive laws of the Colony had suggested itself to other more solid and purposeful people. In the course of 1834 three parties (*commissies*) went exploring to spy out the prospects for settlers in the land beyond. One party went as far afield as Damaraland, through the *Dorstland* (Thirstland), as they justly called it, of the far north-west. A second reached the Zoutpansberg, attractive but malarial country in the northern Transvaal whither Trigardt had gone ahead expecting soon to be joined by Hendrik Potgieter and his party. A third *commissie* under Piet Uys ventured safely, with fourteen wagons, through the heart of Kaffirland to Natal, returning early in 1835 with enthusiastic reports, but to find the further development of their plans interrupted by the outbreak of the Kaffir War—and, just possibly, by the hope that after the war farms nearer home might be thrown open for settlement.

In this of course the frontiersmen were doomed to disappointment. The end of the war brought, rather, grave fresh causes of discontent and early in 1836 the outward movement began again in good earnest. Potgieter, Sarel Cilliers, and others from

---

[1] Theal, *Sketches*, p. 267; Ross to Philip, June 1835; Cory, iii. 53 n. The evidence that Trigardt instigated the Xhosa to continue the war is inconclusive. But such intrigue had a precedent in the undoubtedly treasonable conspiracy of the Slagter's Nek rebels with the Xhosa in 1815. There was also wholesale trade in powder and guns both with Griquas and with Bantu, by Grahamstown traders and others, then and long afterwards.

about the Tarka and Colesberg moved off in February. For a while Piet Retief, the best known and the most competent of them, *swithered* at his home in the Winterberg. On 11 April 1836 he complained to the Civil Commissioner of Albany of danger from savages (the Xhosa), of non-compensation, of distance from the magistracy, of threats to establish a 'militia', and of lack of servants; he added significantly that the state of the coloured classes in general *under the present regulations* afforded 'little security for them to resume with confidence their agricultural labours'. D'Urban himself reported on 'June 9' (probably he actually wrote later) that the farmers had been inclined to emigrate in 1834, that the change in the Commando Law, and the Emancipation Act, increased the dissatisfaction, but that after his annexation of Kaffirland in May 1835 they 'relinquished the purpose of emigration and awaited events (till) one of the colonial journals, *The Commercial Advertiser*, asserted that this change of boundary would not be confirmed'.

In August 1836 the Attorney-General reasserted his two-year-old opinion that the Governor had no legal power to stop emigration,[1] and in September the abrogation of martial law removed the last restriction on free movement. On this there followed a marked renewal of restlessness. In October Piet Retief fell foul of the tactless but harassed Stockenström, originally because of an attempt on Retief's part to use his authority as field-cornet to enforce security by 'firm' treatment of passless Bantu. To the annoyance of D'Urban, Stockenström early in 1837 dismissed Retief from office, but before this he had taken his resolution to be off. By December 1836 a meeting of Trekkers at Thaba N'Chu (near the Basuto border) had elected Maritz, a new-comer, to be *landdrost*. In the following April they were joined by Retief in this eastern corner of the later Free State where deals with Barolong and other tribal groups had given the embryo republic a *locus standi*.

There was more to all this elaboration than a desire to protest against the abandonment of 'Queen Adelaide'. Stockenström, defending his sharp treatment of Retief, might, he told D'Urban on 25 May 1837, have 'soothed' Retief with a definite promise that the slaves should not be free, that the 50th Ordinance be repealed, that Kaffraria be divided up as farms,

---

[1] Eybers, p. 145 and above, p. 117.

that the missionaries be hanged, and the blacks extirpated; even so, he thought, Retief was irreconcilable, and the Trek would not have been stopped. Stockenström's brusqueness can hardly have improved matters but he was so far right. The original cause of this great dispersal of the strength and energy of young South Africa was horror at the equality between black and white so many saw implied in the legislation of 1828 and 1833. Nor was Stockenström far from wrong in his view of the consequences. He 'has it', he writes, 'from Dutchmen, not from over-sensitive philanthropists, that the Boers are likely to reduce the natives to the condition of the Hottentots lately'. Retief and all the republicans after him adhered with unyielding rigidity to the ideas current before 1828; the result was that most of the Bantu were indeed reduced to a condition not unlike that of the Hottentot proletariat of more than a century ago. These forcefully held views were yet to sweep back from the north, to be reasserted elsewhere with vigorous self-confidence nurtured on oft-told tales of the glorious deeds of the founding fathers of the Trekker republics.

The Great Trek happened when it did primarily because of the new official attitude to the indigenous peoples. The peculiarities of the old Cape's economic structure perhaps always made such a movement likely, and certainly gave this convulsion its distinctive character. The Colony, as Dr. Philip was among the first to emphasize,[1] was 'all farms, with no towns forming', and not very many dorps or villages; the farmers accordingly had no markets, no means of transport other than the ox-wagons which for the most part tramped out their own roads, and, consequently, no agriculture except in the immediate neighbourhood of the Cape Town market. Of necessity they were pastoralists, growing enough only for their own subsistence and dealing only in kind. Such cattle-farming, in a dry country where there was no intensive winter-feeding, inevitably needed wide spaces, and land-hunger was very real. The resistance of the Bantu had for nearly half a century stopped natural expansion to the east, so that in the early thirties two generations of sons were clamorous in their demand for farms. Any farms still available were also made more expensive by the change in

[1] There are many references. This quotation is from a letter to Buxton, Feb. 1835.

1813 from the system of one-year leasehold (the marking out as one farm of all land 'within half an hour' of a beacon) to a varying annual quit-rent for a surveyed area. This was designed to encourage more permanent settlement and to facilitate regular sale and transfer, but the annual charge was somewhat higher than before, and farmers had to bear the cost of survey to obtain title-deeds; delay in the issue of titles was a further grievance, and in 1832 the Government tightened the control of Crown Lands.

Land-hunger was thus at least one motive inspiring the so-called *commissie* treks, the reconnaissances of 1834.[1] Even in the less attractive north, which had for a while relieved the pressure, the farmers were now baulked by the new tenderness of the authorities for coloured people's rights. The Griquas of those parts readily enough exchanged grazing rights for oxen if not for guns, or brandy; but in the early thirties the Government, on the representations of the missionaries, for the first time decisively refused[2] to make the time-honoured recognition of effective Boer occupation by extending the boundary to give legal title to farms in 'Griqualand', as had been done so lately as 1826 when the boundary was fixed at the Orange River. Shortly afterwards, to add insult to injury, the Griquas, unlike the Boers, were recognized as a 'free' people though they themselves were only slightly earlier emigrants from the Colony whose normal expansion they now barred. A good deal more was yet to be heard of missionary efforts on Griqua behalf (see Chs. XIII and XIV, below).

The presence of the Griquas was one reason why from the very beginning the mass of the trekkers moved so far away, instead of planting their secession states on the reputedly 'empty' land immediately adjoining the parent Colony. In order to avoid the great mountain knot of the Drakensberg, north of Kaffirland, the streams of Trekkers always tended in the first

[1] Even the western districts were mildly affected. As late as 1847 the Civil Commissioner of Swellendam reported that though 'not many were likely to be affected by the proposal to go to the Mooi River (Potchefstroom) or the Vaal', yet farmers were restless. The reasons he gave were strikingly like those still operative in the 1920's—ten or twelve families crowded on to one farm, with consequent shortage of grazing and of water, and overstocking, at the same time that the relatively high price of land made relief by land-purchase difficult.

[2] Bird, i. 272, for Cilliers's reference to the rejection of a petition from seventy-two householders. Philip MSS.: Memo. on 'Causes of the Boer Emigration'.

instance to converge on Philippolis. But to settle there was another matter. Individual Griquas indeed readily enough granted the Boers leases, but the 'Captains' disapproved of this practice. Had Griqualand been fertile and well-watered the Boers might have run the risk of coming to blows with the only other people in the country armed like themselves with guns, and even of continued friction with the British Government. But this arid country was not after all very alluring, and the double risk drove the Boers farther afield. Once they had taken the further plunge into the beyond, they found themselves on the true *high veld*, the *platteland*, the well-watered country of the upper Vaal River where, thanks to the regular summer rain-fall, the natural ground-cover is no longer scrub but *grass*. They also too readily allowed themselves to hope that after the 'devastations' of the Chaka wars there would be room for many of them, in spite of the Zulus, in the much more genial climate of Natal.

The wide open spaces of the High Veld proper were unques-tionably capable of supporting many more inhabitants, but the firmly-rooted tradition that this country of the trekkers' choice was 'empty' calls for drastic revision. For a moment they them-selves thoroughly accepted the reports of the *commissies* of 1834. Trigardt, for example, in the Zoutpansberg, seems hardly to have been aware of the activities (above, p. 33) of the formidable Moselekatze; he even wondered at the delay of Potgieter and others who were to have joined him there but were rudely in-terrupted by the Matabele in the very heart of the 'empty' High Veld; chance travellers over that huge inland plateau were almost bound to get the impression that they had it all to them-selves. Here and there, after the Chaka wars, they were likely to find human bones and the charred ruins of huts and villages to suggest that the solitude was due to depopulation wrought by man. But much depends on what is being looked for. Dr. Philip, for example, concerned to observe and report upon the facts of Boer emigration, wrote on his 1832 tour of finding 1,200 or 1,500 Boers 'beyond the Colony'; his figures, not to be taken as a precise record,[1] are evidence perhaps that the number of Boers was surprisingly large. On the other hand Boers and

---

[1] Field-cornet Ziervogel in 1835 found '62 families' in the same area (Cory, iii. 257).

other prospective settlers were looking for land unoccupied by potential enemies and undoubtedly believed they had found it. Their evidence does no more than support the view that the Bantu were relatively few[1]—the modern traveller by road or rail might equally well get a similar impression of the emptiness of great stretches of the most highly developed districts in central South Africa. The great plateau of the High Veld is most of it very flat, treeless, open, grass country, with uninterrupted views over immense distances. Its exposure to cold winter winds, the want of shelter for cattle, and, in those unsettled times, the difficulty of lying hidden from human enemies, made it very little attractive to the Bantu tribes except for summer grazing. At any rate those remaining were much weakened by the late wars.

For large numbers the conditions were perhaps neither safe nor comfortable. But the open plains are frequently broken by low ridges, shallow depressions (*leegtes*) and clefts (or *kloofs*); the *kloofs* and *leegtes*, especially those with a north exposure, have patches of sheltering and serviceable bush, and are most likely to have permanent water; in such spots refugees undoubtedly sought refuge and security.[2] And it was precisely these scattered spots that were likely to attract the Boer farmers, to the deprivation of such natives as remained. So far from finding the country empty the trekkers had their first great meeting at Thaba N'Chu, a Wesleyan mission station among Moroko's Barolong; not far off lay 'remnants' of Mantatees under Sikonyela; and the first trekker capital, Winburg, was planted on land 'ceded' by a chief of the Bataung 'in exchange for a troop of cattle and the promise of protection' against the Matabele.[3] The Boers were to strive, and frequently to fight, for many years to clear the eastern Free State of natives professing allegiance to the great Basuto chief, Moshesh, who was strongly ensconced in the

---

[1] The narratives of travellers before the Trek leave a distinct impression that they were constantly meeting 'natives' of one sort or another in a country that was by no means 'empty'. Living tradition indicated that in the sixties and seventies, when the storm had blown over, 'danger from Kafirs' was one of the normal risks of travel even on the High Veld. (See also p. 341 n. 3.)

[2] Strong tradition suggests that native kraals existed at such places as Heidelberg Kloof, the valley under Aasvogel Kop, near Johannesburg, and in sheltered parts of Free State river valleys. That there were also Bushmen and Bushmen children to be 'apprenticed' by the Trekkers (cf. Walker, pp. 212, 213) certainly indicated that the indigenous population was sparse.   [3] *Gie*, ii. 302.

foothills of the Drakensberg. Even in the southern Transvaal early Trekker history is one long story of friction with native chiefs from whom the Boers obtained 'title' by 'treaties'. The open High Veld, therefore, was 'empty' only in the sense that its Bantu, other than the newly arrived Matabele, were as utterly powerless against the white man as the eighteenth-century Hottentots of the Cape Colony—to whose plight trekker 'protection' in time reduced their off-spring, a huge, seldom ill-used but always under-privileged landless proletariat of 'farm natives.'

Only the Matabele were at once a real danger on the High Veld, and they were soon disposed of. Trigardt in the first place steered wide of Moselekatze, but early in 1836 a party of trekkers known as the Liebenbergs were massacred near the Vaal River—Moselekatze, suspecting that there would be no room in that country for him if the Boers once got a footing, had struck betimes. In the same year Sarel Cilliers and Potgieter had to beat off a heavy attack at Vechtkop in the northern Free State, losing their food and cattle. Other encounters cost more Boer lives and led the Boers to take the offensive. Early in 1837 their forces surprised his kraal at Mosega, inflicted heavy losses without losing any of their own men, and recaptured wagons and cattle. In November of the same year Potgieter and Uys made the running so hot that Moselekatze was presently forced to withdraw from the Marico to beyond the Limpopo. This was the end. In 1829 Moselekatze had been visited by Dr. Moffat near the site of Pretoria—whence, apparently, the earlier raids on the Boers. Mosega is far west, on the Bechuanaland border; and the next real stop was only when the tribe had moved *en masse* to become the founders of new 'Matabeleland' (in Southern Rhodesia), thus leaving the Trekkers undisputed masters of virtually the whole of the High Veld.

The scene of the most important activities of the trekkers now changed to Natal which, they had heard, had been 'cleared' of natives by the inter-tribal wars. Piet Retief was elected Commandant-General, and the beginnings of organization, to-gether with their success in chastising Moselekatze, gave the Boers self-confidence; perhaps the well-watered pastures and genial climate of the coastal province made even a clash with the Zulu power worth risking—some of those who had suffered from the Matabele may have felt that the danger could hardly be greater than they had already faced in the north. In the end disputes and rivalry among the leaders themselves decided the issue, and in October 1837, while Potgieter went north to complete the Matabele rout, Piet Retief made the mighty mountain crossing. He trusted to diplomacy to secure from the Zulu chief, Dingaan, a grant of land for another Trekker Republic in Natal.

The Zulus soon made it tragically clear that the trekkers were unwelcome. When Retief first approached Dingaan with his plaint that the colonial farmers were short of land[1] the Zulu, with characteristic Bantu evasion, made his negative indirect. Sikonyela, he said, the Mantatee across the mountains, had stolen 900 of the king's cattle; if the farmers would recover these then they might talk business. Not for the first or last time, the farmers rashly chose to run counter to modern notions of what is expedient and allowed themselves to take sides in a purely Bantu quarrel. In the fatal February of 1838 Retief and some sixty companions, having fulfilled their side of the bargain, returned to conclude the 'treaty' by which Dingaan 'ceded' them the whole of Natal. The chief, however, had different plans, and to him the treaty was but another piece of temporizing. As the episode of Sikonyela's cattle shows, the Zulus were in touch with the people beyond the mountains and knew of the trekkers' doings there;[2] by Retief's

---

[1] 'Our country is small, and we becoming numerous can no longer subsist here...' (D. P. Bezuidenhout's account in Bird, i. 368).

[2] From native sources in Basutoland, Dr. Philip, in Feb. 1842, got an incidental sidelight on Dingaan's murder of Retief. Among the witnesses of Retief's 'recovery' of cattle from Sikonyela, in accordance with his bargain with Dingaan, there was, it appears, one of Dingaan's councillors. Having once got Sikonyela into their power, 'the Boers assumed the fact that he had been guilty of the theft and demanded the stolen cattle, with others as a fine ... forced him into the house of the missionary, in which they bound him, and threatened to carry him to Dingaan ... [keeping him bound for three days, to the] surprise and indignation even of the Zulus, whose respect for their chiefs was shocked by such treatment. . . . "Is this the way in which you treat the chiefs of the people?" one asked. Being answered in the affirmative with coarse and offensive expressions, he asked, "Would you treat Dingaan in this way were he in your power?" To this they made reply: "We shall treat Dingaan in the same manner should we find him to be a rogue." From that moment Dingaan's councillor became restless and uneasy, and as soon as it became dark he disappeared, proceeded with speed to Dingaan, related his story, along with his own impression; and the chief taking fear from his councillor, had made his preparation

own mouth they had news of the defeat of their rebel kinsmen, the Matabele. Now these fellows that were turning the world upside-down were come hither also and Dingaan, as all the world knows, took the shortest way with them. The whole party of those who had put themselves in his power were brutally butchered. Immediately afterwards he sent his *impis* to complete the work by attacks on the Boers in their own camps; a large party were surprised in laager on the site of Weenen (Weeping), where even women and children were massacred. This and further losses elsewhere threw the tenuous Boer organization into utter confusion. Potgieter had come to the rescue, but his first and last love was the Transvaal and he withdrew from Natal altogether; he could not work with the other leaders and designed to found a state of his own. In the course of the year 1838 Boer losses at the hands of the Zulus were not fewer than 362 men, women, and children, besides more than 200 coloured and Bantu servants and 13 English allies—a fearfully high proportion of the very few thousands who had made the Natal venture.[1]

This could not be the last word. The British authorities in Cape Town were filled with anxiety about possible reactions on the Xhosa front, but before they took any action the Trekkers had marshalled their own forces under a new and vigorous leader, Andries Pretorius. Reinforcements came from the Cape to help their fellows in distress and share their fortunes. On a famous date, 16 December (which they vowed to make a national holiday), the Trekkers met and routed Dingaan's army, without loss to themselves, but with such heavy punishment, they claimed, that the river ran with blood (whence Blood River to this day). Six months later, with some diplomatic help from a British agent, Pretorius forced Dingaan to accept a new treaty by which the Zulus recognized Boer claims in a very much enlarged Natal and undertook to pay reparations. Dingaan was no more to be trusted now than eighteen months earlier but, like other tyrants, he had enemies in his own household, and again the Boers seized their opportunity of applying the principle *divide et impera*. They now gave their

for the destruction of Maritz (Retief?) and his party before their arrival with the cattle' (cf. account in *Owen's Diary*, van Riebeeck Society, p. 170).
[1] Preller's *Voortrekkermense*, ii. 52.

support to Dingaan's chief rival, Panda, and encouraged civil war. Early in 1840 Dingaan was defeated, driven into exile in Swaziland, and there murdered. Panda was then recognized as paramount of the Zulus but remained a vassal of the new Boer republic. So within three years the Boers had broken the power of the only two considerable military monarchs in the whole of Bantudom.

But the conquest threw on the victors a more searching test. They had now to deal not only with opposition in the field, but with the puzzle of governing both old opponents and the weaker tribes, the 'surplus' masses who were capable only of indirect resistance by the method of cattle-lifting. The comings and goings in Zululand, or with the Zulus, were the least of it. The Trekkers were now to find that Natal was even less than the Transvaal the 'empty' Elysium they had pictured. Since 1824 English traders and adventurers had had a tiny settlement at Port Natal and occasional dealings with the Zulu potentate Chaka, as well as with his successor, Dingaan. When Retief arrived at Port Natal in 1837 the traders' leader, Captain Gardiner, an ex-naval officer, exercised a vague magisterial authority; the Rev. F. Owen of the Church Missionary Society had a footing at Dingaan's kraal; and about that time American missionaries advised by Dr. Philip were preparing to work among the 'Zoolahs'. In 1835 Gardiner, who had won the support of D'Urban, gave the port the Governor's name but failed to persuade the Home Government to take Natal under its wing.

The Zulu centre lay beyond the Tugela, in districts which included the present Vryheid. The story goes that, presently, 50,000 to 80,000 natives were found to be 'filtering' from Zululand into Natal. It is difficult to see how the Zulus in possession, who had large herds,[1] could have made room for so many dependants—the legend that Natal had been 'cleared' of its native population probably originated with travellers who, on their way through Natal, naturally saw only the central and northern uplands. Great stretches of the country are virtually *high veld* but here at frequent intervals there are secluded bushy valleys. These spots lie for the most part off even modern main roads, and are still, some of them, roadless and inaccessible

---

[1] Cf. Agar-Hamilton, p. 34.

native reserves. In time of stress, and even for choice, natives other than the organized Zulus can never, many of them, have been much farther away than the 'Valley of a Thousand Hills' (admired from afar by modern travellers between Maritzburg and Durban), or the dense bush north of Greytown, the rugged upper valleys of the Mooi and Tugela Rivers, the Umkomaas Valley, and other similar havens of refuge in the very heart of Natal proper.

The overthrow of Dingaan was an undoubted boon to the peaceful natives, allowing the weaker tribes once more to range abroad with less restraint, outside the bushy valleys in which they had been forced to seek refuge and lie low. But the reduced pressure from above created also a strong demand for land. The Boers were glad enough to have a supply of labourers—even squatters who would, with their women and children, supply their labour needs in return for permission to work a piece of the farm—but they soon suffered an *embarras de richesse*. As early as 5 August 1840 the new-fledged *Volksraad* passed the first of a long series of *Plakkers' Wetten* (Squatters' Laws) restricting the allowance of squatters on any one farm, other than that of the Commandant General, to *five families*. If restriction was thus found so urgent, clearly far more than the average of five families were there to be dealt with or provided for. The allowance of five families became a habit. In the 1920's an unrepealed Transvaal Law of 1885 still limited squatters on any one farm to five families—the limitation had never been enforced for the reason that the 'reserves' have never yet allowed for the 'surplus' Bantu population. An American missionary, Mr. Aldin Grout, wrote to the Governor of the situation in Natal in February 1844:

Whatever may be said of previous occupation, the British Government found the people in the Natal district, or they allowed them to locate themselves there, and I am afraid that the Government will find it necessary to provide for them in one way or another.

In 1841 the Natal Volksraad, nothing daunted, returned to the charge with a resolution proposing to deal with the 'influx' by a measure of 'segregation' (in terms much current in the 1960's!). Obviously these natives must either have been returning to their homes, or else were discovered, the moment the

Trekkers broke up their commandos and dispersed to their farms, to have been in the country all the time. The 'surplus' were now to be dumped to the south of the Republic between the Umtamvuna and Umzimvubu Rivers, on territory claimed with reasonable justification by the Pondo chief Faku—a claim the Boers did not waste time in investigating. The numbers of the natives in Natal were in fact an unlooked-for embarrassment and imposed on them a task of government for which they were unprepared, and indeed unfitted. From the very beginning the Trekkers found themselves worse off than in the old Cape. There the thieves were on one side of them only, here they were on all sides at once. In 1845, when at last the British Government had definitely intervened and annexed Natal—when, moreover, the tiny European population was again reduced by an exodus of discontented Boers—the Government was faced with the problem of ruling not 20,000 but 100,000 natives.[1]

This old underestimate of the native population, in the Trekker States generally, probably still tends to vitiate sound thinking. The statistics of slaughter in the Chaka wars are little more scientific than Herodotus' fabulous estimate of the size of Xerxes' army. The troubles in which all the Trekker States were at once involved are proof positive that in the thirties the natives were far more numerous than was commonly believed. The pendulum has now swung back. The modern counterpart (and consequence) of the rooted belief in the wiping out of the Bantu by the Chaka wars came to be the tendency to exaggerate the rate of increase of the Bantu population. The latter-day 'increase' and the fear that Europeans must soon be 'swamped' are correspondingly magnified.

No doubt the Trekkers as a whole wanted only a quiet life. Conquest of the Bantu was no premeditated part of their programme; what they did was for self-protection. The Trekker way with the natives was individual discipline for farm servants (with no legal protection), and the old 'commando system' for the recalcitrant. An affair with the Baca chief Ncapaai illustrates Boer methods. Farmers on the southern border complained of cattle-stealing and traced the spoor to the kraals of this chief, a rival of the Pondo, Faku. In January

[1] Cf. Brookes, pp. 24, 25.

1841 a commando under Pretorius fell suddenly upon Ncapaai and without stopping to investigate the charge against him carried off some 3,000 head of cattle,[1] besides 17 'apprentices'. Faku, fearing his turn might come next, appealed for British protection. The authorities were loath to move, but two years of wars, and civil wars, inevitably had unsettling reactions elsewhere. In mid-1837 Captain Stretch and others reported peace and quiet on the Cape frontier; to the Rev. James Read (whom he last met on the 'Hottentot Parade' in Grahamstown) he writes: 'We are quiet and there is less stealing than has been known for many years past, which is convincing evidence that the chiefs can preserve the colony if they are allowed to go on without commandos continually entering their country.' But when Boer fortunes were lowest, Dr. Philip, fresh from England, wrote on 1 June 1838 to Dr. Thomas Hodgkin, of the Anti-Slavery Society, expressing alarm at 'the discovery of their power and the use to be made of it, by Dingaan and Moselekatze'. Yet, he adds, the Boer emigration continues. 'Compensation money has turned their heads, and they turn it into powder and shot to expel the Canaanite from the Land of Promise. . . . The only part I am taking is that of a spectator, and my only resource is prayer.' A year later unrest in Natal was having its effect and by 1839 there were ominous rumblings of the quarrels of Ncapaai and Faku on the Cape side of Natal; by October 1840 Governor Napier feared the worst for the Stockenström system when he found the whole Xhosa frontier in a ferment.

The immense widening of the area of contact and conflict with the Bantu tribes is indeed the outstanding consequence of the Great Trek, and the aspect most consistently ignored. Most of the difficulty on the old Cape frontier before 1834 arose from the refusal of successive governments to face the problem of setting up a civil administration to control the relations of colonists and natives. The establishment of a settled frontier government now devolved on a scattered community of farmers who had in truth only their guns to trust to; having no vestige of a professional class, the new states were almost utterly lacking in political and administrative experience. There being

---

[1] The 3,000 head, far more than Ncapaai's alleged 'theft', were designed to 'pay the expenses' of the expedition (Agar-Hamilton, p. 142).

no longer even a nominal *line* of frontier, farmers were for the first time settled actually *among* the Bantu they succeeded really only in rendering helpless; being much isolated they were vaguely nervous, yet took no responsibility for the well-being of their involuntary subjects. So far were the governments from being able to hold a fair balance that the conquered Bantu were subject in practice to the caprice of individual Boer masters. All but irresponsible adventurers among these accepted the prohibition of slavery, but the slave-owner mentality persisted which could hardly conceive of an educated 'Kaffir', or of an order of society in which 'Kaffirs' had legally enforceable rights. The argument was often heard in 1910 that only a single, united South African Government could hope to deal effectively with the twentieth-century Native Problem; but the need for unity of control was still more clamant in 1840, when it was also more possible. The powers, the coherence, the machinery and resources of the mushroom republics, then and for a long time to come, were such that only the Government at the Cape could even have tried seriously to control the situation as a whole, as was so necessary. In the later forties the British Government looked momentarily like accepting some part of its responsibility. We shall see how in the early fifties Her Majesty's Government, having started on its task, was turned aside. The tangled skein left for the twentieth century to unravel is a direct consequence.

The emigrant Boers in the thirties and forties were after all undoubtedly still British subjects. At the very beginning Lord Glenelg himself (29 October 1837) scouted as naïve their plea to be treated as 'a separate colony'. The claim was 'so extravagant that I can hardly suppose it serious; they are subjects of the Queen, who put themselves beyond her protection, and if reports be true, they are no longer useful citizens but freebooters'. But to bring Government and subjects into effective relationship over the wide spaces of South Africa demanded more than pious assertions: it needed administration, a strong efficient system of magistrates and police such as the Trekkers could not and the British Government would not be at the expense of providing. In times of peace the Cape Colony barely paid its own way and Her Majesty's Government now set its face against extending its responsibility to cover the cost of social disturbance, if not of more wars, which the action of its own subjects made inevitable. In other words, the very weakness and irresponsibility of these Bantu neighbours were the warrant for letting alone.

In spite even of the Aborigines Report (below, p. 212) the facile plan that came into vogue about 1835 still ruled, that *treaties* were to be concluded with African (as with Indian) potentates, defining the boundaries of their territories and recognizing them as 'allies' in the task of preserving stability. The first of a long series was the treaty with the Griqua Waterboer in December 1834. Early in 1836 Dr. Andrew Smith, a well-known medical traveller, gave less formal recognition to the Matabele, Moselekatze—to the great satisfaction of the Secretary of State who (on 3 September) fondly hoped such treaties might suffice to 'cultivate an amicable intercourse with the Colony', and thus at once to secure peace, and 'to promote civilization among the tribes on our immediate frontier'. The Stockenström treaties with the tribes on the eastern frontier were thus not isolated experiments but part of a set policy. Stockenström himself (above, p. 180) advocated treaties on the ground that, while outright annexation was likely to be welcomed by people like the Griquas who were sufficiently advanced to appreciate the advantages of civilized government, such action might provoke resentment and rebellion if applied prematurely to self-contained Bantu tribes. It had been his intention, he wrote, 'to enter into alliances with all tribes with whom we were likely to come into contact, and who were strong enough to have, or to organize and maintain, a government of their own'; the basis of such agreement was to be the '*acknowledgement of the right to the territory of its then actual possessors*'. Ultimately, he hoped, they would 'see cause and be glad to throw up their independence and embrace British supremacy'.

'Wherever British subjects have already settled,' Stockenström continued, 'or the tribes are broken and weak', the British Government ought to take control. This was likely to be opposed both on the grounds of expense and as appearing to sanction 'dispossession'. But it would be better than the alternative, 'extermination', and in any event, Stockenström concluded, till the *system* is settled 'no sort of title (for British subjects) to any of the land ought to be either directly or tacitly admitted . . . and then only by purchase'. As a consequence of Stockenström's personal distractions in the time of his lieuten-ant-governorship his plans were never really tried out; this was in no way because in 1837 the Aborigines Report had expressly, and vainly, entered its warning against 'compacts between parties negotiating on terms of such disparity [as were likely to make these] rather the preparatives and the apology for dispute than securities for peace'. Yet treaties became and remained so much the established policy of the Colonial Office that the experiment in the forties, still known as 'Dr. Philip's Treaty States' (see below, Ch. XIV), and the outcome of his 'interfer-ence', were the most his urgent representations were able to wrest from a reluctant Government.

Before ever the Great Trek had developed, and as a comple-ment to treaties, the Government had already enacted, for the compassing of the occasional actual evil-doer, the measure known as the Cape of Good Hope Punishment Act. This Act 'for the punishment of crimes'—and saving the 'sovereign' rights of tribes or rulers—made the Cape Laws applicable to offences committed by any of His Majesty's subjects in territory adjacent to the Colony 'to the southward of the 25th degree of South latitude', providing at the same time for the grant of commissions to persons to act as magistrates for the prevention of crimes and the bringing of offenders *and witnesses* to justice *on British soil*. Inevitably the Act was a dead-letter.[1] Magis-trates under the Act were few and far between, their effective power negligible. The Boer advance, even their proscriptive colonization of Bantu land, was in no sense a 'crime'. The only remedy for untoward results was to establish some strong authority capable of governing civil intercourse between an advanced and a backward people.

D'Urban's successor, Sir George Napier, soon concluded that nothing short of the annexation of Natal, and strong govern-ment, could meet the situation. The Punishment Act was irrelevant and the Trekkers themselves were adepts at 'treaties', which were really deeds of *cession*. For this reason the murder of Retief, who had a newly signed treaty in his wallet, wrung from

---

[1] Cf. complaint by Rawstorne, the officer in charge at Colesberg: 'I beg to express regret that the Act of 1836 has been allowed to remain unemployed' (to Govern-ment Secretary, 18 Sept. 1840).

Lord Glenelg nervous and qualified permission to intervene. In the end of 1838 a company of British troops was sent to occupy Port Natal. At that moment the Boers' fortunes revived; Dingaan was overwhelmed at the Blood River. A year later Governor Napier found it necessary to withdraw his troops and, left to themselves, the Boers had been able to settle accounts with the Zulus, to establish Panda in place of Dingaan, and to secure from their vassal the cession of an even larger Natal than before.

At this point the official British attitude began to stiffen. Lord Normanby and Lord John Russell (1839) were stronger secretaries than Lord Glenelg and, after 1841, the Tory Ministry, with Lord Stanley at the Colonial Office, was more conscious and watchful of British interests. As early as June 1839 Lord Normanby had ordered an investigation of reports of surface coal in Natal as of potential importance to 'steam navigation'. In August 1841 an American ship appeared at Port Natal, and in 1842 the intrigues of a Hollander adventurer named Smellekamp, who made various descents upon the coast in a Dutch brig, roused hopes in the minds of the Trekkers of Dutch protection and support. The novel interest shown at the Admiralty, an influential Department, in the possibilities of Natal strengthened the hand of the Colonial Office; but just then the humanitarian interests, their only potential allies in matters affecting only the interests of native tribes, were either engrossed in those of an ill-starred philanthropic expedition up the Niger, or merely silent.[1] Very little first-hand information about the doings and effects of the Great Trek was in fact to reach the outside world till after the middle of 1842 when Dr. Philip returned, full of it, from the greatest of his tours, an eleven months' pilgrimage through much of the country north of the Orange River.

Meantime, in December 1839, just when Sir George Napier had decided to withdraw his skeleton force from Port Natal, Lord John Russell penned the first of a number of dispatches which showed some weakening of the will to resist intervention; six months later[2] Russell expressly ordered immediate

---

[1] The Philip MSS. may have been incomplete for the years 1839–41, but Dr. Philip would seem to have been absorbed by the domestic affairs of the missions and of his church in Cape Town.   [2] 18 June 1840 (Bird, i. 605).

reoccupation; but Napier—unwilling to weaken his garrison on his eastern frontier by the removal of a force of the strength which experience suggested to be necessary—used his discretion and held his hand. Early in 1841 the affair of Ncapaai, and Faku's appeal, induced him to order a force under Captain Smith to advance into Pondoland for the protection of Faku. In the middle of the year the Volksraad's threatened experiment in 'segregation' caused further alarm for the security of the Cape frontier and, after yet another dispatch from Lord John Russell, Napier at last ordered the reoccupation of the port. This time the Boers proved less friendly—or more sure of themselves; in May and June 1842 Captain Smith, who had moved up from Pondoland, was besieged in his camp near Durban. Only after one Dick King had made a famous and desperate cross-country ride to Grahamstown to give the alarm Smith's little force was relieved by the frigate *Southampton*.

The Boer resistance then collapsed, but now the Government held back; in January Mr. James Stephen had written a minute for his new Tory chief, Lord Stanley:

It is very ill policy to enlarge this ill-peopled and unprofitable colony and . . . to make a new settlement at Port Natal where there is not even an accessible port or a safe roadstead . . . [with a danger also of] warfare alike inglorious, unprofitable and afflicting.[1]

On 10 April Stanley followed Stephen and renewed the offer of amnesty to all Boers who would return. Napier then confidentially (25 July) urged the need for the annexation at least of coastal Natal; a month later Dr. Philip's report led him to press for action in the north as well. In December Stanley gave way, decided against the recognition of Boer independence, and agreed to the annexation of Natal. In June 1843 Mr. Henry Cloete was commissioned to proceed to Maritzburg and negotiate a definite settlement with Boers. He found them wavering, prepared to agree that slavery must cease, and even that military action against the natives should be undertaken only with Government sanction. But it was also proclaimed:

There shall not be in the eye of the law any distinction or disqualification whatever founded upon mere distinction of colour, origin, language or creed, but the protection of the law, in letter and in substance, shall be extended impartially to all alike.

[1] Colonial Office 48/214. Public Record Office.

The words were the starkest possible enunciation of the principle which, as formerly applied, had served above anything else to give the Great Trek its truly revolutionary fervour; this was indeed *gelijkstelling*, forced and as it seemed to the Boers even scandalous 'equality' of black and white.[1] By 8 August a Rump of the Volksraad at Maritzburg had despairingly accepted even this condition, but not long afterwards this body ceased to function, and died. Commissioner Cloete struggled on with problems of land settlement till August 1845 when Natal received its own Lieutenant-Governor and entered on a period of eleven years as a separate district, dependent on the Governor and Council of the Cape of Good Hope. But by this time a large proportion of the Trekkers had withdrawn to asylum across the Drakensberg, and the centre of interest and activity shifted to the country of the Orange and the Vaal.

[1] Cf. comments of Dr. S. F. N. Gie in *Gie*, ii. 341.

XIII

THE TREKKERS IN THE NORTH—
GRIQUAS, BASUTO, BECHUANA, AND
DR. PHILIP'S GRAND TOUR, 1841–2

THE serious political and social repercussions of the Great Trek
more quickly made themselves felt in the relatively confined
space of Natal than on the High Veld. All the emigrants were
British subjects who, renouncing their former citizenship,
'asked only to be left alone'. Their Government's difficulty
about accepting this simple solution was complex; unlike the
Trekkers, the only responsible government in the land could
not merely ignore the presence of a large indigenous population
and leave them without any recognized legal status to face
the expansive Boer way of life which must leave them without
secure homes of their own. In the end intervention became inevitable when events proved the indigenous peoples capable of
resistance, whether murderous like that of Dingaan or, like
Ncapaai's, only by cattle-reiving. Chronic disturbance and
even overt war so near its own troubled eastern frontier at any
rate gradually awakened the Cape Government to see the
doings of its errant subjects as a serious threat to its own internal peace. If it is asked why the Government which had
lately 'recognized' earlier emigrants like the Griquas refused to
recognize the Boers it must be said that, in spite of their treatment of the Bushman aboriginals, the continuance of the
Griquas on their Orange River lands was now the only hope of
stability—a mere recognition of the *status quo*; but to recognize
the Trekkers' government either in Natal or beyond the Orange
River would be to pronounce a sentence of deprivation on the
coloured people who were there before them. This unorganized
body of farmers was expressly repudiating the laws enacted
lately by the Government for the protection of the coloured
races, and was entirely without efficient law-courts of their own.
It was many years before any of the Trekker Republics was in a
position to satisfy, even for Europeans, the accepted canons and

obligations of 'independence' once summarized by M. Clem-
enceau as 'those elementary rights of all its subjects which are,
as a matter of fact, secured in every civilized state'. In the
forties, and long after, all such rights were expressly denied to
'people of colour', as such.

Events on the High Veld developed more slowly than in
Natal. Except in the foothills of the Drakensberg climatic conditions may have made dense population impossible; but there
was no geographical obstacle to impede free movement—so
when Boers from the Colony began to spread slowly over this
area, mere distance made for the development of distinct communities almost as completely out of touch with one another as
with the parent Colony. Before 1836, therefore, and for some
years afterwards, northern developments created little stir;
there was no danger of international complications or of British
naval interests being compromised as in Natal. Yet it was here
the future of South Africa was perhaps decided. The original
Bantu population of the High Veld proper, though habitually
underestimated, was relatively small, and the comparative
absence of native opposition steadily attracted white settlement.
In time these High Veld settlers extended their authority over a
vast Bantu population, including those either indigenous to the
Transvaal *bush veld* or driven there from without. None could
guess that, eventually, the whites of the High Veld would not
only rule directly some 44 per cent. of the total African population, but become so strong as to a great extent to determine the
characteristic outlook upon its so-called 'Native Problem' of
the predominant part of the South African electorate.

Any pre-Trek colonization of the High Veld there had been
was by colonial farmers pushing out, after the manner of the
eighteenth century, in search of pasture. Unlike the so-called
Voortrekkers of 1836, these men had no violent political bias and
no burning wish to escape from British control. For a good many
years, indeed, the settlers of the southern 'Free State', under
Michiel Oberholster, made a distinct party sharply opposed to
the die-hard Trekkers under Jan Mocke who pressed on
beyond them to Winburg, and in greater numbers to the Transvaal. Oberholster's men were sometimes called 'loyalists'; with
them at least a satisfactory and amicable settlement ought to
have been possible.

The Bantu to be considered were at once few and weak; with goodwill, and some contrivance, there was ample room for many more people, black or white. The Griquas of the Orange River were estimated about 1840 at barely 5,000 in all. The Basuto were a good deal more numerous than the Barolong and Mantatees of the central area, but even then were largely concentrated in one compact eastern area under one strong chief. The remoter north and west had a more considerable sprinkling of Sechuana-speaking tribes than the very sparse modern population of British Bechuanaland and the Protectorate would suggest; Sechuana is still the language of the very considerable 'farm native' population of the western Transvaal, much of which was conquered from these tribes only in the fifties. But the causes of division lie beneath the surface, being in the first place economic. The Scots artisan missionary, James Clark, a shrewd observer, urged on Dr. Philip in 1841 the desirability of instruction in weaving 'as an industry for leisure hours and to teach regular habits'; his motive was that while 'at the colonial stations even the women can get plenty to do', at such a distance from any market the people were necessarily pastoral, and employment scarce. Thus the Moffats' letters from Kuruman in the thirties and forties often speak of parties of Bechuana going to or returning from work in the Colony. Moshesh, in his talk with Dr. Philip at Thaba Bosigo in February 1842, expressed appreciation of the protection afforded by the Colonial laws, contrasting the defencelessness of his people in the surrounding country. In the Colony,

if they enter into a contract for a year they are not detained beyond that period; if they enter into an agreement their wages are paid; if they are beaten by their masters they can apply to a magistrate for redress. *They return home with the cattle they have earned.*

In other words, even then, as this direct evidence confirms, the northern peoples were glad to improve their living by wage-earning. The immediate effect of the scarcity of employment near at hand was that Griquas and Bantu alike were very ready, for present gain, and without any idea of the ultimate cost, to give settlers permission to use their springs and land. At the next stage the Boers, once they were established, suffered from the same economic disabilities, absorbed more and more land by way of remedy, and very soon left too little to meet the needs of the original population. Only the demarcation of inalienable 'reserves' by a strong government could have saved the situation. The farmers, and the whole of South Africa, must have benefited immeasurably had they been forced thus early to more intensive occupation and, in one missionary's words, to make '*permanent* settlements'.[1] We might then have begun to learn the truth of the paradox that much of South Africa is 'unable to support a larger population *because* its population is so scanty'. Few were so far-seeing as to seek this solution. The farmers at any rate showed no will to find it.

The economic background to these early phases of South African growth has perhaps seemed too obvious to get serious attention. But the neglect may be in part at least because according to the 'authorized version' a second divisive influence was solely responsible for all that ever went wrong. It never entered the heads of the northern farmers that those who were in possession before them had needs not merely as individuals but as societies, primitive perhaps, and yet *societies*. When missionaries took it on themselves to give utterance to such a view they were indeed 'interfering'. The pre-Trek settlers, hard beset by difficulties, were in no wise politically malcontent; but they had to struggle so hard for their own existence that they had no time for refinements. To their eighteenth-century traditions and ways of thinking the Griquas were of no more account than the Hottentots and Bushmen whom their fathers had displaced before them. So far as it had views at all the Dutch East India Company had been of the Boer way of thinking. But now the new factor vitally affected the issue. The older Hottentots had had no spokesman; but the very weakness and unwarlike bearing of the Griquas, the Bechuana, and the Basuto was the missions' opportunity and brought it about that, unlike Natal, the lonely High Veld was linked by a continuous chain of mission stations which were standing witnesses of a newer world outlook. From these centres the rights of the

---

[1] 'The roving disposition so universal among the colonial farmers exerts its influence upon our Griqua people . . . who leave their farms on which, with some labour, they could subsist, to go in search of stronger springs, to places, away from the station, where less labour is required and game is more abundant. Could they be induced to build substantial homes this might be checked. . . . It is our constant endeavour to portray the advantages of *permanent* settlements and industrious habits' (P. Kolbe to Philip, July 1835).

coloured peoples were steadily proclaimed. The Government was itself no longer insensible of its obligation to stand by the principles of its own reforming measures in the parent colony; it was no less important that the missionaries provided regular current frontier news. The Griqua communities—'states' they were not—had grown out of the London missionaries' attempt to fix a nomadic people in villages; they stretched from Bethulie westwards to Griquatown, with Colesberg as at once a base and a colonial outpost. Beyond them to the north-west Robert Moffat and other L.M.S. men worked among the Bechuana. To the north-east French missionaries, in close alliance with the L.M.S. through their common local agent, Dr. Philip, had stations among the Basuto—one at Moshesh's stronghold, Thaba Bosigo. For a while, first Americans, and then Francis Owen of the Church Missionary Society, the eyewitness of the murder of Retief, worked at Mosega, Moselekatze's halt on the Marico. Finally the Wesleyans, though somewhat aloof from their brethren, were established as patrons of Moroko and Sikonyela, petty chiefs of the middle east, weaker rivals of Moshesh. It hardly matters that the missionaries were not always at harmony among themselves; the important independent evidence they furnished was the new and direct means of drawing attention to events in these parts.

The Griquatown of Waterboer was strategically perhaps the least important of all the coloured communities,[1] yet in 1834 it alone was given official recognition and support. The real storm centre was Philippolis, and its history illustrates at once the economic complexities of the High Veld and, in the end, the hopelessness of the attempt to leave the control of black and white relations to any petty coloured chieftain. By ill chance, the death of the elder Adam Kok in 1835 gave rise to a disputed succession and at this most critical juncture the rival claims of Abram and a younger Adam Kok—which were not unconnected with the comings and goings of new-comers—left the district without any settled authority to complete the 'treaty' still vaguely contemplated by the Government.[2] According to

[1] In July 1845 Waterboer reported to Montagu, Colonial Secretary, 'not a single Boer in Griquatown territory'.
[2] Colonial Secretary Bell to the Civil Commissioner of Graaff-Reinet, 1 Apr. 1836.

Stockenström (to James Read, June 1845) a Griqua treaty, and one for Moshesh, would in fact have been negotiated 'if I had not left the Colony in 1838'. Sir George Napier, he adds, intended to act, and 'one of the main features was the *acknowledgement of the right to the territory of its then actual possessors*', with protection for the Bushmen, whose actual reinstatement 'had become for ever impossible.' To make matters worse, the missionary Kolbe fell into disgrace and was dismissed in 1837, whereupon a younger man, Atkinson, seems to have had to divide his time between Philippolis and Colesberg. A domestic feud with Robert Moffat of Kuruman made help from that quarter unavailable (below, pp. 227 ff., 242 ff.). Only in 1842 Peter Wright, who had useful experience as Government Agent with Waterboer at Griquatown, accepted a transfer to the mission at Philippolis; there he devoted what were the last months of his life to the now very hard task of restoring harmony and order.

As early as 1835 Kolbe had written lamenting the action of the Griquas in hiring out land to incoming Boers. In October 1840 Mr. Atkinson, writing from Colesberg, more than confirmed the growth of this practice. The Boers, he says, are 'coming in very fast'. The Griquas[1] are 'leasing their farms to them for six, eight and ten years', in spite of their own law against such leases, and he fears that 'at this rate the Boers will soon get all the land'. A year later: 'I fear there is no way of helping the Griquas in that district.' Ultimately the Directors were appealed to and pronounced a forlorn judgement:[2]

That the Dutch Boers are getting quiet possession of Philippolis seems very manifest, but the Directors do not see how they can prevent it. The Boers have gone there by arrangement with the natives and on payment of some stipulated amounts. That this occupation may involve the final loss of freedom and territory on the part of the native population is by no means improbable—but no case arises out of the present state of affairs with which the Directors can go up to the Government. We have [nothing] to elucidate or substantiate a charge against the Boers which refers to Philippolis. We are not now speaking as to their general measures to obtain possession of territory beyond the Colonial boundaries, but as to the serious point

---

[1] This letter distinguishes between 'Griquas' and 'Bastards', the latter being more dependable. Mr. Atkinson also notes 'trouble' caused by the 'English here' who wanted 'races', and were 'naturally' prevented by the Church-Wardens!

[2] Freeman, L.M.S. to Dr. Philip, 20 Apr. 1841.

mentioned in your letter, namely—the restoration of slavery in that
part of Africa by the intrusion of the Boers. . . . The Directors are
quite ready to appeal to the Home Government, but regret that the
Colonial Government is thought to be useless in the matter.

In September 1841, shortly after receiving this letter, Dr.
Philip set off to the north to see for himself; arriving on the
spot towards the end of the year he was certainly reasonable
about Boer needs and claims and at once began to think of a
settlement which would define and perpetuate the *status quo*:

Let the Boers have guaranteed to them the lands they possess and
forbid them to make any addition to them except by *purchasing*, and
all that is desirable may be done without bloodshed or confusion.

In Griqua country, at Glisson's Drift, 90 miles from Colesberg,
he wrote again: 'The Boers are masters of this country, and
except in Waterboer's and Moshesh's territory as thick as in the
Colony itself.' After this an early letter retails an ominous story
from Natal:

It is a well-known fact that in the late raid on Capai [Ncapaai] the
Boers carried off fifty children,[1] and some of these were seen by Mr.
—— in families by whom they had been purchased. [Pretorius,
indeed] made a proclamation of severe penalties for the practice, but
my informant says the price was from 100 to 250 rix-dollars
(1 R.D. = 1s. 6d.), and the Boers laughed at the proclamation as
meant to *gull the English* and never intended to apply amongst the
emigrants themselves.

Second-hand reports of the use made of native children
agreed with more immediate evidence of the plight of the
Bushmen east of Philippolis:

Not only has an active slave-trade been carried on among the
Boers residing at Natal; but it is well known that an active trade in
children has been carried on between them and the Boers spread
over the Bahurutsi country from the Vaal River to the borders of the
Colony. Mr. Rolland at Beersheba, and even in the country of
Moshesh, is not able to protect the Bushmen in his neighbourhood.
[Giving details of a raid . . .] Mr. Rolland is as much feared and
respected by them as any missionary in his station can be; and yet they
have taken Bushmen children from his kitchen. . . .

---

[1] The number is usually given as only seventeen. On the question of 'apprenticeship', see Agar-Hamilton, ch. ix.

As his tour progressed Dr. Philip said little more on the vague general charge that the object of the Trek was to re-establish slavery—though had his travels taken him as far as the Zoutpansberg he might have found practices not entirely at one with responsible Boer professions even in this matter.[1] Things were far from satisfactory among the Griquas themselves. At Philippolis he found that a party 'composed of the old *Bergenaars* and those they could influence' had newly returned from a 'commando in which they have killed many people and taken 20,000 head of cattle and many sheep and goats'. Nothing, in short, Dr. Philip consistently maintained, could meet the situation but effective British Government control.

There was ground enough for apprehension. Beyond Philippolis Philip came into personal touch with Boer extremists— real Trekkers; noting their hatred against the English he expressed the fear that they 'will continue to infuse it into their children from generation to generation'. Unhappily his fears were in some measure realized. But the missionary movement which has been blamed for promoting hostility did no more than call attention to facts as they were. In the light of history it appears that Philip and the missionaries, not their opponents, were substantially right in their foresight of the social consequences of leaving Boer encroachment to run its course.

Philip's vindication of the equal human rights of the coloured people of the old Cape Colony clearly helped to provoke the Trek itself;[2] and the issue in the north was the maintenance of those same principles. In all the districts affected the Boers as the stronger party were in a position to take, or it may even be to acquire, a virtual monopoly of the land. Except under pressure—sometimes by the formidable resistance of the stronger Bantu chiefs, sometimes as a reward for services rendered, and occasionally, as in the later Transvaal, by the direct intervention of the British Government[3]—they showed little disposition to recognize prescriptive native rights, or to provide in any way for the needs of the weaker. Having themselves left the Colony rather than accept the principle underlying the emancipating 50th Ordinance,[4] they now left dispossessed

---

[1] See Agar-Hamilton, pp. 192 ff., and Walker, p. 290.
[2] Cf. *Gie*, ii. 341; Walker, p. 207.   [3] Brookes, p. 126.
[4] Much of this Ordinance was at last embodied in the Transvaal Masters and

persons with the old choice between 'vagrancy' and totally
unregulated conditions of labour service; children, if not dealt
in, were 'transferred' for long periods of unpaid domestic service
under the guise of 'apprenticeship'—in either case without the
hope of appeal to independent courts of law. In Philippolis, for
example—with which as an L.M.S. district Dr. Philip was
particularly concerned—the immediate future seemed to
threaten a complete undoing of the hard-won rights and freedom of the coloured people. As things stood, all the land must
soon be under European control, and the Griquas either driven
out or reduced to the status from which the Hottentots had
been so lately raised.

Dr. Philip's great tour of 1841-2,[1] providing as it did the
first eyewitness account, was the direct means of forcing upon
the notice of the British authorities not only the hard case of the
Griquas of Philippolis but the hitherto neglected problems of
the High Veld and the northern districts generally. As he
travelled Dr. Philip soon saw for himself the close tie-up between the Boers in the north and those in Natal: he noted in
particular the disturbing effect on the native mind of recent
events in that country—it was after all but a few days' journey
away and the great mountains were easily, and apparently
often, crossed by men on foot or on horseback. More clearly
than ever he saw, and set about impressing on the unwilling
authorities, the essential unity of the trans-frontier region. His
journey was not wholly free of actual obstruction. Near Beersheba, in country the Boers themselves acknowledged to belong
to Moshesh, Philip's party was 'stopped by some Boers who
insisted on our turning back'. With judicious use of his snuff-
box, Dr. Philip persuaded them to meet for a 'conference' at the
station of the French missionary, Rolland, who duly sent out
invitations to all the farmers in the neighbourhood. Philip himself being the stumbling-block, he left his companions, James
Read and Rolland, to begin the interview with sixteen or
eighteen of them, and after 'an hour and a half' was informed

Servants Law, enacted by the short-lived British administration in 1880 (*Cape Col.
Qn.*, p. 213).
    [1] References following were to a full and carefully kept 'Journal', which deserved
to be edited for publication. His main suggestions were embodied later in letters to
the Governor and other officials.

that he would be 'allowed' to proceed, on the understanding that should war result within three years he would be held responsible. Thereupon Philip joined them, explained his pacific intentions and left them 'much softened' after further 'friendly conversation' in which, incidentally, the visitors 're-fused to be convinced that the world was round'. The spokes-man of the party, he adds, had told a Mr. Maider in the Colony two years ago that:

he must trek, that Dr. Philip had spoiled the Hottentots, that he had got a law passed which would oblige him to marry his daughter to a Hottentot, that he would rather shoot her than see her so degraded, and that Dr. Philip had taken all his slaves from him and that he wondered at the mercy of God in suffering such a man to live.

Philip 'hopes his views have modified since their late interview'. His conclusion was that 'the real grounds of the Boers' opposi-tion to my journey were not that they were afraid of me and my party, but that they felt they were intruders in the grounds of Moshesh and they trembled for their security if I induced that chief to drive them out'.

This unusual episode did not long delay the resolve Philip had formed of pushing on from Philippolis to pay a visit to the great Basuto chief, Moshesh, at Thaba Bosigo. 'The future peace of the country', he wrote, appeared to him to be 'involved in the future relations between Moshesh and the Boers', that chief being far and away the most effective in a wide area.

The fundamental question everywhere, as he most clearly saw, was the land; the occupation of the Boers, wherever they got a footing, tended to be so extensive and complete as to raise at once the old, and ever new, problem of the dispossessed. 'So far back as 1828', he writes, 'the attention of the Colonial Government was called to the injuries inflicted upon the natives beyond the frontiers by the practice of the Boers who were in the habit of going across the boundaries in the dry season. . . .' Nothing at all was done. At that time the Boers were still mere colonists, taking advantage of official weakness, or connivance, to extend the boundaries of the old colony. Now the difficulty was far greater—to control a movement rooted in disaffection to the Government. The Boers, it is true, were yet by no means at one with each other. 'The immigrant Boers', Philip writes from Basutoland in February 1842, are divided among themselves, the opposing parties are violent against each other, the collisions which arise from differences of opinion make them fear each other. . . . They are in fear from the Colony, and they are in fear from the natives, and this fear will unite them in one body when the time shall arrive to take possession of this country as they have done at Natal.

'Whether they retain Natal', he continues cheerlessly, 'or whether the British Government take possession . . . the result will be the same.' The annexation of Natal is necessary, but

the Boers who are opposed to the British Government, which many of them are, and these the most ferocious of them, will fall back upon this country [Basutoland]. On the other hand, should the Boers be allowed to retain Natal, the only difference in the event will be in regard to time. In the former case the destruction of the native will be more rapid, but *in either case the crisis is near, and inevitable unless prevented by foreign (British) interference.*

A few months later he wrote, almost prophetically:

If their property and land are not secured to the Griquas, and the protection of the Colonial laws, before ten years there will not be a single Griqua in the country.

In face of these things Dr. Philip's ideas soon began to crystallize. The one thing needful, he wrote from Basutoland in February, was to 'give the Griquas the protection of the Colonial laws'—then, at worst, they might continue as free labourers, with adequate and efficient courts to which to appeal. As in 1833, 'incorporation in the Colony' remained his first specific. But the British authorities continued to fight shy of annexation as the obvious means of keeping control of the errant Europeans, for whose doings as British subjects it was responsible. Only then Dr. Philip fell back on the policy to which Downing Street was wedded and suggested that existing rights in the land might be secured by treaty.

From Thaba Bosigo Dr. Philip turned on his tracks and proceeded, by Philippolis again, to the Bechuana mission stations of the north-west. The Bechuana had not at this time begun to feel the full force of the impact of the Boers of Potchefstroom and Rustenburg. Philip's Journal, none the less—though primarily concerned with mission work, and rendered difficult by variant spellings of the names of a bewildering number of small tribes and petty chiefs—throws light on conditions beyond the Vaal where, in the end, the clash with the Bantu was left to take its own course almost entirely uncontrolled. This array of insignificant names is indeed of the very essence of the matter. In Bechuanaland there was one petty chief at 'Old Lattakoo', another at Motito, yet another at Taungs, and others equally important (or unimportant) scattered about in all directions—sometimes, like one Mahura, given to troublesome little raids on their neighbours—always hopelessly weak and divided. At this very time Gottlieb Schreiner, father of a distinguished family, was restlessly seeking a more congenial station than Philippolis, and was warned by Dr. Philip of the difficulties of settling where there was no reliable chief to maintain some kind of stability. In his Journal, indeed, written at the *kraal* of the Batlapin in April 1842, Philip noted one feature probably characteristic of the Bantu generally before the advent of the military and despotic type of chief—'the extreme freedom of speech allowed at their *Pitso*' (folkmoot). This, he considers, is a 'safety-valve', and 'a corrective to the extreme absolutism of their chiefs'. Even Robert Moffat, it seems, having made a new venture on his own account when he moved to the great spring at Kuruman, had signally failed to persuade the chiefs Mahura and Motibi to move with him and get the benefit of this wonderful 'eye' of pure water.

In this arid and shapeless northern region Philip got less mission help than he needed and deserved. The good Robert Moffat put all his trust in the Lord, but often it would seem sulked in his tent while awaiting the Divine pleasure. In 1842 Moffat was away on leave, but the atmosphere in the region where his was the dominant personality was hostile to the Mission Superintendent. Stout Independent as he was, Moffat was for self-government by a 'district committee' (which the distances to be travelled made impracticable). When the missionary at the Griqua station, Campbell, proved a failure, and was also charged with flogging a Bushman, Moffat resented the disciplining of one of his colleagues by the Society's Cape Town Agent. Hearing of yet another charge of 'interfering in politics', Moffat protested at such a 'ludicrous' accusation to come from Dr. Philip! This drew an acid retort: 'What are politics in the affairs of a chief without subjects and a missionary without people?'

The comment of the greatest L.M.S. man of them all deserves to be recorded. On the eve of the 1841 tour Dr. David Livingstone, newly arrived, was the Philips' guest in Cape Town and wrote:[1]

I had heard many things calculated to awaken unpleasant feelings. I lived in their house a month. I came to it full of prejudice against them and I left with my prejudice completely thawed, my fears allayed and my mind imbued with great respect for (their) upright Christian character. The charge I had heard reiterated again and again in England that they are spiritual despots, upon all that I can learn, appears decidedly false and calumnious. In all our intercourse I could perceive no attempt to usurp authority . . . or dictate . . . (but) the very reverse. The Dr.'s faculties appear to be now a little impaired by age, but Mrs. Philip is much stronger and very active and energetic. One charge is, therefore, quite true, that she is the chief agent in transacting business (i.e. routine business).

The letter continues on the troubles of the Cape Town pastorate, amply confirming other evidence that this disturbance was due to the burdens of his official position in the L.M.S. and to the 'active part he has taken in securing the rights of the coloured population'. The activities of the next years suggest that the congregational distractions of 1839–41 (themselves not unconnected with Kaffir War disputes) were partly responsible for his faculties then appearing 'a little impaired by age'. It may well be that in the next years, 1842–5, the last in which he was fully active, he waited even too much for business to come to him. Moffat's District Committee was approved by the Directors, but rarely so much as met. In 1843 Philip offered his resignation, but though this did not take effect the breach was never healed. Moffat after his return still stood aloof, withholding such frontier information as he had, or should have had, from Philip, the one man who was in a position to use it to advantage.

The Kuruman station, to be known before long as the Gateway to the North, was at that time still so remote that its staff may not in fact have been well posted in the strategical intelligence of which they were also indifferent distributors. Even thus early the traveller, David Livingston (so he then spelt his name), was seeking a station farther north, in the region which had

---

[1] T. Hughes's *Livingstone*, pp. 12–13. The original letter of 13 May 1841, to Mr. A. Cecil, was in the J. G. Gubbins Collection.

been abandoned by the French missionaries ten years before on account of the disturbing of the Bahurutsi and others by Moselekatze. As if unaware of the Matabele's great trek Philip was apprehensive and discouraged any move to those parts where Americans and Anglicans as well as the French had tried and failed. Moselekatze, he wrote, had thought Moffat useful as a protector but was alienated by the withdrawal of the Americans; yet 'little more than a twelve-month ago' the Boers had already informed the Anglican who tried to reassemble the Bahurutsi at Mosega:

that he might continue to teach there for the present but was not to forget that the country belonged to them; he was to consider himself as occupying their ground by sufferance only until they should require it.

The Boer account of this episode is that they feared to have natives congregated at this station, but were prepared to take the whole tribe under their protection at some point farther afield.[1] The missionary Edwards,[2] who early in 1842 had accompanied Livingstone to the north, now assured Dr. Philip he exaggerated the dangers since Moselekatze had already withdrawn '500 or 600 miles farther north than you state', adding that the Boers were not likely to want to occupy the country of the Bakwena and the Bangwaketsi which was 'dry and unsuitable for sheep and horses'. But Philip was correctly enough informed, on the Boers' own showing, that 'the Boers lay claim to all that was claimed by Moselekatze' on the ground that the Bechuana 'retired before the arms of Moselekatze into the desert, where they remain'.[3] As a proof that the Boers 'do not intend the claim to lie dormant' he cites their pursuit of Griqua hunters, whom they warned that 'the country was theirs and they were never again to visit any part of it to kill game of any kind'. A permanent mission, Dr. Philip concluded, was, therefore, inadvisable:

Men may look at the eruption of a volcano from a distance, and they may think of one day settling near it, but not till the eruption shall have ceased. . . . Should the Boers prevail to the extent that

[1] Agar-Hamilton, pp. 120-1.
[2] Letter of Aug. 1842, on missionary matters; he also accuses a colleague of 'propagating tittel-tatel' [sic]!   [3] Cf. Agar-Hamilton, pp. 50-53.

they meditate, our missionaries will not be allowed to remain in the part of the country under their authority.

Just ten years later Edwards himself was to learn to his cost that the warning was just; in 1852 he and his colleague Walter Inglis were summarily expelled, with clumsy formality, by order of the Volksraad, from the newly recognized Transvaal Republic.

Philip's own trek through much arid country was clearly sufficient, in spite of unhelpful colleagues, to impress on him the futility of trying to preserve the Bechuana tribal lands by any sort of 'treaty'; none of the chiefs had effective authority, and the climatic conditions made the real extent and the validity of their land claims dubious. The ineptitude of the Bechuana, and perhaps, he may have judged, also of their missionaries, probably made Philip too hopeful of Waterboer—he seems to have remained under the impression that the Griquas had been strong enough to save the Bechuana, back in 1823, not merely from raiding Bafokeng but from the whole Mantatee 'horde', and later even from Moselekatze. Philip's hope was apparently to get the Bechuana as a body to acknowledge Waterboer as their leader, and he even seems to claim they were prepared to do so. This proposed aggrandizement of Waterboer and Griquatown added fuel to the fires of discontent burning among the Kuruman missionaries. Remote as they were from the realities of South African life, cherishing their 'independence', and already chafing at control by Philip and Cape Town, they were jealous of Griquatown as being too much of the Cape Town faction. Disregardful, or unaware, of the political danger that threatened their whole parish, they sorely harassed Dr. Philip with trivial domestic missionary feuds, yet offered no vestige of an alternative plan for protecting the future of the Bechuana. Almost in despair, Philip began in June to press as fast as oxen could carry him back to Cape Town. In all the next years, which were critical, the affairs of the Bechuana got none of the attention they emphatically demanded. The future of the Bechuana was in reality bound up with that of the *Transvaal*, the only home, to this day, of a large section of that people. In 1852 (below, Ch. XVII), without further parley the Boers of that Republic were left to 'manage their own affairs', and its Bechuana to fend for themselves as best they might.

On the way south in 1842 Dr. Philip remarked that the
country about the *Berg* (north of Graaff-Reinet) had been 'in a
great measure forsaken':

> The emigration mania still continues. Within about 100 miles of
> the Orange River we met thirty Boers trekking, and a great pro-
> portion of the places they deserted are now used as cattle places by
> proprietors who do not reside upon them but leave them and their
> cattle in charge of freedmen, Bechuana and Bushmen.

The softening influence of his February interview (above, p.
225) was momentarily strengthened by the 'great civility' he
received from a Boer at whose house he conducted a Sunday
service:

> My own countrymen [he comments] who were born in a land of
> liberty I have invariably found to be most virulent in their prejudices
> against me for my exertions in favour of the rights of the coloured
> population in this country.

Philip's tune changed abruptly when, nearing Grahamstown,
he found all the news was of Dick King's arrival (above, p. 214)
with his appeal for help for the beleaguered garrison of Port
Natal. He was at once caught up in interviews, and in the
writing to which these gave rise. The Lieutenant-Governor,
Colonel Hare, was evidently glad of first-hand frontier information—what little other news he had was causing him anxiety.
On 24 June he had reported to the Governor that three or four
hundred Boers were said to have left the Mooi River (Potchefstroom) for Natal where Captain Smith was still besieged;
from Smith, moreover, news had passed to the Governor[1] of the
disturbing influence of the Hollander Smellekamp; about this
time Colonel Josias Cloete reported a letter from Pretorius
announcing the cession of Natal to the King of Holland.[2]
Philip's reports were no more comforting. Alarmed as he himself had been by the hostility of the Natal Boers, he now feared
that firmer British action in Natal would make certain, as he
had foreseen, that the Griquas and Basuto would be pressed,
not merely by moderates, like Oberholster, but by the hostile

---

[1] Smith to Napier, 14 May, and Napier to Secretary of State, 13 June 1842. And
above, p. 213.

[2] Letter of 4 July, sent to Secretary of State in dispatch of 11 Nov.

Trekkers from Natal. These fresh developments made what he had himself seen acquire a more ominous significance:

You must be aware [he writes to Colonel Hare] that a political organization has already been formed among bodies of the Boers, reaching from the Orange River to Natal, by Pretorius; that they have taken oaths of allegiance to him as president of their republic,[1] and I am credibly informed they boast that they will soon have back by their arms the farms they sold to the English.[2] ... As it is they occupy the country between the Caledon and the Vaal Rivers, and covet the portion occupied by Moshesh which is small in comparison, but good for breeding horses because it is high and horse sickness is unknown. (They have made) tempting offers to Moshesh for part of this land, but finding they have nothing to hope from his goodwill, they are meditating an attack upon him.

Stressing the dangers of allowing the Boers to get too firm a hold on Basutoland, he asks Hare to correspond with Mr. Casalis of the French Mission about the possibility at least of a 'treaty' before they have established their republic on the great stretch of country adjoining the colonial boundaries: 'It would be much easier', he concludes, 'to keep out the Boers now when a little assistance to the native tribes will enable them to defend themselves. . . .' Supplementing Philip's sober representations to the senior local official, a private letter of the same date, 12 July, reveals his own personal anxiety: 'Tragedy', he fears, 'is imminent since the tribes have no common bond of union': and, very unusually, one significant scrap of his *talk* survives—reporting his conversation with Wesleyans as he passed through Somerset East earlier in the month, a letter from Major Warden (18 July) makes it clear that Philip's personal remedy for the frontier trouble was '*annexation up to the Tropics*'.

Thus, beyond any doubt, 'treaties' bulked so largely in the

---

[1] An undated letter says Pretorius's tour was 'preparatory to the establishment of the new republic they talk of'.

[2] Summing up eastern districts' opinion Philip wrote later: 'The agitation caused by the newspapers contributed largely to the emigration of the Boers.' In the panic thus created, 'they sold their farms much under their value to English settlers, while those who had created the panic became purchasers, and are now selling the farms again at three or four times the prices at which they bought them. They expatriated themselves originally under a delusion created in the first instance by the supineness of the Government, later under the influence of disaffection created by those who wanted (?) their farms at a low price.'

years that followed only because the British Government could never be brought to do more than flirt with the new responsibilities forced on its unwilling attention by the doings of its emigrant subjects. The way out it preferred was hopeless, all the more so when it came to negotiating treaties not only with Faku in Pondoland (January 1844) but with the northern tribes. The Boer die-hards who began to turn north from Natal in mid-1842 to escape British interference had now to be reckoned with also across the Drakensberg where the underlying principle of the Stockenström treaties of 1838 could not apply. This principle had been,[1] *simpliciter*, 'the acknowledgement of the right to the territory of its then actual possessors'. Precisely because possession of the northern lands was the point in dispute, treaties concluded after the hostilities provoked in Natal and beyond by the Boer encroachments acquired even a sinister aspect; inevitably they have been subject to one-sided criticism ever since. It seemed to the Boers at the time, as it has to too many historians since, that Kok, Moshesh, and Co. were taken up by the British Government as military allies against the Boers—which is frankly preposterous. On the other hand the scraps of paper recording the 'agreements' of the Trekkers with the tribes of the interior[2] are treated with solemn respect. The difference between the British and the Trekker treaties is that the former were at least an attempt to preserve the tribes and to prevent their 'extermination'—to prevent indeed the wholesale intermixture of black and white areas which the Boers' successors profess to deplore; those concluded by the Trekkers were instruments designed to legalize *dis*possession.

The great difficulty in the way of the British policy was that it appeared to contemplate subjecting the Boer farmer to the jurisdiction of a shadowy government of coloured peasants—at a time when the strongest of the African potentates was utterly unequal to the task of governing even his 'Native' state in the confusion caused by an influx of European settlers. Philip's letters of February 1842 still looked forward to the consolidation of the *status quo*, including the rights of Boers to land in their actual possession. The wholly justifiable object of

[1] In the correspondence of Stockenström and Fairbairn in 1838 (J. G. Gubbins Collection), and again in letters to Dr. Philip in Aug. 1842, and to James Read, Jan. to June 1845.   [2] Agar-Hamilton, pp. 21 *et passim*.

subsequent treaties—doubtfully possible of attainment by such means, and certainly attempted too late—was to prevent precisely such intermixture of black and white throughout South Africa as their failure in the end brought about. They might at least have secured even the adequate 'Bantustans' now deplorably lacking.

In July or August 1842 Dr. Philip was so abnormally disturbed that, for the first time for many years, several letters to Fowell Buxton and others refer to the possibility of making another appeal to the British Government direct. But this time his reception in Cape Town was favourable; his factual details so impressed Sir George Napier that they were forwarded at once to the Secretary of State by the Governor himself. Philip's suggestions, first made in conversation, were apparently by the request of the Governor embodied in a letter (25 August) supplementing that of 12 July, to Colonel Hare, which dealt more especially with the position of Moshesh. With this went a personal appeal from Kok of Philippolis,[1] and one from the French missionary Casalis on behalf of Moshesh. Dr. Philip's letter betrays considerable alarm. Moshesh is in danger of 'annihilation', the Griquas of Philippolis of even more imminent attack from 'an enemy who are united in their hatred against them, and in their determination to embrace the first favourable opportunity to exterminate them and to possess themselves of their country'—unless the Government intervenes to prevent 'the bloody tragedy'. Government mediation is favoured, however, by 'the better part of the Boers themselves . . . who are too few in number to have any influence over the dispositions, councils or proceedings of their brethren'. The protection of Philippolis is especially urgent:

since if country on the colonial borders passes into the hands of a hostile Boer republic, the free trade with friends in the colony will keep the hostile Boers so well provided with arms and ammunition that it may render all attempts nugatory, which may afterwards be taken, to save Moshesh and Waterboer and the numerous tribes of the natives in the interior.

Later letters show Dr. Philip hoping to put something like a

---

[1] The date of Kok's letter, 5 June, was so nearly that of Dr. Philip's departure from Colesberg (where it was written) that it was no doubt drafted under Philip's supervision.

'ring fence' of protected tribes between the Colony and the Trekkers, not indeed to set the tribes against the farmers, but to protect them by controlling and restricting the supply of weapons of war. His first remedy, however, was to take the Griqua country within the Colony as he had proposed to Sir Lowry Cole years before in 1833; so long ago as 1819, he says, he hoped for this consummation; only on seeing the progress they had made under Mr. Wright between 1825 and 1832 did he begin to think it possible; now, he concludes, it is the 'only possible expedient of safety'. But should the Government hesitate to adopt this plan 'till it shall have received more mature consideration'—'as a *substitute* for the first plan, in the *meantime*, I beg leave to recommend to Your Excellency that Treaties should be entered into with Moshesh and Adam Kok'. Disputes with the Griquas about leases 'may in my opinion be easily adjusted' by the Government acting as a mediator. By submitting their leases to the Government the Boers themselves had made an 'acknowledgement of its right to interfere in this case'. But the Treaties ought to be strictly limited in number; referring to a conversation with the Governor about the advisability of recognizing Lepui of Bethulie, Dr. Philip pointed out that Lepui was there 'on sufferance only', and his case should 'remain in abeyance':

Were Treaties with the Government to become a common thing . . . they would lose all their value and cease to answer any good purpose, and for that reason I would recommend that none should be made at present except with Moshesh and Adam Kok. . . . As there are few points in which these *two* chiefs can come into collision with each other, the soundest policy the Government can pursue will be to strengthen (their) hands; but should the Government enter into treaties with other chiefs beyond them . . . they will find nothing but rivals in those in whom in other circumstances they may find allies who may be useful to themselves, to their people and to the Colony.

The tribal groups consistently (see Ch. XVII) left out of all this protective planning are the Transvaal Bechuana; and so it was to be in those fatal early 1850's, when even Dr. Livingstone found no redress when his station was ransacked by Transvaal Boers. The rooted belief persisted that the missionaries were putting them in danger by supplying the natives with *guns*.

As if to justify Dr. Philip's immediate fears, things began to happen in Griqualand very shortly after his return to Cape Town. Early in September the Governor took the preliminary caution of issuing a Proclamation warning Her Majesty's subjects against any attempt to molest or injure the native tribes, or to take unlawful possession of land belonging to them—mentioning in particular the Basuto, the Barolong of Moroko, the Batlapin of Lepui, together with the half-breeds and Griquas. Meantime the republican leader, Jan Mocke, had returned from Natal and began to make his presence on the Orange River so much felt that 'the better part of the Boers themselves' took alarm and through their spokesman, Oberholster, wrote to the Civil Commissioner of Colesberg early in October warning him of Mocke's intention to proclaim as a republic the whole of the country beyond the Orange River. A few days later Mr. Justice Menzies, in Colesberg on a circuit tour, arrived independently at Dr. Philip's preferred solution, and on very similar grounds:

I believed that every person, black or white, who would not take the oath of allegiance [i.e. to the threatened Republic] would be compelled to leave the country, that they intended no longer to recognize the right of any native tribe or chief, within their assumed territory, to the land in their possession, and to reduce them to a state of servitude.[1]

Deeming the situation critical, Menzies even took it upon himself to make a proclamation annexing, in the Queen's name, all territory east of 22 degrees and south of 25 degrees, 'not being Portuguese dominion or in lawful possession or occupation of any native chief or ruler, *more particularly and especially such portions of the said territory as are now in possession or occupation of any subjects of the British Crown*'.

Meantime the Governor had reported to the Secretary of State on 15 September, enclosing Dr. Philip's letter of 25 August. In his own dispatch he emphasized, what Philip also recognized, that the Griqualand Boers were colonists who had no desire to throw off their allegiance but were being driven by numbers and land-hunger to cast greedy eyes upon Moshesh's country. At the same time, knowing well the dead set against

---

[1] Letter to Governor enclosed in dispatch of 11 Nov. 1842.

extending British dominion, he inverted the order of Dr. Philip's recommendations:

The two modes of overcoming the difficulty are either by extending the protection of the Government by means of treaties with the native chiefs, and the promise of armed support in giving effect to those treaties, or by spreading our influence over the whole of that country by subjecting both the natives and the Europeans to British law and authority.

Judge Menzies's proclamation, too precipitate to have any hope of gaining approval, was inevitably disallowed, though the Governor's private opinion hardly admits of doubt: on 11 November he wrote, immediately after hearing of Menzies's action:

I again take the opportunity of expressing my firm conviction that there is only one mode by which effectual check can be given to this system of slavery which, under the name of *apprenticeship*, prevails over a great part of the country where the emigrant farmers have located themselves, and that is the colonization of those territories.

Even more specifically, on 13 December:

Your Lordship is aware that I am favourable, as a question of expediency, to the extension of British supremacy as the only means of averting calamitous consequences to the native tribes.

This December opinion was called forth by a continuance of acute unrest on the Philippolis front. The numbers involved were small and insignificant but the Governor could not remain indifferent to the news that reached him. In the course of November he must have heard through Dr. Philip how the French missionaries, J. P. Pelissier and Samuel Rolland, were complaining that Boers were ejecting natives from their fountains. Rolland was blunt: 'I am no advocate for war, but I fear the Boers must feel the weight of the British arm before they will come to their senses. . . . Proclamations are of no use. They are so much waste paper.' More ominously, Mr. Atkinson of Colesberg wrote expressing a fear that 'the Griquas will not tamely submit' to the Boers, and may start a war to the extermination of one side or the other. Casalis next, from Thaba Bosigo, reported a rumour that 'the missionaries would be compelled either to acknowledge the authority of the Natal

Volksraad or to leave the country'. Moshesh had no official message from the Boers and there was no rupture, but Casalis, while regretting the necessity for dragging Moshesh out of 'an obscurity so favourable to the reception of Divine Grace', considered action necessary, since 'Boers still creep in silently and settle in the west where they are aware he has least control'.

On 5 December the Lieutenant-Governor, Colonel Hare, reported that 'rebellion' threatened in Colesberg. The trend of official opinion was further reflected in a letter from Theophilus Shepstone (to Dr. Philip, 2 December): 'There appears no human possibility of the natives of any mission station being preserved except by the prompt and vigorous interference of the Government.' In the course of December, therefore, Colonel Hare was sent up to Colesberg with a force of 300 infantry and 100 mounted men—whereupon the hostile Boers at once dispersed and the military danger, such as it was, passed. In March, after another warning Proclamation by Colonel Hare, Atkinson reported first a 'temporary lull', both sides awaiting some Government decision in the matter, then, on the 31st, that the Griquas had collected at Philippolis, 'expecting the Boers'. At last, on 21 and 26 April Napier received dispatches. Lord Stanley had the last word. His instructions, while sanctioning the annexation of Natal, laid down that 'you will be careful not to engage in operations at a distance from the settled parts of the Colony'; measures for the protection of the natives in the north must be strictly limited to '*treaties* entered into for the purpose with the chiefs'.

XIV

'DR. PHILIP'S TREATY STATES', 1843–6

THE next three years, 1843–6, were unusual in being undisturbed by any major crisis in any of the potential storm centres. The Xhosa front had so long been in a state of unrest that comparative quiet, some of it the result of exhaustion and some perhaps of a mild 'boom' (above, p. 193), served only as warrant for neglect. Natal, on the other hand, where pressure was relaxed, even saw the slender beginnings of settled administration. In these years, therefore, Governor Napier and his successor, Sir Peregrine Maitland, tried hard to act on Lord Stanley's instructions and stabilize a fluid situation in the north by formal recognition of the *status quo* in Griqualand and Basutoland. Neither Governor was really satisfied with the limited discretion allowed him; Napier, we know (above, p. 237), was for asserting a general British supremacy and Maitland, when submitting revisions of his treaties in 1845, showed almost deprecating awareness of the ban imposed on any extension of the Colony's administration. No one could know that this was to be the last chance there was ever to be of bringing the Trek under some control and checking at least the worst social consequences of unrestricted expansion—still less that the High Veld, then sparsely peopled, was destined to be the economic centre of a future South Africa. At least the Governors rightly saw the necessity of central control of the situation. But within a year of Maitland's 1845 dispatch the Xhosa front relapsed into chaos. In the prolonged ferment which followed the hope of unified order finally dissolved.

The vast extent of the High Veld, and its remoteness, made against good administration, but at least there was room for manœuvre. The legitimate concern of the Cape Government was to guard itself against the effects of such wholesale (or even piecemeal) 'extermination' of the weaker people as must reduce them to the former state of the Cape Hottentots. To this end the Government must keep itself informed and, having no representatives of its own in the region, naturally drew on the obvious if not the only possible source of current news; the missionaries alone were regular letter-writers. Equally naturally such information came to the authorities through the Superintendent of the many London missions who was also the local agent for the French stations and, in addition, was himself the only person with wide first-hand knowledge of much of this country. Dr. Philip was of course foremost (see Ch. XIII) in calling official attention to the urgency of the situation as he saw it developing. For his pains, almost invariable tradition has it that the only outcome of two Governors' efforts in these years was the futility (alternatively the base plot) known as 'Dr. Philip's Treaty States'. Once again, tradition calls for the closest re-examination.

Beyond any doubt Philip was closely consulted by both Napier and Maitland at every stage of the northern negotiations which took up much of their time in these three years. No less certainly the solution he preferred was known to them and, indeed, notorious all along. In May 1845, when Maitland was setting out to attempt a fresh settlement in Griqualand, a Mr. Merrington suggested to Attorney-General Porter that Dr. Philip should be consulted. According to Mrs. Philip (16 May 1845) Porter replied: 'O! we know what Dr. Philip thinks. He wants us to take in the whole of the country under the Colony, but that we cannot afford to do. There would be no end of that.' Dr. Philip himself the same week restated his opinion from Port Elizabeth: 'The simplest and the only method is to take the Griquas into the Colony, and to get Moshesh to agree to have a fort in his territory to keep the way to Natal open.' 'The Government', that is to say, had its own views and was, besides, bound by instructions imposed on it from London. But there was nothing to stop the Governors taking Philip into their confidence in such intimacy as he had not enjoyed since very early days, except in his fateful and almost secret dealings with D'Urban in 1834. This unusual experience greatly pleased him and led him to write over-optimistically (and indeed almost smugly!):[1]

having brought the Colonial Government to a sense of impending danger, I have succeeded [in getting action taken] to place the Boers

[1] To J. Thomas, Esq., 4 Apr. 1843.

at bay till the Governor shall receive more ample means and powers from Home to enable him entirely to defeat their designs. As the documents I had drawn up at his request were sent to Downing Street *with his recommendations*, we are not without hope as to the result.

A year later: 'Formerly the Government was opposed to me, but things are so far changed that I have now the Government with me' (to Dr. Thomas Hodgkin, Aborigines Protection Society, May 1844), and to Sir T. Fowell Buxton (1844, undated), 'At present the Colonial Government does nothing as to relations with the independent native tribes without consulting me.'

Philip, in short, worked for choice with the local authorities, when they would allow him to, rather than against them. His position was stronger at this time by reason of his good relations also with a capable Colonial Secretary, Mr. John Montagu. Just possibly Dr. Philip's advocacy helped to secure for the Colony its civilian Secretary: 'Lord John Russell ought to see the need for sending a civilian and enlightened Secretary with a military Governor like Napier, not a soldier and a Tory and a nervous-minded man like our (present) who I am sorry to say does as he pleases' (to Buxton on the dismissal of Stockenström, 22 November 1839). The popular new official's memory lives in the name of a town, and of the still impressive Montagu Pass.

In this short phase, the last of Philip's active career, he would seem to have been so ill-advised, or even so puffed with vanity, as to neglect his opportunities of doing what he could to stiffen, as it sorely needed, the attitude of the Home Government without whose backing his official friends in Cape Town were helpless; his letters to Fowell Buxton, or even to the Buxtons, were few and hurried. But there were sadly cogent reasons for his inaction. Buxton, now a baronet but no longer M.P., was in failing health—he died in 1845—and the anti-slavery movement he so devotedly led was quiescent if not dead; its great feat of winning freedom for the slaves at a cost to the state of £20 million was a triumph not to be repeated; the cause of 'Humanity' now faced an increasingly uneven battle with the ever-growing forces of Victorian 'Economy'. The frontal attack on the wickedness of slave-owners had aroused such popular emotions as were much less easily moved to show concern for the land rights of African tribes led, possibly, by a savage murderer like Dingaan. They were at any rate already 'free'.

Even 'Exeter Hall', the formidable evangelical wing of the anti-slavery forces, was almost out of action in so far as Philip himself, the best possible source of guidance and inspiration on Cape affairs, was, as he had reason to know, out of favour. It could not be without its effect that D'Urban's version of the Kaffir War and its sequel was widely current, disturbing some even of his own congregation (above, p. 213 n.). Soon the Directors of the L.M.S. took fright—evidently influenced by Robert Moffat who was on Home leave between 1840 and 1843—it shocked them to hear their leading representative accused of 'meddling in politics'. By 1843 they had approved Moffat's district committee which implied some check on the authority of the Superintendent in Cape Town. One of its rare meetings may have been the occasion for Philip protesting in 1843 at the delay, 'for months', of the confirmation of W. Y. Thomson in office 'at that most important station, Philippolis'. He even made formal resignation of his post and, though the domestic storm blew over,[1] only the staunch support he had from some of the most competent missionaries (Edward Solomon, W. Y. Thomson, Atkinson of the L.M.S., Casalis and Dyke of Basutoland) and also his good relations especially with Mr. Secretary Montagu, kept him at his post till the end. But the L.M.S. in London continued to stand dumbly aside even when, just after Philip's death, its own missionaries were bundled bag and baggage out of the Transvaal Republic.

The persistence of a false tradition makes so much background matter relevant to the story of 'treaty'-making in the northern region. Had the Government still had to deal only with the old peaceful penetration by individually trekking colonists, and with Boer moderates like Oberholster, a settle-

---

[1] The passing of the storm was not without Philip showing himself, as son-in-law Fairbairn once wrote, a man of sound and liberal principle but 'sometimes hard-mouthed!' In Nov. 1843 he wrote to his friend, Miss Wills: 'It is a curious fact, now that I have both the Home and the Colonial Governments at my feet, that my last and the severest of my conflicts should take place with the Directors of the L.M.S. At this moment when the Governor is consulting me and taking my advice on the most important affairs of South Africa, the silliest creatures connected with our missions in this country, men whom it would be charity to the missions to allow them to spend their salaries in England, have more weight in the Mission House in Blomfield Street than I have.'

ment should have been relatively easy. But when at last Napier's instructions authorized him to take measures for the protection of the Griquas the position was more complicated. The acute excitement which brought the troops at least as far as Colesberg in the end of 1842 (above, p. 238) was caused by the more aggressive tendencies of the die-hards under Jan Mocke. The Great Trek, that is to say, was beginning to show itself in its true colours. Rather than submit to the authority of what was after all their own Government the Trekkers in Natal had forcibly defied the Queen's commission, showing that their exodus was of the nature of a rebellion. Its character was disguised so long as the vastness of South Africa made it possible for the malcontents to withdraw unhindered from the control they resented. All the time no doubt the majority of the Trekkers wanted nothing so much as a quiet life—to acquire farms and work them in peace; even their overbearing attitude to those there before them may have sprung from a wholly intelligible nervousness. But when land came to be obtainable only at Griqua or Bantu expense there was conflict; and conflict on the Borders inevitably aroused Government concern about the doings of its Trekker subjects.

Part of the alarm in Griqua territory was probably fortuitous. In this lonely country of vast distances game abounded and lions were still common; not even missionaries travelled unarmed. Boers as a matter of course carried guns with them wherever they went if only to keep themselves supplied with food, so that the frequent semi-political meetings of these unsettled times tended to be assemblies of armed men. In times of excitement, indeed, these armed meetings were customary; long years afterwards, apologies were made for the rebellion of 1914 as originating in nothing more serious than an 'armed protest' that could never have been so grossly misunderstood in the old days of the Republics. By the forties, however, the Griquas, unlike the Bantu tribes, also had guns and, like the Boers, were given to holding meetings. When Boer and Griqua meetings happened near the same time and place the guns were apt to go off—with little or no premeditation on the part of their owners.

It may be, therefore, that Oberholster, rather than Mocke, was the typical Boer, a man governed by considerations of

safety more than by ambition or politics. In the opinion of Mr.
W. Y. Thomson, a young and competent missionary who took
charge after Mr. Wright's death in April 1843, Oberholster was
'weak', and 'liable to be turned by too strong an opposition',
but also 'a humane man, sincerely desirous of preventing
bloodshed'. The same witness wrote in July 1844:

> The firm adherents either of Oberholster or of Mocke are ex-
> tremely few. With the great mass of the emigrants it is a matter of
> indifference whether they belong to Government or to the 'Modder
> River Republic' and they will assuredly adhere to the strongest
> party. A strong demonstration of Government on behalf of the chiefs
> or Oberholster would, therefore, leave the heads of rebellion desti-
> tute of adherents. . . . (Already) some who were formerly the avowed
> adherents of Mocke have declared themselves neuter, and some have
> given in their allegiance to Oberholster. And further, the Boers know
> that to engage in war with disciplined troops in this country, where
> there is neither bush nor woody ravine to afford protection to their
> flocks and herds, or cover to their persons in their peculiar mode of
> fighting, would be utter madness. The Boers know their own tactics,
> and the local advantages requisite to their success, and it was this
> consideration that caused their formidable force to vanish, as at the
> wand of an enchanter, when the Lieut.-Governor with the troops
> appeared at Colesberg (in Dec. 1842).

However this may be, the advent of Mocke on the Griqua
border made any British intervention much more likely to
provoke opposition. At the same time anything like weakness on
the part of the British authorities might, as Mr. Thomson feared,
have the effect of throwing the moderates into the arms of the
more extreme faction. Mocke's party, moreover, as the Griqua
attitude shows, was more utterly regardless of the rights and
interests of the weaker peoples, and the mere addition to the
number of claimants intensified the land shortage. It has been
argued that at the time of the Treaties there were in Griqualand 'actually more white people than Griquas'.[1] Why then, it is
asked in effect, such extreme tenderness for the rights of a handful of Griquas? Oberholster himself, it appears from Mr.
Thomson's letters, pressed merely for 'equal rights'. But the
relatively large and increasing number of Boers was precisely
the difficulty. Even in those days experience had shown that

---

[1] Theal, ii. 419.

equal rights must very soon make an end of Bantu or Griqua land-holding.

The increased pressure, in fact, made the situation almost menacing. Weak and divided though the Griquas may have been they were the descendants of men who had fled from the Colony rather than submit to the very conditions that threat-ened again to engulf them. In their independence—as hunters or traders in ivory, as landholders, or it may be by leasing their land to Boers—they had acquired horses and guns, and some practice and skill in using them. They were by no means certainly disposed to submit quietly to being dispossessed. Several times in the latter part of 1842, when no doubt they had been better employed looking after their own farms, they collected excitedly in Philippolis to prepare to meet the Boers with united resistance. After December the unaccustomed ap-pearance of troops in the north provided them with a little ready money, some of which was spent on house-building, and some, no doubt, on arms and ammunition. In March 1843 Mr. Wright reported great activity. The Griquas having received £578 from the Government for the use of their wagons, they had '25 houses in course of erection'—'but not a glass of brandy!' Nor were they without resources. In May Mrs. Wright reported that, with a view to evacuation, the Government had made a fresh requisition for 50 wagons—a surprisingly large number for such a despised community. Complaining that even Boer leaseholders had taken up arms in order to expel their Griqua lessors, Wright still feared a disastrous clash in the early months of 1843. Dr. Philip, while continuing to keep the Governor in-formed of the rather alarming news that reached him, had to act at the same time as a moderating influence—urging patience both on Mr. Wright and on the Griquas:

The Griquas must not expect too much. . . . The mad proceedings of the Boers in this instance have damaged their cause with the Government, but that is what they will soon get over, as on former similar occasions, and the Griquas will be sacrificed as a peace-offering to the Boers. Government has never withstood the tide of colonial feeling. . . . On the subject of the leases, therefore, the people must be fair and reasonable. Anything unreasonable will transfer the sympathies of Colonel Hare to the side of the Boers. . . . Supposing the farmers are obliged to leave their farms at the expiration of their leases, what is to be done? The land cannot lie empty, and the natives are not in a position to fill the farms with stock.

To Mr. Wright's further remark that the Griquas were 'not in a state to be played with', Philip rejoined that he hoped they were 'not adopting any rash counsels'.

However futile Griqua resistance must have proved, the Government clearly had to reckon with such rashness as an imminent possibility. Missionary letters show that they by no means welcomed the prospect of a return to rule by Boer field-cornets. The section among the Griquas long known as *Bergenaars*, virtually bandits, had been on active commando against Moshesh's neighbours so lately as 1841 (above, p. 223); if their numbers were to be increased seriously by Boer pressure they might easily start more widespread 'depredations', producing in the north the same effects as 'extermination' on the old Xhosa frontier. In the end an exterminatory feud between the Boers and the Griquas was in all probability prevented only by the restraining influence of the missionaries; but even the possibility of a feud was not to be contemplated so lightly by the Government of the day, nor indeed by the Trekkers themselves, as it has been by some historians. The Government had good reason to know also that Griqualand would not long satisfy Boer land-hunger. The turn of Basutoland must come next and, as the history of the Free State was soon to prove, war would then be inevitable.

Such considerations moved Governor Napier in the course of 1843 to show himself disposed to meet appeals from the Griqua leaders, and also from Moshesh. For a moment negotiations were interrupted by the death of Mr. Wright in April; even the Griquas, it appears, were nervous of treaties when left without a spokesman. 'With no one to assist us,' writes one Hendrik Hendrikse, who had *Bergenaar* leanings, 'in a written agreement between two nations, one of which is highly civilized, and the other not so civilized or enlightened, it never goes well.' In a letter dated 25 August, however, Adam Kok himself formulated his appeal, and his questions demanded a serious answer. The Griqua settlement, he claimed, was sanctioned by General Bourke in 1826 and recognized at various times by later Governors. Now its integrity was threatened by colonial Boers,

British subjects; and whereas the Griquas had 'ever been faithful in their adherence to the British Government' these Boers had, in 1842, 'assembled with an armed force to throw off their allegiance, and employed both threats and promises to induce us to join them . . . but though in great danger we un-hesitatingly refused and waited in patience till Colonel Hare freed us from our difficulties'. In particular:

The insults and injuries inflicted on the Griquas by the Colonial Boers have convinced me that should I attempt to execute the laws of my country[1] respecting the lands of Philippolis, at present held by the Boers, when the leases shall have expired, nothing but the interference of the Colonial Government can prevent a war which must end in the destruction of one or both of the contending parties.

Kok's letter was, no doubt, the result of earlier consultations, and even before it can have reached Cape Town the Government Secretary was in communication with Dr. Philip and the missionaries about the terms of the contemplated treaty. For example, on 29 August Dr. Philip, referring to recent conversations, suggested to Montagu that Kok should have at least the same salary as Waterboer (below, p. 267). In the middle of October draft treaties were sent for signature, both to Kok and to Moshesh, and formalities were completed—at Philippolis on 29 November, and at Thaba Bosigo on 13 December. The chiefs now became allies, pledged to friendship, required to preserve order in their own territories, and to co-operate with the Colonial Government in maintaining peace and order on the frontiers; to this end they were allowed small supplies of arms and ammunition. In addition, to bind them to their alliance, and to give them standing with their own people, and with the Boers, they were put on salaries of £100 and £75 per annum respectively (sums by no means trifling at that time and place).

Such treaty-making in truth gave little hope of an effective settlement. This creation of Griqua and Basuto 'states' even had some of the weaknesses of the old plan of making 'para-

[1] An earlier appeal from Kok, sent in with Dr. Philip's letter of 25 Aug. 1842, makes more of the vain provision of Griqua 'laws' which expressly prohibited 'burghers' from leasing their land holdings to colonists. No doubt much of this Griqua correspondence was inspired and guided by missionaries (and more important people than Kok have letters and speeches prepared for them). But several letters exist that appear to have been *written* (in Dutch) as well as signed by Adam Kok himself.

mounts' of Gaika and Hintza. The land question was clearly fundamental. But the treaties not only set up no machinery to deal with disputes in Griqualand where Boers had already acquired a footing; they failed also to effect even a strict delimitation of the boundaries of the new states and this flaw, though perhaps inevitable, was fatal. Primitive peoples can have only vague ideas of territorial limits; even Moshesh's power and authority were weak on the outskirts of his domains, precisely where European encroachments were most considerable. Mr. Casalis, indeed, on behalf of Moshesh, lost no time in asserting the chief's full claims. On 13 December, the very day the treaty was signed, he wrote pointing out that the boundary assigned in the draft treaty excluded several miles of country which, although at present occupied with his permission by the Barolongs under Moroko, 'are undoubtedly within the territory of Moshesh'. Moshesh, therefore, signed only with reservations—in the full expectation that the matter would be adjusted. Equally promptly, however, the Rev. W. Shaw, Superintendent of the Wesleyan Missions in the disputed area, wrote protesting that his protégés were independent of Moshesh. The result was that early in January the Governor was consulting Dr. Philip about requests for separate treaties, not only with Moroko, a respectable chief with some 10,000 followers, but with lesser fry like Sikonyela, as well as with completely insignificant mixed breeds called Carolus Baaitje, Pieter Davids, and Gert Taaibosch, who had only two or three hundred followers each.[1]

But to multiply treaties must destroy any effectiveness they might otherwise have had. The French missionaries, co-operating with Dr. Philip and the L.M.S., were undoubtedly right in principle in holding that Moshesh was the only chief in those parts capable of maintaining his position; Sikonyela and the mixed breeds would be helpless to make a fair bargain with Boers wishing to settle among them, and quite incapable of fulfilling the treaty obligations of 'co-operation' with the Colonial Government for the preservation of peace and order. Their only hope was to stand together, and to consolidate the pacific authority of the stronger Basuto. On the other hand the effective power of Moshesh did not really extend so far as his

---

[1] Report by Field-Cornet Joubert in 1845 (quoted Cory, iv. 319).

supporters claimed. Population pressure was already so great that many of Moshesh's vassals had begun to encroach upon the lands of their neighbours—so that Sikonyela, for example, was perpetually at feud with Moshesh. The champions of the Basuto potentate failed to make sufficient allowance for the fears of the weaker chiefs, or to convince and carry with them their Wesleyan colleagues whose first concern was, naturally, to safeguard the special interests of their own little communities. At the same time, in pressing as they did for separate treaties the Wesleyans showed such lack of statesmanship as threatened to reduce the treaty policy to absurdity. The upshot was that no progress was made with the definition of the Basuto boundaries before the treaty policy as a whole was virtually abandoned and Sir Harry Smith came to try new ways in 1848.

In the Griqua country where the Europeans were already strongly established the treaty threw upon the shoulders of an improvised 'government' of semi-civilized Griquas a task like that which has vexed even organized Western States from that day to this, the ordering of a 'plural' society. From the beginning the Griquas showed themselves just sufficiently informed— by their knowledge of Dutch and by contact with the Colony— to be fearful and suspicious. In September 1843 W. Y. Thomson, like Wright before him, reported that only the hope of a treaty, and the prospect of Government assistance, restrained them from attacking the Boers who refused to vacate the fountains before the reinforcements of Trekkers should come in from Natal. At the same time they were nervous of Government measures:

What little news I can scrape together from Natal seems to say that a peace has been made in which the interests of the tribes in this quarter have been utterly overlooked and that we are consequently left to the tender mercies of the Boers. The consequence is that the very worst characters are leaving Natal and are trying to get a footing here and frightening the people with the story that Government will take Philippolis within the boundary and guarantee to the Boers the lands and fountains on which they now reside.

Incorporation in the Colony, he now fears, may make many Griquas 'turn *Bergenaar*'. 'The leases and written agreements on which the Griquas would ground their claims would be mere waste paper in a court of justice. . . . The Veld-Cornets, &c.,

would be appointed among the Boers . . . and the coloured people are not sufficiently civilized to cope with the Boers in cultivating the land, so that they would soon become mere labourers.'

Two months later the treaties had arrived and were 'well received'. But Atkinson, writing from Colesberg on 17 November, at once had doubts:

> There seems to be a lull, but I cannot think it will be permanent peace till something more shall have been done with the Boers (and their lands claims). The great fault and the chief difficulty is with the Philippolis government and people themselves. *They* let the Boers in, and gave them the footing they have, and now they cannot get them out if they would; and I do not believe many of them are sincere in wishing to get rid of them so long as they can get a little temporary advantage by letting their farms to them. I am afraid for them, they are so very weak and unstable.

About the same day Edward Solomon wrote from Griquatown regretting the spirit and attitude of the Griquas; they resent any advice or interference in their temporal affairs by the missionaries; if they were ripe to manage their own affairs all might be well but they 'obviously are not'. These unfortunate people were now left to themselves to straighten out the tangle in their district.

Just at first Mr. Thomson's letters indicate that even this show of British protection had eased the situation. Oberholster and the 'moderates' were anxious to vindicate their rights to land, but had no desire for conflict either with the British Government or with the Griquas themselves. They resisted, therefore, the more extreme counsels of the Republicans in their midst; as late as 7 March 1844 Mr. Thomson professed to fear nothing—the Boers being sharply divided among themselves. The first serious trouble arose, as might have been expected, about the effect of the treaty in subjecting Europeans to the now legally recognized authority of the Griqua chief and Council—an issue on which, as it happened, Oberholster and Republicans were in large measure agreed. In January 1844, two Europeans having quarrelled, one, Mills, was killed, the other, van Staden, was arrested by Kok and, strictly in accordance with the treaty, and with the terms of the little used Cape

Punishment Act of 1836, sent to Colesberg for trial. Thereupon the Winburg Boers in uproar threatened Kok with vengeance, raising a storm that blew over only after van Staden's release.

Other cases, less well known, served to reduce Kok's legal powers to a farce and on 28 March the Chief made an almost pitiable appeal to Cape Town. The immediate occasion was a complaint that certain Boers, in defiance of a newly enacted 'law', were not only introducing 'large quantities of ardent spirit' (a notorious temptation to the Griquas), but 'threatening to fire on any subject of Adam Kok who shall attempt to carry into execution the order of his chief mentioned above'. Shots, in fact, had already been exchanged between one Hans Rabie and certain Griquas, and Kok is 'grieved to inform His Excellency that he expects similar conduct from many others of the farmers from the threats and insulting language they employ'. In these circumstances the Chief asks:

Does His Excellency consider Kok justified in regarding all colonists resident in his District amenable to his laws? What assistance will His Excellency be prepared to render to Kok should the violence of farmers render dangerous the maintenance of order and execution of laws in his District? What advice can His Excellency give with regard to such colonists in his district as refuse obedience to his laws?

As the Governor could hold out no promise of help, but only advise great caution, the first effect of the treaty was, in truth, to define and make patent the state of anarchy that had long existed. It subjected the Boers in this area to a government as powerless to enforce its behests as they were determined to repudiate its authority. The Boers in this case had some cause for complaint. In the Boer Republics, for a long time to come, natives were subjected to their masters without any court of appeal. Here the Boers found themselves under the jurisdiction of Griquas who had no real courts at all. On the other hand in October 1843, before the Treaty took effect, Jan Vries, a Griqua, was summoned before the Circuit Court for debt on the application of a Boer. 'As the Attorney-General denies the right of the Griquas to indict a Boer because the jurisdiction of the Court does not extend beyond the boundary, this is giving the Griquas the severity of the English law without according them its protection.'[1]

---

[1] Thomson to Philip, 24 Oct. 1843.

Even in face of their united refusal to submit to such Griqua jurisdiction, divisions among the Boers continued so acute as to delay a crisis. When the treaty was first signed, Oberholster and his friends—258 'heads of families'[1]—had petitioned to be taken under direct British jurisdiction on the terms then being applied by Advocate Cloete in Natal. To this view of the matter they adhered, even proposing to Adam Kok, at a meeting in June 1844, to refuse to allow in Griqualand any who repudiated British allegiance. But they also protested to the authorities that they could not hold out indefinitely against the Republicans unless prompt measures were taken to support them in their old loyalty.

Out of the chaos there came one ray of light. Dr. Philip himself had always considered the long-vexed land question a matter for Government arbitration. Mr. Thomson elaborated the suggestion.[2] In October 1844, or early in November, Thomson and two colleagues discussed a plan of separate Boer and Griqua areas with the Lieutenant-Governor; the latter, apparently agreeing in principle, stipulated only that the Griquas must be prepared to accept the Government's decision and probably to 'forfeit the northern part of their land already occupied (hired?) by Boers'. The missionary Hughes in reporting this conversation commented that a 'population basis' would secure substantial justice for the Griquas and 'compel the Boers to condense'; the Griquas were to be left to 'manage their own concerns upon the principles of our municipalities in England'. In December somewhat similar proposals were made to Kok by the Republicans. In substance this was the plan adopted by Sir Peregrine Maitland seven months later.

In February 1845 the Council proposed a Land Commission and this was appointed in April; but the Government could not be persuaded to make a real move till its hand was forced by yet another and this time a more serious 'armed protest'. The occasion was Kok's rather tumultuous attempt, with a 'commando' of about 100 armed men, to arrest a Boer named Krynauw on a charge of ill-using a native servant. There seems to be no question but that Krynauw had administered a brutal

---

[1] Theal, ii. 422. Apparently also in Aug. 1842, when some of them claimed to have been there as early as the Griquas themselves (Cory, iv. 283).

[2] Thomson to Philip, 17 Oct. 1844. Also Hughes to Philip, 7 Nov. 1844.

flogging. On the other hand, finding their bird flown, the commando seems to have made free with some of his property. Thereupon, early in 1845, with marching and counter-marching, protesting Boers came together in camp at a place called Touwfontein, some thirty miles from Philippolis. By April the Griquas had assembled in opposition and there was virtually a state of war.[1] In a country crying out for decent administration the Government had delayed to intervene till the fire which had smouldered while it tarried burst into flame. In May British troops had to be rushed up to the Orange River. After one sharp skirmish at Zwartkopjes the Republican Boers withdrew to the north; the way was then apparently clear for Sir Peregrine Maitland to make some attempt at settlement when he arrived at Touwfontein in person in the middle of June. The restraining influence of London, however, severely hampered his freedom of action; his own report on his doings in the north[2] shows its paralysing effect:

My object was no less than to secure their land and freedom to the numerous native tribes, inhabiting the country hundreds of miles beyond the Colony to the north-east, against the encroachments and aggressions of self-expatriated British subjects, superior in combination and arms, and too often ready as well as able to dispute successfully with the rightful owners of the soil for the simple necessaries of a half-civilized life. [Of the Emigrants he notes, moreover] their independent and migratory habits, their disaffection towards the British Government, their readiness to plunge into the interior to escape the least pressure of an external power upon them, and their contempt for the natives, their indifference to native rights and native life. . . .

I cannot keep too prominently in Your Lordship's view the extreme scantiness of the means at my disposal, for I felt bound to lay aside as utterly impracticable any plan which involved any considerable expense *either for a Civil or a Military* establishment.

Dr. Philip's 1842 report on the 'Transvaal' problem was clearly not forgotten.[3] After meeting the chiefs at Touwfontein

---

[1] It is significant that the Boers did not have it as much their own way as with most Bantu tribes. In petty skirmishes the casualties seem to have been 1 Griqua killed and 6 taken prisoner, and 10 Boers killed and wounded (Cory, iv. 307).

[2] To Secretary of State, 1 Aug. 1845.

[3] The Governor must certainly have seen also a report from the missionary Edwards, made after a long journey to the north-east in Oct. 1844, to the effect

on 26 June the Governor reminded his superiors that unrest had come to a head in the Griqua country but was 'of much wider extent—stretching over the greater part of the country inhabited by Bechuana and Coranna tribes up to the Magaliesberg and French Mountains north of Delagoa Bay'; he urged also that a settlement in Griqualand 'should be framed on principles applicable to the intermixture of British subjects and natives . . . up to 25 degrees S. lat.' In Griqua country, he adds, there was 'scarcely one Boer' who had not obtained his farm, 'generally on lease, from an individual Griqua or their *Raad* (Council) by the payment of a valuable consideration as stipulated by a contract'. Elsewhere, however, 'the Boers generally paid nothing for the lands on which they located themselves, and in many instances held them not only without the Chief's permission but by force, in defiance of his power to remove them'. A temporary pacification would serve no useful purpose. It became necessary 'to do something with these numerous and scattered farmers to prevent fresh quarrels and collisions with the native tribes, and to put a stop to the gradual process of shoving the latter out of their lands and either exterminating them or reducing them to slavery'. The Boers could not be brought back to the Colony, and to expel those settled in Griqualand would only drive them on to adjoining tribes. 'The continued location of them, therefore, among the tribes, *under some restraining regulation*, seemed the only plan open for any consideration.' 'Extension of British sovereignty' being equally out of the question, he concluded that since there was 'land enough for both', they should, in effect, be 'segregated'— by measures 'confining the farmers within certain defined limits, and reserving for the natives an ample tract within which no foreigner should be allowed to acquire land'.

The faltering treaty of 1843 which in time elicited this first clear official statement of the real issue and one possible way of dealing with it cannot after all be written off as wholly vain.

that 'all the Bechuanas east of the Marico are in subjection to the Boers'. One 'Pilane', for example (probably about the 'Pilandsberg'), had said to him: 'I can do and say nothing (relative to the placing of a missionary). I live in the country of the Boers for fear of Moselekatze. I am their servant.' The Boers had then 'all gone to seek powder, and even ordered me (Pilane) to send my warriors'. According to Edwards, 'They are evidently preparing for a struggle with the English and could easily turn us all out of the Bechuana country.'

Nor, as tradition likes to assume, was it in any way *anti*-Boer; so far from being a cause of Griqua–Boer conflict this feeble instrument was an attempt to restrain a conflict which was already acute, so acute as to compel the Governor's attention and move him to this vain attempt to press improvements on his superiors in London. But Lord Stanley's instructions were really only stock pattern; the Colonial Office, a junior in the official hierarchy, was powerless against the Establishment's fixed preference for 'informal' Empire;[1] trade must always be fostered, but without involving the national government in burdensome responsibilities; the local magnate might be buttressed by the use of 'influence' to ensure a necessary degree of stability, but new colonies were definitely not wanted and those in being must by hook or crook be made to pay their own way. Maitland's task was to persuade the far from open-minded Home Government that the potentates now concerned were very weak, at best limited in their range, and at any rate, all of them, utterly incapable of holding the balance even between their own people and new-comers who were emigrants, but at the same time still British subjects. With the devoted help of Philip and his missionaries he was able to get so far as to outline a plan which, with goodwill and good guidance, might have prevented the break-up which was so soon to follow and enabled South Africa to continue on its way as a political unit.

The basis of the settlement was that proposed earlier by W. Y. Thomson. The native territories were to be divided into two portions, one inalienable, the other open for European settlement on terms to be agreed upon with the Colonial Government. The inalienable reserve was to be 'amply sufficient for the present and future wants' of the tribe; that open to lessors was to be defined by treaty and selected, as far as could be, so as to move as few of the existing occupants as possible. An Agent, backed by the force of the Government, was to be on the spot to deal with disputes as they arose; his authority, however, was to be a delegation of that of the chief, not an extension of British sovereignty. Colonists—'clusters of British subjects in their locations'—were to have 'self-government', but were to pay an annual quit-rent, half the proceeds going to the chief,

---

[1] R. Robinson and J. Gallagher's phrase, *Africa and the Victorians*, Macmillan, 1961.

half to defray the expenses of the Agent. Almost anticipating some latter-day Indirect Rule, the 'sovereignty' of the land as a whole was to remain vested in the chief, he ruling his people in accordance with their own law and custom. On these terms a new treaty with Adam Kok was signed in February 1846. Moshesh agreed in principle to the new plan sketched by the Governor at the Touwfontein meeting in June 1845 but his territorial disputes with his neighbours stood unresolved. Barely a month later the Xhosa had provoked a declaration of war. As in 1835, official attention was totally diverted from north to east, again making further progress hopeless.

This revised treaty policy was nevertheless an advance on anything that had preceded it, including, notably, Governor D'Urban's 'locations'. For almost the first time it was recognized that black and white must inevitably share the land between them, but that their different standards placed the backward race at a hopeless disadvantage in unrestricted competition; therefore a minimum of native land must be made inalienable. Unfortunately most of these peoples' well-wishers tended to make the provision of 'reserves' an end in itself, with never a thought for the use to which they were put. Even the rules against alienation were, at first at least, imperfectly enforced, as in Griqualand. After all, the best economics of the day taught the virtues of free competition so fervently that freehold tenure of land, being a highly prized right, was pressed on the unfortunate free Cape people who thus lost virtually all the tenuous acreage they ever had, even that of the old 'Hottentot Institutions'.[1] Many Africans too were rewarded for their services with land held on free 'native title'; this is practically all now in European ownership. *Laissez-faire* principles also forbade purposeful development by local or any other authority, with the result that traditional agricultural methods were left to provide as best they might for an expanding population. The 'development' which became the fashion only in our day has in consequence had to begin by undertaking wholesale reclamation and restoration of Reserves threatened with the approach of (as one Commission was to put it) 'desert conditions'. The existence of Reserves served in truth for many years (see Chs. I and XVIII) to warrant almost forgetting the presence of

---

[1] For examples see *Cape Col. Qn.*, pp. 252, 284-6.

millions of Bantu. As lately as 1930 a Southern Rhodesian Land Apportionment Act was claimed in all sincerity to be forestalling the troubles already besetting South Africa by making 'ample provision', betimes, for future African development. Modern South African leaders must wish in their hearts, when planning their 'Bantustans', that their Republican predecessors had shown any similar forethought.

The revised northern treaties of 1845 which provided for inalienable reserves never became sufficiently operative for the complex administrative details necessary for their efficient working to mature. Even before the major diversion on the old frontier early in 1846 Dr. Philip fell out of action. In the preparatory months of 1845 the missionaries who spoke for the people concerned, and had successfully floated the idea of 'reserves', strove hopefully for a reasonable settlement, one moreover which fully recognized the legitimate claims and interests of the Boer farmers. Edward Solomon, trained by Dr. Philip, and married to Mrs. Philip's niece, rejoiced that the protection of neighbouring tribes would no longer rest on the none too strong shoulders of the already almost forgotten Waterboer. 'Additional treaties', he writes to Dr. Philip from Griquatown on the eve of the Touwfontein meeting, 26 June 1845, 'will rouse our people to see that their superiority must be maintained, not by a mere treaty with the Government, but by a steady progress in civilization and religion.' Mr. Solomon was pushing on with an irrigation furrow from the Vaal River to help them in their hard struggle for existence. 'If the means of civilization were at hand I believe our people would make rapid strides.' A large body of irrigation workers from other parts, he believes, 'would settle here if they could only find means of supporting themselves'. He concludes:

Now is the time for the interference of our Government on wide and comprehensive principles. Now or never. I think that Sir P. Maitland may now by some bold and decided step settle the affairs of the Boers which have given so much trouble to his predecessors. . . . The Boers must be brought under British rule and must be separated from the Griquas. This is the only foundation on which peace can be established in this country. You will, no doubt, be using your influence with Government to direct them aright, and I thank God that you are still in the country at this critical period.

It was a great misfortune that precisely at this crisis Dr.
Philip was no longer fully available to advise upon the difficult
adjustments involved in the signing of new and more elaborate
treaties. Early in July 1845 the old man of 70—full as ever of
affairs—had travelled as far as the Kat River, on his way to the
north, when he was summoned back to Hankey by a tragic
event, the drowning of his eldest son, William, and his 11-year-
old grandson (Johnny Fairbairn). Letters from W. Y. Thomson
and others indicate that even after this blow Dr. Philip was
instrumental in securing (unspecified) 'material alterations' in
Adam Kok's treaty.[1] In one of his last reports to the L.M.S. he
was still of his old opinion: 'The tribes are for the present
preserved from the destruction that threatened them. . . . The
treaties will, I hope, afford protection *till they shall become
colonial subjects, the only thing that will place them beyond the reach of
danger.*' Thus Philip on 26 March 1846, immediately before the
outbreak of the Kaffir War, a calamity of which he wrote little;
though still Superintendent he was only 'waiting for a successor'
(till 1850) and never his old self again. In January 1846 he was
presented on behalf of the Basuto with a lamp—for his help in
'bringing them light'. But his second visit, on the journey
actually begun, never was made. His 1842 tour was mainly
instrumental in first putting the northern region on the official
map at all. Now he was unable to follow up such success as he
had had. It must have made a difference had Dr. Philip been
able, for example, to clinch the matter of the 'inalienable'
reserve, to help in the settlement of Moshesh's boundaries, or
even to talk over with the Governor in Cape Town the full
letters that continued to reach him about the administrative
difficulties of the frontier Agents. It was above all for want of
help and guidance that the short-lived Orange Sovereignty
was finally engulfed. 'Dr. Philip's Treaty States', so called,
were, at the last at any rate, like ships sent to sea without a
navigating officer.

The usual view is that the treaty policy was unduly consid-

---

[1] Mrs. Philip's letters during her husband's absence in 1845 throw incidental
light on happenings not recorded when he was on the spot. On 2 May, for example,
she sent Thomson's letters 'first to the Governor', before forwarding them. A week
later 'the Governor sent to ask if we knew anything of the happenings at Griquatown'
(where the Boers were supposed to be creating a diversion to keep Waterboer from
coming to help Philippolis).

erate of Griqua and native interests, and correspondingly provocative of Boer resentment.[1] The relative strength of the emigrant Boers, if not their actual numbers, made Boer co-operation and consent the first essential of any permanent settlement, and at Touwfontein no doubt, Sir Peregrine Mait-land, like any good Army officer, was severe towards those subjects of the Queen who claimed to treat with him as spokes-men of an independent Republic. But the die-hards, as their quarrels with Oberholster proved, were only a section of the European settlers in Griqualand, and a good deal less important at that time than the later history of the Republics would sug-gest. The important thing just then was to keep the goodwill of the 'moderates', and the fact is that so far as their first objective, land, was concerned, *bona fide* settlers got very good terms in-deed.

In Griqualand proper the area open to lease was markedly larger than the inalienable 'reserve'. At the very beginning missionaries and Griquas protested[2] at the ear-marking of half the quit-rent accruing from leases—hitherto all their own—for the maintenance of an Agent (as it seemed to them) 'for the protection of the Boers'. The Agent was, indeed, too weak, had he wished it, to put any serious pressure on the stronger party in the territory—the Boer farmers. Mr. Thomson continued to complain, too, not only of the feebleness of attempts to use the Punishment Act to protect natives against ill-usage, but of the failure, sometimes even of the absence of any desire, to clear the 'Reserve' for native occupation. By a later decision of Sir Harry Smith[3] farmers might be required to vacate lands in the Reserve, but only on receiving 'compensation for improvements'; and as the Griquas were either too poor or too improvident to make this payment, Maitland's hope that 'in forty years the Reserves will be free' proved too optimistic. Government by a mere Agent was a further fundamental weakness of this settle-ment and could not be a permanent *modus regendi*. An Agent could never have the legal and moral authority of a regular

[1] Cf. Cory, iv. 314.

[2] (Thomson to Philip, 1 July 1845.) In November Thomson said the Griquas were rather against annexation on the ground of the Attorney-General's 'special pleading', i.e. tenderness for Boer interests. He wrote similarly in Feb. 1847.

[3] Dr. C. W. de Kiewiet MSS., 'The British Government and the South African Republics', later published as *British Colonial Policy*, Longmans, 1929.

magistrate, having the backing neither of troops nor even of police. But it was not the Boers' interests which chiefly suffered from this weakness.

For a very short time the unlooked for outcome of the Xhosa disturbance was even to improve the prospects of a comprehensive settlement. In December 1847, when Sir Harry Smith took over as Governor, his ripe experience made him decide that the right course was at last to take full control of the frontiers. Having proclaimed a new Province of British Kaffraria and, as he hoped, pacified the chiefs, he marched north to the Orange River country and, having dispersed 'die-hard' Boer opposition at Boomplaats, annexed the whole of the region between the Orange, the Vaal, and the Drakensberg as the Orange River Sovereignty. What was more, the Colonial Secretary, Earl Grey, was for once sufficiently forceful to override critics in the Colonial Office and to carry the Cabinet with him in such a drastic change of policy. It of course strengthened Grey's hand that, by this time, the combined influence of liberal sentiment in favour of self-government and more self-seeking economical considerations had the country fully committed to a policy of colonial devolution; preparations for the establishment of representative institutions in the parent Cape Colony were well advanced. In the middle of 1851 a draft constitution for the Orange River Sovereignty actually reached Cape Town,[1] but this was held back by Sir Harry Smith, and apparently its very existence was overlooked by his successor, Sir George Cathcart. Had all gone well the extension of parliamentary government to the people of the Orange River Territory, whose interests were identical with those of the parent Cape Colony, must have followed as a matter of course. In that event, since their right to the land had been acknowledged, there was neither reason nor inducement for the really solid, peace-loving majority of the Orange River Boers to join the irreconcilable Republicans. The influence of Mocke and Co., cut off from the later Orange Free State and frowned upon by the official Dutch Church,[2] must have been weak and negligible in face of a

---

[1] de Kiewiet MSS.
[2] Letters from Rev. A. Faure to Dr. Philip (e.g. on 1 Jan. 1844) afford fresh evidence of the well-known dislike of the Dutch Church for the Trek movement, or, it is sometimes said, of a 'lack of sympathy' between ministry and people.

liberal Cape Colony reaching to the Vaal. The die-hards might then have been left to come to their senses at their leisure, and to some 'common South Africanism'.

It was not to be. In the late forties South Africa was nearer to recovering and retaining its unity than it ever was again, even in 1910. This hope was blasted, not by the imperfections of the attempted settlement in the north, but because Her Majesty's advisers were driven to despair by events in the Xhosa east. On 1 April 1846, within a month of the signing of the second Kok treaty, Governor Maitland left Cape Town to take charge of operations in the east; for the next two years he and his successor, Sir Henry Pottinger, had so much to occupy them there that they left the newly appointed Government Agent in the north almost entirely to his own devices. The Agent's authority was so very slender that he could hope to make good only if he was sure of backing from the Cape Colony. The war, however, absorbed not only the Governor but all available troops. It also encouraged the more refractory Boers to persist in a restless agitation. Thus further embarrassed, the hapless Agent made little progress with the Griqua settlement, and none whatever farther afield on the much disputed boundaries of Moshesh's country. Sir Harry himself may have had little leisure for the details of land and boundary disputes; and before his downright policy had had time to prove itself, late in 1850 the pent-up grievances of the Ama-Xhosa burst into fiercer flame than ever. Like the administrators of those early forties, historians give all their attention to the Great Trek; but the political consequences of that venture were determined in very large part by the resolution with which, not the voortrekkers, but the Ama-Xhosa tribesmen they so lightly regarded, fought to maintain *their* independence.

XV

THE TREATY SYSTEM ON THE EASTERN FRONT, 1838–42— MALADMINISTRATION AND DROUGHT

On the principles dominant in modern South Africa relations with the tribes on that vexed Cape frontier should have been easier stabilized than those of the scattered peoples in the north. The Ama-Xhosa had their internal divisions,[1] but were yet a compact, homogeneous community, living in areas which were 'their own' and had fairly definite boundaries. The problem was apparently only to keep peace on the border where black and white met, whereas in the Griqua country Europeans and coloured people were not only in perennial danger of a physical clash, but had to find a *modus vivendi* side by side in the same country. The obstacle to an eastern settlement was of course that South African colonists of that day saw the Bantu's 'own areas' only as wastefully used grazing land and poached on it freely. The Ama-Xhosa for their part, rival pastoralists all of them, and better placed than their fellows on the open High Veld, equally freely used the ample cover afforded by their bush-country to retaliate on a considerable scale by well organized, or merely random, cattle-stealing.

In origin the 1836 Treaties, like those of the forties, were a compromise between humanitarians seeking to protect the native tribes, and economists concerned above all for the interests of the British taxpayer. In the event economical motives had the certain effect of starving efficient administration, making the treaties in all their history a poor substitute for the full responsibility and control which missionaries and others vainly pressed for. The treaties, moreover, had a bad start. In the excitement of 1836 land-hungry colonists were blind to the Xhosa's need for land, and were gravely disappointed that their own hopes of new farms in Kaffirland were frustrated, fearful

---

[1] Treaties were signed separately in 1836 with the Gaikas, Ndhlambis, and Gunukwebe—later with the Tambookies (or Tembus).

at the same time that the retention of the borderlands by the 'Kaffirs' would mean a continuance of cattle-stealing. They were prepared apparently to have taken that grave risk had the boundary been extended to the Kei. From the beginning colonial opinion was almost derisively hostile to the 'Glenelg policy' and, seeing in it only the cloven hoof of humanitarian distrust, unwilling ever to give it a fair trial as even a possible remedy for frontier disorders.

The treaties as framed undoubtedly showed the influence of humanitarian and other critics of the lack of policy that had led to the war of 1834; Xhosa land-hunger being recognized as a real thing, even the long-disputed 'Ceded' Territory was given back to them, not indeed in full ownership, but on 'loan'— during good behaviour. Military posts on the border, like Fort Beaufort, were to remain but, for the rest, the control of the frontier was thrown on the chiefs; colonial interests were represented by Agents, resident near the principal chiefs but armed only with 'diplomatic' authority. On paper, at least, there was a reversion to the policy of non-intercourse; British subjects must enter Kaffirland only with permits, at their own risk, and remain there subject to Bantu law; Bantu on the other hand were to enter the Colony only with 'passes' from the Agent.[1]

The cattle-stealing provisions were at least elaborate. Any Bantu caught red-handed in the Colony was to be dealt with under Colonial law but even shot at if necessary. With former usage in mind the treaty-makers now laid it down emphatically that 'on no occasion whatever shall any Patrol, or armed party of any description, be allowed to cross' the boundary, either for the capture of alleged criminals or for the recovery of stolen animals. On the Xhosa side of the line the law of the chiefs must prevail, colonial interests being watched or sponsored only by and through the Agents. Thus, if colonial pursuers traced thieves or cattle to the boundary, two courses were open to them; they might cross, unarmed, enlist the aid of the nearest *pakati* (councillor or headman) and, having with his help traced the spoor, report on oath to the Agent, carry off their own property (and no more), leaving the exaction and

---

[1] In practice the colonial need for labour, and distress in the tribal areas, led to a considerable influx of Bantu on passes issued apparently under the 49th Ordinance of 1828 (see pp. 87 ff. and 300).

payment of compensation to the chief; alternatively, complainants might appeal to the nearest military post for an escort and, having traced the spoor as far as they could or dared, lodge a complaint, on oath, with the Agent, thus throwing the whole responsibility on to the chief direct. The burdens thrown on the victims of thefts seeking lawfully to recover their stock were onerous, or even clumsy. The hand of Stockenström (possibly of Dr. Philip) appears in the provisions which require, for example, a formal declaration, on oath, not only of the precise number of animals missing, but also that they were properly guarded by day,[1] or adequately secured in kraals or stables at night; if the theft was at night pursuit must be commenced, at the latest, early next morning—this last, no doubt, to make sure that the animals' traces were reasonably fresh, and to check the notorious ingenuity of 'spoor-finders'.

These not in themselves unreasonable regulations made little allowance for the natural difficulties of farmers scattered over an unfenced frontier. At the same time, the scheme threw such a burden of responsibility on the chiefs as could only be borne by them if the civilized government did its share in trying to prevent cattle-stealing. But the frontier line was open, virtually without police protection.[2] To operate these paper treaties must have taxed the resources of even a very strong latter-day colonial administration, but the staff available at the Cape was virtually nil. Thieving inevitably continued, and changes made to meet constant demands were always in the direction of heaping more responsibility on to the chiefs without offering them anything in return; prolonged wars and unsettlement must in any case have impoverished their people—it is not to be forgotten how short a time had elapsed since the clearing of the Zuurveld in 1811; men driven from their homes at the age of 20 when old enough to feel violent resentment were only 55 in 1846, in their full strength and vigour at least as leaders and councillors.[3] This Government, which had for years allowed its

[1] 'The frontier farmers should remember that they got *good* land *cheap*, and they should not complain of having to protect their flocks as they knew they would have to do' (Stockenström to Philip, 25 Aug. 1842).

[2] Capt. Stretch, e.g. on 28 Sept. 1839, complained to the Governor's Secretary that a body of 60 native police was not properly remunerated. In 1836 they had been paid with cattle taken from delinquents, but this 'fund' ceased when 'Queen Adelaide' was abandoned.

[3] e.g. 'His rights to the Kat River is a theme Maqomo delights to dwell on, [and,

subjects to encroach on what the Bantu had reason to look on as *their* land, now expected law and order from the long harassed tribes—even that they should police colonial farms on its behalf.

On his first trip to the frontier in 1838 Sir George Napier seemed to accept unreservedly a colonial view, that the farmers were blameless—that the Xhosa had 'no excuse for their continued and daring depredations', and that the chiefs did not do their part in checking them. His report to Lord Glenelg on 12 July 1838[1] saw mainly a task for soldiers—'to defend the Colony from any sudden rush of Kafirs'—in fact he could not see how to make the troops 'at the same time a police force to check the constant stealing of cattle which must, if not speedily put a stop to, force farmers who reside on the immediate frontier to emigrate or be reduced to absolute want'. For the present he contented himself with warning the chiefs and trying to strengthen the patrol system. Returning to Cape Town in October, evidently with the firm impression that the treaties were a hopeless failure,[2] he decided in January 1839 on one step of very doubtful wisdom. In his desire to test the efficacy of the treaties in preventing thefts he instituted a 'Not Reclaimable List' of animals stolen (or alleged to be), but 'irreclaimable' because their owners had failed to comply with the undoubtedly rigorous stipulations of the treaties. In practice this list grew inordinately because farmers were able to submit records of losses 'by theft' without the need for proof, thus inevitably keeping excitement alive on both sides. Colonial discontents were doubled by such 'official' evidence of their sufferings, and the much advertised 'D'Urban System' came to be idealized by contrast. On the other hand the Xhosa were alarmed by this (unsifted) testimony against them and protested, like Maqomo on one occasion: 'Our people steal oxen and cows but the Government steals with the pen.'[3]

Maqomo being] of a warlike and ungovernable disposition, [he and others] if Sandile's countenance be obtained, would scarcely reflect on the fearful and ruinous consequences to them of attempting to recover the lands Gaika lost in 1819, and which, I reiterate, I believe to be the source of existing irregularities on both sides of the Border' (Stretch to Lieutenant-Governor, 6 Mar. 1845).

[1] Quoted Cory, iv. 329.

[2] To Secretary of State, Sept. 1840. 'Never were treaties more strictly and pertinaciously adhered to', he writes, yet 'it has been impossible to prevent depredations.... But God forbid that I should ever be an advocate of the unjust or inhuman policy which calls for seizure of the land.'

[3] As early as Sept. 1839 Stretch begins to complain of 'unofficial' returns in the

Nearly two years later, in October 1840, the Governor set out once more for the frontier, armed this time with a carefully annotated memorandum by Judge Menzies, and hoping to secure modifications in the Treaties.[1] As a result, a Proclamation of 28 January 1841 (sanctioned by Lord John Russell in a dispatch of 17 April 1841) announced that, by agreement with the chiefs, armed herdsmen would no longer be required, that *bona fide* pursuers of stolen cattle might cross the boundary, in small parties and unarmed, without the formality of procuring passes, and that 'on recovering cattle they should be allowed to take something more than the exact quantity lost, by way of compensation for time and trouble'.[2] These changes seem to have been helpful in the recovery of stolen cattle, but they had the defect of lessening the need for the Government to improve its defective police system.

The evidence is, however, that Napier's views were considerably modified by what he learned on his second frontier visit;[3] while trying to keep the peace by winking at the payment of compensation for 'irreclaimable' losses, he now took the alarms of Grahamstown more calmly; not all the murders reported were the work of 'foreigners'; besides 'strays', many of the thefts complained of were the work of Hottentots, Fingos, and ex-slaves, or of Xhosa whom the farmers 'harboured' for their own convenience in defiance alike of pass laws and of the wishes of the chiefs.[4] Stretch afterwards reported that according to Napier himself the Governor had come to Kaffirland disposed to proclaim martial law and get Stretch hanged.[5] A new note began to be heard. In Napier's dispatch of 7 January 1841

Press gaining credence, while the Agents were ignored. In support he forwarded 'statements' from Maqomo, Botman, and Tyali, complaining of 'claims' for cattle and horses that had not been adequately traced. Such claims, he concluded, were 'the cause of the last war'.

[1] Memo. in Gubbins Collection.   [2] Cory, iv. 353.

[3] Napier may possibly have met Stockenström, who returned from England to his farm near Bedford just about the time of the Governor's visit and on 29 Oct. wrote to Fairbairn claiming that, thanks to the treaties, the frontier was unusually peaceful, and that the Boers of the Colony rejoiced in their immunity from service on commandos. The 'Eastern' party, however, were pressing for changes, and must be carefully watched lest their importunity make the Governor depart from the *principles* of the treaties and make a big war inevitable (letter in Gubbins Collection). To Dr. Philip on 26 Feb. 1841 he 'refrained from comment' on the revised treaties—'the amendments, appendages or whatever you call them'.

[4] Walker, p. 233.   [5] Memo. on Treaties, Gubbins Collection.

he remarked on 'the excitement kept up in Kaffraria by the movements of the emigrant farmers', and noted the likelihood that 'especially the Gonaquabi' will soon 'make a formal application' to be brought under 'the authority and control of H.M. Government'. In the following December: 'No important merchant in Grahamstown has not within the last few years invested in sheep farms along the border'—one, Cypherfontein, sold by the Government for £1,975, resold lately for £3,500; another, on the Fish River, bought for £300, had sold for £1,100. 'Thefts', he adds, are largely 'for food'. In October 1843 he wrote:

It is the object of a party on the Frontier at present to exhibit the Kafir character in the most unfavourable light in order to prove that the effect of the treaties has been to degrade rather than elevate them in the scale of civilization.

And he promised statistics to prove the contrary.

Almost on the eve of his departure, 4 December 1843, Napier definitely challenged Colonel Hare's faith in 'coercion, prudently, justly, and judiciously conducted', urging that this was a mere reversion to the 'Commando System', and that 'every armed patrol would be to postpone the great object of the treaties, namely, to raise the Kafirs by an appeal to their sense of justice'. He would rather the punishment of robbers rested, not on the chiefs but on colonial tribunals, and concluded by expressing approval of the suggestion made by Dr. Philip in a letter of August 1843 to Montagu:

I consider the want of what is here recommended [a salary for Kok], to be the grand defect of the Caffre treaties. Had a few of the powerful chiefs been subsidized by having small salaries allowed to them we might by this time have had the affairs of Caffreland in our own hands.

This advice was actually followed later by Governor Maitland in his revised treaty.

The truth is that the treaties were by no means the unqualified failure that tradition would suggest. Futile as a permanent solution, they yet marked an undoubted advance on the *bellum in pace* of the years between 1811 and 1834. The reprisals and commandos of all those years contributed their share to the insecurity and unrest out of which the Trek developed;

the burghers who remained now had a rest at least from military service. In 1839 there was a fresh development of mission work, even by the L.M.S. which in 1830 had expressly diverted the French missionaries to a less unsettled area.[1] In particular these years brought prosperity (see p. 193) to the much complaining Eastern Province. The rise in land values remarked upon by the Governor as well as by Stockenström[2] and his friends owed a little to 'compensation', but was due in the first place to the introduction of sheep-farming; and though some frontiersmen abandoned their farms, whether to go on trek or to seek a safer zone within the Colony, the development of the wool industry could not have come about without some measure of practical security. Before long the very success of the treaties in keeping relative peace gave rise to a new demand for native labour; then difficulties about 'passes' and about 'squatters', and also (since according to Napier[3] squatters sometimes stole in order to live) a new chain of 'thievings', started a renewed attack upon the treaties themselves.

The original sin which finally led to the breakdown of the treaties was European as well as Xhosa, and the causes of failure a good deal more complex than the colonial critics, by whom they have always been summarily condemned, ever allow. The first blow to this policy was the (hardly blameworthy) failure, and the fall, of Andries Stockenström, who framed but did not originally suggest the treaties, and undoubtedly thought of them as a mere preliminary. The Philip Papers[4] made it clear that in the Lieutenant-Governor's view they were to prepare the minds of the Xhosa tribes for willing acceptance, presently, of the advantages of civilized government within the Colony. Thus, in a long apologia to Philip on 25 August 1842: 'This abominable Natal affair frightens me. . . . I see our political and normal advancement retarded half a century.' He pours scorn on Lord Normanby for his desire to treat the colonists with 'Conciliation'; fancying he could establish a firm government on a mere ephemeral 'popularity'(!) (which Stockenström

---

[1] New stations were planted by Messrs. Calderwood and Birt (see also above, p. 95).   [2] *Cape Col. Qn.*, pp. 79, 80.   [3] Below, p. 279 and note 1.
[4] The Philip MSS. included important letters not only from Read and Calderwood but also from Stockenström, Stretch, and many others.

lacked), he unhinged the confidence of all friends of order . . . and shook the foundations of good Government and left us with almost *none at all'*. . . .

I speak and feel strongly. Is not this my native country? Have not the Boers always been dear to me? Are not the English my fellow subjects and adopted countrymen? Are not all the victims of rapacity and savage cruelty, of whatever colour and class, my fellow-creatures? Might we not all improve and prosper together? . . .

After a long defence of the Boers as potentially 'the best disposed and easiest managed people in H.M. dominions', he urges the systematic 'colonization of all depopulated territories'. As for the tribes, 'I confess that (with Sir B. D'Urban) I should be glad to see the whole of Africa one immense British Colony with our laws in full vigour through every nook of it. But . . . it is folly to talk of reversing the order of nature. . . .' Hence:

Where you have depopulated territories, over which there may be scattered remnants of tribes who have lost all order or law, or never had any, and are altogether powerless against your own subjects, whom you cannot keep away from them, and who show their superiority merely by oppression and plunder and slaughter, then you must either leave those enormities to take their course, until the original population of the soil shall be completely rooted up, or enslaved, and the moral degradation shall have come to such a depth as to act injuriously upon the parent state which sent forth the venom; or you must interfere by applying the only antidote at your command; —you must '*swamp*' the bad by an ample supply of the good, and adapt the orphan race to a full participation in the benefits of the laws and improvements which this superior population will bring along with them, thus forming a nucleus to which thousands of the oppressed will gradually draw for protection, and planting the seed from which British law and British institutions may in process of time spread far and wide, as their virtues become known and felt and the soil becomes prepared for their culture. . . . For example, the Griquas are already thoroughly convinced of the superiority of British rule, but to force Moshesh and his tribe to become British subjects forthwith might be disastrous.

In normal conditions Stockenström might have been trusted to keep a fair balance. Himself a frontier farmer he could not disregard frontier security, and as administrator he must also have been watchful of the effects of his policy on Bantu interests and feelings. But conditions were far from normal. In the two years of his lieutenant-governorship he was so persecuted by his Grahamstown critics that though indefatigable in organizing his department he was absorbed and over-wrought: citing similar colonial persecution of Maynier, Philip, and Fairbairn, 'May the D——l pity me!' (he writes to Fairbairn, October 1837). 'I am quite done up' (28 February 1838), 'I can go on no longer.' Also—'I know my own temper.' His enemies are getting the officials 'in their fangs'; their evidence against him is taken 'in holes and corners'. In March 1838 when Grahamstown was celebrating, with illuminations, the failure of a libel action he brought against the Civil Commissioner Campbell, he writes: 'I never humbled myself before any man. . . . There lives a God who will settle all this in defiance of the whole fraternity.' By July he had decided to take leave of absence, not without the satisfaction of finding the Governor comparatively sympathetic:

> The malicious and stupid faction will be disappointed in their hopes of setting the Governor and myself by the ears. As I despise *them* and their meanness and see them with pity and contempt flourish in their disappointed fury, so much I reverence and venerate the true gentleman and man of honour.

This being Stockenström's state of mind as revealed in his confidential letters to John Fairbairn,[1] he was naturally inclined to seize on every fragment of evidence that went to justify the treaty experiment. From the Chumie in October 1837 he noted the surprise of Sir John Wylde, the Chief Justice, at finding that at a conference with the chiefs he and Captain Stretch went all *unarmed*, quite safe among those 'irreclaimable monsters'. Like Stretch he insisted that a ' "Cabal" and "War Party" *want* a blow up—that they may share in the scramble'— more than once, that 'the price of land continues to rise'. The frontier is almost always 'quiet'—'only six head of cattle this week' (January 1838). Again (27 April)—'the fellow who pretends to believe that the Hottentots and Caffres are preparing to *eat us up* gives £200 for a sheep farm *bordering on the Fish River Bush*'. In July, on the eve of departure: 'The Government sees more and more through the trick of frontier dangers', one Major Charters having returned 'delighted' from the front

[1] J. G. Gubbins Collection.

where '*unarmed* Boers have gone into Kafirland, got a commando from the chiefs, and returned successful' with the cattle. Finally on 10 August he encloses Reports 'to enable you to judge whether I have any cause to blush at the fruit of my labours'.[1]

One whole-hearted supporter, Captain Stretch, as Agent among the Gaikas, the most 'turbulent' of the clans, was in a position to know the facts and no less emphatic about the 'tranquillity' of which Stockenström boasted.[2] The farmers' complaints undoubtedly ascribed to the 'Kaffirs' all losses whatever —animals straying in an unfenced and broken country or coming to grief in holes and dongas, together with the 'sins of jackals, wolves and tigers' now being laid to the charge of the Xhosa, as in other days to that of 'vagrant' Hottentots. But peace in Kaffirland was not incompatible with thefts and 'depredations' in the Colony itself; it was therefore easy enough to charge Stockenström with crying 'Peace, Peace', where there was no peace. One effect of the persistence of his critics was thus that Stockenström himself came to judge the treaty policy by their standards—his own emphasis supported and confirmed the impression that Xhosa cattle-stealing was the beginning and end of the matter. Napier (for a time at least), and Maitland after him, absorbed to the full the still almost universal delusion that cattle-stealing was the fundamental cause of the whole long tragedy of the Kaffir Wars.

The cattle-stealing was of course the sympton of frontier unrest rather than its prime cause. As the Gaika chief, Sandile, protested to Sir George Grey in 1855: 'The patrimony of a chief is not cattle. It is land and men.' History and experience have since proved the Bantu to be singularly amenable to just government. Stockenström at least understood how much depended on humouring them; they could only be convinced gradually of the incalculable advantages of civilized government, of which they had no direct experience. What little they had seen, heard, and felt, was not encouraging. The emancipation of the Hottentots was too recent, and still too insecure, to afford unquestionable proof of the benefits to be expected; the

[1] He rejoices also that not only did Maqomo and Eno come to say 'Farewell', but Governor and staff, with Colonels Peddie and Hare, were present at a farewell dinner 'given me' by the 72nd Highlanders.

[2] 'With the exception of the slanderer's tongue, everything is quiet on the frontier' (Stretch to Philip, 22 July 1838).

Xhosa's own experience was only of their country being 'cleared' by commandos, and of military 'reprisals'. The significant tribal judgement of Hottentot history is preserved by Captain Stretch who, in July 1845, warned the authorities that even Tembu and Ndhlambi chiefs agreed that they must 'stand by the House of Gaika, *lest we be broke up as the Hottentots were*'.

But if even Stockenström set such store by evidence that 'depredations were on the decrease', their continuance, not surprisingly, became the all-absorbing fact with his successors. On the fall of Lord Glenelg in 1839 the best efforts of the humanitarians in England[1] failed to save the one official who could be trusted to give their policy a fair trial. He was superseded by a soldier under whom the independence and prestige of the lieutenant-governorship steadily declined, Colonel Hare. This faithful soldier, never original nor creative, had no special qualifications for his highly difficult administrative task and was soon convinced of the necessity for coercion, having but little appreciation of the wider aims that were an essential part of the treaty policy as conceived by Stockenström. Hare was not hampered like his predecessor by personal unpopularity, but neither was he so independent; indeed, the claims and clamours of his neighbours in Grahamstown so filled his communications to the Governors as to shut out from their minds the need to consider also the effect of frontier policy upon the interests of the Bantu. Both the Governors of the time, Napier and Maitland, were honest and painstaking but apart from official reports, especially those from Captain Stretch, received little independent evidence from the frontier. The missionaries, unfortunately,[2] were unusually silent. Scots and Wesleyans, who between them had many important stations in Kaffirland, had

---

[1] The dismissal of Stockenström is a commentary on the evergreen South African tradition that British ministers trembled at the nod of 'Exeter Hall'. 'We have done all we could to sustain Stockenström by urging the Governor to sustain him', writes Freeman of the L.M.S. to Philip (14 Aug. 1838)—'we' being the newly reorganized Aborigines Protection Society. A year later, 5 Sept. 1839, Fowell Buxton, no longer an M.P., reported to Dr. Philip his despairing effort to change Lord Normanby's decision against the most trusted of humanitarian officials: 'By Stockenström's desire I made an effort to do him service with the higher powers, but as usual with my applications, no good came of it.'

[2] Dr. Philip himself made a short visit to eastern stations on his return from England when Stockenström was going, or just gone, on leave in 1838. Any 'Journal' there was of this tour and, it would seem, much correspondence of the years 1838–40, were missing from the main collection.

no obvious spokesman; the L.M.S. was represented chiefly by the Reads, father and son, on the Kat River, and by Mr. Henry Calderwood,[1] at Blinkwater, near Fort Beaufort, but he and the Reads were in such sharp antagonism that their reports were largely about their own quarrels, and any time and energy Dr. Philip's mounting northern preoccupations left him were devoted to keeping them at peace. Calderwood, moreover, seems to have been dictatorial and, resisting the blandishments to which so many others fell, failed to make a friend of his important parishioner, Maqomo, actually alienating him by the changes he advocated in the treaties.[2] Dr. Philip's former close watch on the workings of frontier policy was sadly missing.

Thus the treaties were judged more and more exclusively as police measures for the protection of the farmers; this is evident from the constant (and unsettling) demands for their amendment; and yet, as Captain Stretch complained,[3] the Government failed to find money even for the police. The chiefs were still sore about their earlier losses[4] rather than elated by the respite of 1836—lacking any intimate guide and spokesman they were inclined to brood suspiciously, as if even the treaties were measures subtly designed against them for their still more complete undoing. As their first experience of anything but naked military force the experiment of the Stockenström treaties and, in particular, the retrocession of the territory conquered in 1835 must even have set them wondering. Since 1778, especially under the more intensive régime of the years between 1811 and 1834, there had been nothing to demonstrate

---

[1] Henry Calderwood, who joined the L.M.S. about 1838, seems to have had abilities above the average, and considerable ambition. In his early days on the frontier he unburdened himself boldly to Dr. Philip (from Grahamstown, May 1839): 'I see it is *impossible* for a missionary with a conscience and a heart to live in Caffreland and refrain from doing what will be *called political*. And if it be political to stand between oppressor and oppressed I am determined by the Grace of God to be *political*.'

During Dr. Philip's absence on tour in 1841–2 Calderwood 'supplied' for a time at 'Union Chapel' in Cape Town. On his return to Kaffirland he disliked and disapproved of Read's conduct of the Kat River and his 'familiarity' with the coloured people, but he himself never quite won their confidence. The friction with Read drove him to take his own line and in 1846 he found a new 'field' as a Kaffrarian magistrate.   [2] Philip to L.M.S., 11 Mar. 1845.

[3] Notably in Memo. on the failure of treaties. In Gubbins Collection.

[4] Maqomo's heart was always 'sore about the land', especially the Kat River valley (Cory, iii, pp. 52, 276—fully confirmed by Stretch and others in letters on eve of the war of 1846).

the benefits of just and efficient civil government. The new policy had to live down the not unnatural feelings of suspicion and distrust engendered by all the mere repression which had gone before. The idea that the Xhosa saw the European withdrawal as a sign of weakness makes them too sophisticated; this deduction, natural perhaps to the 'powder and ball' school,[1] was no more than this school's faith in the efficacy of repression differently expressed. At best frontiersmen were nervous of 'treaties'—and nerves were on edge on the frontier throughout those ten years.[2] The chiefs' already noted fear of suffering the fate of the Hottentots shows how watchful they were of events on the colonial side of the frontier, and even beyond it. Colonists for their part, constantly on the look-out for 'trouble' from the Xhosa, undoubtedly magnified what there was; and the incessant agitation in Grahamstown inevitably had the effect of persuading the Xhosa that the lull they seemed to be enjoying was only temporary and to be viewed with suspicion. Both chiefs and people soon had reason to believe that the change of attitude in 1836 was too good to be true. Before the treaties were two years old Grahamstown had succeeded in making things too hot for Stockenström, one man the Xhosa knew to be their friend; a year later it was known he was gone for good and Stretch, another obvious friend, was threatening to resign.[3] As Dr. Philip at once prognosticated,[4] a process of tightening up the treaties soon began and changes invariably threw more responsibility on the chiefs; these instruments, always imperfectly understood, became more and more bewildering. Almost incessant 'nagging' shook the prestige of the chiefs, and their already weak hold over their own people. As early as October 1838 Rev. J. Brownlee reported inter-tribal fighting and this he ascribed to the loss of authority by chiefs as a result of earlier happenings; Gaika, a weak Paramount, was dead, and Maqomo only a Regent. Among many later references, Stretch in December 1844 reported Gaika's heir Sandile as saying: 'I am not as your Governor. If he speaks he is obeyed. My people are

---

[1] Phrase used by Duncan Campbell, later Civil Commissioner of Albany (*Cape Col. Qn.*, p. 121). [2] Cory, iv, *passim*.

[3] To the dismay of Dr. Philip and the missionaries (Philip to Buxton, 22 Nov. 1839; Birt to Philip, 13 Sept. 1839; Calderwood to Philip, 11 Nov. 1839).

[4] 'Captain Stretch is likely to resign,' and if so, 'the last link that binds the Colony and Kafirs on amicable principles will be dissolved' (Philip to Buxton, Nov. 1839).

disobedient and will not hear.' Such chiefs were too ready to try to impress their followers by some show of bravado—or even by cattle-raids that brought new demands and more outcry from Grahamstown about the futility of the treaties. The news percolating from beyond the Colony was even more disturbing. The trek itself was no doubt a defiance of the Government; and the overthrow of Moselekatze and Dingaan, the occupation of large tracts of land both in Natal and in the north, the pro-longed war and unrest behind them in Natal and, latterly, in Griqualand could not but make the Xhosa uneasy for their own security. Such tales would lose little in the telling.

The Xhosa country, still very attractive, must have been beautiful before so much of it had been ruined by the over-grazing and deforestation forced upon its original inhabitants; in parts where the dung of the cattle has had to be used as domestic fuel instead of fertilizing the soil, even agriculture has only added to the ruin. In its former condition the Xhosa's European neighbours inevitably judged them to be wasting good land (as no doubt they were), but this view ignored or refused to see the well judged attachment, say, of Maqomo's people to the Kat River as their *homeland*. The farmers, besides being better armed, were wealthier, and the Xhosa, instead of fighting them, took to raiding their cattle: for their pains they lost very many of their own,[1] and often had their villages burnt as well.

It was so much worse for these tribes to be caught (above, p. 133) between two fires just when they had reached the geographical limit of what their own tradition makes a general Bantu migration from farther north. At the very moment pres-sure from the West was mounting internal pressure (perhaps like that which caused the earlier migrations) was raised to a peak of intensity by the Chaka wars behind them in Natal. All through the 1820's they had to make room for, fight, or other-wise deal with a succession of organized 'hordes' or 'broken tribes' killing or stealing or seeking new homes, or all these

---

[1] Statistics of cattle taken by one side or the other are equally worthless. The estimate by the Rev. W. B. Boyce (quoted Cory, iii. 129) deserves notoriety. Having proved to his own satisfaction that the 60,000 head said to have been captured by troops early in 1835 could not have been more than 30,000, he adds laconically the *precise* number stolen from the Colony, 111,418. Mr. Boyce obviously took the un-checked 'Not Reclaimable List' (above p. 265) at its face value.

things together—Bacas, Tambookies, Fingos, and others. The Tambookies (or Tembu) presently settled down to the north of the Xhosa and behind them. The Fingos were beginning to do so when, so far from bringing peace, the D'Urban settlement opened the long feud between them and their former masters or protectors (above, pp. 89–90); the last clauses of the Stocken-ström Treaties expressly required the Xhosa to 'abstain from molesting' not only the Fingos remaining on Gaika land 'near the Gaga' but those more firmly planted among the chief Pato's hitherto almost unoffending Ndhlambis at Peddie. This humane provision was unfortunately wholly at the expense of the Xhosa, both in land and in cattle.

The straitened conditions the Xhosa had now to face could have been fully met only by purposeful 'development' (blessed word! unknown in those days) and this had demanded a speedy and virtually impossible revolution in their whole way of life. They actually made room for, or were even assimilating, numbers of Fingos and other refugees, but only the Colonial Government could possibly have controlled the clash with its own farmers. An equitable apportionment of the land between so many rival claimants would or should have been quite practicable, but it is hard to imagine this circumscribed Government ever being allowed to provide the close adminis-tration which could alone have made this plan work. So the Ama-Xhosa were left to deal with their emergency without any help from without. None of the so-called *colonial* peoples was ever subjected to such intense pressure for so long—or none except perhaps the North American Indians.

Pure mischance contributed at last to the tragic denouement. Any hope there was of peace and recuperation was dashed by the cruel hand of nature. There is evidence that, throughout the story, occasional dry years were years also of unusual unrest and of 'Kafir cattle-stealing'.[1] On this unlucky frontier the early and middle forties seem to have been a time of prolonged drought; had there been nothing else of note these years might have been memorable for an acute famine. In the winters of 1841 and 1842 the Civil Commissioner of Albany so far relaxed restrictions as to allow two friendly chiefs, Kama and Zibi, to

---

[1] Statistics both of cattle theft and of rainfall are too unreliable to detail. But there is no doubt about the droughts of the critical years 1834, 1845, and 1846.

reside temporarily and graze their cattle in Bathurst, at the source of the Koonap, and even in Albany itself.[1] Early in 1842 Dr. Philip, on tour, described devastating swarms of locusts beyond the Stormberg. In the end of 1844 drought distress was still acute and, according to Stretch's Diary, crops failed both in 1845 and 1846. In July or August 1845 snow and cold rain played havoc with the starved animals. After four such years the provisioning and the movements of the troops in the campaign of 1846[2] were gravely impeded by the impoverished condition of the transport cattle, and the effect of drought would be particularly sharply felt on the more densely populated Xhosa side of the frontier. It was as in the days of the prophet Joel:

> That which the palmerworm hath left,
> Hath the locust eaten,
> And that which the locust hath left,
> Hath the cankerworm eaten; . . .
>
> The fire hath devoured the pastures of the wilderness
> And the flame hath burned all the trees of the field.
> For the water brooks are dried up,
> And the fire hath devoured the pastures of the wilderness.

These lean years, following on others which may have been less lean but were none of them fat, hit both colonists and Bantu. The conditions are not easily conveyed to those who are incredulous when told how cloudless days of unbroken sunshine can pall; but memories of African droughts are, rather, of days when the clouds bank up promising a storm of rain but yield only searing winds which carry off the good earth in whirling 'dust-devils' hundreds of feet high. Colonists, with tempers already frayed by their experiences, faced enforced idleness and stagnant trade; having time on their hands many took to airing their remedies for frontier disorders (below, p. 285);[3] and one remedy widely favoured was that the Xhosa be expelled, finally, from the Ceded Territory. Acutely conscious as the Xhosa were by this time of the pressure on their *land*, they fell at last into a mood of mere reckless desperation.

[1] The vagaries of South African climate make it quite possible that, for example, Albany had benefited from local showers that missed Kaffirland.

[2] Cf. Cory, iv. 463.

[3] See also Cory, iv. 377, for the 'Springbok' speech by Mr. J. M. Bowker, who declared that to 'see the Kafir *sink* before the European, as the herds of springbok had already vanished, could occasion me no feeling but pleasure'.

XVI

THE DRIFT TO WAR AND CONQUEST, 1842-8

A PERIOD of comparative and perhaps deceptive calm had followed Governor Napier's amendment of the treaties in the end of 1840, allowing the boast that 'no shot was fired' during Napier's term of office. But in the middle of 1842 the Colony had one of its periodical war scares;[1] in May charges of witchcraft implicating the Queen-Mother Sutu in the death of the important chief, Tyali, and the beer-drinking and fighting which accompany such great occasions among the Bantu,[2] gave Colonel Hare some cause for anxiety. A year earlier Gaika's heir, Sandile, had come of age; he does not seem to have had very striking gifts or presence (he had a deformed foot) but Maqomo was shaken in his regency and became restive;[3] at the same time probably the younger bloods were roused to greater bellicosity. None the less towards the end of the year troops could be moved from this frontier to deal with the Griqua and Boer disturbances about Colesberg and Philippolis (above, p. 238) even if in May 1843 they were rather hurriedly recalled. A few months later Colonel Hare had reached his conclusion that 'just and prudent coercion' was a necessity. The Governor, on the other hand (above, p. 267), was more disposed to agree with Stockenström and Stretch, reinforced about this time by the Wesleyan missionary W. B. Boyce, that the rumours of unrest were spread chiefly by a war party among Europeans on the frontier: 'A war and nothing but a war' will satisfy these people.[4]

The decisive factor, however, was more and more the drought.[5] Because of this it became increasingly difficult for the

[1] Alarmist rumours reached as far as W. Philip at Hankey, May 1842.

[2] The months May, June, and July are the time of harvest, and the new season's beer, brewed from Kaffir corn or millet, often gives rise to local disturbances and faction fights.

[3] Calderwood repeatedly, and on 29 May and 19 July 1842 even the Reads (both to Philip) suggest the restlessness of Maqomo.

[4] Stockenström quoting Boyce to Philip, 9 Aug. 1843.

[5] It is probable that, for example, the South African rebellion of 1914 would

Colony to absorb Bantu labourers forced across the border by starvation. This influx, so far as it meant cheap labour, was not unwelcome to farmers; for years Mr. Justice Menzies had been pointing out to the Governor how farmers liked to encourage a 'reserve' of labour, trying also to tighten up the administration of the old 49th Ordinance. In a fashion which still survives, families were readily given land, grazing, and hut-room, as 'squatters', in return for unpaid services—if need be those of the whole family. But in times of dearth such people, being cut off from the communal life of any tribe, were often driven to steal in order to live.[1] In the early months of 1842, when the magistrate of Fort Beaufort roused himself to put pressure on Mr. Read to secure the removal of Fingo and 'foreigner' squatters from the Kat River Settlement, Read's protests[2] raised some pertinent questions. Why, he asked, should the 'Hottentot burghers' and not the Boers lose the valuable services of 'squatters'[3] for herding and harvest? To remove them at that moment would deprive them of their *pay*—their own harvests. The Fingos themselves protested that if forced out they would leave the Colony altogether, presumably to 'live by their wits'. Practical considerations like these, and land shortage such as already existed in Kaffirland, have made unavoidable much of the squatting still practised on South African farms.

By 1844 the authorities were becoming increasingly troubled. On 10 June 1844 Mr. Moore Craig in an official Memo. ascribed most of the alleged thieving, like Menzies before him, to 'wandering natives encouraged to squat by farmers, in defiance of repeated orders of Government and of Ordinance 49'. The law of passes was in fact in utter confusion (above, p. 87), and the Tembu Agent, Mr. Fynn, presently showed how and why.[4] In terms of the treaties passes were to be issued by the Agents; in practice they were obtained, ostensibly in terms of Ordinance 49, from any magistrate, field-cornet, or J.P. on a

never have happened had the drought-breaking rain which made the campaign a double misery come a month earlier and set the farmers in the affected area ploughing.

[1] Menzies to Napier, 12 Oct. 1840, and Jan. 1843, the latter quoting a 'Report' of Oct. 1838. Also Napier to Secretary of State, July 1841.

[2] To Borcherds, 14 Jan., and to Philip in January and February.

[3] Read makes early use in this connexion of the now familiar Dutch term—*bijwoners*.

[4] Memo. on Ordinance 49, 20 Sept. 1844.

printed form—this, incidentally, ignored the stipulation of the Ordinance that passes to natives going 'in search of work' should be valid for only fourteen days. Thefts, he concluded, were often due to 'natives who, having served in the Colony and acquired a knowledge of Dutch, ingratiate themselves into the favour of the Dutch colonists by whom they are too frequently permitted to rove the Colony without passes'. Considerations of convenience were too strong and the legally defunct Ordinance continued in use: 'No description of servants', wrote Mr. Fynn, '—or such an abundant supply—could be so well suited to the wants of the frontier farmers. The colonists are materially benefited and many a native in times of need is saved from famishing.' In spite of redoubled outcry against 'thieving', district reports and the diaries of Agents like Fynn and Stretch[1] continue throughout 1844 and 1845 to record 'streams of Kafirs passing through to seek employment in the Colony'— and presumably to find it.[2] In the end of 1845 the Rev. R. Birt, making his annual report to the L.M.S. from his Kaffirland station, gave another side of the picture: 'The great difficulty of finding some means of employment for the natives becomes more pressing every year.'

South Africans were in truth having their first experience of the complex they learnt to take all too calmly as a matter only for the perorations of their political leaders' speeches—the Native Problem. Thus early the prolonged unsettlement in Kaffirland and the ferocious drought which followed had strained the social system of the Colony's nearest neighbours to breaking point. Since those days experience and dire necessity have taught the Bantu to accustom themselves to even more straitened conditions than those of the forties. European neighbours came to accept their endurance as a matter of course, but the intense resentment roused even among these long-suffering Bantu by the restrictions of the Land Act of 1913 (see Ch. XVIII) was a conscious echo of the protest their fathers made in the more spacious days when they first felt such pressure, but were yet *free*. Even then there was much coming and going; many needy men or adventurers (Xhosa and Fingo) were

---

[1] Stretch especially, in a very full Diary in Cape Town archives.
[2] According to Stretch, 11 Nov. 1844, the 'normal' pay for twelve months' service was 'one cow and calf, with keep'.

ready to try the experiment of seeking an outlet among the farmers of the Colony—and some, no doubt, went looking for peace and quiet; squatters of those days were economically better placed than now, land and grazing rights being more generous. But at that time, when firm control was especially necessary, the administration was most ineffective; magistrates were few and feebly supported, and were sorely needed not so much to make the white man's law feared as to teach the natives to value its impartial justice. Severely shaken as they had been, there was a limit to their endurance—in his Diary for 11 February 1846 Captain Stretch was to record that the farmers' servants had 'suddenly deserted'.

The crisis came suddenly at the last but was long preparing. Ever since the fall of Stockenström even Governors and officials had tended to concentrate more and more on the absorbing and troublesome practice of cattle-reiving. Sir George Napier's more alarmist views were modified after 1840, but in the last months of his governorship he took a well intentioned step which in the long run did more to rouse Xhosa anxieties about their land than to give increased security to the Colony. Frontier disturbances so alarmed Colonel Hare that, when he failed to persuade the Governor to sanction the removal of the Gaikas altogether from the Fish–Keiskama country, in October 1843 he induced the chiefs to agree to have a fort, Post Victoria, in the heart of the Ceded Territory. This was for the better control of a chief Sir George Cory calls 'the horse thief Tola' but who later showed special interest (see p. 290) in a stolen 'axe'. From this point Security definitely dominated Policy.

In March 1844 Sir Peregrine Maitland took over from Napier at a time when, as the Agents' reports show, distressed natives were steadily seeking work in the Colony and 'depredations' were being loudly complained of. The frontier trade in guns,[1] it also seems possible, helped to make the younger braves more daring. In July a farmer named de Lange, who had gone in pursuit of his stolen horse, died of wounds received in an exchange of shots near the Fish River. Shooting made this a more serious affair—'the Lieutenant-Governor (Hare) moved with alacrity'.[2] 'He decided, at length, upon the military occupation

---

[1] Cory, iv. 336 ff.

[2] de Lange undoubtedly suffered violence. But the occasion was reminiscent of

of the Ceded Territory'—and this time there was no Napier to
say him 'Nay'. Instead, Maitland himself proceeded in haste to
the frontier, arriving at Port Elizabeth on 10 September.
Barely a week later he reached Fort Peddie and, on the 19th,
summarily abrogated the old and dictated new treaties, first to
the chiefs of the Amagunukwebi (Pato and Co.) there assembled. From Peddie he went on to Fort Beaufort and made
similar new treaties with the Tambookie chiefs who met him
there;[1] it was only then he turned to deal with the Gaikas. They,
as much the most important of the frontier tribes, took occasion
afterwards to feel aggrieved at this slight on their dignity.

The broad intent of the new provisions was the same in all
the revised treaties. The Bantu were left as before in possession;
but Post Victoria was regularized by a clause which gave the
Government permission to plant forts in the Ceded Territory.
The cattle clauses were similarly stiffened up; animals identified
in Kaffirland might now be reclaimed, with compensation, even
if not followed up at the time they were lost; the Chief too was
made responsible for cattle that were definitely traced to his
territory whether actually discovered there or not. Alleged
thieves and criminals, moreover, even those belonging to
Kaffirland, were to be tried *in the Colony*, and a Court of Appeal
was to be established, independent of the Agents. This clause
caused considerable difficulty since, as the Kaffirs protested, the
Agents they at least 'knew'. The Gaikas also objected strenuously to an attack on their authority by a clause specially safeguarding the rights of their Christian subjects. The clause as
drafted made a rather sweeping and old-fashioned attack on
Native Custom (for example on the payment of *lobola*, long
criticized as 'the sin of buying wives')—rightly or wrongly the
Native Administration Act of 1927 showed the modern trend
by recognizing established Custom as law for the Union. This
clause was of importance too for its effect in putting missionaries
out of favour, especially Calderwood: 'The Gaika chiefs have
no advisers, no intercourse with the missionaries, and no con-

---

old Scottish Border forays. In the pursuit of his horse he came upon Kaffirs
driving 'a large number of cattle, *presumably stolen*' (Cory, iv. 375), thereupon
'hurriedly returned and collected a number of farmers', gave chase, and, in the
inevitable mêlée that followed, was shot. Such was Cape border law and practice.
   [1] A few weeks later, to complete the 'chain' of 'Treaty States', Mr. Shepstone
concluded treaties with Kreli for the Gcalekas and with Faku for the Pondos.

fidence in them, because at the time of the Governor's visit they in a body recommended changes in the treaties in a way that the chiefs disliked.'[1]

On every ground the Governor would have been well advised to move more slowly. The Colony's joy at the abrogation of the Stockenström Treaties, and at new 'shackles for the Kafir',[2] did nothing to help matters, serving rather to rouse suspicions at 'changes' not very material in themselves merely because they were changes. The innovations, perhaps, gave some warrant for uneasiness; Captain Stretch was afterwards of opinion that the Governor's visit was 'disastrous', and the final doom of all hopes of making a success of any treaty policy.[3]

The onus of carrying out the treaties again lay too much with the chiefs; but the weakness of the new order, like that of the old, was as much due to the deficiencies of administration on the colonial side of the border as to the sins of the Xhosa; relying on its new treaty rights the Government did as little as ever of its own share of 'prevention'. Captain Stretch again gives the clue, in a frankly worded private letter:

> The Dutch farmers are dissatisfied with the treaties because they would like to be their own magistrates in deciding cases of theft. On the other hand the English . . . are in favour of rubbing in the military side of civilization. . . . The troops are likely to have plenty to do—for they have been allowed to slumber for the last five years and *not a thief was caught in the Colony by either* the civil or military authorities, all being demanded from the unfortunate Caffre chiefs. £200,000 has thus been enriching the Grahamstown shopkeepers while they were calling out at this outlay on account of the 'Treaties'

Stretch wrote in November 1844; his 'not a thief' may be questionable but the substance of his criticism stands. In the year that followed there was no substantial improvement in the efficiency of Government preventive measures and by unanimous testimony 'depredations' were worse. During, or because of, Boer and Griqua excitements, in the hard winter months of 1845 Stretch,[4] Fynn, and Shepstone alike reported

---

[1] Philip to L.M.S., 11 Mar. 1845.   [2] Cory, iv. 380.
[3] Stretch, Memo. on Treaties.
[4] Stretch takes occasion to note also (July 2) that animals alleged to be *stolen* but found *strayed* are not reported found. One de Lange, he says, having told Col. Somerset of 50 horses stolen, afterwards reduced the number to 20 in Somerset's presence in Stretch's office.

numerous thefts; and by the end of the year, or the beginning of 1846, thefts gave place to deeds of violence which gave some warrant for fearing a general attack on the Colony. It is all too clear how these poor Xhosa people were driven to the folly and violence which were their own undoing. They already had some, doubtless highly coloured, knowledge of what was passing in the Colony; now the true inwardness, as it seemed to them, of colonial designs was forcibly brought home to the 'man in the kraal'. In October 1843 Colonel Hare, as above, had obtained leave to plant 'Post Victoria' in the Ceded Territory, but it was only during the Governor's treaty-changing visit about a year later that the modest fort was erected and troops sent to garrison it. Coming together with the new treaties in this way the fort was ominous. Notoriously, leading colonists and their newspapers had long assumed that the only real remedy for their grievances was the expulsion of the Gaikas from the Fish River Bush[1] and the Fish-Keiskama country (which included what little remained to the Ama-Xhosa after 1829 of the delectable modern districts Bedford, Adelaide, Fort Beaufort, Stockenström (the Kat River), and Victoria East). Here then was another step in the execution of this well-known programme. In March 1845 Captain Stretch emphasized to the Lieutenant-Governor how difficult it was for the young Paramount, Sandile, had he wished, to control the 'National Party' of Maqomo and the late Tyali who chafed at Gaika losses—'more particularly' (he underlined the words) 'as (depredations) *have been principally confined to the country they always speak of*' (i.e. Bedford, Adelaide, &c.).

In the middle of that year 1845, when unrest was considerable, the *land* came more and more to be the issue. 'I feel convinced', wrote Fairbairn to Dr. Philip, who was then on his way to the frontier, 'there is a design for handing over the best part of the country between the Colony and Natal to the colonists'—to the 'final destruction of the natives from sea to sea'. Fairbairn, missing the help of Fowell Buxton, whose health was gone, now suggested an appeal to Lord John Russell. On

---

[1] Cory, iii and iv, *passim*. An extreme, but common, view is recorded in a conversation of 1843. A farmer pressing for 'the D'Urban System' was asked: 'If we did return to it, and the lands of the Caffres were secured to them—what then?' 'Oh,' he observed, 'what better would we be then? we want the country.' (Enclosures, Stockenström to Philip, 3 Aug. 1843.)

6 July rumours had reached not only Stretch, but the Rev. J. Brownlee at King William's Town; this good Scot found the frontier position *aquard* (awkward!); a message, he says, has threatened chiefs who protect thieves with 'forcible ejection from the Ceded Territory'. The same day Stretch tells Dr. Philip, as he had already told the Governor, how the Kaffirs all fear to be 'broke up as the Hottentots were' by expulsion from their lands: 'You must eat your corn', they are saying to Botman, 'and make yourselves strong; prepare *veld schoenen* (shoes) also that may stand fast.' On the 13th to the Governor: 'Allow me to solicit' no patrols in the Ceded Territory 'till the excitement has subsided'.[1] Next day Maqomo thanked the Government for 'reassurances'—'we hear now it is only against thieves'. On the 31st Stretch 'refuted' in an interview with the chiefs the current statement that the 'Gaikas had been threatened with expulsion', but added in his official letter: 'It is obvious that considerable efforts have been made at Fort Beaufort to involve the Kafir chiefs in war, which, it cannot be concealed, is more desired by the colonists than by the Gaika chiefs.'

The charge that colonists wanted war is facile. There were a good many who believed that force was the only remedy; on the other hand Maitland complained that the fears of the farmers 'may even have given the Kafirs self-confidence'. It is at least certain that in their own anxiety colonists saw nothing of the effect their ideas of policy had on the other side of the frontier. In August and September farmers' meetings 'broke out' once more[2] and petitions poured in from the Eastern Province; one of these, from Albany and Lower Somerset, wanted 'the immediate removal of the Kafirs from the Ceded Territory', another held that 'savage hordes are quite incapable of appreciating treaties'—a half-truth that overlooked the failure of the civilized government to do its share of the police work. In reply, both the Government Secretary (Mr. John Montagu) and Attorney-General Porter held the farmers' complaints to be 'exaggerated', the latter taking a philanthropic view 'without being a philanthropist'. But the complaints made their mark and the Governor, forwarding petitions to London on 17 November, agreed that, though exaggerated, the charges

---

[1] On the same day he adds that 'the Rev. J. Laing alleges' that Boers were 'inciting' Maqomo.   [2] Cory, iv. 400 ff.

were partly true, 'depredations [being] inevitable so long as an uncivilized race greedy of cattle . . . lies along such a frontier'.

The Governor's first thoughts at this time, like those of Dr. Philip, were still for the danger in the north; troops had had to be moved there, he said, if he 'would not suffer our allies the Griquas to be exterminated by the emigrant British subjects':

Should affairs North [he continued] again demand an armed force, an entrance into the Colony by Kafirs in force might not be unlikely. Treaties are no good unless to work on the fear or interest of the chiefs, and a line of posts is useless on such a frontier. I do not mean I think an inroad probable, at least while the present force is maintained. But it is difficult to calculate on the movements of an uncivilized race—to a considerable extent irritated by our endeavours to control their plundering habits.

This dispatch shows Sir Peregrine Maitland fair-minded and just in intention, but as far as ever from understanding the essential cause of unrest. Like his predecessors—soldiers all of them—he conceived the tribes as first of all a serious military danger. Since at least 1838 such exaggerated fears of a systematically planned invasion had in effect immobilized the troops; since they must be kept together, at considerable expense, as a garrison they were not available, as Napier had foreseen, to act as a police force; nor were there funds for additional enrolments, for magistrates, even for prisons. The Governor had all the same thoroughly absorbed the fallacy that his prime task on the frontier was to check cattle-stealing.

Meantime, the elements that found an outlet in cattle-lifting had Kaffirland in a ferment, made worse by the continued failure of the summer rains and the threat of famine. In October 1845 Sandile raised objections to Post Victoria: 'The country is now quiet', he urged. 'I therefore wish the soldiers to go home . . . where they were useful against thieves.'[1] In November a German missionary, a Mr. Scholtz, was murdered in the country of the once friendly chief Pato; that his assailants mistook their victim for the ex-Government Agent Shepstone made the deed no less ominous. In the end of December two hundred natives were reported as casualties in a collision with troops near the unwanted Post Victoria. On 13 January Sandile himself made a 'raid' and helped himself to goods from a store

[1] Stretch's Diary, 2 Oct. 1845.

near Captain Stretch's house—Stretch reporting two days later
that the culprits said of 'stealing': 'We are only taking what
belongs to the Kafirs and Hottentots.' Next day 'missionaries
report kraals of observation, building'. On the 25th 'traders are
preparing to leave'. On the 27th Fynn reported that his Tambookies were excited, the Gaikas and Ndhlambis having promised
Pato help in refusing to surrender the murderers of the missionary
Scholtz. On top of all this the Government took a disastrously
false step. So far from agreeing to abandon Post Victoria they
proposed to move it to a more convenient site near 'Block
Drift'. About 20 January engineers arrived and, apparently by
the mistake of a subordinate, began a survey *on the Kaffirland
side of the river*.[1] Had it been intended to provoke a native attack
no surer way could have been taken and yet on 7 February
Stretch reported that Sandile was 'sleeping in the bush for fear'.
Next, on the 14th, Colonel Hare himself reported one Captain
Smith as advising against 'provoking a collision' by the establishment of a new post; on the 24th traders and even missionaries arrived at Fort Peddie, 'feeling insecure under the present
excited state of the country'.

As this crisis was developing Henry Calderwood wrote Dr.
Philip a letter showing real insight and understanding for
which much may be forgiven him, even if most of the missionaries, and some officials, were severely critical of his attempts
to combine the missionary with the official:

BLOCK DRIFT,

18 *January* 1846

Several of the Brethren have wished me very much to visit Cape
Town with a view to converse *privately* and *fully* with those who may
have influence in the Government, but the way does not seem quite
open. . . . In the meantime I wish on my own responsibility to state a
few things to *you* in the hope that you may be of some use . . . if you
have the ear of the Government. There is, however, a serious difficulty in the way. . . . I cannot *at present* see my way clear to *write*
nearly all I know, and therefore *much* caution is necessary in saying
anything to Government. But it is the unanimous opinion of the
Missionaries that unless the Government determine to *understand*
the Caffre Question better than they *now* appear to do, it is almost

---

[1] The site was that of 'Fort Hare', later happily transformed into a University
College for Natives—and later still reduced to the status of a college for Xhosa-
speakers only.

certain that the Caffres will be destroyed, and our missions too, but
not before a terrible blow shall have been inflicted on the Colony.

We have most certain evidence that the great bulk of the Caffre
people were bent on war a few weeks ago. . . . The feeling is deep and
bitter in the extreme. The approaching famine—and the somewhat
formidable preparations on the part of the Government and the
farmers—appear to have overawed them in the meantime. I have
seen Macomo very often just now and he sent most of his chief men
to me to speak on the present state of things. He very urgently de-
clares that he will not fight and that *most* of his *people* will sit still with
him. Perhaps he himself would really sit still—but he certainly could
not restrain the great body of his people in the event of war—unless
it should happen that the Caffres were *instantly* repulsed, and this
they could not well be.

The feeling of the *Nation* seems now to be against all *white* men,
and in the event of war mission property would all be destroyed, and
even the lives of missionaries would be placed in extreme peril. I
fear that the *political* circumstances of the people are now such that
until a decided change is effected the success of our mission will be of
a very limited description. It is deeply to be regretted the Government should so easily have fallen into a false position with the Caffres
in the affair of Sandile's violation of the treaty the other day. The
Government with much simplicity allowed the vexatious land question to be mingled up in the dispute. The Government had no *just*
power to send engineers to survey ground for a Post (*Block Drift*) in
Caffreland, and this leads me to notice two or three other points,
which deserve serious consideration, without attempt to illustrate
them.

(1) Amongst all the vexatious questions between the Colonial
Government and the Caffres, the most vexatious is what may be
styled the *land question*. The Caffres are evidently so sensitive on this
point that they *cannot* and *will* not consider *any question calmly* when
that is mixed up with it.

(2) The Caffres are, either from ignorance or design, exceedingly
disposed to mix up the *land question* with every other between them
and the Government. Thus the movements of Government are
rendered much more intricate and liable to misconstruction than
they otherwise would be.

(3) The agitation of the *land question* is a powerful engine by which
the war party can work upon the feelings of the more peaceably
inclined and thus effectually endanger the peace of the country.

(4) It is equally clear that the Government in all their interviews
with the Caffres have by their language fostered this feeling in the
Caffre mind by *always threatening* the *expulsion* of the Caffres from their

country, if the demands of Government were not complied with. The difference between the neutral territory and any other territory is only one of words, and at this moment the *mind of the nation* is in a perfect fever on the land question. There never can be a really sound understanding between the Caffres and the Colony until this is set at rest and that for ever.

The Government ought instantly to use any possible means to cause the mind of the Caffre people to comprehend and believe this fact—that the colonial boundary cannot on any consideration whatever be extended so as to deprive the Caffres of *one inch* of ground. There must be no more *threatening*. The Caffres *never threaten* when they *really intend* to do anything. Expulsion must never be thought of— far less threatened. . . .

Let the Government place the land question on its only proper footing and take their stand simply on cases of theft and oppression of Europeans received by themselves into the Caffre country—and punish *vigorously* and *promptly* all such cases as are *well authenticated, even at the risk* of war. Let this be fully understood, and the evil-disposed in Caffreland will stand more alone than they do now.

The Caffres can understand what it is to be punished for *stealing* and *murder*—but no argument will ever convince them that it is either *just* or *reasonable* to take their *land* from them. It will be a hard task to teach a barbarous people that there is very great harm in taking the cattle of the Colony so long as it is threatened to take their land from them—seeing, as they say, *so much has been taken from them already*. If the Caffres require to be punished—as I think a very large body of them do—in the name of *mercy* and *justice* let them be punished *where they are*. Let the policy of the Home Government have a fair trial on its own merits. But it *cannot* have that if the Caffres *can* be every now and then threatened with *expulsion* from their *lands*. . . . [Second sheet of letter missing.]

This letter of Calderwood's almost certainly reached the Governor and made its impression. On 21 March he wrote to Lord Stanley, clearly recognizing now the importance of the land question:

The hint that they hold the Ceded Territory only on good behaviour has them ready to *unite* to oppose our endeavours to put down depredations, on the ground that the land is the object aimed at. Expulsion is likely to keep up an irritation about the land, which is better avoided.

It was too late now to save the situation. Almost before this dispatch can have left Cape Town, the episode of the Axe had happened. The 'Seventh Kafir War' was not begun, like that of 1834 and the momentous war which followed in 1850, by the Xhosa. In March the aforesaid Tola (see p. 281) attacked the escort taking a prisoner from Fort Beaufort to Grahamstown for the theft of an axe—whence the popular name, the War of the Axe. This mere police affair was a real turning-point; coming when it did it served to convince the Governor of the need for a definite departure from the treaty policy of 1836 and made him decide to strike first. According to the Manifesto which he issued on leaving Cape Town for the front, this was only the culmination of a long chain of 'causes which rendered it impossible to refrain any longer from punishing the systematic violation of justice and good faith on the part of the Kafirs'. On 21 March Colonel Hare had decided to take action, and on 1 April the Governor sanctioned a declaration of war. There was no question this time of the war bursting on an unsuspecting Colony. The Xhosa had been so refractory that even missionaries had fled betimes and Maitland was satisfied that the tribes, if left to themselves, 'would probably have assumed the offensive in the spring or summer'. He knew also that it would not be possible to fight the Gaikas alone, that even beyond the Kei Kreli was alarmed, and that he 'must be prepared to grapple with the whole Caffre nation'.[1]

Nor was there any excuse for the dominant party among the colonists to complain of the 'machinations' of an Anti-Colonial Party. The restrained though negative and unimaginative treatment of the Xhosa in the last ten years seemed to have put them in the wrong and now united all parties against them; in the end, in their hour of overwhelming defeat, they were left without any effective advocate. Captain Stretch was sad at their sullen recklessness and almost silent. Sir Andries Stockenström presently led the burghers against them. The Reads also were definitely alienated[2] by attacks that did not spare the Hottentots of the Kat River; they were driven for many months to the shelter of the fort at Elands Post (now Seymour).

---

[1] Hare to Maitland, 4 Apr., and Maitland to Gladstone, 15 May 1846.

[2] Joseph Read, a mission teacher, shocked even his father by serving as a combatant. But the old man wrote in July of the 'national antipathy' of the Hottentots against the Kaffirs on account of 'aggressions by their ancestors'.

Fairbairn and the *Commercial Advertiser* supported Maitland's policy,[1] not without some eyebrows being raised; on 10 October his sister-in-law, Mary Christie, wrote to her mother Mrs. Philip remarking on his attitude and that of the Reads: 'It seems so very strange!' Yet the restraint of so many 'philanthropists' was inconsistent chiefly with the popular conception of their policy in 1835. Dr. Philip himself wrote to the L.M.S. (13 May):

You will remember that, while I was opposed to the last war as a war of extermination, I was also decidedly of opinion that the Kafirs having given in their adhesion and taken the oath of allegiance to the British Government, ought to have been retained as British subjects, and that the expense of such a measure was the only objection urged against it. *Every one here is now of my opinion,* but the result might have been no better had it been acted upon. . . .

In spite of an unusual consensus of opinion in the Colony, and of ample warning, the opening military offensive was marked by more than traditional muddle and incompetence. A whole series of 'unfortunate incidents'[2] in April and May cost the troops two large baggage trains and gave the Xhosa such confidence that they even took the initiative. Wholesale, partly defensive, destruction of the property of traders and missionaries in Kaffirland was prelude to their exacting toll once more in the Colony, burning houses, raiding cattle, and forcing refugees to take shelter in towns and villages.

The ruin effected by Caffres upon mission property erected for their salvation is most striking and lamentable. I dare say most of the mission property has been destroyed that the invading force might have no shelter. Except near Peddie and Block Drift, all stations of London, Scottish, Wesleyans and German Societies this side of the Kei have been destroyed. It is a sad blow to us all.[3]

[1] For the paper's differentiation between this war and the policy it had fought in 1835 see, for example, *Commercial Advertiser*, 14 Oct. and 2 Dec. 1846.
[2] Cory, iv. 428 ff. Some responsibility attached to Col. Somerset, who first appeared on this frontier in the time of his father, Lord Charles Somerset. One of his earliest semi-independent exploits (1825) was known as '*Somerset's blundering Commando*' (Cory, ii. 239). For his share in precipitating the war of 1834 see above, Ch. VIII; for his doings in this war see Cory, iv. 434 n., and below, p. 298). It may be significant of the power of 'uncles at the Horse Guards' (Stockenström's gibe) that Somerset, now a Major-General, was still active in a subordinate capacity in the war of 1850-2.   [3] Calderwood to L.M.S., 13 Aug. 1846.

The troops were on the defensive when 28 May was ordained a 'day of humiliation and prayer', moving Dr. Philip in his old age to show a gleam of grim humour: 'The question is not what to do with the Kafirs, but what will the Kafirs do with us?' On 11 June, Maitland commented: 'We or they must abandon the country.'

The Xhosa plucked up courage for a futile attack on Fort Peddie in the end of May but had soon shot their bolt. In June unusual carelessness or over-confidence on their part exposed an 'army' to severe punishment by a surprise cavalry charge 'on the Gwanga'—this episode, the nearest approach to a set 'battle'[1] in the whole campaign was followed by a long series of 'Smithfield Market cattle-driving' expeditions; these scoured Kaffirland but met with little further active opposition. The Xhosa, indeed, whatever the Zulus may have been, were never an organized offensive military power; yet their deeds in the early days of 1846 served to confirm the fixed idea that the only way of safety for the Colony was to appropriate more of Kaffirland.

The British campaign continued to be very badly conducted. Drought and transport difficulties gave some excuse for burghers and regulars to quarrel among themselves,[2] especially as the burghers were half-hearted, knowing in advance that Governor Maitland held out no prospect of farms for Europeans[3] if only because he justly deplored the weakening effects of the former Boer emigration and the loss of so many of the stoutest fighting men. Yet it was the scattered farmers who, to protect themselves or their cattle, had been fain to invoke the organized power of the Government to take still more native land and to break up and disperse the tribes who had retaliated, inevitably, in their own way. Against organized military attack the Xhosa now fell back on non-resistance, the attacking column of troops being met and surrounded by crowds of women and children 'begging for food', sometimes in return for bundles of fuel or thatching. Many chiefs protested, as Maqomo had done even in 1835, that they were not fighting, would not fight, and asked only for peace.

[1] The attack on Grahamstown in 1819, the ambush of a column in the Boomah Pass, 1850, are almost the only 'Battles'(?) in the whole series of Xhosa wars.
[2] Cory, iv, chs. ix and x.
[3] Maitland to Stanley, 21 Mar. 1846 and 20 Jan. 1847.

But the tragedy had to be played out—the 'power' of the tribes broken. Even the short-lived 'treaty' settlement of 1836 had made the worst of both worlds, offending the colonists, without giving the Xhosa any feeling that their human interests and feelings were really safeguarded. Yet this was the only attempt in more than seventy years to give this essentially administrative and police problem other than rigidly military treatment. The one thing never tried was honest civil government which recognized the Xhosa as subjects with a secure place in their own land, and punished wrongdoers, in Mr. Calderwood's phrase, *where they were*. The policy of such a course, tried and abundantly justified since with many only very partially conquered tribes throughout Africa, was learnt—if it has been fully learnt everywhere even yet—only after the sacrifice of the alert ad cheerful Ama-Xhosa.

In August or September 1846 Sir Peregrine Maitland was seriously thinking of the 'ultimate settlement' for which the situation had not been ripe when he reported on 11 June. By September Maqomo and others had surrendered; the discontented burgher forces were disbanded (or seized an excuse for going home); after this, rain made fresh movements of troops possible but any Xhosa still in the field made no resistance. It now fell to this mild and humane Governor to make a decision which was so generally approved at the time that, even yet, its consequences have never been appreciated. All agreed, even the Colonial Office,[1] that British control must once more be extended to the Kei. But for additional security the Governor resolved to set about 'clearing' another slice of country and 'filling up' instead with Fingos, friendly or 'mission Kaffirs', and Hottentots. The country to be cleared included the whole of the 'Ceded' Territory and, in addition, 'the Amatola fastnesses'—the most beautiful country in all that area and the cherished home of many Gaikas. Since, in Sandile's words, 'the patrimony of a chief is land and men', the chiefs felt that they might as well resist where they were as accept another and more drastic uprooting; the new 'locations', to be assigned by the Governor at his own pleasure subject to the good behaviour of their already unruly tribesmen, meant an end to their dignity and independence. The Governor's resolve left nothing

[1] Grey to Pottinger, 2 Nov. 1846. See p. 295.

for it but war *à outrance*: 'How in the world', wrote James Read[1] to Dr. Philip on 6 October, 'could Sir Peregrine think of trying to come to such terms of peace just after all the Boers and many of the coloured people [i.e. all the colonial forces] had left the frontier and he and Colonel Hare retreated to the Colony?'

It was not for this that Sir Andries Stockenström had come out in April 'to serve his country'. The task assigned him was to organize and conduct a march through the heart of the drought-stricken country to deal with Hintza's successor, Kreli, the great chief beyond the Kei. As commandant of the burgher force he was allowed some discretion and he agreed that the tribes needed punishment—a forcible reminder of the power and efficiency of the white man—but he had never contemplated a war of conquest and extermination. His hope was to get Kreli's sanction for annexation up to the Kei River by a treaty which would give the Government a warrant, such as they now lacked, for compelling him to do his share in keeping the Ciskeian tribes in order. He fulfilled this mission, but when he returned in the end of August the Governor was leaning to a more drastic policy and bluntly repudiated the treaty he had made with Kreli. To add to Stockenström's easily roused chagrin one of his companions, Colonel Johnstone, contradicted his version of the interview with Kreli. He found, too, that posts he had planted for the protection of the roads into the Colony had been moved in his absence, and an expedition sent off to the north to chastise the Tembu chief, Mapassa. This diversion he resented as at once an encroachment on his sphere of campaign and liable to prejudice the success of his own mission. With a parochial zest for petty personal details the South African account of Stockenström's second withdrawal has fastened on the 'acrimonious' letters which Stockenström presently inflicted even on the Governor.

Stockenström was notoriously touchy; he 'knew his own temper'; but the difference with the Governor which soon brought about his resignation went deeper than 'personal pique';[2] it arose from the Governor's growing determination to

---

[1] Read soon got over his 'anti-Kaffir' phase. From this point letters which reached Dr. Philip from Read, Stretch, Stockenström, and others show that Maitland and his two successors had begun to have their critics.

[2] 'You need not fear that I shall resign from personal pique', he wrote, explaining his views to Read on 12 and 17 Sept.

embark on what Stockenström knew by experience must be a prolonged and costly effort to hold the tribes in peace, not by reason and good government but by crushing them into helpless subjection. Calderwood at this time (to the L.M.S., 26 September) claimed to have made the Governor see the justice of leaving the Xhosa on their land; on 7 October he wrote to Dr. Philip that the Governor had put his name to a message, declaring '*he will not give the land to white people*'.[1] Next day Calderwood had accepted office as a magistrate to do his best for the location of the Gaikas; in doing so he bound himself also to take official orders and by the 14th Maitland had hardened again and wrote to the Secretary of State that the Gaikas must go; their passive resistance made it necessary to continue 'systematic devastations' and drive them across the Kei; there, he airily assumed, there was 'plenty' of land for them. A month later he had hopes that 'famine' would compel surrender. In the same week he accepted Stockenström's resignation.

The flame of philanthropy which Stockenström had struggled to keep alive could not survive his second departure from frontier office. The authorities again found, as in 1835, that the extreme measure of driving the tribes across the Kei was impracticable; but forfeiture of lands now came to be the normal penalty for 'rebellion'. After another year of 'war' the Xhosa were compelled for the time being to submit. But seeing nothing that was '*intended* for their benefit', they were left with so little to lose that the train was well laid for the 'terrible war some years hence' (no later than 1850) which Calderwood had prophesied in his pre-official days (13 August to L.M.S.) would be the inevitable consequence of uprooting them, or even holding over their heads the threat to drive them from their home land.

In the course of 1846 a new Colonial Secretary, Earl Grey, decided not only that a younger man was needed at the Cape but that he must be armed with a wider discretion as High Commissioner for South Africa. This extension of the Governor's authority was a recognition also of the necessity of annexing Kaffraria, since 'the welfare of our uncivilized

[1] Maitland (to Secretary of State, 18 Sept.) is against white farms, but favours towns and artisans.

neighbours, and not least the welfare of the colonists, require
that the Kafir tribes should no longer be left in possession of the
independence they have so long enjoyed and abused'.[1] In
October and the months remaining to him Sir Peregrine
Maitland persevered with his plan of redistributing the lands of
the still protesting Xhosa among 'Fingos, Hottentots and
friendly Kafirs in some measure organized for defence under
British supervision, and supported by the military posts': a
missionary would be 'a desirable addition'.[2] On 14 October the
Commercial Advertiser, satisfied that the object was 'not the
acquisition of territory, but self-defence', agreed that 'a different
class of settlers must be interposed between these two races'; it
also understood 'Fingos, Hottentots and others, hostile to the
Caffres as any could desire, to be ready in thousands to accept
frontier locations'.[3] Maitland got no further; for the rest of his
time his energies were fully absorbed in continuing the war.

Sir Henry Pottinger, who took over in January 1847, was a
good deal less favourably disposed to the Hottentots or
'Coloured People'; he was presently describing them as
'pampered and spoiled'. Even Genadendal, the widely approved of Moravian settlement in the West, was a 'Hottentot
Elysium' where they got 'three or four times what they would
receive as soldiers'. In February and March he insisted on their
serving in 'levies' instead of as 'free burghers', thus sowing
seeds of discontent that produced the Rebellion of 1851. The
Kat River Settlement, which had suffered very severe losses by
deaths on service, by drought, devastations, and interrupted
industry, was soon (12 March) 'memorializing' against the new
policy including a threat to stop war rations; the very next day,
had they but known it, the Governor was listening receptively
to new demands for laws against *vagrancy*[4]—'the laws in force',

[1] Grey to Pottinger, 2 Nov. 1846.
[2] This was in accordance with a 'Memo.' by Mr. W. Shaw, communicated to Dr.
Philip by Brownlow Maitland, the Governor's son and Private Secretary, on 19
Oct. Dr. Philip gave qualified approval to a 'swarming off' of Hottentots from the
Kat River and remarked to the L.M.S. on the 23rd: 'You will see that I shall find
some work to do on the frontier of Caffreland.'
[3] Fairbairn had some difference with his friend Stretch on this issue; on 26 Dec.,
on Stretch's retirement, he noted the disappointment of 'his expectation of a *peaceable*
union of Caffreland with the Colony'.
[4] Pottinger to Secretary of State, 13 Mar., 14 April 1847 (*Cape Col. Qn.*, 276,
279 ff.).

he wrote, 'do not impose such restraints as are desirable'. The new Governor, therefore, was disposed to accept the verdict of Mr. Biddulph, a Settler magistrate, who in October sounded the knell of fresh 'Kat Rivers' by an adverse report on that settlement. Sir Andries Stockenström thereupon wrote in its defence, even to Earl Grey (20 November); and Dr. Philip momentarily roused himself to write in protest to the Governor, also more generally to L.M.S., 18 January 1848: 'The new plan turned out to be a system of *Martial Law*; but it received no countenance from the coloured people. They would have been between two fires, between the white man and the Caffre.' Thus Maitland's plans for the Hottentots miscarried and nothing was left for it but to 'fill up', as his successors soon began to do, with European farmers.

The resettlement or 'location' of hostile Xhosa made still less progress. In the closing months of 1846 Maitland began a system of registering those who gave up their arms and made submission as British subjects; he planned to ignore the authority of the chiefs and to place these under the direct rule of magistrates. Some 3,000 Gaikas submitted and got crops planted; but it was estimated that 7,000 Gaikas remained, besides Pato and others nearer the coast, who never even asked for terms. On 6 January an order from Downing Street recalling Maitland found him still superintending cattle-driving expeditions[1] on the far side of the Kei at Butterworth.

If Maitland definitely came down on the side of stringent military enforcement of tranquillity on the Xhosa frontier he did so almost in amiable despair; his peppery successor, Sir Henry Pottinger, sought to apply the remedy ruthlessly. When the new Governor took over early in 1847 the Colony itself was war-weary, disappointed of its hopes of farms,[2] and sore at quarrels with the regulars; the pressure applied to the Hottentots was, perhaps, more relentless because of the poor response[3] made to his frequent appeals for burgher help in bringing the Xhosa to complete submission. His first concern was Pato. When Colonel Somerset attempted in April to clear this chief from the country towards the mouth of the Kei, Captain Stretch

---

[1] Cf. Theal (iii. 35) for numbers of cattle taken, and how few Xhosa.
[2] Cf. Maitland to Grey, 20 Jan. 1847.
[3] Cf. Theal, iii. 40, 45. Read to Philip, 13 Oct. 1847.

snorted at the prolongation of the 'campaign'[1] and gibed at Colonel Somerset for whom, said he, Pato was 'as good as a walking annuity'.[2]

But besides the last-ditcher Pato, poor Sandile was not done with. Once more in June, the time for beer when they had reaped the crops grown by those who had submitted to Maitland, some of his people seem to have stolen 'fourteen goats' from the Kat River Settlement. Sandile, who had been ignored if not deposed by Maitland, was now held responsible by Pottinger for restitution of the goats and the surrender of the thieves. When he only partially complied with the demands made upon him the Governor ordered his arrest. A patrol sought him out, but Sandile, mindful (said James Read who is borne out by the frontier tradition) of the fate of Hintza, fled to the bush and the patrol was fired on. Sandile now sent a 'peace-offering' of twenty-one head of cattle, but 'the season was favourable for military operations' (says Dr. Theal) and the Governor resolved on drastic measures for his total expulsion.

On 27 August Sandile was proclaimed an outlawed rebel and, for their encouragement, volunteers were promised that cattle were to be kept by their captors as *booty*. On 7 September General Sir George Berkeley was given confidential instructions; the Governor thought the 'booty' Proclamation would suffice, but any cattle that could not be driven off were to be *killed*; hostilities would cease only when all arms were surrendered in token of complete submission. When on the 24th the Governor further demanded complete renunciation by Sandile of his claims west of the Kei even the General (Berkeley) protested—unless Sandile was given a fixed location his 'predatory hordes' would impose an impossible strain on the military machine. In fact, even with a great chain of cattle-receiving depots as bases 'all that the forces could accomplish in the Amatolas was to destroy the huts and prevent the Kafirs

---

[1] 'Whoever writes on the Caffre tragedy to be acted yet will have to record British Justice to her Colonies' (to Philip, 14 Apr. 1847). Also, 'You did not record the 100th part of the sufferings of the Hottentots in your *Researches*.' He thought Stockenström's return 'the only hope' (26 June).

[2] For Somerset see above, p. 291, n. 2.

[3] Read, writing to Philip from Kat River on 29 June, says categorically that the goats *and cattle* sent by Sandile as fines 'miscarried', but 'have since been delivered'.

from settling anywhere';[1] but in less than a month Sandile surrendered at discretion.

In October the troops moved on to the Kei to carry out a 'similar plan' against Pato. Stockenström was now moved to protest (20 November to Earl Grey) that the *loot* policy was 'worse than commandos'—they at least professed to recover stolen property—this, on the contrary, allowed thefts and murder 'by men who never lost nor possessed a cow or a shilling'. Scouting 'the surrender of a miserable starving chief' and scoffing at 'newspaper victories', he warned Earl Grey that the result would be to leave 'four or five times fifty thousand robbers' on their hands, with the chiefs on Robben Island and their cattle in the Colony, and endless expense to 'keep the Kafirs conquered'.[2]

The 'similar plan' against Pato was the end for the time being. Sir Harry Smith took over from Pottinger on 17 December 1847 and for him it remained to make definite Proclamation (on the 23rd) of the annexation of 'British Kaffraria', and to dictate terms of peace. Kaffirland and its tribal system were now in ruins. Throughout 1847 the Agents' or the new magistrates' reports had shown the social consequences of a prolonged period of drought and war, unrest and instability. In March and April Henry Calderwood, now Commissioner with the Gaikas, noted that among these tribes (the 'strongest' in Kaffirland, and occupying the 'best' of the country), there was a breakdown of tribalism. Many natives had taken up residence on one chief's land while still professing allegiance to another. If a census that was taken is any guide, the Gaikas, who in 1846 were estimated at 55,000, had shrunk, two years later, to 30,000, many being absent owing to 'the scarcity of food'.[3] At the later date, 1849, natives of Kaffraria were required to choose between assigned 'locations' and 'service';[4] thus the characteristic modern 'search for work' caused by landlessness and hunger had fairly begun. Earlier the Government had allowed Calderwood to engage

---

[1] Theal, iii. 48.

[2] To Dr. Philip, on 11 Dec., he wrote in similar strain, adding, 'The Gospel may follow the guns and do good in the end, but the Gospel might have got in without the guns.'

[3] In an 1849 Report Calderwood estimated that another 20,000 Gaikas were dispersed with chiefs beyond the Kei as well as in the Colony. The Ndhlambis had surprisingly grown from 10,000 to 34,000. At the later date Calderwood and others remark on land-hunger even among the Tambookies north of the mountains where there had been an influx of Europeans.   [4] Smith to Grey, 26 Oct. 1849.

even the lately independent Xhosa for service with masters who were prepared to 'take charge of and provide for them on their own premises'. In spite of passes (and 'thieving') other Commissioners[1] found at the same time that farmers being 'in great distress for servants, gladly welcomed' war refugees. The Government itself met the farmers' wants, and its own embarrassments on the frontier, by encouraging recruiting through the Commissioners.[2] The evidence is, too, that wages were not rising —the 'cow and calf' per annum referred to earlier by Captain Stretch had by one account become 'one cow' only.[3] It was incidental to this attempt to control the comings and goings of these working Xhosa that the authorities at last discovered that the 49th Ordinance was no law at all (above, p. 87). Further convincing evidence of the acute distress in the new *Kaffraria* comes from far-off Griquatown whence, on 15 August 1847, Edward Solomon reported the arrival of a 'party of Caffres who had come 250 miles', located themselves under Waterboer 'near the Great River and were asking for instruction. We are at a loss', he tells Dr. Philip, 'how to meet their wants.'

Dr. Philip recounts a shrewd remark made some years earlier by an old native: 'The Boers are like buffaloes; they have hard heads, but we see them before they attack us. But the English are like the tiger; they have too much here' (pointing to his head), 'they spring upon us before we see them.' The effect of the 'peaceful penetration' of Hottentot and Bantu land by the earlier Boers was indeed as nothing to the systematic havoc wrought among the Ama-Xhosa;[4] even the later Republics got

[1] Fynn to Government Secretary, 17 May 1847.
[2] Cf. reply to one van den Berg of Riversdale (Private Letters, 1847, Cape Town Archives) who was recommended to take *not* children but *families*. On 18 Nov. Calderwood despatched 170 natives and expected many more applications; he too recommended that *families* be sent, and 'as far into the Colony as possible', though another Commissioner, Col. G. H. McKinnon, later of Kaffraria, reported that natives were against going to the west. After the war a Proclamation of 27 Jan. 1848 referred to 'the present attempt, by a system of "apprenticing" young natives, to add to the scanty supply of labour', and at the same time 'reclaim a number of the youth of British Kaffraria'. This was also to 'contribute to the peace of this important province'. Applications presently came from as far afield as 'Piketberg' and Colesberg. Beaufort 'could use four times as many'.
[3] In 1848 B. Moodie of Swellendam has a note on wages: for the first year, one cow; for the second and third years of *contract*, two cows; for girls, six she-goats; *or*, for men, £1 per annum.
[4] Rev. T. D. Philip, in a draft 'Life of Dr. Philip' written about 1900 but never published, remarked on the efficacy of British policy for wringing from the Bantu

their way without needing to shatter the tribal system of the Bantu
so utterly (see below, pp. 359 ff.). In the Cape the power of the
chiefs was completely broken; later commissioners inevitably took
virtually full charge from the beginning, even if—once the 'tiger
spring' was complete—the disastrous effects of this policy of
Thorough were in some measure mitigated by scrupulously fair
administration and, in the Cape, by the boon of political freedom.

When Sir Harry Smith took charge at the close of this
devastating war there was of course no political freedom even
for the Cape Colony, and political rights were meaningless to
the Bantu. War and unrest made it hard for officials, and still
harder for colonists, to think except of the need for 'security';
Sir Harry's system was Martial Law. A stroke of the pen (and a
spectacular show of Sir Harry's fireworks) had finally swept the
treaties aside and annexed the land to the Crown as 'British
Kaffraria'; 'I make no treaty, I say this land is mine.'[1] The
chiefs were at the same time given to understand that their
'locations' would be where they were sent; they also solemnly
bound themselves (under *force majeure*) to repudiate 'witchcraft'
and 'the sin of buying wives'; other conditions, 'subversive of the
whole framework of Bantu society', says Dr. Theal, required
them to acknowledge *no* chief but the Queen of England.[2] It is
little wonder that a magistrate reported them 'slow to believe'
when a few months later they saw the Ceded Territory—the
fair Chumie Valley above the later Lovedale, towards the Hog's
Back—being planted with villages of soldier settlers (the same
Auckland, Woburn and the rest where they were to perpetrate
a massacre on the Christmas Day of 1850, below, p. 321). By
way also of tidying up, the north-eastern district of Albert (long
contested by farmers and Tambookies),[3] was finally incorporated in the Colony in January 1848.

the two things they possessed—land and labour; having taken up a position on the
outskirts of Bantu country, the British became involved in war for the suppression
of cattle-stealing; in the war they destroyed Bantu wealth in cattle, at the same time
seizing land as a penalty for theft. Thus one blow reduced the native people to
economic dependence which forced them to supply labour, or starve.

[1] *Sandile*: 'Your children require land as they are crowded.'

Governor: 'All up to the Kei' (i.e. up to 100 miles *beyond* the old 'Ceded' Territory)
'is Sandile's.'   *Sandile*: 'I do not know that country.'
Whereupon, Smith threatened total expulsion from Kaffraria (Smith to Grey, 7
Jan. 1848).   [2] Theal, iii. 57.

[3] Read to Philip and to the Lieutenant-Governor throughout 1843.

The acquisition of British Kaffraria at once threw on the Governor and his staff the burden of finding ways and means of carrying on the Queen's government for the benefit of people who neither possessed cash nor needed it, and had little reason to expect to profit from the services rendered by this new authority. For this first 'High Commission Territory' Smith on 23 March 1848 told Earl Grey of a stop-gap 'financial expedient': 'Frontier farmers having generally speaking acquired large fortunes by the war expenditure, they are prepared to pay large prices for these lands'; and he proposed to sell them farms in the former Xhosa country. His next move was more important, was indeed a fateful experiment destined to a very long life. The bright idea was to kill two birds with one stone; it would bring in revenue, and at the same time give the tenants of the new *locations* a steadying sense of ownership, if they were required to pay an annual quit-rent for their holdings, £1 per annum. Old James Read, in the fray for the last time, at once protested that 200 Fingos in his neighbourhood would be paying £200 for 2,000 *morgen* (well under 5,000 acres) which would cost a European farmer only £4. A year later Calderwood urged at least a temporary reduction to 10*s.*; but even the £1 rate had come to stay for most of a century. Little more was heard of the educative value of land tax; but the African *poll* tax of about £1 became almost general practice, sometimes with a smaller *local* tax added. About the time (1930's) the experts were at last becoming critical of the poll tax as 'regressive' taxation, it fell to the credit of the keen Indirect Rulers of northern Nigeria to set a fashion of graduating the tax, thus reducing the load on the people of poorer districts.[2] In the prosperous South Africa of the 1950's higher earnings (and improved social services) were held to warrant an increase in the traditional basic rate, but the system was left unchanged.

Once introduced the poll tax persisted, even if it was (the late Sir James Currie used to protest) 'taxing a man for the offence of existing!' Perhaps the old Cape officials had some idea of the reason why when they made their vain attempt to give their people some individual interest in their land holdings; the Xhosa and almost all other African people lived at or so near subsistence level that they had to be self-sufficient; producing

[1] W. M. Macmillan, *Africa Emergent*, chs. xi, xii; *Road To Self-Rule*, ch. x.

no appreciable surplus they had virtually none of the trade that is normally the source of government revenues. Most of the *colonial* peoples had no need to practise any but 'shifting' cultivation, and had no idea of the agricultural methods they must acquire to make a success of the peasant small-holdings the new *locations* forced upon them; it was many years before any colonial administration seriously tried to nurse them into using better technique. So it may be that even a poll-tax fulfilled some educative function. The commercially active Gold Coast, almost alone, lived entirely (and latterly quite well) on customs duties; but independent Ghana was left, in consequence, under the painful necessity of itself teaching its people to pay direct taxes. For the Xhosa, and in the long run for most of these tribes, the effect of the tax was to leave them only a stark choice: either they must subsist as best they might on their own remaining land (where some of the pressure was directly due to the natural growth of the population); otherwise, and more immediately, they must undertake the only paid employment then offering, poorly paid (and rather prospectless) service on a colonial farm.

Sir Harry Smith was well aware of this, or even meant it so.[1] No one in those days knew enough of Bantu ways and thinking, or even about the 'ecology' of their vast continent, to foresee the cumulative effects on the soil, and in the first place even on food production, of the continuous application of extensive methods to the increasingly straitened locations to which the Xhosa were now confined. The first condition of the peaceful co-existence required of the Xhosa, not only with the stronger white colonists on their western front but with their own kith and kin in their rear, was that they adapt themselves to new agricultural methods, and to the changed ways of life these must necessitate. Sir Harry Smith's previous experience, so far from helping him in this new crisis, may even have been his undoing, tempting him to suppose it would suffice to carry on the 'system' he had regretfully had to abandon in 1836. A forceful personality, this Governor was also of too impatient a nature to work out the details of the proposals designed to help them in their 'first step to civilization'; he was presently consulting Dr. Philip and others about how best to teach them to

[1] Smith to Grey, 26 Oct. 1848.

plough and to follow habits of industry, to see 'the necessity of wearing clothes', and the use of money, how also 'to establish schools on such a footing as would ensure hereafter teachers from among themselves'; 'too much pains' cannot be taken to wean them from the use of blankets and, 'of all things His Excellency requests' the use of English in the schools 'to the total exclusion of the Kafir dialect'.[1]

As things were in those days, when no Government had any of its own functional departments, only the missionaries—many of whom shared the Governor's simple faith in the virtues of civilized clothing—were in a position to help these almost high-falutin schemes. But the widely scattered missionaries were now also leaderless. Dr. Philip was virtually out of action—six months before Sir Harry took office a valedictory letter to the Buxton ladies showed him in an unaccustomed mood of pious resignation: 'My own health is very precarious, but if the Lord has any more use for me He can yet give me a few more days: if not He can carry out His work without me.' But one function remained to Philip so long as he continued 'awaiting a successor'. Much troubled by a 'shake', he tells Miss Gurney (one of the Buxton connexion), in July 1847, he is able only to 'collect information'—for Dr. T. Hodgkin, of the Aborigines Protection Society in London, who made no obvious use of it. Whether the Governor so much as saw this information is uncertain; he and Philip occasionally exchanged notes but apparently never 'talked things over' together. Yet Dr. Philip's 'collection' was of the first importance including, as it did, a mass of letters from key points all over the country; not only Calderwood, Niven, the Reads, and others on mission stations but Stretch and Stockenström supplied a continuous stream of evidence showing clearly, and betimes, how Kaffrarian policy was misfiring. No less clearly E. Solomon, and Casalis, Dyke, and Rolland of Basutoland, chronicled in detail the mismanagement and muddle which were the undoing of the Orange Sovereignty venture. Without a Philip to marshal so much material or, even better, to view events on the spot, this all went to waste; and, save only the first gleanings recorded in these pages, none of it remains for historians.

It may be that even the missionaries knew little of the

---

[1] Circular by Richard Southey, Secretary, 17 Apr. 1848.

stirrings of the Xhosa mind, of the significance, for example, of the rise of the prophet Umlangeni, who was a power in the land as early as 1850 (and the inspiration of the final cattle-killing delusion of 1857). But they recorded quite enough to supplement the deficiencies of official intelligence and make it inexcusable that the authorities were again caught off balance (as they were in spite of warnings in 1834), by the renewed outbreak in 1850. The causes at any rate of continuing unrest were obvious. In the very first days of the 'peace' the Rev. R. Niven returned to his station near the Chumie to find only Burnshill reoccupied. 'War', he wrote to Dr. Philip on 18 January 1848, 'has changed the missions sadly for the worse.' He was, he felt, 'walking among tombs and haranguing the dead'. Writing of the settlement and of the prospects for the future, he deplored the 'evil of depriving them of so much land and giving the Europeans a position in the little that is left, which will, I fear, end in the Caffres becoming a nation of degraded servants on their own soil':

Our Governor is attempting too much, denouncing social evils which his system cannot punish, and which in that case had better be left to the progress of light among this unhappy people, who have suffered equally from themselves and others. Time is needed and must be allowed for maturing an incipient scheme in the hands of such an *ex tempore* character as Sir Harry Smith.

But within six weeks of his assumption of office this '*ex tempore* character', having launched British Kaffraria, dashed off through the Orange Territory. On 3 February he was writing of his doings from the banks of the Tugela in Natal, blissfully unaware of having left behind him a 'peace' founded only on poverty and prostration.

XVII

THE ANNEXATION AND ABANDON-
MENT OF THE NORTH, 1848–54:
ASSESSMENT OF JOHN PHILIP'S WORK

OFFICIAL attention had of course far too long been diverted
from the complex issues raised in the north by the Great Trek.
Sir Henry Pottinger's short term of office was fully taken up by
his exertions in Kaffirland; his one if not only contribution was
to northern *un*-settlement—the Transvaal leader, Andries Pretorius, was refused the interview he had journeyed some hundreds
of miles to seek. Sir Harry Smith at once set out to use the
authority vested in him, as High Commissioner for South Africa,
'for the settling and adjustment of the affairs of the territories . . .
adjacent or contiguous . . . to the frontier'. The institution of the
high commissionership was in itself an advance, and in private
talk before he left England the new Governor must have discovered that as Secretary of State Earl Grey had definite and
constructive notions of colonial policy. But even Earl Grey was
in no position to carry through a 'forward' policy unless this
could be done with a minimum of expenditure and lighten the
financial load for the future.[1]

The attitude of the British Parliament was very different from
what it had been in the thirties when humanitarians, almost
alone, took even a passing interest in any colonial affairs. The
direct and continuous influence of this body of opinion, even at
its zenith, has been much overrated and now Fowell Buxton had
no successor as watch-dog for 'Exeter Hall'. Dr. Philip, who
retired finally in 1850, died at a remote mission station in 1851;
whereupon—so little was his life's work appreciated by his own
folk—even the L.M.S. stood aside from any debate for fear of
being 'branded as political'; this phrase is from R. Niven's
letter from London in 1852 telling Captain Stretch how he
failed to get any hearing at all for the plea he entered on behalf

---

[1] The 1846–7 war had already cost a round £1,000,000.

of the Xhosa. On the other hand the Colonial Office now had a variety of persistent critics who were at one in knowing little and apparently caring even less about Bantu tribes, certainly stopping far short of making their welfare a British responsibility. By this time the colonies, in general, were a constant parliamentary theme. Gibbon Wakefield and his 'school', the advocates of *systematic* colonization, had diagnosed the inescapable weakness of all *colonial* rule when they insisted that *local* affairs can best, if not only, be settled by the people locally concerned, not from afar by a London office. But their experience and their concern were the colonies of settlement, entirely excluding the Cape and its frontiers where the nostrum of self-government could not readily be applied to the Bantu portion of the 'self' to be governed. This school, at any rate, and its active spokesman, the Benthamite Sir William Molesworth, had influential support from the Cobdenite Free Traders; their commercial interests, and those of the British tax-payer, would, they considered, be best served by devolving colonial responsibilities upon colonial legislatures. Against so much *laissez faire* a forward-looking Colonial Secretary could look for no help in those days from highly placed sponsors of 'Imperialism'. We have it on the authority of Earl Grey himself that pillars of society like Sir Robert Peel and Sir James Graham and even Benjamin Disraeli 'betray' a leaning to the heresy that we have no interest in preserving our colonies and ought, therefore, to make no sacrifice for that purpose.[1]

Faced thus by the cocksure 'colonial reformers' who had a sovereign specific for all colonial ills, and by others who were yet to win elections with promises of 'Peace, Retrenchment and Reform', Earl Grey perhaps lacked the political flair needed to win popular support for a policy more closely related to the situation with which he had to cope in southern Africa.[2] In Sir Harry Smith, moreover, he had in that anything but stock-pattern colony a Governor apt to move with such speed and decision as were likely to run into obstacles. Before ever Grey had heard of the annexation of Kaffraria he had drafted a note (March 1848) warning Smith that the Colony would in future

[1] Grey to Elgin, 18 May 1849, quoted by J. L. Morison, *British Supremacy and Canadian Self Government*, pp. 266–7, from the Howick Papers.
[2] *Colonial Policy of Peel and Russell*, by W. P. Morrell, O.U.P., 1930.

be held responsible for its own expenditure. Yet by January the Governor was already dashing from Kaffraria to his hardly less troubled northern frontier. At Philippolis, on his way to Natal, he made time (with no Dr. Philip to check him now, and W. Y. Thomson removed to Grahamstown) to set aside Kok's treaties as of little importance (above, Ch. XIV) and deprive him of control beyond the 'inalienable reserve'. He also acted the part of a confiscatory land-reformer, giving Kok permission to eject time-expired Boer lessees, but only on payment of compensation for improvements[1]—'as if', remarked Sir Andries Stockenström, 'by *lending* a room in your house, you forfeit the whole'. To Moshesh, a 'great chief', Smith was more polite, gaining his 'magnanimous' concurrence in the view that 'some great and paramount authority' was necessary for 'peace, harmony and tranquillity', for the purpose also of 'maintaining inviolate the hereditary rights of the chiefs, and of effectually restraining the Boers within limits and upon the locations they now possess'.[2] Being satisfied, further, that at least the considerable Oberholster party of Boers was well disposed, and having apparently 'sounded' even the Transvaalers, through Pretorius,[3] he tarried no longer; a Proclamation issued on 3 February from the Tugela extended the Queen's sovereignty over the whole of the country of Moshesh, Moroko, Kok, and others between the Orange, the Vaal, and the Drakensberg—this

with no desire or inclination whatever on the part of Her Majesty to extend or increase her dominions . . . but on the contrary with the sole view of establishing relationships with those chiefs and protecting them from any future aggression . . .

British subjects, it was laid down,

were to be subject to the laws of the colony of the Cape of Good Hope, and guaranteed the *full possession of the rights of citizens of the said colony*, subject to the payment of an annual quit-rent for the lands they now occupied; the proceeds of this revenue were to go first *to the fair and honest remuneration and indemnification of the native chiefs*, secondly, to defray the expenses of (British) government; any surplus, with the

[1] Stockenström was moved to indignation: 'What statesmanship we are at the mercy of!' 'Hiring', he had written to Earl Grey, 'was preferable to trespass.' (Quoted by Read to Philip, 11 June 1848.) This was 'contrary to all law', comments E. Solomon (Dec. 1848).

[2] *Agreement* with Moshesh, 27 Jan. 1848. Eybers, p. 269.

[3] Walker, p. 240.

proceeds of traders' licenses (at £50 each, as in Kaffraria), was ear-
marked for churches and schools, 'for the exclusive benefit of the population north of the Orange River'—loans being also promised to supplement
any sums locally subscribed for church building.[1]

With surprisingly little demur, Earl Grey on 28 June approved
of Smith's action, though in March he had taken alarm at the
extension of 'risks' likely from the annexation even of the north-
eastern district of Albert; he even rejoiced in the 'success of the
measures for bringing the emigrant Boers once more within the
control of regular government'. And so, had fates proved kinder,
the hesitations of ten years or more might have been ended by
the effective re-union of far the greater part of this divided
South Africa.

Sir Harry Smith was at every stage full of consideration for
the welfare of 'his children', the Boers; this prompted for
example the high-handed treatment meted out to Kok and the
Griquas. Edward Solomon, the judicial father of two well-
known South African judges, was concerned for native welfare
and considered Smith's policy, as a whole rather than in particular, 'too dogmatic and bullying'. James Read, the younger,
wrote with less restraint:

Many sensible men on the Frontier begin to think that he will
inflict a more severe blow on the rights of the natives of this country
than any former Governor. . . . What does he mean in one of his
familiar epistles to the Boers, I think to Potgieter, by saying that he
would locate some of the natives among them? Some years ago such
hints would not have escaped the eagle-eyed Philanthropists here
and in England.

In spite of this, the irreconcilable northern Boers were the first
obstacle to South African reunion. In the winter Sir Harry was
forced to dash post-haste all the way from Cape Town to the
rescue of Major H. D. Warden, the British Resident Agent,
who had been ejected from his capital Bloemfontein by Andries
Pretorius and a force from beyond the Vaal. In August Smith
dispersed the malcontents near the Orange River at Boomplaats,
put a price on the head of Pretorius, whom a little earlier he had
tried to bait with the offer of a land commissionership in Natal,
and drove them out of the Sovereignty to nurse their grievance

---

[1] Eybers, pp. 270 ff.

and to continue their quarrels with their own friends beyond the Vaal.[1] On this episode Edward Solomon commented again from Griquatown (to Dr. Philip on 9 September):

> I think it is fortunate for the natives that from the first this outbreak has assumed the character of decided opposition to the Colonial Government. Sir Harry Smith appears to me to have formed too favourable an opinion of the Boers, looking upon them rather as unfortunate than as criminal, and inclined to side with them when their interests and those of the natives clash. He appears anxious to clear them from the imputation of being rebels, but now in spite of his conciliatory manners and the really kind measures adopted for their benefit, they have put themselves in a posture of opposition and insulted the British Government by expelling its agents. . . . I rejoice that this has not originated in any dispute between Boers and Griquas (but in) open hostility which necessitates a real settlement and the removal of the ringleaders from this country.

Still the Governor was long-suffering, refusing to eject even rebel lessees of Griqua land; yet in the end Mr. Solomon advised Dr. Philip (March 1849) that it would be wiser to 'encourage the Griquas to make what use they can of the lands that are left to them than to go on quarrelling about what they have so unjustly lost'. 'This', he concludes, 'is advice the Griquas little relish and is, therefore, the more important.' And there the long political battle fought by the L.M.S. on behalf of the Griquas virtually ended. In the sixties and later the Rev. William Dower shepherded the trek of the Philippolis Griquas to a new home (and short-lived separate existence) in Griqualand East (Kokstad).

In 1849 and much of 1850 Sir Harry's attention was diverted, this time to Cape Town, by the hectic agitation of all parties in the Colony against Earl Grey's plan of making the Cape a convict settlement.[2] During these fateful months difficulties that demanded the care of a wiser and a stronger man than the Resident Agent, Major Warden, came near destroying all hope of a satisfactory permanent settlement in the newly annexed Orange River Sovereignty. The Griquas, as the Governor had quickly divined, were weak and submissive, and their discontent made little difference; but the delay caused by the Kaffir War in carrying out the revised Treaty policy of 1845 had

[1] See, e.g., Walker, p. 257.   [2] *Cape Col. Qn.*, p. 260.

by this time made the fixing of Moshesh's boundaries a more intractable question than ever. Even Moshesh, a Bantu chief, who had done wonders in binding broken fragments of tribes into a Basuto nation, enjoyed no precise territorial sovereignty. On the undefined borders where his authority was necessarily weak European colonists had now considerably enlarged their claims by bargains with lesser potentates, and insidious and by no means disinterested flattery had elevated some of these into rivals who appeared of greater importance than they actually were.

As in Kaffirland, the real dispute was not merely about land but about access to the very best land in all those parts. The broad valleys of the Caledon and its tributaries are much the best watered and most fertile in this part of the country; these are one of the only two or three considerable wheat-growing districts in the whole of the later Union. Originally the rise of the Basuto power, following hard on the Chaka wars, was possible only because of the security afforded by the mountain fastnesses of the Malutis, an off-shoot of the Drakensberg. But the people of Moshesh, as times became more settled and their confidence in the chief's protection more assured, had by this time spread once more over the agriculturally much more tempting (but less easily defended) open country lying to the north and west. In this area the lesser people like Moroko and Sikonyela and other ill-organized refugees had a footing; and here also, through the very weakness of these chiefs, Boer farmers had staked claims characteristically wide, and out of all proportion to their numbers. For straightening out this tangle Major Warden's authority was pitifully inadequate. He was, moreover, largely dependent on the goodwill of the burghers on whom, for want of a garrison, the defence of the territory rested. In spite of Sir Harry Smith's optimistic appropriation of the revenue due from quit-rents, funds were very short; and both Smith and Warden knew very well that in the last resort Earl Grey was prepared to tolerate the experiment of the Sovereignty only so long as it was self-supporting.

Warden's first step was to appoint a Land Commission composed exclusively of officials and burghers. In spite of the 'native danger', farmers and natives were inextricably mixed up together and any line that sought merely to recognize the *status quo* must have made an impossible frontier. Very careful handling was needed to secure a workable compromise. The French missionaries were the constant advisers of Moshesh but, as foreigners, needed such backing as Dr. Philip had given them. In 1848, moreover, Revolution in France left them so short of financial support that there was a danger of their giving up altogether. The consequence was that, in the absence of any even unofficial sponsor, Basuto interests received short shrift in the delimitation of the boundary long known as 'the Warden Line'; this took no account of how an actual shortage of land was the prolific cause of rivalry among the natives themselves. 'For three years', wrote the Rev. Hamilton Dyke of Morija to Dr. Philip on the Christmas Day of 1848, 'the Government had promised arbitration' to settle a dispute about an area claimed by the Basuto though occupied in part by Mantatees under Sikonyela; 'but the delay and recent acts of the Government in reference to other parts of the country were but little calculated to inspire confidence (as) unfortunately Sikonyela has never been long without giving provocation'. An 'act of hostility' followed the Boomplaats rebellion in September[1] and led to a Basuto counter-attack in which about twenty Mantatees were killed and two or three thousand head of cattle captured. In this and other instances Moshesh made reparation to his troublesome neighbours; but Mr. Dyke continues:

We have just heard of a plan for a boundary proposed to His Excellency by Mr. (later Sir Richard) Southey and one of the magistrates in these parts. . . . To facilitate the Government of British subjects who have emigrated into Moshesh's country, these gentlemen kindly propose to take in all the part of Moshesh's country in which emigrants have set themselves down, and who in very many cases are living side by side with villages of native Bassoutos. The plan says that emigrants living in (areas) not embraced by the new British line will have to remove. . . . Naturally the natives taken in by the line must retreat over it so as to leave room for new emigrants—a cunning plan certainly, and very fair, seeing that for five or six families of Boers to be displaced, thousands of natives must remove. . . . This scheme is the more unjust as Moshesh never

---

[1] E. Casalis had written from Thaba Bosigo on 1 Sept. 1848: 'Moshesh having ever been faithful to his treaty has naturally been an object of great suspicion to the rebels who have kept him closely watched, endeavouring at the same time, by every means, to stir up the Mantatees and other tribes to attack the Bassoutos.'

took a farthing from any emigrants who have settled in his country. His limits were settled by treaty in 1843, after which he was requested by Sir Peregrine Maitland to grant a portion of land which would be exclusively for emigrants. This he did and now he is told by Mr. Southey that he proposed to the Governor to set aside all former limits and establish another which cuts off half of Moshesh's country, or rather the Bassouto country—that is, of the habitable part of it. . . . The Governor may perhaps see the enormity of the plan proposed and try by his answer to Moshesh to allay the angry feeling which is already excited. . . . I only trust the Bassoutos will be patient and see what can be done without war. War must ruin them but who would wonder if they resort to it, seeing that they know not where to look for redress.

Mr. Southey's proposal concerned the extreme south-west of what was then Basuto country, the area round the mission station of Beersheba. Two months later Mr. Casalis, Moshesh's most intimate adviser at Thaba Bosigo, wrote with rising indignation of the delimitation of a boundary that involved the removal of 'at least forty villages (*Basuto*, not Mantatee or Barolong)', and threatened to leave the great Morija mission station, chosen as it had been for its *central* position, on the very border outskirts of Basutoland (where it has remained). Indeed, the crowding of the modern Basuto population into the narrow strip of habitable country along the Union border points again to the real significance of the long feud of the Basuto with the Free State; the mountainous interior has begun to fill up only in our own overcrowded day: Mr. Casalis's letter, like that of Calderwood from Kaffirland (above, p. 287) makes it clear that in Basutoland too the dispute between colonists and Bantu was for possession of the *land*.

The Rev. Dr. Philip
Dear Sir,
    That Sir Harry Smith should feel vexed at the manifestation of dissatisfaction among the natives is by no means surprising. But His Excellency is very much mistaken as to the personal dispositions of the French missionaries, and the amount of influence they possess on the minds of the natives in such matters, if he supposes that this dissatisfaction originates in any interference on our part.
    Up to the conclusion of the late wars with the Boers the natives have given the most satisfactory proof of their confidence in Government. The rebels used every exertion to induce them to join in the

revolt. On the other hand, had the natives not felt assured that Sir Harry would regulate the affairs relative to their territory with uprightness and equity, they had it in their power to burn the houses and destroy the gardens of the emigrants interspersed among them—most of the farms having been abandoned and left entirely unprotected by their owners. It appears then that there must have been something in the working of the present system which has created suspicion with regard to the real intentions of Government.

All men who believe that generosity and a disinterested interference may yet find their place among political principles understood that the Sovereignty proclaimed beyond the Great River, being neither the result of conquest nor the infliction of a deserved chastisement, was the extension of a wholly paternal impartial authority over parties who might well be taken in the light of children in a state of minority. Could it have been suspected to be anything else every honest heart would have repudiated it as the most refined piece of imposition ever contemplated. The possession of the places they already occupied was secured to the Boers, and this the native chiefs (the Basuto chiefs) consented to, because they were assured both in private conferences and through public proclamations that no further encroachments should be suffered, and that their rights and authority over their people should be respected.

One of the first acts of the magistrate of Smithfield has been to seize the person of a subaltern chief belonging to the family of Moshesh, because he refused to allow a veld-cornet to take an account of the number of the people and of their property. The chieftain was afraid that this might be a preliminary to making soldiers of his men, and insisted on the contemplated measure being first communicated to Moshesh. The chieftain was seized and dragged to Smithfield and only released when one of his people offered to stand bail for him. The incident created great excitement among the natives.

At the same critical moment the disaffected Boers were using every means in their power to work upon the feelings of the natives, telling them that the sovereignty of the Queen had bereft them of all rights to their own country, that they would be placed under British Law, be obliged to pay taxes, to serve in the Cape Corps, &c. On another hand the boasting and haughty behaviour of the farmers, who were willing to abide by the new regulations of Government, their utter disregard for the feelings of the natives among whom they lived and whose rights they had till then outwardly respected, seemed to confirm the interpretation which the dis-affected gave of the new system of policy. At the same moment rumours were rife that it was intended to draw a limit between the Boers and the natives. The latter were under the impression that the object of Sir Harry Smith in changing the former treaties and proclaiming the sovereignty had precisely been to preclude the necessity of a boundary. They understood that *intermixed* as the Boers were with them, it had been found impracticable to operate a perfect separation, whence flowed the necessity of bringing black and white under the general protection and supervision of Her Majesty.

Moshesh had, himself, expressly asked His Excellency what would be done in the case of the Boers living near native villages, to which it had been *explicitly answered* that each party were to remain as they were. Thus the natives were led to think there would be between them and the farmers nothing more than a moral limit—that Government would accurately ascertain the number of Boers already settled in their country, define the extent of their farms, restrain them from further extension, govern them where they were, and leave to the natives the free occupation of all those portions of their territory which remained yet in their possession. They felt conscious that if a boundary was established, some one must be removed, and they thought from indications which they had already observed, that they had much reason to fear that necessity should be laid on them.

Hence I suppose the reluctance of Moshesh to meet personally the land commission to make a limit. But had he no reason to demur before becoming a party to any such arrangements? I received information of the boundary proposed by the Commission and found to my utter amazement that it is such as will require (if carried out) the removal of at least 40 villages of Bassoutos including the personal residence of a brother of Moshesh. That boundary would pass within 25 miles of Morija, one of the most central stations. It detaches entirely from the remainder of the tribe the stations of Beersheba and that of Hebron. It deprives the inhabitants of Beersheba of 23 cattle posts, actually occupied by them, and from which their flocks must be driven. It places at the disposal of Government a large portion of territory in which only a few families of Boers reside at the extremities, whilst the central parts are occupied by the natives. Happily the Commission have left to Moshesh the liberty of expressing his opinion to Sir Harry, before the proposed limit be confirmed, and I hope he will have availed himself of that his right.

My conscience has not allowed me to remain silent and I have taken the liberty of respectfully stating my opinion to the High Commissioner by a letter. No one laments more than I do the estrangement of the confidence and the affections of the Bassoutos from the British which even the mere proposal of such measures must unavoidably occasion. It will eventually prove the ruin of the natives, and if improved by the disaffected farmers may very soon involve the Colony in great difficulties. I apprehend it will also materially impair the credit of the missionaries in the tribe, as we have always endeavoured to persuade the Bassoutos that the British Government was animated with the most generous and upright intentions towards them.

I have long been convinced that the natives, brought as they have been in close contact with a white population, are unable to govern themselves, and I believe they had a sufficient perception of this to have yielded to the authority of Government, had they not been threatened of being dispossessed of the very fields they cultivate. I fear much confusion arises from the very limited and erroneous ideas generally entertained respecting the statistics of the Bassouto country. The population is underrated, the actual and future wants of the tribe are not taken in consideration. It is no childish debate about useless wastes that takes place at this moment. The present lamentable war of the Bassoutos and the Mantatees which originates in nothing else than a land question, shows sufficiently how keen and deep are the feelings of the natives on that subject.

Excuse this long letter, and believe that in thus frankly expressing myself, I only yield to the desire of acknowledging the proof of interest you have given us by writing,

I remain, Reverd. and dear Sir,

Yours most respectfully,

E. CASALIS

GRAHAMSTOWN,
22nd *February*, 1849

Another two months later (25 April 1849) M. Rolland of Beersheba, a less regular correspondent of Dr. Philip's, put the truth about the land in a nutshell, that this was:

not even a question of boundary between Colonial territory and native land, but of *taking a certain part*, hitherto in their undisputed possession, *from the natives*. . . . The new line takes in nearly all the white inhabitants (and decrees) the removal of *some hundreds* of native villages, inter-mixed with their farms, including our mission station of Hebron with the whole of its population.

These letters were more than the fulminations of missionary philanthropists. Major Warden had insufficient power behind him to interfere with European farmers, or to enforce their removal, therefore he let himself be guided exclusively by their interests and advice. Without, it would seem, in a single case disturbing farmers in actual occupation,[1] Warden's Commission issued certificates of possession, giving the Sovereignty a definite boundary and the farmers a legal title—one to which they clung even after the abandonment of the Sovereignty a few years later. At the same time while, as missionaries protested and officials affirmed,[2] the Government paid little regard to the rights of native occupants, it was yet powerless to carry out the evictions it proposed. In part from fear or jealousy of Moshesh, and usually at the expense of the Basuto,[3] the 'settlement' was unduly tender to the claims of the petty tribes, giving them more than they really required. The farmers' legal title to the land remained, but masses of Basuto and others became squatters without rights, a rare legacy of native discontent which had to be lived down by the later Free State.

It was hardly for this that Moshesh so readily agreed in 1848 to Sir Harry Smith's proclamation of British Sovereignty 'for the purpose of effectually restraining the Boers within limits and upon the locations they now possess'. As Dr. Philip had pointed out in the beginning, and as the Governor at first realized, Moshesh was the one chief whose friendship and co-operation were worth keeping. If only because of the Government's eastern preoccupations, the so-called 'Dr. Philip treaty' had in nearly two years in no way relieved the boundary situation; now the Governor's abrupt setting aside of that with Kok cannot have passed unnoticed. His firmness in and after the affair of Boomplaats promised better things; but a moment later the never very effective agent, Major Warden, was thrown once more on his own resources while the Governor fenced with anti-convict politicians in Cape Town. Even so Moshesh showed himself not only sincerely anxious in spite of all provocation to keep the peace; over and over again, for the sake of good relations, he used the restraint of one both willing to keep a bargain and able to enforce it on his own people. For years Boers and Basuto

---

[1] Clerk to Newcastle, 10 Nov. 1853, and de Kiewiet, *British Colonial Policy*, ch. v.
[2] de Kiewiet, op. cit. Basutoland Records, ii, pp. 29–30.
[3] One Molitsani, who in the end adhered to Moshesh, having been crowded out by the 'Warden Line', was given a 'slice' of Basuto country, 'that a recognized chief should not be without a country' (de Kiewiet, ibid.). On the other hand, Warden was unable to make room for some 12,000 Barolong except at Basuto expense, because he was unable to remove 'two or three Boer farmers' who between them claimed 'some 100 sq. miles' (Warden to Smith, 23 Dec. 1848).

had in fact been living side by side with a minimum of disturbance; in 1848 isolated Boers were left unmolested during the excitement of the Boomplaats campaign; Sikonyela was even reimbursed for not unmerited losses at the hands of the Basuto. In 1849 Moshesh agreed, under protest it is true, to the new boundary line, even when Major Warden perversely recognized the petty chiefs (who more readily consented to white occupation) as independent rulers and, presently, as 'allies' against the Basuto.[1] The restraint and control maintained by Moshesh were remarkable; but his followers, threatened with dispossession by weaker tribes they probably despised, in the end inevitably came to blows with their old enemies, now the special protégés of 'Government'.

Worse was to follow. In the last week of 1850 war flared up with renewed violence on the eastern front. In spite of this, perhaps even suspecting collusion, Warden persisted in seeing the continued unrest in his region as due, not to his own dispositions, but to the greed and ambition of the Basuto. First he demanded compensation for what were certainly not unprovoked Basuto attacks on Sikonyela and the Barolong Moroko. Moshesh meekly paid 2,500 head of cattle, but inter-tribal fighting continued (always in the disputed corn-lands) and Warden next decided to take 'strong action'. Though the forces were now being heavily drawn on for the Xhosa war he called up the burghers and his native allies and prepared to march against the Basuto chief. Many of the farmers would undoubtedly have welcomed a British garrison to protect them in the enjoyment of their new lands, but Downing Street tolerated the Sovereignty only so long as it was self-supporting and self-protecting. As for the burghers, Basutoland farms were one thing, the suppression of the unrest to which their occupation gave rise quite another; this was an inter-tribal quarrel and no concern of theirs. The burghers, therefore, obeyed the summons in very small numbers, and in June 1851 the punitive expedition was sharply checked at Viervoet on the very borders of Basutoland. Warden was then forced to fall back on Bloemfontein, and to remain there on the defensive, till the High Commissioner should find men and leisure for the vindication of British authority and prestige.

In this nearly desperate situation Major Warden seems to

[1] For other instances and references see Walker, pp. 254–5, 259, 267.

have fulminated from Bloemfontein against those burghers who had left him in the lurch. The burghers for their part saw the frontiers in confusion and the Basuto once more in effective occupation of the lands assigned to the native 'allies'; even if the tumult and unrest were not all of Bantu making the tribes were fighting each other and farms were unsafe.[1] Some of the Boers, still hankering after independence and freedom from the inconvenient obligations of British rule, appealed for help and protection to the outlawed Transvaaler Pretorius; but he, with a forbearance that was to bring him a quick reward, refused to intervene. Others objected not to British rule as such but to the autocratic rule of Major Warden. Had this indeed been all, the Letters Patent of a liberal parliamentary constitution for the Orange Sovereignty needed only to be promulgated. But a blind unreasoning fear of the Basuto power stood in the way. In spite of the high-handed blundering of which he had been the victim Moshesh was steadily for peace; but the memory of the unlucky incident at Viervoet so rankled in many small minds that they persisted in seeing this chief's unbroken power as a standing threat to any settlement, and Moshesh himself as a new embodiment of an ever-present 'Native Menace'. So the state of the Sovereignty was judged to make the medicine of a liberal constitution inappropriate and, almost incredibly, the Letters Patent seem to have lain in Cape Town till their very existence was forgotten.[2]

In the upshot the unrest on the Basuto border was to play only a minor part in determining the fate of the Sovereignty and of Sir Harry Smith's plans for a comprehensive settlement. This once at least, the decisive factor was the effect on political opinion in London of the more immediately disturbing news of renewed turmoil in Kaffraria. In that long-harassed province the Governor's almost blustering settlement endured just over two years.

[1] Some who had marched with the expedition were harried by the 'disaffected', Warden being powerless to protect them (Warden to Smith, 24 Aug. 1851). Other evidence indicates that Zulu levies did some 'thieving' and that even European adventurers 'fished in troubled waters' (de Kiewiet, op. cit.).

[2] Dr. de Kiewiet notes that in 1853 the Law Officers were in some doubt as to the legality of abandoning the Sovereignty except under an Act of Parliament, till it was pointed out that the Representative Assembly under this draft had never been formally constituted (*British Government and Boer Republics*, ch. vi).

The later months of 1850 seem to have been another period of drought[1] and, therefore, probably of 'stock-theft'. The intrusion of this new term about 1850 points to the growing value attached to sheep; but the losses persistently complained of by the present-day farmers especially of this Eastern Cape suggest that much of the earlier 'cattle-stealing' was by half-starving Africans drifting into the Colony through wide open farms (as certainly in 1849–50) 'in search of work'. The drift in 1850 was in fact so heavy that it strained the pass system to breaking-point; in October Ordinance 49 was at long last discovered to have lapsed; 'Vagrant' laws[2] were threatened and, to the further alarm of the Kat River Hottentots, an attempt was made to root out their 'squatters'[3] (above, p. 279). Hard times, moreover, were little favourable for the collection of the new quit-rent (above, p. 302), which caused some discontent even among loyalists. The Bantu, Smith pronounced again, must choose between service with farmers and their newly defined 'locations'.[4] The younger Read was apprehensive; in August 1849 he wrote a friendly warning:

I fear (this) stringency will bring another collision with the Kafirs. A conquered people should be ruled with leniency. . . . I saw Macomo the other day. He said: 'I did not fight in the last war. I fear not death, as I would rather die than have Smith's foot on my neck—but I fear God.' There is a certain point at which nations become reckless of death and would rather commit *felo de se* than be exposed to indignity.

Both in April and June 1850 the Governor had felt able, notwithstanding, to report peace and great progress. Then, in October the Governor called a general meeting of chiefs at King William's Town; but Sandile, the Paramount Chief, mindful once more of the fate of Hintza, failed to appear. The chief was summarily deposed and in November came 'reassuring notices' by frontier officials. In December Sandile was to be 'fetched';

---

[1] In this crisis, another veteran was falling out. Old James Read wrote to Hankey in Sept. 1850 that he would fain see Dr. Philip 'once more in this world'. But he could not ride, and the oxen were unfit to travel 'owing to the severe drought'.

[2] Enclosures from Smith to Grey, 7 and 28 Aug. 1849: on 27 Sept. Mackinnon urged Proclamation in restraint of passes, whereupon (3 Oct.) Attorney-General gave opinion, quoted above, p. 87.

[3] Read's letters to Philip, especially in March and April, brought personal re-assurances in a private letter from Smith to Philip, 2 Apr. 1849.

[4] Smith to Grey, 26 Oct. 1849.

but on Christmas Eve the fetching expedition was ambushed, with heavy loss, in the bush of the Boomah Pass; on Christmas Day the soldier settlers of the villages in the Chumie Valley were horribly butchered; and not long afterwards raiding parties got to work in the Colony itself. In January, on top of this, came the unprecedented news that numbers (much exaggerated)[1] of the Hottentots of the Kat River and Theopolis had joined the rebel Xhosa. In spite of the apparent danger to the Colony the European farmers were slow and unwilling to turn out once more on commando in adequate numbers.[2] The reluctance of the burghers to serve was partly due to the lapse of the old Commando Law, whose amendment was disallowed in 1834 (above, p. 104), and partly perhaps to the withdrawal of so many on trek. But a cry of the 'country in danger' could not have evoked so poor a response had it not been clear that the Xhosa were seen to be already a broken people. Nevertheless, when left with such troops as he could muster to bring the rebels, as they now were, to sufficiently abject submission, the Governor's campaign made little or no progress, and in May 1851 he wrote cheerlessly that the attempt to 'civilize the Gaikas' (all in two years) had proved an 'awful failure'.

Bowing to the storm which broke over Westminster the moment the news arrived in March of the outbreak of an *eighth* Kaffir War, Her Majesty's Government had already come to much the same conclusion. Sir William Molesworth complained that leniency had only made the Xhosa better fighters but worse savages and, almost in the Governor's words, denounced any attempt to civilize such 'barbarous and sanguinary wretches'. Mr. W. E. Gladstone, a rising star, joined in to attack a policy which 'for no possible benefit to South Africa . . . ensures the recurrence of war with a regularity which is perfectly astounding'.[3] As such critics saw it, every possible plan had been tried. The Bantu original sin which made them cattle-stealers had provoked 'reprisals' which issued in war. A neutral belt, naïvely assumed to have been genuinely tried as a means of keeping the races apart, had broken down. Treaties, similarly assumed to have been 'equal', had led, after more war, to British military rule which had issued quickly in a peculiarly

---

[1] *Cape Col. Qn.*, pp. 279 ff.   [2] Smith to Grey, 21 Jan. 1851.
[3] Quoted by C. W. de Kiewiet in loc. cit.

bloody rebellion and, indeed—when news from the Basuto border presently followed—war on two fronts. The Government's one major policy move had been to assume responsibility for this northern fringe and increase the risks now to be paid for.

Earl Grey himself had so lately had Sir Harry Smith's usual hopeful reassurances that the December news came as a rude shock, upsetting his hitherto implicit faith in his Governor, and even his own self-confidence; instead of a Minister pushing a considered policy of his own he appears as one under strong outside pressure. When Sir Charles Adderley, one M.P. with South African experience, pressed for a commission to investigate the relations of colonists and Africans on the spot the Government temporized and proposed a select committee; but before the end of May Earl Grey had decided at once to strengthen and to check Sir Harry by sending out two Assistant Commissioners, Major W. S. Hogge and Mr. Mostyn Owen; they were to help the Governor to restore order and settle the country on a more permanent basis.[1] Grey's parliamentary critics, however, had their own convictions about what that basis should be. It particularly galled them that first the burghers of the Cape, and a few months later those of the Sovereignty, were failing to do their stint of military service in their country's hour of need. It was common knowledge too that their traders, and even farmers, habitually 'did well out of' wars of any kind. The fashionable and widely approved cure for such irresponsible conduct in *colonies* (then a totally undifferentiated class) was *responsible* self-government. [Exactly a century later, in the 1950's, British public opinion was still, or again, ardent for self-rule and the abandonment of inexperienced African states, with one difference; instead of these latter paying all their own way they must be provided with, or found, the capital needed to promote their *development*.] There surely never was such a total silence in the British Parliament on this or any other aspect of Africans' needs as that which left almost only Earl Grey himself with reservations. Acutely conscious of British responsibility for the African population, he continued to fear 'the destruction of the less civilized races', and much suffering to the Boers themselves in the process. Yet even he began to reconcile himself to the abandonment at least of the Orange Sovereignty, and in

[1] Grey to Hogge and Owen, 31 May 1851.

September, on hearing of the feeble support given to Warden's unlucky expedition, he expressly warned Smith that unless the colonists were prepared to accept their full share of responsibility for the defence of the country no British interest would be served by continuing the British connexion. A month later, on 12 October, without so much as waiting for the new Commissioners to report, Lord John Russell himself minuted: 'The ultimate abandonment of the Orange Sovereignty should be a settled point of British policy.'[1] By 12 January 1852 Grey had decided to recall Smith and minuted, a little less finally, for the instruction of the new Governor, Sir George Cathcart:

It is a question for serious consideration whether the attempt (to civilize the natives) which has thus failed can be renewed, or whether the exercise of British authority in South Africa must not be restricted within much narrower limits than heretofore. . . . Apart from the very limited extent of territory required for the security of the Cape of Good Hope as a naval station, the British Crown and nation have no interest whatever in maintaining any territorial dominion.

Only Sir Charles Adderley was left, and for all that he was a stout 'colonial reformer' his was a voice crying in the wilderness when he deplored 'abandonment' as a short-sighted plan for shaking off 'present difficulties'.

In February 1852 the Russell Ministry was defeated and Sir John Pakington took over, under Lord Derby. As Lord Stanley, Derby had made the first notable concession to humanitarian concern for the Bantu by his instructions to Sir Benjamin D'Urban in the end of 1833. But the Bantu were now 'the enemy' and the good Sir Harry Smith was foremost in so classifying them. On 12 November 1851, the moment he received Grey's dispatch warning him that the Sovereignty might be abandoned, in his anxiety to save his own creation he had written:

If H.M.'s Sovereignty over this territory were rescinded, the step would be regarded by every man of colour in South Africa as an unprecedented and unlooked for victory to his race, and be the signal for revolt and continued resistance to British authority.

By chance, some of the first letters to be dealt with by the new Colonial Secretary reported the appeal of the still outlawed

[1] Draft of a reply to Smith's dispatch of 20 Aug.

Transvaaler Pretorius to be allowed to enter into regular peaceful relations with the British Government. Major Warden thought he was not to be trusted, but Pretorius had shown good faith and refrained from taking the opportunity of stirring up more trouble in the Sovereignty. He might yet make difficulties by working on the feelings of the 'disaffected'; on the other hand, these Africans, Smith was telling his superior, were not so much a responsibility as a danger to be dealt with. Two months later, near the end of his term of office, he went on to stigmatize the Ama-Xhosa as 'perfidious, treacherous and bloodthirsty', quite regardless of the sustained pressure on their homeland which had made this easy-going people a danger. Thus Pretorius might be an invaluable ally against them. It went for nothing that the Transvaalers were those who had gone farthest into the wilderness to escape restraint—in its first week the new administration gave decisive evidence of its conversion from humanitarianism in African affairs to a policy of uncompromising military repression. A minute of 4 March welcomed the prospect of agreement with Pretorius expressly on the ground that:

If we could obtain the co-operation of men trained in and accustomed to Bush warfare, *the Caffres would no longer appear such dangerous enemies*. No time should be lost to *repair the errors* that have made these men our enemies instead of friends and invaluable allies.

This was really the end. Interpreting, or anticipating with accuracy the wishes of their superiors in England, Earl Grey's Commissioners, Messrs. Hogge and Owen, though without precise instructions, had already on 16 January 1852 signed the Sand River Convention. By this instrument the Transvaal Boers received their independence, with a pledge of 'non-interference' which was to be mutually binding on British and on Boers. 'As we should object', wrote Governor Cathcart in approval and support,

to the Boers beyond the Vaal forming alliance with Moshesh . . . so it appears to be just that we should disclaim alliance with those North of the Vaal River, amongst whom the Boers can only live by exercising a requisite supremacy for their control. . . .

Not long before this Dr. Livingstone had complained of the loss of his household goods at the hands of Boers 'exercising requisite control'; within a few days of submitting the Convention for approval Sir George Cathcart was pleased to reply that the injury he had sustained was but 'incidental to a state of war or to life in remote regions'. Livingstone was not yet a famous popular hero and his protest could be disregarded. All that 'Exeter Hall' stood for, and a faintly uneasy official conscience, were paid the homage only of a supererogatory clause in the Convention by which, in return for Her Majesty's Government's repudiation of 'alliances with the coloured nations', the Transvaalers agreed neither to permit nor to practise *slavery*. With this embellishment the Convention was received in Downing Street with 'great satisfaction' and the Transvaal was free.[1]

In fact Hogge and Owen's original hope, and still more that of Sir Harry Smith in lifting his ban on Pretorius, was, if possible, to save the Orange Sovereignty. Pretorius, as an enemy, might rally the malcontents of Winburg and threaten not merely Bloemfontein but Natal; his benevolent neutrality must be bought. But the whole object of the Sovereignty had been, in Earl Grey's words, to bring these emigrant British subjects 'once more within the control of regular government', and to save the natives from oppression or 'extermination'. There now remained no obvious reason why if these principles were renounced for the Boers beyond the Vaal they should be maintained, possibly at heavy cost, in the Orange Territory. The overwhelming desire of the Molesworths was 'that a limit be put to the extent of the British dominions in South Africa', and the Orange River was a more effective limit than the Vaal. Thus guided Sir George Cathcart, when he had sufficiently beaten the Xhosa to be able to turn some of his attention northwards, plumped at once, on 12 October, for withdrawal, without qualification:

An acknowledged foreign state will be far more easily . . . and economically controlled by respect for the power of H.M.'s armed forces within the Colony, and will form a more secure barrier against barbarians from without than can ever be accomplished by British political interference and attempted Government, without an expensive military establishment for its support.

[1] Cathcart to Grey, 12 Apr. (for Livingstone), 20 Apr. (enclosing the Treaty), and to Pakington, 28 July 1852.

This 'barrier against barbarians' dispatch arrived on the eve of the fall of the Derby Ministry and Sir John Pakington left his successor a minute approving Cathcart's recommendation.

The new minister was still getting his bearings when Cathcart, like Smith before him, walked into further serious trouble. When he reached Bloemfontein in October he must have seen, had he examined the evidence even then available,[1] how hardly and unjustly the land claims of Moshesh were dealt with by Major Warden, and how conciliatory he was in spite of this. The Governor, however, met him only by somewhat cutting down the colonial claims against him and immediately gave Moshesh three days in which, without parley, to collect 1,000 horses and 10,000 head of cattle from his scattered dependent chiefs. Within the time-limit Moshesh duly paid 3,500 head of cattle. When asked for longer time, the Governor refused and marched against Thaba Bosigo. As in Kaffirland war meant cattle-driving, and cattle in this instance were the Governor's undoing in spite of all his wide experience. In December 1852 the invading force became 'entangled' with captured cattle at Berea and was forced by the Basuto to withdraw. Moshesh, protesting his honest desire for peace, then persuaded the embarrassed Governor to let his former captures meet the bill and, further, to agree to a peace which left the chief still the Queen's ally. News of this ill-starred attempt to vindicate British authority was just in time to clinch the matter. The Duke of Newcastle at once pronounced for abandonment of the Province and, considering the principle as settled, he appointed yet another Commissioner, Sir George Clerk to see it through.

The first need was to induce the settlers as a whole to undertake the responsibilities of self-government, and to persuade those who disliked the enforced loss of their rights as British subjects to fall into line. At various meetings of delegates 'loyalists' were fully more vocal than the republicans. To the end the Boers showed no marked enthusiasm for the 'independence' thus thrust upon them; even in the Volksraad of the later Republic the old 'loyalists' continued to have a fair share of the representation. The defence of the country was the crux, and the Boers were as hesitant to assume this dangerous responsi-

---

[1] Theal's *Basutoland Records*, 3 vols., published, and three more volumes, *Miscellaneous Basutoland Records*, in Cape Town Archives.

bility as the British authorities seemed determined to escape it. There was still, various delegates reminded Sir George Clerk, an only partially settled land dispute with the Griquas; and there were the Basuto. In the following year Moshesh once more kept his own people in control, besides chastising Sikonyela and other disturbers of the peace.[1] At last Sir George Clerk, recognizing the injustice of the Warden Line, but unable to reach a new agreement with the burgher delegates and anxious only to be gone, left the matter as he found it.[2] Moshesh, for all the 'wily astuteness' with which he is credited, took this to mean that his old 1843 Treaty making him the Queen's ally, and its wider boundary, stood. The burghers, however, strong in their possession of land certificates, felt that they were free to deal with the Basuto as occasion demanded or offered. The Free State wars with the Basuto were the not long delayed, and inevitable, consequence.

The treatment of Kok and his Griquas was similar, but more immediately final in its results. The unstable Griquas not only failed to pay the 'compensation for improvements' demanded of them for the time-expired leases of their land but continued under the Sovereignty to make new leases and sales, even in the 'inalienable' Reserve. On the flimsy pretext that leases and sales were the practice, not only was written promise made of 'measures affording every facility' for such land transactions, but privately Clerk left it to be understood, *not* by Kok, that land sold by the Griquas would henceforth form part of the Free State. When even a pension of £300 failed to persuade Kok to agree to his measures the Commissioner at last left him and his people to fend for themselves—with the result Dr. Philip had seen to be inevitable, that within ten years (see below, p. 356) they had been crowded out and trekked *en masse* to a new home. A convention signed in February 1854 recognized the independence of the Orange Free State. Even this did not quite complete the dismemberment of South Africa. The new state destroyed the land bridge between Natal and the Cape and two years later, in 1856, this so-called Garden Colony was cut adrift as a separate Crown Colony.

[1] Walker, p. 266, and references.
[2] Sir George Clerk, in dispatch of 3 Dec. 1853, having his doubts, comforted himself and his superiors as follows: 'So long as Moshesh and Sikonyela maintain the degree of control they now exercise . . . their wars either among themselves or with Europeans will not deserve to be characterized as exterminating or atrocious.'

Sir Harry Smith's bold unifying movement ended thus quickly in anticlimax. By a deliberate exercise of British authority the diversified but natural unity of the Cape Colony was shattered—and for two whole centuries the Cape had been (as for many it long remained) all *South Africa*. A breach between Boers and Britons was not the cause of disruption. The frontier Boers and the British authorities had sharply conflicting views on the place of the dependent peoples in the body politic, but widening of the rift came only later and was a direct effect of setting the Republics on their separate ways with this vital difference unresolved. The Boers in general stood unrepentantly for a simple master-and-servant relationship. British rulers, reflecting British public opinion, were no less insistent on Bantu 'rights', but had never been able to define these clearly. Thus the Boer view had the merit at least of being readily understood. Boer masters were decidedly more tolerant of Bantu lapses, understanding (and having Scriptural warrant for it) that it was the nature of servants to be unprofitable; but Britain's dependants' ill-defined rights were assumed to carry with them the heavy obligations of an organized state. Thus the frequent failure of Bantu tribes to carry out ill-understood agreements tended to be visited by British governments with such crushing severity as Boers might have thought inappropriate had they had Britain's resources.

The Ama-Xhosa, by such British reasoning, had by 1846 come to merit chastisement for their treaty-breaking, and then they took two years to bring to terms. Within three years, in December 1850, at a time when, however unjustly, the attitude of Moshesh was giving rise to apprehension, the Xhosa were renewing the fight with such violence as was to keep an army in the field against them for most of four years. The necessity felt for an alliance with the Boers came of sheer desperation. British statesmen never accepted or even condoned the Boer master-and-servant relationship with the weaker race; but they clearly also spared no thought for the future of either the Xhosa or any other of the Bantu tribes. The now splintered South Africa of which such tribes were a part rested on foundations ill laid to weather the storms that could not fail to blow.

Even in their haste the British statesmen responsible had in mind, as always, some well considered principles of traditional policy, but they applied these with unusual, almost Teutonic logic which momentarily ignored the no less deep-rooted traditional concern for the well-being of such dependent peoples. A dim awareness, even now, of this moral obligation served only to strengthen a resolve to avoid accepting any further responsibility for the doings of those Boers trekking, beyond control, ever farther into the wilds of Africa. The resolute Transvaalers had in fact already reached a limit set by the vast stretches of malarial 'bush' beyond and below the 'edge of the berg'. The few who had made that venture had already named their High Veld place of retreat *Lydenburg* (*lijden* = suffer); but few except perhaps Dr. Livingstone then knew enough about tropical health to understand—and Livingstone was 'especially' (below, p. 334) not wanted in the Transvaal.

An over-simplified faith in the newly discovered virtues of colonial self-government was perhaps the decisive argument for the policy of 'abandonment'; because the magic of local responsibility promised to suit the totally different colonies of European settlement, therefore the Cape, the republics, Natal, and presumably at least Kaffraria, must all go their separate ways and, it was confidently hoped, be self-supporting. The common and inevitably closely linked interests of these separate units were so far recognized as to be left to a High Commissioner for *South Africa*—it was the surest possible way of getting the blame for any mishandling of inter-state differences firmly turned on to that official's master, Her Majesty's Government. In the final 'scuttle' of 1854 the draft constitution which would have converted the well-tried and efficient Cape law court into a Supreme Court of South Africa and ensured at least a unified legal system was (see p. 319) *mislaid*.

The withdrawal of British authority was at last almost disingenuous—though, in face of the differing status of the parties at that date, quite innocently so. Governor Cathcart's dispatches sufficiently show the underlying assumption that the *de facto* British supremacy, not to say suzerainty, remained unaffected, making it a simple matter to resume full sovereignty if and whenever that seemed necessary or convenient. The colonial self-government of that day conferred no such status as that conferred much later by the Statute of Westminster. It was thus in the spirit of the age that it was also assumed by British statesmen

of all parties, then and much later, that recognition of two distant and land-locked republics could not and could never be
allowed to affect the one British interest they all agreed was
vital—secure and exclusive control of the Cape sea-route.[1] It
certainly appeared to Lord Grey at the time to warrant the withdrawal from the distant interior that all such vital strategical
interests would be served by retaining control of little more than
the naval base at Simonstown. Even at the very outset it was not
without an eye to British interest in the Natal coast that Moshesh
remained an 'ally' after 1854. Years later the Transvaal, to its
chagrin, was repeatedly headed off from Swaziland and Zululand. Thanks in part to the irritation of such pin-pricks the
convenient moment for reasserting British supremacy never
came. In consequence, the very desirable reunited South Africa
became steadily more remote—the political isolation actually
forced on many of the Boers reinforced their old-time isolation.
Their fundamentally different view, in particular, of the status
of the dependent peoples became a great bond holding them
together, and more aloof. The Transvaalers, finding themselves
the masters of more Bantu than they had at first realized, were
touchily assertive of their right to manage these people and all
other affairs as their own responsibility, in their own way. Since
this was not always that of the rest of South Africa, mounting
strain produced at last the war of 1899–1902. British supremacy
was then temporarily restored at a cost which would have paid
for any number of the frontier wars the abdication of 1854 was
intended to obviate.

The almost total silence of the British Parliament and people
in the 1850's on the moral obligation to the weaker peoples is
strangely out of keeping with a tradition dating back, past the
Act of Abolition of the Slave Trade, to the struggle of British
administrators, against Colonial opposition, to save the American Indian 'reservations'—the prototype of African 'reserves'.
The high tide of humanitarian influence which forced Emancipation on the 1833 Government had not ebbed so quickly; the
Colonial Office could hardly, without such support, have reacted
as it did in 1835 to D'Urban's frontier policy. Two years later
Buxton's Aborigines Committee was conventionally hard on
'grasping' colonists, but gave more sage advice on the danger

[1] Robinson and Gallagher, op. cit., passim.

that treaties, such as the Colonial Office was by then sponsoring, might be ill understood and thus *un*-equal. The setting up of the *Aborigines* Protection Society in 1837 was a recognition that British responsibilities must now cover Africans other than slaves. Almost at once Buxton's loss of his seat in Parliament cost the Society its most effective link with and spokesman on public affairs. But even Buxton could not evoke a policy appropriate to a distant colony like the Cape out of his own inner consciousness. Since the days of the 50th Ordinance, and indeed since the earlier moves on behalf of the 'free people of colour', he had constantly relied on letters from or personal discussion with Dr. John Philip, by far the weightiest exponent of a carefully considered new deal for the dependent Cape peoples. This Buxton–Philip partnership suffered an accidental check in 1837 when the imminence of the death of King William IV forced Buxton to drop the joint draft of the Aborigines Report, 'our South Africa' (above, 188 ff.). No copy of this survives, and it was at any rate too late to affect D'Urban's interpretation of the 'Glenelg policy', which was not Philip's; but early the next year Philip returned to the Cape to face the full blast of almost nation-wide unpopularity—as if he had indeed been personally responsible for this misconceived and precipitate withdrawal.

The comparatively few letters surviving from the next years (above, p. 102, n. 4), were sufficient to show that Philip had had to lie very low. In part this meant that the status of his Cape People promised well (above, p. 17) but still needed watching. There were, however, dissidents even in his Cape Town congregation whose doings needed attention. One unfortunate result of this period of inaction was that developments on the Xhosa frontier went almost unobserved. By 1841–2, when he made his major investigation of all the frontiers, there were two changes. The tragic failure of the Niger Expedition, Buxton's great 'positive' effort to counter slavery by a civilizing mission, caused a breakdown in his health which ended his career; and the Board of the L.M.S. chose this moment to adopt Robert Moffat's attitude and stand aloof from public affairs for fear of being 'branded as political'. Philip was now left doubly alone—at the Cape and—since no one at all remained to speak with authority in support of the reasoned approach to South African matters he had championed for the past twenty years—also in London.

The silence of Parliament in the fifties, and the positive discredit into which the very idea of a 'humanitarian' frontier policy had fallen, are not to be explained without taking account of these changes. Even the two Xhosa wars following in such quick succession were an effect rather than a cause; they were the outcome of years of heavy-handed maladministration, most of which passed almost unobserved. Yet the consequences of all this blundering were taken at the time, and often are still, as the warrant for a policy of almost unqualified repression. The story will in truth never be read aright so long as the 'Dr. Philip' of Afrikaner mythology is allowed to pass as the real John Philip of history. The mythology may claim to take account of numerous Philip letters and formal memoranda surviving in public archives, if not at least of the appendices to his published *Researches* which throw some official light on the disabilities of his Hottentot parishioners; but these reveal nothing of their sources, a mass of letters received from far-flung mission stations or from public men, including Governors, and notes made on his own wide travels. The short-lived emergence of these Philip Papers from under lock and key originally led to the writing of the present book; its first gleanings from this mass of new evidence having done little to explode the myth, and since this supply of fresh material runs dry about 1849, it becomes desirable at this point even to recapitulate shortly in order to focus attention on the significance of the fresh material.

It still passes as gospel with many that Philip had a meddlesome itch for prejudiced and ill-informed 'interference'. Yet from the day in 1821 when he cast aside his Philosophical Review of Missions and resolved that his case must eschew building on 'particular' grievances, he never took any action without having first made investigations, both extensive and intensive, in the field concerned. It was only after four visits to the Xhosa frontier, two of them intensive, that he so much as warned Buxton to make the representations to Mr. Spring-Rice and Lord Stanley which resulted in Sir Benjamin D'Urban being given instructions to consider some reform. From first to last Philip's themes were land and livelihood, sometimes the state of the law, but always *life*, and the means of living it. His most severe and persistent censure even of the frontier Boers related to their rapacious and uneconomical use of land; his evidence hurt, when it did, because it was hard-headed and, above all, comprehensive. An Exeter Hall spokesman calling himself Justus was driven to make a more suitably emotional appeal by writing on *The Wrongs of the Caffre Nation*. In its simplest terms, Philip's plea was that if the Xhosa were ever to be tolerable neighbours they must themselves be able to live tolerably.

The history of the Cape People stands as the monument to the wisdom of the 'Cape Policy' of which Philip was the principal architect. But the very success of his most decisive achievement won him also such enduring unpopularity, or even hate, as was the undoing of all his efforts to establish frontier conditions on a similar basis. The alleged and so quickly forgotten 'vagrancy' of the Hottentots brought his unpopularity to its early height in 1834, at the moment when D'Urban was deputed to examine the frontier system and situation. The Governor therefore chose to make his dealings with him on frontier affairs a closely guarded secret. Philip's carefully studied and reasoned proposals thus got no public attention or debate at the time. Almost immediately the outbreak of war, which the Governor's delays did nothing to prevent, meant no doubt that some adaptation of earlier plans might reasonably be needed; but straight away the very fact that plans had been under consideration was overlooked and, indeed, buried under clouds of misrepresentation which have survived uncontradicted to this day. Worse followed Philip's alleged doings in London; there the Colonial Office had in fact taken action before ever he reached it, action which ignored his consistent advice to retain control of 'Kaffirland'. D'Urban meantime had not only originated a too precipitate withdrawal, but no less consistently adhered to his theme that 'the Glenelg policy', like Glenelg's dispatches, were (above, p. 160) 'all Philip'.

When the culprit returned to the Cape in 1838 this policy, the bitterly resented 'retrocession' of the conquered territory, had become 'the Philip policy', still often so called. The Great Trek itself, which caused little stir in any British circle, was in effect a Boer national revolt aimed at stopping the spread of the Cape system beyond the frontiers. Finding himself now in the extraordinary position of an *Athanasius-contra-mundum*, in reverse, Philip could only wait and see. So far from 'interfering', he unfortunately allowed the Xhosa frontier to escape the close attention for want of which its deterioration went unchecked. At last, however, concern for his trans-frontier mission stations took him off on the great tour of inspection (see Ch. XIII) in the north. As the first independent eyewitness of the Great-Trek-in-being he was able this time to win such attention from Governors Napier and Maitland for his highly relevant observations as apparently made him think it unnecessary to find a substitute for Buxton and his own Directors in London. Having by his perseverance won amendments to the two northern treaties ('treaties' being the most he could get accepted), he was actually on his way back to the north when he was struck down by a family calamity and a personal breakdown of health. Thereupon, for want of such watchful guidance as he alone was in a position to give, as well as because of the diversion created by neglected Kaffraria, the northern situation deteriorated in its turn.

On one vital point of northern policy Philip was unfortunately silent, failing to make it clear that matters affecting the scattered Bechuana tribes could be appropriately settled only by dealing with the Transvaalers—the same fervent seekers of independence who were so quickly set quite free in 1852. The reason for Philip's avoidance of the Bechuana or, in reality, the *Transvaal* issue was undoubtedly the uncooperative attitude of a number of his own missionaries who shared the a-political views of their senior Robert Moffat. In almost the latest of the original Philip Papers, 19 March 1849, Edward Solomon reported to Philip, still nominal Superintendent, how Hughes *told* him that *he* had heard from Moffat that 'Mr. Potgieter, who calls himself Commandant' had written demanding the withdrawal of missionaries, 'especially Livingstone', from the interior—on the ground that they were supplying natives with guns and ammunition. Moffat was best placed to know the pressure on the Bechuana and was apprehensive (below, p. 357), but he stood aloof. Solomon's report came too late; when Philip was silent, protest ceased and three years later Governor Cathcart spurned Livingstone's own complaint (above, p. 325). Barely six months after this the L.M.S. itself, in the persons of Inglis and Edwards, was ignominiously expelled from the newly fledged Transvaal Republic. This summary ejection of the L.M.S., as well as the whole course of British policy after 1846, would have been unthinkable so long as John Philip held his watching brief on behalf of the dependent peoples. No voice was raised in any responsible quarter to question the assumption that dealings with the Bantu peoples were impossible until the 'menace' of their military power was finally broken.

The normally sensitive conscience of British opinion on these matters was at last revived by enthusiasm for the work of David Livingstone and, after him, of a notable chain of African missionaries from Mackay of Uganda to Laws of Livingstonia. The L.M.S. itself appropriately regained its strength in Bechuanaland, in the person of John MacKenzie.[1] In spite of a disagreement with C. J. Rhodes about the policy to be adopted, MacKenzie took a leading part in the moves which stopped the Transvaal from swallowing up more of Bechuanaland and spreading across the Road to the North. In 1895 his superb stage-management of chief Khama's London visit sent his client home in triumph; what remained to the tribes was vested not in Rhodes's Chartered Company but in the Crown, as the Bechuanaland Protectorate. The protective role taken upon itself as in this instance by British public opinion can be formidable, but is unsure: it was caught off guard again owing to an equal tenderness for Boer susceptibilities in the post-war settlement of 1902, and finally so with regard to the Act of Union in 1910. British opinion has rarely warmed to men like John Philip whose genius was for facing the hard facts of any situation without emotional or sentimental bias.

At this point the evidence of the Philip Papers ends. There is, however, little dispute about the later course of so-called 'native policy'; disputes rage, significantly, almost entirely about the ins and outs of Boer–British relations. That feud has little relevance to the study of the effects of the country's stolid refusal to be guided by earlier experience and to follow on the lines Philip struggled to establish. The consequences for the country as a whole were and are above all *social*. It remains accordingly to note the insensate crushing of the Bantu front line, the Ama-Xhosa, and thereafter to trace the development of the so-called Native Problem thus early and fully *made*.

[1] John MacKenzie calls for special mention in this place for the deplorable reason that an important collection of his private correspondence, newly acquired and little more than glanced at, went up in flames at the same time as the Philip Papers. Like Philip and for similar reasons, in a more limited field, MacKenzie remains a target for abuse in certain circles. His own defence survives in the book *Austral-Africa*.

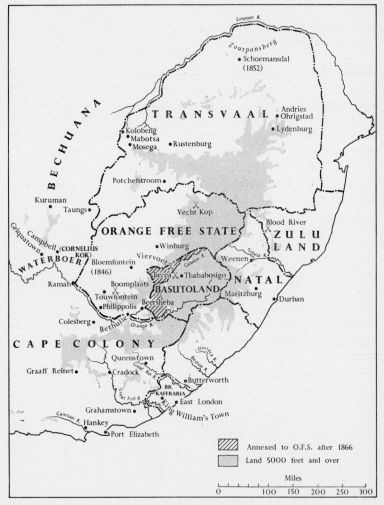

MAP 3. South Africa, 1856.

XVIII

THE SHORTEST WAY WITH THE BANTU—AND THE CONSEQUENCES

THE British authorities had little need of help from their Boer allies once they had decided that the shortest way with the Bantu was to make an expensive recurrence of war in the British zone as nearly as could be impossible. Sir George Cathcart, the last as it happened of the long line of soldier governors, at once set out to reduce the tribes to impotence by systematic invasion and confiscation of their lands. In vain the Scots missionary Niven urged: 'Let the Government show that it does not conquer in order to dispossess.' Even while the northern Bantu were in process of being handed over to the Republics who were to exercise the 'supremacy requisite for their control'—requisite also 'to preserve proper relations between master and servant'—the tragedy of the Ama-Xhosa was played out with a devastating thoroughness which the more limited resources of the Boers could never match. It was the economic consequences of such peace by conquest that came at last to be called the Native Problem.

The facts of the Xhosa story stand out starkly from Dr. Theal's bald and unimaginative pages.[1] Sir Harry Smith achieved little in his last year, 1851; troops and burghers were short and raids on the Colony continued for some months. But when reinforcements arrived and 'active operations' began, the 'forests and jungles were scoured'—and scoured again, if only for cattle 'most of which had been driven across the Kei' to the Gcaleka Paramount Kreli. In December 1851, accordingly, 'two columns were directed to that quarter, with the double object of punishing Kreli and depriving the rebels of their sources of supply'. Thus true to type, this Kaffir war, like each of its predecessors, had its storm centre just a little farther east than the one before it; first the conflict was near the Gamtoos, then, in succession, in the Zuurveld, the Fish River Bush, on the Keis-

[1] Theal, iii, pp. 98 and 111 ff.

kama, twice in the Amatolas, now beyond the Kei, finally, in the rebellion of 1878 which ranks as the 'last' war, on the Bashee and beyond. So now Kreli's country was 'scoured ... with great damage to the crops and kraals'—and some to the Gcalekas themselves. In January General Somerset, old hand that he was, 'returned to King Williamstown with 30,000 head of cattle, a few horses and 14,000 goats'; the second column 'brought out 7,000 Fingos, with 15,000 head of cattle, which these people had seized from the Gcalekas and were allowed to retain for themselves'.

Still, says Dr. Theal, only a small number of burghers responded to the Governor's appeal in February 1852 (the month of the epic disaster to reinforcements on the troopship *Birkenhead*). For the heartening of the Xhosa, moreover, and of their 'prophet', Umlangeni, the summer was a good one, and the crops cut down by the troops early in the season sprang up again, giving them new courage to prolong the agony. In the winter the campaign began again in earnest with the burning of Kreli's principal kraal and the capture of 10,000 head of cattle. Now also, improving on the 1847 device of cattle depots, and anticipating the blockhouses with which Lord Kitchener helped to end the Anglo–Boer War of 1899–1902, the Governor hit on the plan of throwing up numerous 'small defensible turrets in commanding positions on the line of march'. These 'proved themselves most admirably adapted for South African warfare', and made the next scouring of the Amatolas and other 'fastnesses' so effective that in October surrenders began. By November only 'a few wretched fugitives' remained to be dealt with and the Governor felt able to withdraw 2,500 troops to watch Moshesh who was anxiously watching these events.

In February 1853 the Governor returned to dictate peace. Now that the tribes were broken he provided the frontier with what Captain Stretch had so much needed, a thoroughly efficient police force, the famous Cape Mounted Rifles. But the best of the Ceded Territory and the Amatolas were now indeed 'forfeited for ever' and, says Dr. Theal, 'the Gaikas having lost most of their cattle as well as the rich valleys of the Amatolas, were poor and weak'. Wiser at least than the D'Urban of May 1835 Sir George Cathcart refrained from attempting total expulsion and promised them *locations* 'in the large tract of open

mines became the mainstay of all the tribal peoples of those parts.

Sir George Grey's disastrous handling of this matter of Xhosa rights in land is one blot on the record of his deservedly popular and even distinguished governorship. First, if not almost alone, Grey saw the dangers of the dismemberment of South African unity which came of the policy of abandonment; at some risk to his own career in the public service he wrote a famous dispatch urging Her Majesty's Government to change course and follow rather a plan of Federation. A great library in Cape Town, and several public institutions, keep his name in honoured memory. But he drove the Xhosa to desperation. Some even of his beneficent social works were of the nature of unavoidable poor relief, made necessary, as his chequer-board resettlement of Xhosa country was only made possible, by the hunger and distress and the rude dispersal of that people by the shocking episode known as the Cattle Killing. In times of stress the Bantu peoples were too readily led astray by 'prophets'. After the expulsion from the Zuurveld it was Makana. Lately it had been one Umlangeni, but he 'sank into contempt and died an object of derision'[1] in 1853. The mantle then descended upon a young girl called Nonquase and her uncle Umhlakaze who now began to dream dreams and see visions of revenge. Inspired by these two national enthusiasts the leading tribes in the course of 1856 prepared themselves, killing their cattle freely and squandering their stores of grain; they were to eat and make themselves strong against a day in February 1857—a Great Day of the Lord when grain was to sprout, cattle were to spring out of the ground, warriors to come back from the dead and, with the help of a 'great hurricane', sweep the white man into the sea. The Day came and the sun went down as usual; but 'when the chiefs called upon their warriors, they were answered by the wail of a starving people'.[2]

The Ama-Xhosa were now broken indeed. 'Immense numbers'[3] died of starvation, and whole districts were, for the time being, depopulated. A census of Kaffraria was said to show a

[1] Theal, iii. 117. [2] Professor Walker's phrase, p. 298.

[3] Dr. Theal, iii. 198, estimates the number of dead at not fewer than 25,000, and 'possibly double that number'. The likelihood is, as usual, that contemporary estimates would be exaggerated.

The significance of any figures would depend on the total of the population and

drop in population from 105,000 in January 1857 to 37,000 in July; in the course of the same year of famine Sandile's clan had decreased by death and flight from 31,000 to 3,700; Pato, Maqomo, and one Stockwe between them could muster fewer than 10,000 in all; Umhala's people were reduced from 23,000 to 6,500.[1] Clearly this was dispersal not disappearance. 'Thousands', as Dr. Theal himself says, 'poured into the Colony begging for food—nor did they ask in vain.' Many more scattered beyond the Kei—anywhere out of the old war zone; poor to begin with, this zone was the scene of the most thorough cattle-killing and destruction. Now if ever was the time for a mild and generous settlement, but it was not to be. Deliberate policy completed the scattering they themselves had so effectually begun.

The military danger to be feared from the tribes having become the general colonial obsession, even officials short-sightedly chose to see the cattle-killing as part of a plan for a general rising and, taking the will for the deed, set about punishing them as rebels. In spite of the native 'menace' frontier colonists saw much coveted land at last within their grasp when the Governor himself, full of ideas of civilizing by example, confiscated the larger part of such land as remained to the rebellious chiefs and planted it systematically with Europeans. King William's Town was thrown open not merely to the thousand men of the German legion planned for in 1856, together with their Irish wives, but to another 4,000 peasants obtained direct from Germany. Grey was at the same time for keeping the Basuto in check by planting Europeans and Griquas in the sub-mountainous no-man's-land.[2] He even hoped to carry

this, for reasons suggested above (p. 208), tends to be underestimated, just as the modern increase is probably exaggerated. Polygamy is one of the reasons often suggested as making for an inevitably rapid increase in time of peace. Its effect is no doubt to reduce the number of unmarried women, but the effective increase depends not on the crude birth-rate, but on survival, i.e. on the excess of births over deaths; and all the evidence shows that under adverse conditions of health and over-crowding the native death-rate continued to be abnormally high. In a passage which throws light on much South African thinking, Dr. Theal (v. 255) cites as evidence of 'the enormous *rate* of increase' of the Bantu (once they were 'prevented from killing each other in war and on charges of witchcraft') the bare fact that 'in 1904 the population of the Transkei *was* 817,867'. The *apparent* modern increase of the native population depends on proof that the population in earlier days has not been grossly underestimated.

[1] Theal, iii. 197.
[2] The modern districts Barkly East, Elliot, Maclear, Mount Fletcher, Matatiele

on the work of civilization by promoting European land-settle-
ment in the Transkei itself—an area which, Dr. Theal adds in
an inadvertently illuminating aside, 'it is surprising that the
Cape police had been able to keep open as long as they did'.
The doubts of Downing Street, and the sound sense of Grey's
more humdrum and unpopular successor, Sir Philip Wodehouse,
put a term to this madness. To the grievous disappointment of
'hopes that were raised throughout South Africa, particularly in
Kaffraria, that vacant land beyond the Kei would at last be
allotted to European settlers and the influence and power of
the civilized race thus increased',[1] Wodehouse in 1864 decided
to keep the Transkei as 'reserve'. Europeans got a firm footing
in the country about Queenstown. But Umtata, the capital of the
Transkei, became the centre of a new Tembuland, and the
Transkei itself survived to become the proudest boast of South
African native administration.

The mischief in the 'Cis-Kei' had already been done. Confiscation of sufficiently tenuous locations[2] confirmed the effects of
the dispersal of 1857, finally preventing the reunion of the fragments, and ending the possibility of preserving a decent nucleus
of the Ama-Xhosa as a people like the Basuto. The Cis-Kei could
never become even a compact unit of administration like the
Transkei. Again the stark facts stand out from Dr. Theal's
narrative.[3] Kreli, first, was too far away to be himself a cattle-
stealer but must be punished, like Hintza, for aiding and abet-
ting his kinsmen in the west; it must be put out of his power to
do more harm, so a strong force was sent over the Kei 'to expel
him', with the remnant of his people, 'from the territory that
had been the principal abode of his tribe for many generations'.
The police 'kept possession of the country between the Kei and
the Bashee' till 1865 when Kreli was allowed to 'occupy a portion' of his old land; but his former dependants, the Fingos, converted the bulk of it into 'Fingoland' (which it still is). In 1877
the Xhosa not unnaturally came to blows with their dispossessors,
the Fingos, in consequence also with the Government; and

and Griqualand East, the last taking its name from Adam Kok's people who were
planted there in 1863. This area, good in parts for agriculture, and admirable for
sheep, was gradually alienated in large part to Europeans. Its relatively scanty
population is in striking contrast to the crowding of the very similar country to the
north of the mountains, which is Basutoland.   [1] Theal, v. 44; Walker, 312–13.
     [2] See note, p. 340 above.   [3] Theal, iii. 200 ff.

so Kreli, 'tall, erect and splendidly formed . . . deeply versed in traditionary lore and ever ready to impart his knowledge' (to Dr. Theal among others), was driven once more to live on a 'small tract of land' given him by a lesser chief in 'Bomvana-land' (Elliotdale)[1] beyond the Bashee, where he lived on till 1893. His son, Sigcawu, succeeded him in the chieftainship, 'but the dignity of the position was gone for ever'.

The fate of some other well-known figures in this frontier story was more tragic. Maqomo, 'the most intelligent of all the Rarabe chiefs, brave in the field and exceedingly capable as a guerilla leader, though addicted to drunkenness . . . wandered into the Colony and was arrested' in August 1857[2]—like so many humbler Bantu since—*'for being without a pass'*. For this dire offence 'he was sentenced to imprisonment for a *year*'. But such a doughty prisoner could hardly escape even so lightly, and 'he was afterwards convicted of having been accessory to the murder of a petty chief who refused to destroy his cattle . . . and was sentenced to transportation for twenty-one years'. It is good to read that on Robben Island the old charm, which had impressed people so different as Colonel Somerset, Sir Harry Smith and Captain Stretch, and many missionaries, seems to have reasserted itself; he was treated there 'more as a prisoner of state than as a convict', being allowed 'the company of his favourite wife' and other indulgences. In 1870 'under pro-mise of good behaviour' the veteran was allowed to return 'to the country of his birth'; but he 'began immediately to foment disturbances' and was removed once more to Robben Island, where he died 'at an advanced age' in 1873. His son, it seems, then prospered sufficiently to *buy* a farm, again in the old family home near the Kat River. There the clan again gathered 'increasing strength', but this was its final undoing. Like so many others Maqomo's son and people joined Kreli against the Government in the war of 1877–8. This time their leader was taken in war and banished to Cape Town 'as a convict'; there-upon the members were 'dispersed', and the 'history of the clan came to an end'.

The Gunukwebe chief, Pato, the loyalist of 1835 but 'last ditcher' ten years later, was, Dr. Theal adds, 'utterly ruined', his

---

[1] In the 1920's the most overcrowded district in the populous Transkei.
[2] Theal, iii. 202.

people either joining his more consistently pacific brother Kama or being 'dispersed' in the Colony. For *an* offence he also visited Robben Island, returning only to find himself 'almost forgotten'; 'his allowance from Government', however, 'supported him till he passed away almost unnoticed'.

Finally Sandile—the crippled heir of Gaika, ally of the British in 1819 when he was Western Paramount—was graciously allowed to retain a 'portion' of his former share of some 500 square miles about the modern Stutterheim. His clan very naturally began to come together again as soon as the crisis of 1857 was past—Dr. Theal's version was that it 'grew rapidly under British rule'. But Sandile, too, and a great many more including one considerable chief Umhala, son of Gaika's old rival Ndhlambi, and lesser people like 'Anta and Botumane', became involved on the side of Kreli in the conflict of 1877. In this war, which began as a fight with their supplanters the Fingos,[1] Sandile 'was killed in an engagement with the colonial forces'. The Xhosa being now British subjects, most of them suffered what was long the normal penalty for the offence of rebellion. As in 1857 Sir George Grey had been 'enabled to give complete protection to the long harassed farmers of Albany' by filling vacant (rebels') land with farmers, so twenty years later what remained of their locations were confiscated, one by one, divided into farms and 'sold to *Europeans*'. The people, like their predecessors in 1812, were 'removed' or 'dispersed'.

The full consequences of this dispersal are still being reaped. The clans were not wiped out, as the precise reckoning of 1857 would suggest; Dr. Theal himself says 'the greater number of the young men and women 'remained in service in the Colony';[2] it was all they could do. Nor is the comforting assurance that there they 'lost their (old) antipathy to Europeans' and 'gained some knowledge of civilized ways ... and acquired habits of industry' much more to the point. Such there were, and are; but the Cape almost more than any other part of the former Union has also far more homeless natives than farmers can fully or efficiently employ. The excessive supply of labourers made wage levels in the Cis-Kei too miserably low to support as

[1] Local tradition suggests unmistakably that this Government patronage of the Fingos helped materially to provoke one last rising of the tribe of Pondomisi in Tsolo, east of Umtata, in 1880.   [2] Theal, iii. 200.

much progress in civilized ways as might have been hoped.[1] Cis-Keian farmers continued to complain as constantly of 'stock-theft' as their predecessors did of 'cattle-thieving'; for Bantu must live and, as judges and police alike have asserted,[2] they steal to supplement inadequate wages. Since women and children must have a home the men are not free to take their labour to a better market; if they leave the farmer they expose their families to the risk of eviction. The very number of these under-employed Africans called into being, in addition, one peculiar Cape institution, the so-called 'private locations'; in these some of the 'surplus' natives (to use the word beloved of the Trekkers in the north) eked out the revenues of European land-owners in districts like Komgha by paying rent for the right to live their own life as semi-independent peasants, some of them no doubt on ancestral land from which they were never 'cleared'; but the final result was that the steadily increasing poverty of its Africans became a heavy drag on the well-being of the whole Eastern Province.[3]

In the Cape generally the process of confiscation begun in 1853 was intensified in 1857 and continued, sometimes for quite trivial offences, long afterwards. Social disintegration was further intensified by the systematic transplanting of fragments of 'unruly' tribes,[4] a good many of them, in early days, to take their chance 'beyond the Kei'. In the Cape, it is true, Africans were not prevented from relieving congestion by purchase; but they were quite unfitted to face the free and open competition of Victorian *laissez-faire* and farms they held on individual title were nearly all sold and lost.[5] The conditions fastened upon these people once their military power was broken were by any way of it ruinously uneconomic. The nervous government,

---

[1] In 1926 wage rates ran as low, in some districts, as 6s. a month, with 'keep'; even at 10s., the evidence was that servants rarely saw cash, their wages going to pay the employer for additional food. Ploughing or grazing rights might or might not go with the wage, but 'development', especially the growth of sheep farming, definitely restricted such privileges both for native and for European squatters.

[2] *Cape Col. Qn.*, pp. 30 n., 239.

[3] Ibid., pp. 177–8, and pamphlets there cited.

[4] Like the Pondomisi in 1880 (above, p. 345 n.). One late example was the confiscation of a large block of comparatively good farms in the Langeberg, west of Kuruman, for a trivial Bechuana 'rebellion' occasioned by tactless handling of *rinderpest* (cattle-plague) regulations in 1896.

[5] In Kaffraria I have seen the title deeds of land now owned by Europeans on 'title' expressly described as 'Native'. In barren Gordonia land granted 'in per-

having relied always on martial law, utterly neglected the constructive civil administration which alone could have equipped them to face life anew.

The manifest inequity of the final settlement made this conquest in truth no more than the prelude to the long drama being played out in our own day. Till the events recounted in these pages are seen in better perspective, and the experience of these thirty crucial years given its due weight, this drama will be in danger of taking a more tragic turn. This Cape frontier was no doubt a severe test. The ruling powers, successively Dutch and British, had to operate from afar with neither precedent nor experience to guide their steps. The invasions recorded in history were normally by land forces which were content, once they had brought the invaded people into subjection, to live on what these produced, if necessary under direction. But in America, as now at the Cape, the struggling self-sufficiency of *colonists* left the indigenous peoples with whom they clashed no satisfying function, nor even land on which to live a life of their own. The Federal Government of the U.S.A. quickly gave over its British predecessor's abortive attempt to maintain central control—whereupon the well-distributed local units, leaving all to highly mobile forces endowed with intimate local knowledge and strong local interests, at last virtually annihilated the Indians. At the Cape the colonists were many fewer in number, and in those early days faced their rivals on a narrow front far from base; the colonists were also more law-abiding and self-disciplined than American frontiersmen and, originally at least, looked as a matter of course to the central government to help and if need be protect them. We know how the slow-moving, often heavy-handed government, and its never highly mobile forces, did their part. To the credit of all concerned, including the colonists, the resort to force was always regarded only as a means to a higher end, *law and order*. The Bantu, accordingly, unlike the American Indians, survived with their numbers little if any reduced. But they emerged as an almost heavier responsibility than before, having been rendered virtually incapable themselves of helping to raise and better their position.

petuity' to men of colour for services in Bechuanaland in 1885 has been largely absorbed by Europeans in the same way (article in *Rand Daily Mail*, May 1922). See also *Cape Col. Qn.*, pp. 284–6.

The years of the major 'Kaffir' wars were in this respect decisive. The all but total neglect the Bantu suffered for most of the
next century was the natural reaction to follow such storm and
stress. Once it was 'peace', the overcrowded and even more over-
grazed locations deteriorated; but the process was so gradual as
to pass unnoticed or, if casually observed, to give further warrant for refusing to squander money on roads or railways to help
the development of such wretched (and 'lazy') husbandmen.
The Xhosa were difficult neighbours to act with on the golden
principle 'live and let live', but it was the white society which
failed to apply the 'let live'. There was ample warning. John
Philip's most consistent plea was that the tribes be left land
enough to supply a livelihood. Andries Stockenström would
fain have had a period of well-ordered quiet to prepare the
Xhosa for incorporation in the civilized society. It was in vain.
Philip's unforgivable sin was to lead and win a struggle for
the rights of 'Hottentots', an unwarlike people already closely
bound up if not 'integrated' with the white society. Rather than
tolerate similar freedom for the Bantu a solid body of the
frontiersmen went off into exile, shattering the unity of their
own South Africa. Many years later some of Philip's still very
bitter critics were loud for a further subdivision. They wanted
the 'separate development' of the Bantu in (non-existent)
'Homelands' of their own, apparently unaware even yet that
had their fathers not spurned Philip's advice their experiment
had at least been possible. Instead, before ever the Ama-Xhosa's
Hundred Years War had dragged to its end in the rebellion of
1877-8 the country's four separate units were set on diverse
ways, all except the Cape clinging with pathetic conviction to
some variant of the bankrupt ways which made the Cape Cis-
Kei locations the not untypical South African 'native areas'.

The actors involved and the outcome of their dealings varied
in detail from province to province. The broad freedom for all
which the Trekkers rejected was the making of the Cape, including the Transkei. The almost vaunted success of this unique,
tribally composite but roomy 'Bantu Homeland' as a model of
Native Administration had, indeed, its drawbacks; the peace and
quiet ruling there materially helped to lull public opinion and
confirm the authorities in their attitude of almost studied neglect

of economic development. None the less the Africans of the Cape were in a position to enter the Union of 1910 with confidence, loyal and law abiding, justly holding their heads high. Educationally the long harried Cis-Kei was actually foremost, the first University College 'for Natives' being inevitably sited there within reach of its three notable senior schools—at Fort Hare, on the grounds of the most famous of these, Scotland's contribution, Lovedale. But the reunion of the Cape with its neighbours unhappily gave renewed strength to the out-moded Trekker tradition; leaders like the Prime Minister, Mr. J. X. Merriman, were fatally mistaken in their confidence that the manifest superiority of the Cape policy must quickly commend it to the Union as a whole. Even in that old warrior's lifetime the long campaign was gathering head which was ultimately to succeed, not in raising the status of the Bantu generally, but in bringing those of the Cape down to the political level deemed appropriate by the fathers of the Afrikaner republican tradition.

Natal, the second province, had a strong British tradition but brought little or no help to those who strove to maintain that of the Cape. Geographical isolation, which was emphasized after 1856 when the infant colony was left to make it own adjustments, cut Natal off from the liberalizing influence of the Mother Colony's riper experience, sorely needed though guidance was through a sea of inherited troubles.

The first matter demanding the attention of the British authorities back in 1843 had been a relic of the spacious days of the early Boer Republic; on the comfortable theory that Natal was 'empty' of natives the Volksraad had promised burghers two farms each, together with a town *erf* or building-plot—for a 'Sunday house' to be used on visits to market and *Nagmaal* (Holy Communion). Commissioner Cloete at once found their leaders claiming not merely two, but ten (in one instance forty) farms each,[1] and the standard Boer farm was 6,000 acres; his task was to limit and apportion these extravagant claims.[2] It became imperative also to provide for the 'surplus

---

[1] Cloete to Napier, Private and Confidential, 20 June 1843 (Bird's *Annals*, ii. 191). Pretorius claimed 10 farms, Commandant Rudolf 40.

[2] Cloete at once offered to register claims to 6,000-acre farms for all who could prove occupation for twelve months previous to his arrival, limiting other grants to only 2,000 acres. The confusion of these twelve months, however, made it difficult

natives'; but a Land Commission appointed in 1846 to mark off reserves inevitably included in the native areas farms claimed by Boers, besides leaving others of them uncomfortably close to unwelcome African neighbours. This tenderness for native rights was so ill received that probably a majority of the Trekkers withdrew rather than abate their full claims. Later, Sir Harry Smith's efforts[1] especially helped to retain a small permanent colony of Afrikaans-speaking farmers.

From the earliest days of Mr. Cloete's administration American missionaries had been watchful of native interests. To Dr. Philip in September 1843 Mr. Aldin Grout quoted the opinion of the Rev. Daniel Lindley who, soon after this, gave up his mission work and devoted himself entirely to the service of the pastorless Trekkers:

Mr. Lindley says if the natives are located in small bodies as proposed, it will be simply that they may become servants to the Whites, and root them ultimately out of the land as was done to the Hottentots, and he consequently says that if the Government so locates them he would not on any account work among them as he thinks they can never become *Men* under those circumstances.

Mr. Grout himself wrote to the Governor on 11 February 1844 that

were the question of right to be decided by previous occupation, a great proportion of the present inhabitants would be claimants by right of birth or previous residence, but that the testing of such claims would be utterly impracticable; any attempt to enforce the expulsion of the 'surplus' from Natal would either expose them to the remorseless vengeance of Umpandi (the Zulu chief), drive them upon the assagays of Faku (the Pondo), or precipitate them upon and leave them to the mercy of the (northern) farmers.

Mr. Grout also argued strongly against the proposal to 'place the natives under the authority of chiefs', holding that few things

to prove effective occupation, and the offer was accompanied or followed by demands for an annual quit-rent of £4, and the payment of survey fees, together with mention of an 'upset' price of 4s. an acre for Crown Lands—innovations which in the old Colony had helped to provoke the Trek itself (Walker, p. 204 and references).

[1] These included the offer of farms on the larger 6,000-acre scale to those who would take occupation within six months and undertake not to sell or mortgage them within seven years.

could be more unfavourable to their improvement. For my own part I see no difficulty in placing them at once under British Law and in that case there would be no objection against placing the most intelligent and best characters among them as local magistrates, removable at pleasure. . . . The sooner we can weaken (old prejudices) by withdrawing from their minds what has a tendency to strengthen them, and familiarize their minds with British forms, principles and ideas the better.

In October 1843 Mr. Montagu had already given assurance through Dr. Philip 'that the determination to respect the claims of the natives to the lands in that territory was distinctly and emphatically announced' in Mr. Cloete's original instructions. He also enlcosed a supplementary directive, dated 11 October:

I am to request you will make it known to the Emigrant Farmers and native tribes that you were directed in May last to cause the claims of the natives to lands which they either held or occupied to be scrupulously respected. You will also make it known that . . . the natives are not to be restricted in locating themsleves to any particular spots or districts nor are they to be excluded from occupying any land whatever which remains at the disposal of the Crown. The Government will neither disturb them, nor permit them to be disturbed in their occupations or selections.

In spite of this the Commissioner seems to have leaned to the Boer Volksraad plan of complete 'segregation', being disposed— by one missionary account—to make 'any sacrifices, concessions or compromises that he consistently can for the sake of peace. . . . Many say he gives the Boers reason to believe that things may be arranged far more to their advantage than there can be any reason to believe possible.' The Boer plan was for a time favoured apparently even by Theophilus Shepstone[1] who later, as Native Commissioner, handled the natives with great tact, shepherding a large proportion of them after 1846 into what were for a long time fairly adequate reserves. Instead of subjecting the tribes to European law he set about reconstituting their broken tribal system; he recognized native law and custom but also introduced the precautionary device of vesting overriding powers in the Lieutenant-Governor (1850) as Supreme Chief. The reserves provided included broken and dispersed pockets of good land—and also a proportion of what certain of

[1] Brookes, pp. 28 ff.

their own prophets have described as 'country for baboons'.[1] They were a device in fact for leaving rather more than a fair share of the acreage of Natal open for the 'occupation and speculations' of Europeans. These still number barely one-ninth of the total population.

It mattered little at first that the demarcation of Reserves made no provision for the natural expansion of the native population. Extensive Crown lands, expressly left open to the natives in accordance with the instructions of Mr. Cloete in 1843, were only slowly and gradually swallowed up by new white settlers. European farmers, moreover, or absentee landlords, welcomed labourers or share-paying squatters as tenants on their very broad domains. For a long time, therefore, thanks to the smallness of the European population, all was well. But it was almost in spite of the Reserves. Shepstone's paternal administration was a steadying factor; but it was the abundance of land actually open to native occupation which long served to keep the peace almost unbroken. The traditionally formidable Zulu remained separate and 'independent' till 1887, even the serious war of 1879 passing with no more than a storm of nerves in Natal proper.

The situation changed radically when, as the years passed, Natal really began to come into its own as an agricultural paradise. When the coastal belt was thickly planted with sugar-cane, sub-tropical fruit or vegetables, and the High Veld districts, having a reliable rainfall, filled up with progressive 'mixed' farmers, the old, easy days of unrestricted native 'squatting' gradually ended. The very small European minority, almost inevitably provincial in its outlook, was assuming responsibility for a growing population of physically insecure Africans when in 1893 Natal became a fully self-governing colony; in the astonishingly over-confident spirit of the age the overwhelmingly Bantu Zululand was incorporated with Natal four years later. The burden of responsibility was so little shared, or the safeguards against the risk of the minority being 'swamped' were so stringent, that after ten years of self-government only three Africans had succeeded in qualifying as registered voters.[2] Yet according to the earliest authoritative estimate, that of 1915, barely half the natives of Natal proper were located in the,

[1] R. Russell's *Natal*, p. 203. (See also pp. 207–8, 341, n. 3.)
[2] Native Affairs Commission, 1903–5.

even then, crowded reserves;[1] evictions due to the progress of European farming have ever since continuously increased the pressure on the available land. The artificial tribal system, there is reason to believe (as Mr. Grout feared in 1844), has been rather an obstacle to the advance of civilization,[2] but it tends to break down altogether.[3] The sharp repression of an incipient rebellion in 1906 betrayed a nervous lack of self-confidence which tended to persist. When in 1910 Natal joined the Union her strongly anti-republican sentiments were, at best, muted when voices were raised from the old Boer Republics insisting that the major preoccupation of Union Native Policy must be to safeguard the interests of *White* civilization.

The Orange Free State has long ceased to be embarrassed like its neighbours by any over-spill of 'surplus natives'. Unlike Natal where the European minority is nearly nine times outnumbered, the Free Staters find the barely three to one Bantu majority insufficient, without Basuto help, to meet at any rate the peak demand for farm-labour. As a provision for its Bantu people's reasonable needs the scheduled 'reserves', amounting to less than one-250th part of the area of the Province, would be a mockery; they are of course a survival of remnants of land left to early 'native allies' in the days of the Trek. So far from making (in a phrase current later) 'further provision' for other dependants, one of the first acts of the newly established Republic after 1854 was, almost as a matter of course, to bar any coloured person from holding land or acquiring rights as a free *burgher*. Here, however, Dr. Philip's labours proved to have

---

[1] The estimate of the Beaumont Commission (U.G. 19, 1916, see Appendix VI) was that 12,742 natives were still on Crown lands, 80,070 on *un*occupied European-owned land, 346,641 on occupied European-owned farms, and 37,199 in urban or mining areas; thus accounting for 476,652 out of a total of 823,720. Since 1915 the pressure on Reserves has unquestionably increased owing to the development of European farming in Natal. In 1915 native areas 'scheduled' under the Land Act of 1913 amounted to 2,414,203 acres, out of a total of 15,864,660 in Natal Proper besides 3,887,100 out of a total of 6,651,105 in supposedly Bantu Zululand. This brings the total Reserve for Natal and Zululand combined to between one-third and one-fourth of the whole area.

[2] Even in free tribal Basutoland progressive individuals have been known to seek Government protection against the jealous exactions and persecutions of backward chiefs, and in Natal itself, and Zululand, the 'progressives' used to prefer mission-controlled Reserves or privately owned farms. (See also Brookes, pp. 30, 47.)

[3] In 1927 I found one sugar-belt magistrate tearing his hair to make provision for a 'good little *tribe*' whose huts had been reduced by eviction from European farms from more than 100 to barely 10.

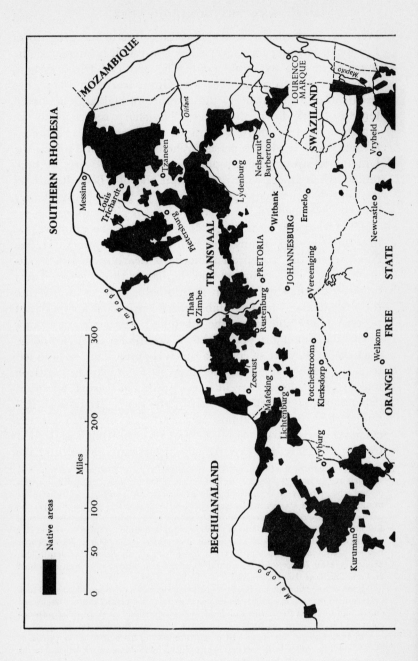

SOUTHERN RHODESIA

MOZAMBIQUE

Messina

Louis
Trichardt

Tzaneen

Olifant

Pietersburg

Lydenburg

Nelspruit

Barberton

LOURENCO
MARQUE

SWAZILAND

Maputo

Vryheid

Witbank

Ermelo

Newcastle

TRANSVAAL

Thaba
Zimbe

PRETORIA

Rustenburg

JOHANNESBURG

Vereeniging

ORANGE   FREE   STATE

Welkom

Potchefstroom

Klerksdorp

Zeerust

Mafeking

Lichtenburg

Vryburg

BECHUANALAND

Limpopo

Kuruman

Molopo

Native areas

Miles

0   50   100   200   300

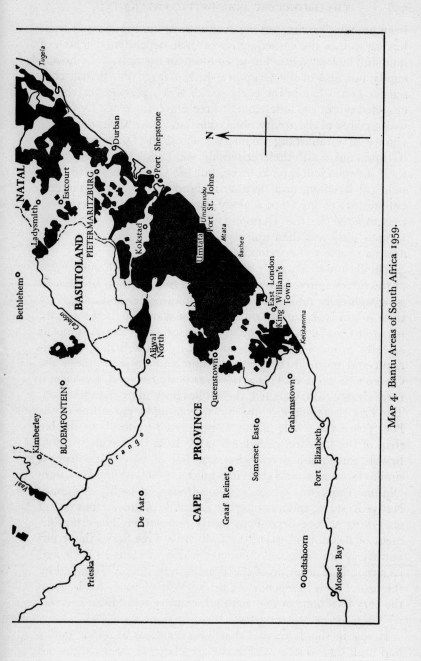

MAP 4. Bantu Areas of South Africa 1959.

been not wholly vain, serving even to save the Free Staters from having to face the consequences of their dependants' dearth of land and lack of rights. The abandonment not only of the Sovereignty but also of the Griquas a little nagged the British conscience and, when in the early sixties Kok's people were being crowded out of the independent Free State, the Cape Governor was sensible of old treaty obligations and gave them one more chance of establishing themselves across the Drakensberg. In 'Griqualand East' their economic weakness again lost them their independent land-holding, but the Griquas retained their political freedom, and became merged in the free 'Coloured' community of the Cape Colony. Even Waterboer's treaty was remembered in the Diamond Field's dispute of 1871; the Griqua state was then quickly absorbed in Griqualand West, and its people too became free Cape citizens.

The Basuto treaty more effectively survived the abandonment of the Sovereignty. Moshesh, who was more favourably placed geographically, and stronger both in man-power and in sagacity than Adam Kok, carried on a desperate war with the Free State till at last, in 1868, when he was hard pressed, his old status as an 'ally' aroused a sense of responsibility in the British Government and induced them to take him and his state under the Queen's protection. This action was hotly resented. But even if mere strategy also weighed, the act has been more than justified. The Free State had already shown its hand by parcelling out as Boer farms the whole of the 'Conquered Territory', a valuable strip of the Caledon corn-lands taken from the Basuto in 1866. British annexation saved what was left of Basutoland from a similar fate and, would the critics but see it, 'solved' the Free State 'Native Problem'—at once guaranteeing a highly necessary Native Reserve, and relieving the Republic of the onerous task of governing a huge dependent native population. The establishment of Basutoland gave 'the tight little Free State' that comparatively homogeneous character which was long its pride and its strength. The pride of the Free Staters, deeply wounded by the loss of their independence in the War of 1900, made them the very backbone of the twentieth-century republican revival.

It was in the Transvaal that Trekker ideas of native policy had it all their own way. For the area beyond the Vaal the old theory of depopulation will not hold. From the beginning the Reports and Resolutions of all the numerous republican *Volks-raads*—and the ascendancy everywhere of the *Krijgsraad*, the military arm of the governing authority—show conclusively that the early settlers in the Transvaal were at once 'faced by the same problem' (of surplus natives) 'that was at that moment confronting the Republic of Natal'.[1] The Boers debouching on the High Veld in the first place separated the Basuto ('Sotho'-speakers) from their near-kinsmen the Bechuana (Tswana-speakers), driving some of the 'Sotho' (Bapedi) far north of their fellows in Basutoland. The Bechuana, many of them, drifted if they were not driven north-west towards the more arid Kala-hari; but many more became subject to the Transvaal where, to this day, tribes like the BaKgatla are more numerous than in Bechuanaland itself. Before ever Boer settlement had begun to have serious effect upon the tribes directly under the influence of the L.M.S. Dr. Philip expressly warned the Government, after his tour in 1842, of the danger of a clash in the north (above, pp. 229 and 253). Moselekatze had newly been expelled by the Boers and the Bechuana had begun to 'creep back' to their old homes, only to find the whole territory claimed, whether occupied or not, by the conquering Boers. By the late forties the clash Dr. Philip had foreseen had come about; even the weak and divided Bechuana were making some show of resistance to Boer en-croachment and constant bickerings and commandos kept the country beyond the Vaal in a ferment. Moffat wrote to the L.M.S. in an undated letter as early as 1847:

No real friend of the Aborigines could give the Boers credit for good intentions, but the very reverse. Their perpetual aim and object is the entire subjugation of the interior tribes, having already appropriated the most fruitful part of the country, while its rightful possessors are driven to the waste places. How Sechele can receive missionaries from the Boers is a puzzle to me ... for certain it is, they care nothing about the eternal interests of either Sechele or his people, but would dance a jig to hear them all, great and small, cry '*Baas*' (a most servile epithet demanded by the Boers of all coloured persons).

He concludes that of course he cannot hinder the Moravian new-comers, or interfere in any way.

[1] Agar-Hamilton, pp. 53, 75, *et passim*.

In the crisis of the early fifties, when Philip was no more, Moffat and even Livingstone, while still less conciliatory of the Boers, failed even to keep the Government informed of what was happening under their eyes. So it came about that, in sheer ignorance of the real situation Her Majesty's Government in 1852 left the unfettered control of all these Bantu fragments to the emigrant Boers, former subjects of its own who had expatriated themselves precisely because their view of their obligations to such people was so diametrically opposed to that formerly pressed upon them by Her Majesty's local representatives. The out-of-date homage paid to 'Exeter Hall' by the clause in the Sand River Convention (above, p. 325) requiring the Boers to repudiate *slavery* only showed Her Majesty's Government's ignorance slightly touched with suspicion born of as uneasy awareness of the dimensions of the task of administering this wide and undefined frontier.

The burden which Her Majesty's Government now set down with relief fell thus upon the handful of inexperienced farmers who, besides being an interested party in the disputes likely to arise, included, as the Government very well knew, no vestige of a professional class, few if any traders, not even so much, for many years, as a settled minister of their own Dutch Reformed Church. The constitution of their Republic, the *Grondwet*, 1858, was six years maturing. It is to be read perhaps as above all a *manifesto*, their first uninhibited statement of the functions they considered proper to any government situated as theirs must be. The most frequently quoted clause of this *Grondwet* is at any rate basically clear—'Het Volk *wil* &c.', 'The People *wills* to agree to no equality between coloured and white inhabitants either in Church or in State.' The immediately preceding clause 8, in which the sovereign people make profession of the obligations of their own religious faith and duty, concludes: 'The people *permit* the spread of the Gospel among the heathen, subject to definite safeguards against fault and deception.' Further (par. 31) 'no coloured persons nor half-castes are admitted to meetings of Volksraad, nor to any civic privileges'.[1] On the other hand the '*Krijgsmagt*', or army, compromises 'if necessary'—as they might be, to keep each other in order—'all the coloured people in this country whose chiefs are subject to it' (par. 96). Native admini-

---

[1] Eybers p. 363 (translation sometimes modified in text).

stration, most vital and absorbing of governmental duties, comes, significantly, under the heading '*over de Krijgsmagt en den Krijgsraad*' (pars. 104 and 105): 'To the Assistant Field-Cornets, and Field-Cornets, is entrusted the *preservation of order*, to the Commandants, the commandos, in case of internal insurrection of the coloured population'—disaffection on the part of Europeans was reserved for the higher dignity of the Commandant-General. 'By *preservation of order*', the next section reads, 'is understood seeing to the observance of the laws, the execution of sentences . . . the observance of measures of general and local concern, *besides the supervision of the coloured population and the suppression of vagrancy and vagabonds in the field-cornetcies*.' There are some definitions: e.g. (par. 104) 'By *commandos* in case of internal insurrections of the coloured population is understood, *keeping the Kafir chiefs to the performance of their duty*.' This duty would include not only keeping their own people in order but requiring them to furnish labour as and when required—obligations which carried no corresponding right even to security of land-tenure.

The arbitrary claim in the earliest forties to the disposal of all the undefined conquests of Moselekatze was typical of the Republicans' general attitude. Land was their first objective, the second a plentiful labour supply, always with 'proper' relations between master and servant. Where the natives were powerless, as in the Sechuana-speaking area, some few chiefs were given lands and 'burgher status',[1] with the right to continue approximately where they had always been. The great majority paid a 'labour tax' which, like that of the *villein* of old, was variable and indefinite in amount. A few weak tribes voluntarily 'surrendered' their independence 'for the privilege of settling within the domains and under the protection of the Republic',[2] for the most part as rightless 'squatters'. It never suggested itself to the Boers that in taking over Moselekatze's conquests they must assume also the civilizing responsibilities of a governing race. *The Bible* made Ham a servant of servants, and servants these children of Ham must always remain.

It may be claimed that at least the Republic suppressed inter-tribal fighting; but that security gained was some return for the

[1] i.e. exemption from the cruder labour exactions, but never 'political' rights.
[2] See Agar-Hamilton, p. 76, and for 'Labour Tax', ch. x.

tribes' loss of independence is belied by the state's continuous record of 'commandos' and 'wars'. It has its significance that while the Cape had its distinctive 'Kaffir' wars, and the Free State repeated wars with the Basuto, the history of the Transvaal is a record of what were for some time almost annual 'commandos' against malcontent but isolated native chiefs—Montsioa, Makapan, Sekukuni, Mapoch, Malaboch; on the very eve of the war of 1899 General Joubert led an almost bloodless expedition to the north and drove the Bavenda chief, Mpefu, into temporary exile across the Limpopo. The Transvaal, that is to say, most completely illustrates the way in which the Great Trek 'turned the flank' of the Bantu, laying the tribes open, one by one, to forfeiture of their lands, and to subjugation—military, economic, and political. The Republic never taxed itself with the task of subjugating all the low veld tribes, and on these it practised 'indirect rule'—to the extent that it left them, without help or guidance, to their own devices. Where tribal resistance in malarial country was formidable, as in the Zoutspansberg, the Boers had by 1870 actually lost ground they once held and in a few such parts tribal institutions remained virtually undisturbed.

The aim of the Trekkers was perhaps a foggily conceived plan of 'segregation'. But, as in Natal at the very beginning, segregation was little more than a warrant for shutting their eyes to the inconvenient presence of a 'surplus' population which disturbed the unity and harmony of their peasant republic. The dream of 'separateness' took shape at any rate only after they had assumed ownership, in total disregard of minimal Bantu needs, of more than all the land they could hope to use themselves; and the sponsors of 'separate development' have never yet, save in some highly academic circles, abandoned the assumption that nothing shall be allowed to interrupt the free flow of all the 'native labour' required or demanded by farms and industries.

Conquest, no doubt, brought the Transvaal Bantu into touch with civilization, and individuals among them reached out, earlier than they might otherwise have done, after all that Europeans could teach them. At the same time labour conditions were what masters chose to make them and, save that supervision by field-cornets and *landdrosts* checked physical ill-treatment, such service, uncertain and variable in quantity, with no effective appeal against the lord and master, was of the very essence of the *unfree* tenures of the Middle Ages. Native rights in land were virtually wiped out in the whole of the central High Veld; from Bloemhof in the west to Ermelo in the east, a stretch of country some 300 miles long, barely 35 square miles remained so definitely 'native' as to come to be 'scheduled' as Native Reserve by the Land Act of 1913.[1] Yet native labour could not be fully used and the Transvaal became the province *par excellence* of the rightless native squatter; in 1915 nearly one-quarter of its rural native population were resident on land *owned* but *un*occupied by Europeans.[2] The current complaint was that companies had amassed great blocks of this land by buying at cut prices from Boer owners and now made their income from 'Kaffir-farming'. Less was heard of how the Republic itself, having promised Her Majesty's Government after its dis-annexation in 1881 to extend its Native Reserves, had done no such thing before its fall in 1900. One wry comment is relevant. The supervision even of absentee landlords served at any rate to save the soil surface from such ruin as it suffered from the inter-nal pressure of population in almost all the official Native Reserves. So grievously were these neglected.

Disregard of the Bantu, as a people divinely appointed to live under direction, was explicit in the Transvaal tradition; but indifference to the fortunes of a class known only as servants was general. When in the 1920's the social disorders resulting from the strain of World War I compelled public attention, the influence of the Transvaal as the most industrialized unit tended to lead in the formation of national opinion; but having so long ignored the Bantu in its midst the country proved to be almost totally ignorant of the facts of Bantu life and means of livelihood. Everywhere the predominantly 'native' areas were accessible only by difficult bush tracks. The one thing generally required of their people was a steady supply of labour and, this being perennially *short*, the easy life the reserves afforded was

[1] 17·8 square miles in Potchefstrom, 16 square miles in Wakkerstroom.
[2] Report of Beaumont Commission, U.G. 19, 1916. Total native population 1,382,285: Witwatersrand (largely mine natives, imported) 272,938; on un-occupied European-owned land 232,082; on farms, i.e. including labourers and 'labour-tenants', 390,332.

held to be responsible. Back in the 1890's even Cape parliamentarians were arguing the need for a labour tax to put pressure, in a notorious phrase, 'on dandies loafing about the kraals'. With such phantasy still passing for knowledge, the world-shaking demand arose that the aloofness so long practised in the old Transvaal be preserved for a new Republic by a policy of *apartheid*.[1]

The so-called *national* movement, as it developed, continued to be nurtured on phantasy which fights shy of brute fact. Even official figures may be at best informed estimates, but that of a strong Land Commission suggested that in 1915 perhaps half the Bantu population, including many of their absentees in urban employment, had *homes* in actual 'reserves'. The term used is advisedly *homes*; over-population being general many had no more than a lien on the family strip, or strips; much even of the Transkei land being subject to the rule 'One man, one lot', economic farming units were rare. Production for general markets was, accordingly, negligible and few reserves were self-supporting even in the staple, maize. Left utterly without guidance, the people had made nothing of the straitened conditions forced upon them; it was in 1932 that an *Economic Commission* bewailed 'approaching desert conditions' in many or most of the reserves. By far their largest export was in truth manpower, *labour*, and wage-earning was their mainstay.

Yet but for the reserves the lot of the old or of the poor and needy had long ago been parlous indeed, and the burden on the State of unavoidable poor relief so insupportable as to have compelled remedial action. As things were, and are, the strips of cultivation have many older men happily occupied, supplementing pensions and keeping tribal traditions in some measure alive. It is a no doubt unavoidable consequence that this home base in the reserve operates as a subsidy which aids and reduces employers' wages bills. The bosses' gain may be offset by the inefficiency arising from the workers' not infrequent absences on visits home; and the fact of having homes to visit at any rate strongly buttresses the economic independence and the self-

[1] The Prime Minister, General Hertzog, was interested in challenging me to correct unfavourable comments on the state of the Cis-Kei by a study of Herschel, a district of his own advisers' choosing, to show, he said, how well the Bantu fared 'in their own areas'. The substance of this study is embodied in ch. xi of *Complex South Africa, 1931*. See also p. 364 and Appendix B, Biographical Note, p. 372.

respect of those who have them—if only it did not also tend to cut the rate of wages and lower the standard for those not so blest.

These dispersed Bantu—the direct result of conquest in the Cis-Kei, and of more gradual extrusion elsewhere—are the crux. The often mentioned 'squatters' are the typical remnant of the dispossessed population, left, where they were, without legal security but practically undisturbed, often on their ancestral land. In undeveloped districts, with a kind (or even a lazy) landlord, 'squatting' may yield a fair measure of comfort and better life prospects than the only alternatives, whole-time labour, or the so-called 'labour tenancy' (90 days' service, not necessarily continuous). The typical squatter has to give his own services, often unpaid, often those of his whole family as well, for the mere right to live where he is, perhaps to plough a small patch of land, or graze a limited number of cattle, and he dare not move for fear of having his family evicted. He cannot readily take his labour to the best market, or even where it is most needed. The shortage of labour so long and loudly complained of throughout South Africa was the direct and inevitable result of the extreme immobility of the great mass of landless Bantu. Long ago, in 1827, when Dr. Philip was asked to put his case for the Hottentots in one sentence he asked for no more than 'a fair market for their labour'. William Huskisson, an able Minister, at once agreed that that 'includes everything else'.[1]

The economic insecurity of the Bantu has of course more than anything else retarded their advance in civilization; an assertive paganism could not otherwise have continued almost to flaunt itself at the very doors of the schools of the depressed and yet sophisticated Cis-Kei. And so, a hundred years after Philip and Huskisson, in the 1920's the wheel came full circle. The Boers of the *platteland* had still not learnt the art of intensive agriculture; their fathers' reckless extrusion of the Bantu left them with an abundance of land which made this extra effort needless; when the days of continuous expansion ceased farmers in occupation readily made room for family and other dependants who were content to subsist at a very modest level as *bijwoners* (squatters). Only after 1914 the steeply rising

[1] *Cape Col. Qn.*, p. 216.

prices of all commodities at last compelled all who possibly could to put their land to better use than was made of it by European squatters—even the Bantu variety were more dependable workers. The modern crisis in South African affairs took form when 'poor whites', streaming in thousands to the towns in search of such employment as their inexperience could command, found themselves in competition with the cheaper and not much less unskilled exodus from congested Bantu reserves. Again this was in spite of John Philip. This people stoned the prophet who toiled hardest to steady the frontier process by which 'the meeting place of civilization and savagery' (in F. J. Turner's unhappy phrase) staged at last this bitter conflict.

'Such has been the unlooked-for result of the "extermination" of so many native tribes. It came not without warning which went unheeded in days when South African society might possibly have been set on a more stable basis. The hard case of the Poor White began to arouse serious attention only after about 1908,[1] and the first result has been to drive South African politicians to short cuts—anything to meet the panic of an overwhelmingly European electorate at the danger threatening their "white" civilization. But civilization is not "white" or "dual", and the talk of segregation today, with its stress on a policy of "separate development", too often merely runs away from the essential problem—the established contact of advanced and backward peoples as parts of one South African community. To increase the "Reserves" may mitigate the rigours of this economic clash; but policy is to be judged by its success in lessening the fatal difference between European and native standards, and raising the mass of landless natives from that state of backwardness which is precisely what makes them a "problem".'

The previous paragraph is printed nearly *verbatim* as it was written in 1928—it followed a description (condensed in this edition) of the conditions of Bantu life as revealed by pioneer investigations made in the 1920's. A great number of official reports and authoritative contemporary studies make it needless to elaborate on later developments. The basic facts remain substantially as they were—the changes any visitor returning to the scene is expected to wonder at are changes of scale only.

[1] Report on *Indigency in the Transvaal*, 1908, much of it by Mr. Philip Kerr, later Marquess of Lothian.

The paragraph written in 1928 may pass as evidence that the policy of South African rulers, in face even of great economic expansion, was no more than a development of trends and tendencies long ago manifest. Thirty years later it seems clear that they have followed all too closely on the lines that were then feared; the condition of the Bantu masses is still what the policies and events described in earlier chapters combined to make it, successive British Governments making their own sorry contribution to the outcome. It was no great help that the distant Colonial Office long retained a direct but uncertain responsibility for the 'Natives'; the Cape was far from enjoying unfettered dominion status when it became self-governing in 1872, and the fear of provoking some assertion of a shadowy British suzerainty favoured a do-nothing policy also in the Republics. The crushing of the Ama-Xhosa in the 1850's and the repudiation of responsibility for the northern Bantu need not have been Britain's last word. The support given to the Basuto in 1868, the assertion of sovereignty in the diamond-fields, and the firm intervention later in Bechuanaland kept the Bantu in general as touchingly hopeful as their masters were apprehensive of British intervention in defence of Bantu interests. But the mood which inclined British opinion to 'abandonment' in the 1850's was never long suppressed. Direct British influence on developments in South Africa ceased finally to count after 1910 when, I have suggested elsewhere,[1] her statesmen made the great refusal; having side-stepped the need to insist on native enfranchisement in the Peace of Vereeniging in 1902, they passed the Act of Union in 1910 still unamended.

For many years before this the legal but rarely exercised right of Her Majesty's Government to intervene had been little more than an irritant, once the days of its possible usefulness in 'Kaffir Wars' seemed to have passed for ever. In the later nineteenth century the effective control of public business devolved ever more completely on political assemblies, and on Ministers elected (except always in the Cape) exclusively by European electors. In practice, all four states came to conduct their business as nearly as possible as if there had been no large Bantu population to be reckoned with. The Cape alone had some excuse for this unconcern; except in the far-off eastern districts

[1] *The Road to Self Rule*, ch. vi.

its Coloured People supplied all the labour necessary—in the capital, Cape Town, a Bantu face was rarely seen. Yet the Cape Bantu came off best. A few were voters, and for others there was always the hope, and an urge, to prosper sufficiently to qualify as voters. The Native Affairs Department had a high morale and gave its people in the Reserves devoted service, almost warranting the popular belief that most of the Cape Bantu were, in the language of later days, not uncomfortably 'segregated in their own areas'. The electors of Natal on the other hand were nervous about the present, without having any clear ideas of what to do about the future of their African population. When the Union of the Provinces came, the Transvaal influence on national policy was bound to be strong; it remained peculiarly its own, even that of the great mining centre on the Rand counting for less than the pure republican tradition. On the Transvaal *platteland*, as elsewhere, the burghers had ceased to be exercised about the Bantu peoples once their military power had been broken. It was indeed on the Rand mines that 'white' labour first began to complain of wage-cutting competition by 'natives'; but at the first hints of such new trouble burgher opinion, always against anything like the Cape solution, began to raise the demand for 'segregation'. This term, first widely current in Edwardian days, covered little more than a demand that the Bantu should remain out of sight—as in the days of the Republic when they were in fact of little account.

Strangely enough the 1910 Union Government's first legislative venture in 'native policy' derived from an earlier tradition. Employers in general and farmers in particular remained convinced that labour was perpetually short of their needs for the sole reason that laziness was the besetting sin of the Bantu peoples. The Natives Land Act of 1913 decreed, accordingly, that native occupation even of unused European-owned land would henceforth be legal only on condition that they be registered as labour-tenants bound to give in return a minimum of ninety days' labour service. The old republican law allowing only five families on any one farm was a dead letter, but although the administration of the new Act was never effective it remained an instrument to harass squatters with for many years. A second provision of the Land Act was more directly due to the influence of the new school of segregationists, and was more devastating in its effects. To forestall any over-ambitious or over-wealthy Bantu encroaching on areas already effectively 'white', no Bantu was henceforth to purchase or rent land except in established reserves, or in additional 'scheduled areas'. No additional land was in fact scheduled till more than twenty years after the Act became law.

The profoundly disturbing Land Act was followed within the year by the first World War, with shattering consequences for the Bantu, but even more immediately for the white rural economy. All had reason to feel the effects of war-engendered monetary inflation. Market scarcities and rising prices at last forced those landlords who could command the means and the knowledge to put their farms to more intensive use. The weaker farmers, and the unwanted *white* squatters, were forced out by hundreds or even thousands; throughout the war years the former trickle off the land was becoming a flood. Many drifted from the arid interior to the less fertile but humid coastal districts where even a garden plot would make them fairly sure of a subsistence crop of 'sweet-potatoes'; some ended in appalling Johannesburg 'yards'—but most of all in 'peri-urban' squalor on the fringes of the bigger towns. These 'peri-urban' areas are surely a South African speciality; the term is fittingly applied to settlements allowing of a shack and a *mealie*-patch, conveniently within reach of odd jobs in the towns, but beyond the range of rate-collectors, *and* of municipal services. Unhappily for the refugees' prospects of employment, they now met the competing flood of Africans whose economy was similarly hard hit, or already reeling from the effects of their rulers' latest folly, the 1913 Land Act. Those 'squatters' who preferred the precarious freedom of a Reserve to a tied labour-tenancy made for the already congested Reserves, where their fellow tribesmen felt bound to receive them. The increased pressure on scanty food supplies, which could be supplemented only at ever-rising prices, forced more and more of the able-bodied to try their fortune in the urban labour market. This unlooked-for exodus effectually checked a long overdue rise in 'native' wages—Bantu labour, far from being in short supply, became cheaper than ever. The almost equally unskilled poor whites found themselves plunged into an unholy contest with poor blacks.

Thus, suddenly, the weaknesses of the whole South African

system stood revealed, on a scale the State itself could no longer ignore—the country's history has turned ever since on the grim struggle to find a remedy. Wage-cutting, a legitimate trade-union interest, rightly took the attention of the Unions, but these were all-white, highly skilled, and had 'done well out of the war'; an acute shortage of skilled men was the opportunity for the craftsmen of the Rand to use their strength. But the one commodity sold at a fixed price was gold, to the embarrassment of the mining industry on which all else very largely depended. Early in 1922 the Chamber of Mines showed itself inclined to risk a major strike rather than make any further concession to trade-union demands. By March strikes had most of the Rand for several weeks in a state of open war which took an anti-Bantu twist. New men, ousting the staider craft-unionists, made the issue the mine-owners' alleged intention to 'dilute' their highly paid white staff by introducing a higher proportion of 'cheap' Africans. The nub of the matter was that during the war years Cornish and other overseas skilled miners kept drifting away and by this time up to 90 per cent. of the mineworkers were home-born Afrikaners, the abler and more venturesome of the white influx from the back-veld. In the revolutionary strikes of March the cry was for a Workers' Republic; but the Republic the most militant had in mind was their all-white Transvaal.

What has followed since is too near us for definitive history, but it is clear how great a part the themes of the earlier chapters played in the approach to modern developments. The essential novelty of 1922 was the incursion of Afrikaners into the industrial field, and since then they have become more and more dominant in new and expanding industries. Political action was, however, more congenial to them than trades unionism, and they have continued to look for political solutions to every problem, whatever its fundamental cause. Nationalism, which in the period between Union and 1922 had been considered out of date and backward-looking, now found a new and wider appeal —to the many nostalgic Republicans, and to workers attracted by a Republic on the old pattern, with 'Natives in their place'. In 1924 this bid brought a Nationalist Government to power but their dependence on non-Afrikaner labour support made them play down the Republic. The programme of the new Government put first a 'civilized labour policy' which ensured preferential treatment, and a minimum wage, for whites; in 1926 a statutory 'Colour Bar' replaced the regulations (disallowed by the Courts) which had in practice sufficed to keep the more skilled mining operations for white workers. In 1927 the Prime Minister, General Hertzog, next introduced draft Bills setting course for a highly *political* form of 'segregation'. One of these Bills was to provide at last some of the additional land promised for 'native' use so long ago as 1913. But the Courts had since ruled that the restrictive provisions of the 1913 Land Act came under the 'entrenched' clauses of the Union constitution protecting the Cape franchise and could not be applied in the Cape. The new Bills, therefore, were put to the two Houses sitting together, the procedure required for alteration to the franchise; but when a two-thirds majority was not to be had for the Bill restricting the solidly anti-republican Cape vote the Government withdrew *all* their proposals, including the long-delayed further provision of land. In 1929 they appealed to the electors and won a clear republican majority in Parliament. Before they could avail themselves of this majority they had made the fatal mistake of clinging to the gold standard in the slump years of 1931–2. In 1933 they were forced both 'off' gold and into a 'Fusion' with General Smuts's opposition South African Party. A new United Party Government reaped the benefits that followed; but in 1936, hoping thus to preserve national unity General Smuts and his followers (surprisingly) allowed Cape *native* voters to be removed from the common electoral roll. For twenty years they had four communal 'Native' representatives, who had to be *white*. To sugar the pill the Africans of the other three provinces were for the first time allowed three (white) Senators, chosen not by direct vote but by means of a complex system of electoral colleges. A short-lived 'Natives Representative Council' was set up (with *advisory powers* only) and at last a Trust and Land Act set in train the long process of acquiring a limited acreage of additional native land, at prices vastly higher than they would have been in 1913.

The Nationalists' chance to pursue *apartheid* came only in 1948, in a much expanded post-war world, and with the South African population about doubled since Union. A remarkable expansion of secondary industries had owed much to adventurous government backing, but more to the increased price of gold which followed the abandonment of the gold standard currency in 1933; the necessity too of making the country as self-sufficient as possible in the war years gave industries a good start. The national income accordingly reached a figure far exceeding any to be explained away as due to currency inflation. Full employment was becoming possible, but was attained only by the whites; the African population of urban or industrial centres greatly increased, but the rapid expansion of industry and modernized agriculture was far from achieving a balanced economy in face of other arbitary factors imposed which made that outcome more difficult. Many of the urban African population found at least semi-skilled work, or employment in mechanized industries where craftsmanship is not essential, at greatly improved wages. But on the ground that increasing urban populations outrun the costly housing schemes embarked on by municipalities and government, the official policy restricted the flow of labour to the towns, and limited the opportunities offered there, by the operation of a rigid, bureaucratic and sometimes inhumane system known as influx control.

The dominant Party neither changed nor adapted their policy one iota to meet new conditions ruling not only in South Africa but in the world. The conviction that their country is unique (above, Ch. I) rests only on the relatively great numbers and the established interests of the white population; but the dependent peoples too are unusual in being the most experienced of their race in Africa; many are fully as 'advanced' as any elsewhere, and so-called 'practical' *apartheid*, involving separate seats in parks and duplicated transport services, besides being wastefully costly, caused insult to just these exceptional people. It thus matters the more that they are expressly denied any say in the political conduct of South African affairs. Self-governing 'homelands' can be little help so long as the grown numbers of advanced people in urban areas have no say in their country's affairs. This exclusion was finally completed after a sustained and ultimately successful attack on the Cape (Coloured) franchise. That barrier gone, 1955, the way was cleared for a referendum which narrowly endorsed the long-sought Republic. The break with the Commonwealth followed.

One sincere and positive move for Bantu development, even if separate development, was made in the authoritative *Tomlin-*

son Report of 1955. The proposed deliberate planning of suitable conditions for *apartheid* was at first cold-shouldered, but in 1962 it received qualified support from Dr. Verwoerd, the Prime Minister, who proposed a grant of £57 million for development and greater local self-government for the Transkei. This was too little and too late to affect the situation which already existed. The rate of wages paid to the individual remains uneconomically low if only because of the vast reserve of imperfectly occupied workers. The 'native reserves', now re-christened the Bantu Areas, have received a little more attention but their congestion remains unrelieved, and soil-reclamation or better use of the land even drives redundant peasants off it. These areas are as far as ever from being self-supporting. Economists plead in vain for the fuller development of African skills, if only in the interests of the potential African market for consumer goods. But South Africa as a whole has not begun to learn the lesson propounded by Adam Smith's faithful follower, John Philip, who long ago deprecated the habit of thinking of the dependent peoples as low-grade 'producers only, never as consumers'. Philip as economist elaborated that case more especially in the long-sustained struggle I detailed in *The Cape Colour Question*, the effort to better the lot of the Hottentots to whose former state so many of the Bantu, as he clearly foresaw, have since been reduced.

It was alarming that even the 1962 programme given the blessing of the Prime Minister was based less, in spite of Tomlinson, on the study of the changing situation than on a theoretical blue-print fabricated in Pretoria offices. *Apartheid* is the counsel of despair conjured up by some of the most generous of the Afrikaners; many of these, not surprisingly, quail before the difficulties inherent in ordering the complex society which has so suddenly replaced the rustic seclusion of quite recent days. Under this sincere but deluded leadership too many of the Afrikaner people have become the victims of a hallucination which comes directly from their misreading of their own past. These pages have, I hope, thrown some light on what actually happened. A new awareness of the responsibility borne by the Trekker founders may reform the inherited habit of laying the blame for what is amiss on outside interference. Only such a change can save those heroes' successors from the folly of trying to build a stable future on dreams of a past that never truly was.

BIBLIOGRAPHICAL NOTE

The account of social and economic conditions given in Ch. XVIII was based on investigations made at the time and embodied in papers and pamphlets—*Economic Conditions in a Non-industrial Town*, Grahamstown, 1915, *South African Agrarian Problem*, Johannesburg, 1919, *Land, Natives and Unemployment*, Johannesburg, 1924, *At the Roots*, articles in *Cape Times*, Cape Town, 1926.

The substance of these pieces was brought together in the book *Complex South Africa*, Faber & Faber, 1931.

For the guidance of readers wishing to follow later developments the following short list is appended:

Report of *Natives Economic Commission*, U.G., Pretoria, 1932.

The Native Reserves and their place in the economy of South Africa. *Report No. 9* of the Social and Economic Planning Council. Govt. Printer, Pretoria, 1946.

Economy of a Native Reserve, by D. Hobart Houghton and Edith M. Walton. Pietermaritzburg, Shuter & Shooter, 1952.

The socio-economic development of the Bantu areas—Summary of (*Tomlinson*) Commission Report. Pretoria, 1956.

Native Reserves of Natal, by E. H. Brookes and N. Horwitz, O.U.P., Cape Town, 1957.

M. Roberts, *Labour in the Farm Economy*, 1958.

M. Horrell, *Economic Development of the Reserves*, 1959—and other publications of the South African Institute of Race Relations, Johannesburg.

Townsmen and Tribesmen (Urbanization in a divided society), by Philip Mayer. O.U.P., Cape Town, 1961.

INDEX

Aberdeen, Philip's years in, 12.

Aborigines Committee: criticism of treaties by, 211, 212; origin and work of, 108 & n., 123, 142, 148 n., 160, 167 & n., 330–1; report on S. Africa dropped, 187–90, 331.

Aborigines Protection Society, 209, 304, 331.

Act of S.A. Union, 365.

Adderley, Sir Charles, 322, 323.

Admiralty, the, on Natal, 213.

Africa, slender links of S. Africa with continent of, 4, 5, 85.

Albany, British settlers in, 89, 130, 193, 198. *See also* ZUURVELD.

Alexander, Capt. (General Sir James), 137, 144.

Amatolas, the, 293, 298, 338.

Ama-Xhosa: as British subjects, 23, 169 n. (*see also* BANTU); attention momentarily diverted from, 193, 239; break-up begins, 278–305, reaches climax, 328, 337–48; distribution and tribal system of, 22–30, 44–51; D'Urban's attempted settlement of, 130 ff., 154, 168 ff.; effect of Chaka Wars on, 89–90; growing unrest among, 262–77; land needs of, 168, 287–9 (*see also* LAND, POPULATION); mounting Western pressure on, chs. V and VI; provocation at end of 1834, 125–7; Sir H. Smith's verdict on, 324; war tactics of, 129–32, 149, 292. *See also* GAIKA, HINTZA, MAQOMO, NDHLAMBI, SANDILE, &c.; CEDED TERRITORY, CISKEI, KAT RIVER; LABOUR; LAND, POPULATION.

American Indians, fate of, and Bantu compared, 73, 276, 347–8.

American missions, 13, 95 n.; in Natal, 206–7, 350–1.

Anderson, Rev. W., 53, 80.

Anti-colonialists, early, 147.

Anti-slavery Movement: confused view on status of free Bantu, 147–8, 158–9, 166, 186; rise and influence of, 7.

Apartheid, *see* SEGREGATION.

'Apprenticeship' in Republics, 222–4.

Bakgatla, 357.

Bantu: as a society, 73, 86, 105, 219; customs and organization of, 26 ff.; effect of Chaka Wars on, 30–37, 275; first clash with Europeans, 25 & n., 45, 75 n.; flank turned by Great Trek, ch. XII, 360; name and geographical distribution in S.E. Africa, 23–26. *See also* LABOUR; LAND, POPULATION.

Barolong, 198. *See also* MOROKO.

Bastards, *see* GRIQUAS.

Basuto, Basutoland: beginnings of, 33; Boer pressure on, 237, 315 ff.; ill-defined boundaries of, 248–9; in Transvaal, 357. *See also* MOSHESH.

Batavian Republic, 7.

Bechuana, 23, 32, 55–56; abandonment of, to Transvaal, 235, 334–5, 357; conditions of life among, 227, 229, 230; early wage-earning of, 32; reports on, 253 & n.

Berea, effect of Cathcart's check at, 326–7.

Bergenaars, 32, 55, 58, 223, 246, 249.

Bethulie, 220.

Black Circuit, 8, 9, 20.

Block Drift, 287.

Bloemfontein, 309, 318.

Blood River, battle of, 19, 213.

Boers, Afrikaner: as a distinct people, 6; attitude to weaker races, 7, 42–43, 71, 94, 243–4, 349, 358 ff.; expansionism checked, 43, 200; Maitland on ways of, 253; opinions clash with British tradition, 14, 328–30, 335; rooted opposition to racial equality, 199, 215, 223; turn to industry, 368; wasteful agricultural habits of, 39, 40, 115 ff., 141, 195, 199–200. *See also* GREAT TREK, NATIONALISM, TREKKER REPUBLICS, &c.

Boomah Pass, 321.

Boomplaats, 260, 309, 318.

Bourke, acting Governor Gen. R.: innovations of, 78, 85; is criticized, 87.

Bowker, Mr. J. M., 149 & n., 184 n., 277 n.

PRINTED IN GREAT BRITAIN
AT THE UNIVERSITY PRESS, OXFORD
BY VIVIAN RIDLER
PRINTER TO THE UNIVERSITY